Lecture Notes in Computer Scien

Commenced Publication in 1973
Founding and Former Series Editors:
Gerhard Goos, Juris Hartmanis, and Jan van Leeuwen

T0238094

Oscar H. Ibarra   Hsu-Chun Yen (Eds.)

Implementation and Application of Automata

11th International Conference, CIAA 2006
Taipei, Taiwan, August 21-23, 2006
Proceedings

 Springer

Volume Editors

Oscar H. Ibarra
University of California
Department of Computer Science
Santa Barbara, CA 93106, USA
E-mail: ibarra@cs.ucsb.edu

Hsu-Chun Yen
National Taiwan University
Department of Electrical Engineering
Taipei, Taiwan 106, ROC
E-mail: yen@cc.ee.ntu.edu.tw

Library of Congress Control Number: 2006930260

CR Subject Classification (1998): F.1.1-2, F.4.2-3, F.2

LNCS Sublibrary: SL 1 – Theoretical Computer Science and General Issues

ISSN   0302-9743
ISBN-10   3-540-37213-X Springer Berlin Heidelberg New York
ISBN-13   978-3-540-37213-4 Springer Berlin Heidelberg New York

Springer is a part of Springer Science+Business Media

springer.com

© Springer-Verlag Berlin Heidelberg 2006

Typesetting: Camera-ready by author, data conversion by Scientific Publishing Services, Chennai, India
Printed on acid-free paper   SPIN: 11812128   06/3142   5 4 3 2 1 0

Preface

The 11th International Conference on Implementation and Application of Automata (CIAA 2006) was held at the National Taiwan University, Taiwan, August 21–23, 2006.

This volume of *Lecture Notes in Computer Science* contains the papers that were presented at CIAA 2006, as well as the abstracts of the poster papers that were displayed during the conference. The volume also includes the abstracts and extended abstracts of three invited lectures presented by Ming Li, Grzegorz Rozenberg, and Sheng Yu.

The 22 regular papers were selected from 76 submissions covering various topics in the theory, implementation, and applications of automata and related structures. Each submitted paper was reviewed by at least three Program Committee members, with the assistance of referees. The authors of the papers presented here come from the following countries: Austria, Canada, China, Cyprus, Czech Republic, Finland, France, Germany, Hungary, India, Ireland, Italy, The Netherlands, Poland, Spain, Sweden, Taiwan, UK, and USA.

We wish to thank all who have made this meeting possible: the authors for submitting papers, the Program Committee members and external referees (listed in the proceedings) for their excellent work, and our three invited speakers. Finally, we wish to express our sincere appreciation to the sponsors, local organizers, proceedings Chair, the editors of the *Lecture Notes in Computer Science* series and Springer, in particular Alfred Hofmann, for their help in publishing this volume.

August 2006   Oscar H. Ibarra
                                                               Hsu-Chun Yen

Preface

Organization

Program Committee

Marie-Pierre Béal	University of Marne-la-Vallee, France
Cristian Calude	University of Auckland, New Zealand
Jean-Marc Champarnaud	Université de Rouen, France
Erzsébet Csuhaj-Varjú	Hungarian Academy of Sciences, Hungary
Jürgen Dassow	University of Magdeburg, Germany
Jacques Farré	Université de Nice - Sophia Antipolis, France
Rudolf Freund	Vienna University of Technology, Austria
Jozef Gruska	Masaryk University, Czech Republic
Tero Harju	University of Turku, Finland
Jan Holub	Czech Technical University, Czech Republic
Markus Holzer	Technische Universität München, Germany
Oscar H. Ibarra (Co-chair)	University of California, Santa Barbara, USA
Masami Ito	Kyoto Sangyo University, Japan
Kazuo Iwama	Kyoto University, Japan
Juhani Karhumäki	University of Turku, Finland
Hsueh-I Lu	National Taiwan University, Taiwan, ROC
Denis Maurel	Université de Tours, France
Mehryar Mohri	New York University, USA
Andrei Paun	Louisiana Tech, USA
Bala Ravikumar	Sonoma State University, USA
Wojciech Rytter	Warsaw University, Poland, and NJIT, USA
Jacques Sakarovitch	CNRS/ENST, Paris, France
Kai Salomaa	Queen's University, Canada
Pierluigi San Pietro	Politecnico di Milano, Italy
Giora Slutzki	Iowa State University, USA
Bow-Yaw Wang	Academia Sinica, Taiwan, ROC
Farn Wang	National Taiwan University, Taiwan, ROC
Bruce W. Watson	University of Pretoria, South Africa
Hsu-Chun Yen (Co-chair)	National Taiwan University, Taiwan, ROC
Sheng Yu	University of Western Ontario, Canada

Additional Reviewers

Cyril Allauzen
Manuel Baclet
Miroslav Balík
Kamel Barkaoui
Samik Basu
Nicolas Bedon
Jean Berstel
Franziska Biegler
Renaud Blanch
Henning Bordihn
Ján Bouda
Bohuš Brim
Luboš Brim
Lin-Zan Cai
Cezar Campeanu
Chih-Hong Cheng
Loek Cleophas
Mark Daley
Akim Demaille
Michael Domaratzki

Ming-Chang Dong
Rémi Forax
Nathalie Friburger
Hermann Gruber
Vesa Halava
Geza Horvath
Geng-Dian Huang
Jarkko Kari
Tomi Kärki
Martin Kutrib
Eric Laporte
Martin Leucker
Chih-Wei Lin
Li-Ping Lin
Sylvain Lombardy
Ian McQuillan
Alexander Meduna
Angelo Morzenti
Gonzalo Navarro
Ernest Ketcha Ngassam

Harumichi Nishimura
Alexander Okhotin
Maciej Pilichowski
Libor Polak
Gheorge Rahonis
Ashish Rastogi
Chantal Reynaud
Matteo Rossi
Nicolae Santean
Sylvain Schmitz
Luc Segoufin
Jason R. Smith
Paola Spoletini
Alain Terlutte
Ming-Hsien Tsai
Ladislav Vagner
Thomas Worsch
Shigeru Yamashita
Artur Zaroda

Organizing Committee

Tsan-Sheng Hsu (Co-chair)   Academia Sinica, Taiwan, ROC
Oscar H. Ibarra   University of California, Santa Barbara, USA
Hsueh-I Lu   National Taiwan University, Taiwan, ROC
Bow-Yaw Wang   Academia Sinica, Taiwan, ROC
Farn Wang   National Taiwan University, Taiwan, ROC
Hsu-Chun Yen (Co-chair)   National Taiwan University, Taiwan, ROC

Proceedings Committee

Oscar H. Ibarra University of California, Santa Barbara, USA
Hsu-Chun Yen   National Taiwan University, Taiwan, ROC

Publicity Committee

Hsueh-I Lu   National Taiwan University, Taiwan, ROC
Farn Wang   National Taiwan University, Taiwan, ROC

Steering Committee

Jean-Marc Champarnaud	Université de Rouen, France
Oscar H. Ibarra	University of California, Santa Barbara, USA
Denis Maurel	Université de Tours, France
Derick Wood	Hong Kong Univ. of Science and Technology, Hong Kong, China
Sheng Yu (Chair)	University of Western Ontario, Canada

Sponsoring Institutions

National Taiwan University, Taiwan, ROC
Center for Information and Electronic Technologies, NTU, Taiwan, ROC
National Science Council, Taiwan, ROC
Ministry of Education, Taiwan, ROC
Academia Sinica, Taiwan, ROC
University of California, Santa Barbara, USA

Table of Contents

Invited Lectures

Technical Contributions

Poster Abstracts

Information Distance and Its Applications

Ming Li

School of Computer Science, University of Waterloo, Waterloo, Ont. N2L 3G1,
Canada
mli@uwaterloo.ca
http://www.cs.uwaterloo.ca/~mli

Abstract. We summarize the recent developments of a general theory of
information distance and its applications in whole genome phylogeny,
document comparison, internet query-answer systems, and many other
data mining tasks. We also solve an open problem regarding the universality of the normalized information distance.

1 Introduction

We live in an information society. Internet has created the cyber, or information, space. In the classical Newton world, we know how to measure physical
distances. Have you thought about the equally fundamental question of how to
measure the "information distance" between two objects: two documents, two
letters, two emails, two music scores, two languages, two programs, two pictures,
two systems, or two genomes? Such a measurement should not be application
dependent. Just like in the classical world, we do not measure distances sometimes by the amount of time a bird flies and sometimes by the number of pebbles
lining up on the Santa Barbara beach.

A good information distance metric should not only be application-independent
but also universally minorize all other "reasonable" definitions.

The task of a universal definition of information distance is illusive. Traditional
distances such as the Euclidean distance or the Hamming distance obviously fail
for even trivial examples. For instance, we (human) perceive a positive photo
to be similar to its negative print, while their Hamming distance is the largest.
In fact, for any computable distance, we can always find such counterexamples.
Furthermore, when we wish to adopt a metric to be the universal standard of
information distance, we must justify it. It should not be out of thin air. It
should not be from a specific application. It should not require amendments for
different applications. It should be as good as any definition for any application,
in some sense.

From a simple and accepted assumption in thermodynamics, we have derived
such a universal information distance [2,18,19] and a general method to measure
similarities between two sequences [18,19]. The theory has been initially applied
to alignment free whole genome phylogeny [18], chain letter history [3], language
history [4,19], plagiarism detection [5], and more recently to music classification
[9], parameter-free data mining paradigm [13], internet knowledge discovery [8],
among many recent applications.

O.H. Ibarra and H.-C. Yen (Eds.): CIAA 2006, LNCS 4094, pp. 1–9, 2006.

2   A Theory of Information Distance

Given a binary string x, the Kolmogorov complexity of x condition on y, $K(x|y)$, is the length of the shortest program that outputs x with input y. When $y = \epsilon$, we write $K(x|\epsilon)$ as $K(x)$. For formal definitions and a comprehensive study of Kolmogorov complexity, see [20]. What would be a good departure point for defining "information distance" between two sequences? What should be the properties it must satisfy? The second question is easy to answer. We can use our common sense of a metric: (a) It must be symmetric; (b) It should satisfy the triangle inequality; (c) The distance of any sequence x to itself is 0, and positive otherwise.

To answer the first question, in early 1990's, we have studied the energy cost of convertion between two strings x and y. Over half a century ago, John von Neumann hypothesized that performing 1 bit of information processing costs $1KT$ of energy, where K is the Boltzmann's constant and T is the room temperature. Observing that reversable computations can be done for free, in early 1960's Rolf Landauer revised von Neumann's proposal to hold only for irreversible computations. We thought about using the minimum energy needed to convert between x and y to define their distance, as it is an objective measure. Thus, if you have x and wish to erase it, then you can reversibly convert it to x^*, x's shortest effective description, then erase $|x^*|$. Only the process of erasing $|x^*|$ bits is irreversible computation. Carrying on from this line of thinking, we [2] have defined the energy to convert between x and y to be the length of shortest program converting x to y and vice versa. That is, with respect to a universal Turing machine U, the cost of converting between x and y is:

$$E(x,y) = \min\{|p| : U(x,p) = y, \ U(y,p) = x\} \tag{1}$$

A natural upper bound for $E(x,y)$ is $K(x|y) + K(y|x)$. Using this (and other reasons), we have defined the sum distance in [2]:

$$d_{\text{sum}}(x,y) = K(x|y) + K(y|x).$$

However, the following theorem proved in [2] was a surprise.

Theorem 1. $E(x,y) = \max\{K(x|y), K(y|x)\}$.

Thus, we have defined the max distance:

$$d_{\max}(x,y) = \max\{K(x|y), K(y|x)\}.$$

Both distances are shown to satisfy the basic distance requirements such as positivity, symmetricity, triangle inequality, in [2]. We have further shown that $d_{\max}$ and d_{sum} minorizes all other distances that are computable and satisfies some reasonable density condition that within distance k to any string x, there are at most 2^k other strings. Formally, a distance D is admissible if

$$\sum_y 2^{-D(x,y)} \leq 1. \tag{2}$$

Then we proved that for any admissible computable distance D, there is a constant c, for all x, y, $d_{\max}(x, y) \leq D(x, y) + c$. Put it bluntly, if any other distance recovers some regularity between two sequences, so will $d_{\max}$.

The remaining question is to demonstrate that such distances are useful. However when we [18] tried to use our information distances, d_{sum} or $d_{\max}$, to measure similarity between genomes in 1998, we were in trouble. *E. coli* and *H. influenza* are sister species but their genome lengths defer greatly. The *E. coli* genome is about 5 megabases whereas the *H. influenza* genome is only 1.8 megabase long. $d_{\max}$ or d_{sum} between the two genomes are predominated by genome length difference rather than the amount of information they share. Such a measure trivially classifies *H. influenza* to be closer to a more remote species of similar genome length such as *A. fulgidus* (2.18 megabases) than to *E. coli*.

In order to solve this problem, we introduced "shared information distance" in [18]:

$$d_{\text{share}}(x, y) = 1 - \frac{K(x) - K(x|y)}{K(xy)}.$$

where $K(x) - K(x|y)$ is mutual information between sequences x and y [20]. We proved the basic distance metric requirements such as symmetry and triangle inequality, and have demonstrated its successful application in whole genome phylogeny in [18]. It turns out that d_{share} is equivalent to

$$\frac{K(x|y) + K(y|x)}{K(xy)}.$$

Thus, it can be viewed as the normalized sum distance. Hence, it becomes natural to normalize the optimal max distance in [19]:

$$d(x, y) = \frac{\max\{K(x|y), K(y|x)\}}{\max\{K(x), K(y)\}} \tag{3}$$

We have called $d(x, y)$ the "normalized information distance" proved metricity properties similar to that of normalized sum distance.

However, a key issue of universality of the normalized information distance, all versions, has remained unsolved. The similar proof for $d_{\max}$ and d_{sum} does not work any more for normalized distances d_{share} and d. In [18], in order to prove the universality statement, we were only able to prove a very weak statement: for any computable distance D, there is a constance $c \leq 2$ such that, with probability 1, for all sequences x and y, $d(x, y) \leq cD(x, y)$. This seemingly innocent statement is actually begging the question: the random sequences have probability 1, whereas it is non-random sequences we are interested in measuring and this statement says nothing about them.

In our second paper [19], we have tried to avoid this problem by rescaling the density conditions changing from

$$|\{y : |y| = n \text{ and } D(x, y) \leq d \leq 1\}| \leq 2^{dn} \tag{4}$$

in [18] to

$$|\{y : |y| = n \text{ and } D(x, y) \leq d \leq 1\}| \leq 2^{dK(x)} \tag{5}$$

However it turns out that Formula (5) is so restrictive that no reasonable distances can satisfy such requirement except our own normalized information distance. Thus the universality statement is again meaningless. Cilibrasi and Vitanyi have tried to further change the definition of normalized admissible distances [9].

3   Fixing the Theory

We did not need to change the definition after all. Using the the original defition of [18], Formula (4), we now prove the full universality theorem, removing the "with probability 1" condition.

Theorem 2. *For any computable distance D, satisfying density requirement (4), for all sequence x and y, $d(x,y) \leq D(x,y) + O(\log n / \max\{K(x), K(y)\})$.*

Proof. For any binary sequence x of length n, Muchnik [21] proved that there exists a (shortest) program x^*, such that $|x^*| = K(x)$, $K(x|x^*) = O(\log n)$ and $K(x^*|x) = O(\log n)$. That is, x^* is a shortest program for x and it does not contain too much extra information unrelated to x.

For any sequences x and y of length up to n, there are x^* and y^* satisfying Muchnick's theorem. Given y, we can compute y^* using $O(\log n)$ information. Then using $K(x^*|y^*)$ information, we can compute x^*, which in turn gives x with $O(\log n)$ information. We have proved:

$$K(x|y) \leq K(x^*|y^*) + O(\log n). \tag{6}$$

The equality actually holds. More general exploration of this is in [12].

Applying Inequality (6),

$$\begin{aligned} d(x,y) &= \frac{\max\{K(x|y), K(y|x)\}}{\max\{K(x), K(y)\}} \\ &\leq \frac{\max\{K(x^*|y^*), K(y^*|x^*)\} + O(\log n)}{\max\{K(x), K(y)\}} \end{aligned} \tag{7}$$

Given D, using the density property of Formula (4) and the computability of D, we know $K(x^*|y^*) \leq D(x,y)|x^*|$ and $K(y^*|x^*) \leq D(y,x)|y^*|$. Thus, from Formula (7) and symmetry of D, we have,

$$\begin{aligned} d(x,y) &\leq \frac{\max\{K(x^*|y^*), K(y^*|x^*)\} + O(\log n)}{\max\{K(x), K(y)\}} \\ &\leq \frac{\max\{D(x,y)|x^*|, D(x,y)|y^*|\} + O(\log n)}{\max\{|x^*|, |y^*|\}} \\ &\leq D(x,y) + O(\log n / \max\{K(x), K(y)\}). \end{aligned}$$

Similar proof gives the universality statement for the normalized sum distance (d_{share}), defined in [18].

Corollary 1. *For any computable distance D satisfying (4), there is a constant $c \leq 2$ such that for all sequences x and y, $d_{\text{share}}(x, y) \leq cD(x, y)$, modulo an $O(\log n / K(xy))$ additive factor.*

4   A Tale of Two Approximations

Kolmogorov Complexity is not computable and not approximable [20]. Two heuristic methods were proposed to approximate $d(x, y)$ in practice.

For sequence data, we [18] demonstrated that normal compression algorithms can be naturally and conveniently adopted to relplace Kolmgorov complexity in the formula $d(x, y)$. Others have subsequently successfully used the popular compression programs such as gzip, jzip and bzip [4,19,13] to apply to similar fomulas. Keogh, Lonardi and Ratanamahatana called this method parameter-free [13] and compared it with 51 different parameter-laden measures/methods from seven major data mining conferences SIGKDD, SIGMOD, ICDM, ICDE, SSDB, VLDB, PKDD, PAKDD, on various standard time series clustering tasks. The simple parameter-free normalized information distance method outperformed all 51 methods for classifying various time series ranging from heart beat signals to stock market curves.

We give the original example presented in [18] on whole genome phylogeny. This is the first success of this method. Traditional method for phylogeny depended on multiple alignment of sequences of different species corresponding to one protein. Often different protein gives different phylogeny. For example, half of the proteins in mammalian mtDNA implied that primates were closer to rodents, and the other half implied that primates were closer to ferungulates. Around the turn of the last century, we started to have complete genomes of many species. We thought about doing phylogeny construction using the whole genome information. However, multiple sequence alignment of complete genomes were out of question for obvious reasons. Partial information of the genomes were used to construct trees: gene order, break points, and segment copying [29]. We took a bold step by bluntly computing $d_{\text{share}}(x, y)$ for each pair of x and y, mitochondrial genomes for 20 species of mammals and constructed the tree in Figure 1 accordingly. The method was very robust and 100% correct on all branches at our first try. The tree confirmed the accepted hypothesis that primates are closer to ferungulates than rodents. Later, the similar experiments were repeated in [19], and many other publications.

Objects can be given literally. A sequence contains information within itself. Names and abstract concepts also contain information, although not within themselves. The name "human genome" implies three gigabases of information. The phrase "*War and Peace* by Tolstoy" perhaps carries information even beyond the book. If "human genome" and "*War and Peace*" can still be asscoiated with some sequences that can be compressed, the concept of "home" or "red" is even more problematic. Behind these names, there lays the common knowledge of the human kind and our civilization. Can we still measure the normalized information distance between two abstract concepts? Cilibrasi and Vitanyi [8]

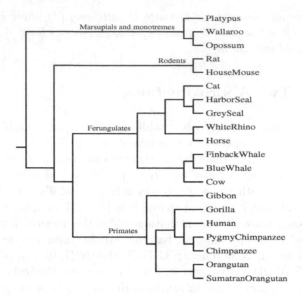

Fig. 1. The evolutionary tree of 20 mammals built from their mtDNA sequences

observed an alternative way of approximating $d(x, y)$. By the Coding Theorem (see [20]), we have

$$- \log \mathbf{m}(x) = K(x) + O(1), \tag{8}$$

where $\mathbf{m}(x)$ is the universal distribution of x. Equation 8 relates the randomness of an object to its probability. While we do not know how to compute $\mathbf{m}(x)$, the natural heuristic now is to use the distribution of x in the world-wide web to approximate $\mathbf{m}(x)$. Let us define such a distribution $g(x)$ to be the probability x appears in a page indexed by an internet search engine. Then the Shannon-Fano code length is

$$G(x) = - \log g(x).$$

Replacing $K(x)$ by $G(x)$ in the definition of $d(x, y)$, with simple rearranging, we now arrive at our second heuristic approximation of $d(x, y)$.

$$
\begin{aligned}
d''(x, y) &= \frac{G(xy) - \min\{G(x), G(y)\}}{\max\{G(x), G(y)\}} \\
&= \frac{\max\{\log f(x), \log f(x)\} - \log f(x, y)}{\log N - \min\{\log f(x), \log f(y)\}}.
\end{aligned}
\tag{9}
$$

where $f(x)$ is the number of pages containing x, $f(x, y)$ is the number of pages containing both x and y, and N is the total number of indexed pages.

Extending formula (9) to its conditional version, it has allowed us to explore the new frontiers of the internet as a knowledge-base, in [12]. In that paper, we have implemented the first Query-Answer prototype based on this theory. The system parses (by natural language processing) a user's query such as "Who invented the light bulb?" into x (who) and y (the light bulb) and a condition (invent). Then it using a search engine to search for names that are closest to "the light bulb" conditioning on "invent", using the normalized information distance approximated by Formula (9). The search result is shown in Table 1.

Table 1. Top 10 answers to "Who invented the light bulb"

Who invented the light bulb?	
Candidates	Distance
thomas edison	0.4801
edison	0.4859
lightbulb	0.6087
thomas alva edison	0.6444
did thomas edison	0.7252
latimer	0.7283
thomas	0.7724
joseph swan	0.7750
incandescent light bulb	0.7876
wilson swan	0.8088

Table 1 is interesting. The top answer Thomas Edison is of course the popular solution, whereas it is amusing to see the name of Sir Joseph Wilson Swan who invented the electric lamp with a carbon filament, 20 years before Thomas Edison. Lewis Latimer's name was also not far fetched; a son of of runaway black slaves, he made decisive improvements to the Edison's bulb.

5 Blossom of Hundred Flowers

The reserach of information distance has developed along two directions: theoretical and practical.

Paper [2] has stimulated the theoretical research. Significant theoretical progress has been reported by an elite group of Russian scientists: A.V. Chernov, An.A. Muchnik, A.E. Romashchenko, A.K. Shen, N.K. Vereshchagin, M.V. V'yugin, and many others. See [21,6,22,27,30,31]. Many of these results will be disseminated in the third edition of our book [20].

Along the more practical direction, initiated by the paper [18], many research groups have reexamined our experiments and experimented on the new ones. We mention a few more recent experiments not already mentioned. Using various versions of normalized information distance, a wide range of applications have appeared: language classification [4,19], hierarchical clustering [9,15], music classification [7], software metrics and obfuscation [14,28], web page authorship, topic and domain identification [25], protein sequence/structure classification [16,17], phylogenetic reconstruction [1,23], hurricane risk assessment [11], SVM kernel for string classification [10], ortholog detection [24], and clustering fetal heart rate tracings [26].

While the method is robust, it fails when there are not enough data to compensate for the compression overhead. Francesc Rossello, J. Rocha, G. Valiente and their colleagues in Spain have experimented on protein sequence comparisons using the normalized information distance. Because the protein sequences are short and simple compression does not take right scoring functions (such as BLOSUM scores) into account, the clustering result is inferior to standard methods, as expected. The universality claim is theoretical. In practice, it may be possible to characterize the data so that some class of compression algorithms approximates the optimal. A typical such assumption is the stationary source in the field of information theory.

References

1. C. Ané and M.J. Sanderson, Missing the Forest for the Trees: Phylogenetic Compression and Its Implications for Inferring Complex Evolutionary Histories, *Systematic Biology*, 54:1(2005), 146-157.
2. C.H. Bennett, P. Gacs, M. Li, P. Vitanyi, and W. Zurek, Information Distance, *IEEE Trans. Inform. Theory*, 44:4(July 1998), 1407-1423. (STOC, 1993)
3. C.H. Bennett, M. Li and B. Ma, Chain letters and evolutionary histories, *Scientific American*, 288:6(June 2003) (feature article), 76-81.
4. D. Benedetto, E. Caglioti, V. Loreto, Language trees and zipping, *Phys. Rev. Lett.*, 88:4(2002), 048702.
5. X. Chen, B. Francia, M. Li, B. Mckinnon, A. Seker. Shared information and program plagiarism detection. *IEEE Trans. Information Theory*, 50:7(July 2004), 1545-1550.
6. A.V. Chernov, An.A. Muchnik, A.E. Romashchenko, A.K. Shen and N.K. Vereshchagin, Upper semi-lattice of binary strings with the relation "x is simple conditional to y", *Theoret. Comput. Sci.*, 271(2002), 69-95.
7. R. Cilibrasi, P.M.B. Vitányi, and R. de Wolf Algorithmic clustring of music based on string compression. *Comput. Music J.*, 28:4(2004), 49–67.
8. R. Cilibrasi and P.M.B. Vitányi, Automatic semantics using Google, manuscript, 2005. http://arxiv.org/abs/cs.CL/0412098 (2004).
9. R. Cilibrasi and P.M.B. Vitányi, Clustering by compression, *IEEE Trans. Inform. Theory*, 51:4(2005), 1523-1545.
10. M. Cuturi and J.P. Vert, The context-tree kernel for strings. *Neural Networks*, 18:4(2005), 1111-1123.
11. K. Emanuel, S. Ravela, E. Vivant, C. Risi, A combined statistical-deterministic approach of hurricane risk assessment, manuscript, Program in Atmospheres, Oceans, and Climate, MIT, 2005.
12. Y. Hao, X. Zhang, X. Zhu, and M. Li, Conditional normalized information distance. Manuscript, 2006.
13. E. Keogh, S. Lonardi, and C.A. Ratanamahatana, Towards parameter-free data mining, *KDD'2004*, pp. 206–215.
14. S.R. Kirk and S. Jenkins, Information theory-baed software metrics and obfuscation, [*J. Systems and Software*, 72(2004), 179–186] and
15. A. Kraskov, H. Stögbauer, R.G. Andrzejak, and P. Grassberger, Hierarchical clustering using mutual information, *Europhys. Lett.* 70:2(2005), 278-284.

16. A. Kocsor, A. Kertesz-Farkas, L. Kajan, and S. Pongor, Application of compression-based distance measures to protein sequence classification: a methodology study, *Bioinformatics*, 22:4(2006), 407–412;

17. N. Krasnogor and D.A. Pelta, Measuring the similarity of protein structures by means of the universal similarity metric. *Bioinformatics* 20:7(2004), 1015-1021];

18. M. Li, J. Badger, X. Chen, S. Kwong, P. Kearney, H. Zhang, An information-based sequence distance and its application to whole mitochondrial genome phylogeny, *Bioinformatics*, 17:2(2001), 149-154.

19. M. Li, X. Chen, X. Li, B. Ma, P.M.B. Vitanyi, The similarity metric, *IEEE Trans. Information Theory*, 50:12(2004), 3250-3264.

20. M. Li and P. Vitanyi, *An introduction to Kolmogorov complexity and its applications*, Springer-Verlag, 2nd Edition 1997 (xx+637 pp).

21. An.A. Muchnik, Conditional comlexity and codes, *Theoretical Computer Science* 271:1(2002), 97–109.

22. An.A. Muchnik and N.K. Vereshchagin, Logical operations and Kolmogorov complexity II. *Proc. 16th Conf. Comput. Complexity*, 2001, pp. 256-265.

23. H.H. Otu and K. Sayood, *Bioinformatics* 19:6(2003), 2122-2130. A new sequence distance measure for phylogenetic tree construction.

24. H.K. Pao and J. Case, Computing entropy for ortholog detection. *Int'l Conf. Comput. Intell.* Dec. 17-19, 2004, Istanbul Turkey.

25. D. Parry, Use of Kolmogorov distance identification of web page authorship, topic and domain, *Workshop on Open Source Web Inf. Retrieval*, http://www.emse.fr/OSWIR05/, 2005.

26. C. Costa Santos, J. Bernardes, P.M.B. Vitányi, L. Antunes, Clustering fetal heart rate tracings by compression, *Proc. 19th IEEE Intn'l Symp. Computer-Based Medical Systems*, Salt Lake City, Utah, 22–23 June, 2006.

27. A.K. Shen and N.K. Vereshchagin, Logical operations and Kolmogorov complexity, *Theoret. Comput. Sci.* 271(2002), 125-129.

28. W. Taha, S. Crosby, and K. Swadi, A new approach to data mining for software design, manuscript, Rice Univ. 2006.

29. J.S. Varre, J.P. Delahaye, and E. Rivals, Transformation distances: a family of dissimilarity measures based on movements of segments. *Bioinformatics*, 15:3(1999), 194-202.

30. N.K. Vereshchagin and M.V. V'yugin, Independent minimum length programs to translate between given strings, *Theoret. Comput. Sci.*, 271(2002), 131-143.

31. M.V. V'yugin, Information distance and conditional complexities *Theoret. Comput. Sci.*, 271(2002), 145-150.

Theory Inspired by Gene Assembly in Ciliates

Grzegorz Rozenberg

Department of Computer Science
University of Colorado at Boulder
Boulder, CO 80309, U.S.A.
and
Leiden Institute of Advanced Computer Science (LIACS)
Leiden University
Niels Bohrweg 1, 2300 RA Leiden
The Netherlands
rozenber@liacs.nl

Ciliates (ciliated protozoa) are unicellular organisms with an evolutionary history that extends back perhaps two billion (2×10^9) years. The unique extraordinary feature of ciliates is that they posses two kinds of nuclei within the same cell: macronucleus containing genes that provide the genetic information needed to maintain the structure and function of the cell, and micronucleus that does not contribute to the maintainance, growth and proliferation of the cell – it is reserved for the sexual exchange of DNA between two mating cells.

When ciliates are starved they may mate. At some stage during sexual reproduction a micronucleus develops into a new macronucleus. This process of transformation of the micronuclear genome into the macronuclear genome, called gene assembly, is perhaps the most involved process of DNA manipulation yet known in living organisms. It is fascinating from both the biological and computational point of view.

The computational nature of gene assembly has attracted much attention in recent years and considerable body of theory has been developed. This theory involves, among others, novel kinds of string and graph rewriting systems, novel sorts of graphs as well as new questions about various known graph families, and novel topics in the combinatorics of words. In our talk we will survey some of the main developments of this theory.

O.H. Ibarra and H.-C. Yen (Eds.): CIAA 2006, LNCS 4094, p. 10, 2006.
© Springer-Verlag Berlin Heidelberg 2006

On the State Complexity of Combined Operations

Sheng Yu

Department of Computer Science, University of Western Ontario
London, Ontario, Canada N6A 5B7
syu@csd.uwo.ca

Abstract. The state complexity of combined operations is studied. We
show that the state complexity of a combined operation can be very different from the composition of the state complexities of the participating
individual operations. However, the estimate through individual nondeterministic state complexities for each of the combined operations being
considered is very similar to the actual state complexity. Several open
problems related to state complexity are also proposed.

1 Introduction

State complexity is a fundamental topic in theoretical computer science. Many
results on state complexity also have important practical implications in automata applications [26]. In recent years, there have been a large number of
papers published in this area of research. Examples include [2-5, 8-10, 13-16, 18,
19, 23, 24, 26, 28]. However, in all those papers, state complexity is considered for
only individual operations, e.g., union, intersection, catenation, and Kleene star.
In [27], the state complexity of combined operations was proposed as one of the
future directions in state complexity research. There have been a few examples
recently, e.g., the state complexity of

$$\{x_1, x_2, \cdots, x_k\}^*$$

is considered in [6] and the state complexity of L^k, for $k \geq 2$, is studied in [20].

In both theory and practice, combinations of operations are as important as
individual operations. It is clear that the state complexity of combined operations
should be studied along with the study of the state complexity of individual
operations.

The state complexity of a combined operation may not necessarily be equal
to the composition of the state complexities of the participating individual operations. For example, given an m-state DFA A and an n-state DFA B, what
is the state complexity of $(L(A)L(B))^*$ (i.e., the number of states of a minimal DFA that accepts $(L(A)L(B))^*$ in the worst case)? It is known that the
state complexity of the catenation of an m-state DFA language and an n-state
DFA language is $m2^n - 2^{n-1}$, and the state complexity of the (Kleene) star of

O.H. Ibarra and H.-C. Yen (Eds.): CIAA 2006, LNCS 4094, pp. 11–22, 2006.

an n-state DFA language is $2^{n-1} + 2^{n-2}$. Then is it true that the state complexity of $(L(A)L(B))^*$ is $2^{m2^n - 2^{n-1} - 1} + 2^{m2^n - 2^{n-1} - 2}$? In fact, it is not true for this combination of operations. The result is even in a different order [7]. However, in some other cases, the state complexity of a combination of operations is very similar to the composition of the state complexities of individual operations.

In this paper, we consider only the combinations of operations each of which consists of only two operations. In particular, every second operation of the combined operations we consider is (Kleene) star. Note that the first operation of a combination may restrict its result to a special type of DFA. Then the worst cases for the second operation in the general setting may or may not be among the outputs of the first operation. Therefore, the state complexity of a combination of operations may or may not be the same as the composition of the state complexities of the individual operations. Each case has to be studied individually.

We also use the nondeterministic state complexity of each individual operation to estimate the state complexity of a combined operation. Surprisingly, all the results of the estimation for the examples we use are very close to the actual state complexities. Although they are not as accurate as the state complexities we have proved, they appear to be good enough for practical purposes.

In the following, we introduce the basic notations that are necessary for this paper and review the definition of state complexity in the next section. In Section 3, we consider the state complexities of two combined operations: star of union and of star of intersection. In Section 4, we consider another two combined operations: star of catenation and star of reversal. We estimate the same four combined operations using individual nondeterministic state complexities in Section 5. We conclude the paper and raise several related questions in Section 6.

2   Preliminaries

A deterministic finite automaton (DFA) is denoted by a 5-tuple $A = (Q, \Sigma, \delta, s, F)$, where Q is the finite and nonempty set of states, Σ is the finite and nonempty set of input symbols, $\delta : Q \times \Sigma \to Q$ is the state transition function, $s \in Q$ is the initial state, and $F \subseteq Q$ is the set of final states. A DFA is said to be complete if $\delta(q, a)$ is defined for all $q \in Q$ and $a \in \Sigma$.

A nondeterministic finite automaton (NFA) is also denoted by a 5-tuple $M = (Q, \Sigma, \delta, s, F)$, where Q, Σ, s, and F are defined the same way as in a DFA and $\delta : Q \times \Sigma \to 2^Q$ maps a pair of a state and an input symbol into a set of states rather than, restrictively, a single state. An NFA may have multiple initial states, in which case an NFA is denoted $(Q, \Sigma, \delta, S, F)$ where S is the set of initial states. An ε-NFA is a further extension of NFA, where $\delta : Q \times (\Sigma \cup \{\varepsilon\}) \to 2^Q$ allows ε-transitions from the states.

The reader may refer to [11,21,25] for a rather complete background knowledge in automata theory.

State complexity ([26]) is a descriptional complexity measure for regular languages based on the deterministic finite automaton model. The *state complexity* of a regular language L, denoted $sc(L)$, is the number of states in the minimal complete DFA accepting L. The state complexity of a class $\mathcal{L}$ of regular languages, denoted $sc(\mathcal{L})$, is the supremum among all $sc(L)$, $L \in \mathcal{L}$. When we speak about the state complexity of an operation on regular languages, we mean the state complexity of the languages resulting from the operation. For example, we say that the state complexity of the catenation of an m-state DFA language, i.e., a language accepted by an m-state complete DFA, and an n-state DFA language is exactly $m2^n - 2^{n-1}$. This means that $m2^n - 2^{n-1}$ is the state complexity of the class of languages each of which is the catenation of an m-state DFA language and an n-state DFA language. In other words, there exist two regular languages that are accepted by an m-state DFA and an n-state DFA, respectively, such that the catenation of them is accepted by a minimal DFA of $m2^n - 2^{n-1}$ states, and this is the worst case. So, in a certain sense, state complexity is a worst-case complexity measure. Clearly, the state complexity of a regular-language operation gives a lower bound for the space, as well as the time, complexity of the same operation.

3 Star of Union and Star of Intersection

We first consider the state complexities of the star-of-union and the star-of-intersection combined operations. It is clear that for an m-state DFA A and an n-state DFA B, the state complexities of $L(A) \cup L(B)$ and $L(A) \cap L(B)$, respectively, are both mn. We know that the state complexity for the star of a k-state DFA language is $2^{k-1} + 2^{k-2}$. Calculating the composition of the complexities of union (intersection) and star, we obtain $2^{mn-1} + 2^{mn-2}$. However, the state complexities of the two combined operations are actually very different [22].

Theorem 1. *Let A be an m-state DFA and B an n-state DFA, for $m, n > 2$. Then the state complexity of $(L(A) \cup L(B))^*$ is*

$$2^{m+n-1} - 2^{m-1} - 2^{n-1} + 1.$$

The idea for proving that the above number is an upper bound can be described as follows. An ε-NFA that accepts $(L(A) \cup L(B))^*$ is first constructed, and then the number of states in the corresponding DFA is counted. Note that each state of the DFA is a set of states of the NFA, i.e., the states of A and B, possibly except the initial state of the DFA. It can be shown that it is the worst case when at least one of the two initial states is a final state and each of A and B has only one final state. In this case, the initial state of the DFA consists of the two initial states of A and B, respectively. Then the states of the DFA consist of the following two parts. The first part consists of $(2^{m-1} - 1)(2^{n-1} - 1)$ nonfinal states, each of which is a set that is the union of two nonempty sets of states of A and B, respectively, and do not contain the final states. The second part consists of 2^{m+n-2} final states, each of which is a set of states of A and B that include the two final states. Then the total number of states in the resulting DFA is

$$(2^{m-1} - 1)(2^{n-1} - 1) + 2^{m+n-2} = 2^{m+n-1} - 2^{m-1} - 2^{n-1} + 1.$$

For proving that the above upper bound can be reached, we choose the following general example for $m, n > 2$:

$$A = (Q_A, \Sigma, \delta_A, 0, \{0\}) \text{ where } Q_A = \{0, 1, \ldots, m-1\}, \ \Sigma = \{a, b, c\}$$

- $\delta_A(j, a) = (j+1) \pmod{m_1}, \ j = 0, 1, \ldots, m-1,$
- $\delta_A(j, b) = j, \ j = 0, 1, \ldots, m-1,$
- $\delta_A(0, c) = 1, \ \delta_A(j, c) = j, \ j = 1, 2, \ldots, m-1,$

and

$$B = (Q_B, \Sigma, \delta_B, 0, \{0\}) \text{ where } Q_B = \{0, 1, \ldots, n-1\},$$

- $\delta_B(j, b) = (j+1) \pmod{m_2}, \ j = 0, 1, \ldots, n-1,$
- $\delta_B(j, a) = j, \ j = 0, 1, \ldots, n-1,$
- $\delta_B(0, c) = 1, \ \delta_B(j, c) = j, \ j = 1, 2, \ldots, n-1.$

DFA A and B are shown in Figure 1 and Figure 2, respectively.

It has been proved [22] that any DFA accepts $(L(A) \cup L(B))^*$ needs at least $2^{m+n-1} - 2^{m-1} - 2^{n-1} + 1$ states, for $m, n > 2$.

Then the above number is the state complexity for the combined operation: star of union. It is very different from our calculation according to the individual state complexities.

Let us consider another similar combined operation: star of intersection. We know that the intersection of two regular languages has exactly the same state complexity as the union of two regular languages. However, we have the following result [22].

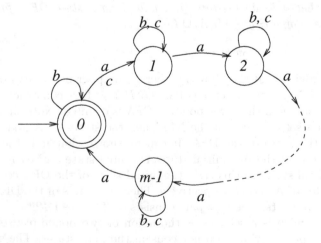

Fig. 1. DFA A

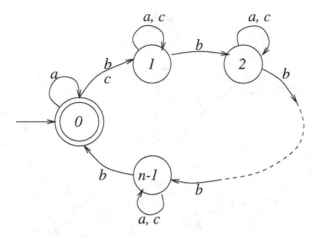

Fig. 2. DFA B

Theorem 2. *There exist an m-state DFA A and an n-state DFA B, $m, n \geq 3$, such that any DFA accepts $(L(A) \cap L(B))^*$ has at least $2^{m(n-2)}$ distinct states.*

This result can be shown using the DFAs in Figure 3 and Figure 4.

Clearly, this result is very different from the result for the star-of-union combined operation. The former is of $2^{O(mn)}$ and the latter is of $2^{O(m+n)}$. It appears that the set of the DFAs resulted from the union operation is different from the set of the DFAs resulted from the intersection. They may not be disjoint. However, the former may not include those that are the worst cases for the star operation. It is an interesting question: what are the properties of the DFAs that are resulted from a certain operation?

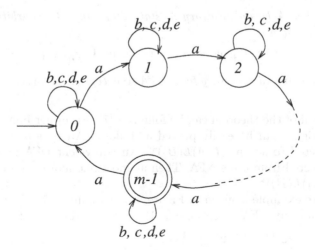

Fig. 3. DFA A in the worst-case example for $(L(A) \cap L(B))^*$

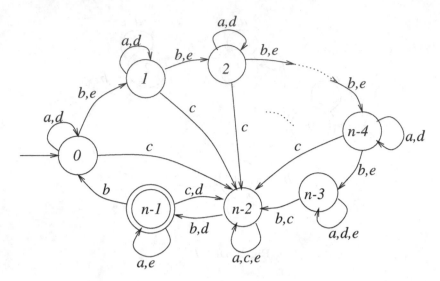

Fig. 4. DFA B in the worst-case example for $(L(A) \cap L(B))^*$

4   Star of Catenation and Star of Reversal

For star-of-catenation and star-of-reversal combined operations, we again start with looking at the compositions of the state complexities of individual operations. We know that for an m-state DFA A and an n-state DFA B, the state complexities for $L(A)L(B)$, $L(B)^R$, and $L(B)^*$, respectively, are $m2^n - 2^{n-1}$, 2^n, and $2^{n-1} + 2^{n-2}$. Then $2^{m2^n - 2^{n-1} - 1} + 2^{m2^n - 2^{n-1} - 2}$ would be an upper bound for $(L(A)L(B))^*$ and $2^{2^n - 1} + 2^{2^n - 2}$ would be an upper bound for $(L(B)^R)^*$. However, each actual state complexity is significantly smaller than the above bound [7].

Theorem 3. *Let A be an arbitrary m-state DFA and B an arbitrary n-state DFA, $m, n > 1$. Then*

$$2^{m+n-1} + 2^{m+n-4} - 2^{m-1} - 2^{n-1} + m + 1$$

states are sufficient and necessary for a DFA to accept $(L(A)L(B))^*$ in the worst case.

A detailed proof of the theorem can be found in [7]. An upper bound $2^{m+n} + 1$, which is not tight, can be easily proved as follows. An $m + n$-state ε-NFA is easily constructed to accept $(L(A)L(B))^+$. An equivalent DFA of 2^{m+n} states can be constructed from the ε-NFA. Then at most one more state is needed for accepting $(L(A)L(B))^*$.

A worst-case example is given in Figure 5 and Figure 6, for $m, n > 1$. It has been shown that any DFA accepting $(L(A)L(B))^*$ needs at least

$$2^{m+n-1} + 2^{m+n-4} - 2^{m-1} - 2^{n-1} + m + 1$$

states, which is exactly the same as the upper bound.

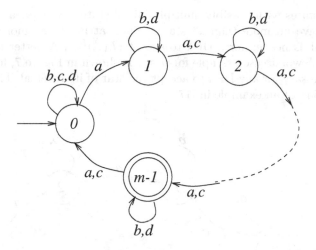

Fig. 5. DFA A in the worst-case example for $(L(A)L(B))^*$

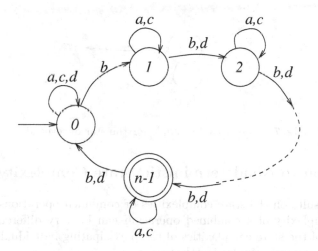

Fig. 6. DFA B in the worst-case example for $(L(A)L(B))^*$

Note that from the above result and several previous results, it appears that the proof of an upper bound in general needs careful observations, which may not be very difficult, and the proof of a tight lower bound needs right examples, which are usually difficult to find. However, an upper bound is shown to be tight only when a general worst-case example is found. The software system Grail+ has played an important role in helping us to find the right examples.

Theorem 4. *Let A be an arbitrary n-state DFA, $n > 0$. Then 2^n states are sufficient and necessary in the worst case for a DFA to accept $(L(A)^R)^*$.*

It is easy to show that the state complexity of this combined operation is no more than $2^n + 1$ by the following arguments. $(L(A)^R)^+$ is clearly accepted by an NFA of n states with possibly multiply initial states. An equivalent minimal DFA would have no more than 2^n states. Then at most one more state, i.e., $2^n + 1$ in total, is needed for a DFA to accept $(L(A)^R)^*$. A better bound 2^n is proved in [7]. A worst case example for $n > 1$ is shown in Figure 7, for which 2^n states are necessary for any DFA to accept the star of its reversal. This example is a modification of an example in [17].

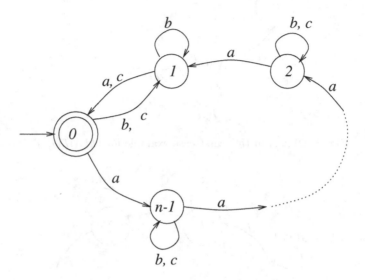

Fig. 7. A worst-case example for the star of reversal

5   Relation to Nondeterministic State Complexity

The above results on the state complexities of combined operations show that the state complexity of a combined operation can be very different from the composition of the state complexities of the participating individual operations in some cases and very similar in other cases.

In this section, we examine a different approach to estimate the state complexity of a combined operation.

In obtaining each of the upper bounds of the combined operations, we first construct an NFA and then transform it into a DFA and count the maximal possible useful states in the DFA. Naturally, we can calculate the composition of nondeterministic state complexities of individual operations first, and then calculate the number of states in the resulting DFA that is corresponding to the resulting NFA.

The nondeterministic state complexities of basic individual operations on regular languages were obtained in [8]. We list them in the following.

Theorem 5. *For any integer $m, n \geq 1$, let A be an m-state NFA and B an n-state NFA. Then*

- $m + n + 1$ states are sufficient and necessary in the worst case for an NFA to accept $L(A) \cup L(B)$;
- $m \cdot n$ states are sufficient and necessary in the worst case for an NFA to accept $L(A) \cap L(B)$;
- $m + n$ states are sufficient and necessary in the worst case for an NFA to accept $L(A)L(B)$.

Theorem 6. For any integer $n > 2$, let A be an n-state NFA. Then $n + 1$ states are sufficient and necessary in the worst case for an NFA to accept the language $L(A)^*$.

Theorem 7. For any integer $n > 3$, let A be an n-state NFA. Then $n + 1$ states are sufficient and necessary in the worst case for an NFA to accept the language $L(A)^R$.

Note that DFAs are special cases of NFAs. For an m-state DFA A and an n-state DFA B, the nondeterministic state complexity of $L(A) \cup L(B)$ is $m + n + 1$ and that of the star of an $m + n + 1$ NFA is $m + n + 2$. Then $m + n + 2$ is an upper bound for the number of states in a minimal NFA that accepts $(L(A) \cup L(B))^*$. Therefore, 2^{m+n+2} is an upper bound for the number of states in an equivalent minimal DFA. This number of states is very close to the state complexity of $(L(A) \cup L(B))^*$, i.e., $2^{m+n-1} - 2^{m-1} - 2^{n-1} + 1$.

We estimate the state complexity for each of the four combined operations through individual nondeterministic state complexities (NSC). These results, compared with their (deterministic) state complexities, are listed in the following table, where A is an m-state DFA and B an n-state DFA:

Operations	State Complexity	Est. through NSC
$(L(A) \cup L(B))^*$	$2^{m+n-1} - 2^{m-1} - 2^{n-1} + 1$	2^{m+n+2}
$(L(A) \cap L(B))^*$	$\geq 2^{m(n-2)}$	2^{mn+1}
$(L(A)L(B))^*$	$2^{m+n-1} + 2^{m+n-4} - 2^{m-1} - 2^{n-1} + m + 1$	2^{m+n+1}
$(L(B)^R)^*$	2^n	2^{n+2}

It is clear from the above table that the estimates through nondeterministic state complexities are very close to the real state complexities for those combined operations. This fact also suggests that the compositions of the nondeterministic state complexities of individual operations are very close to the nondeterministic state complexities of those combined operations. Although the tight bounds or the accurate state complexities still need to be rigorously proved, those estimates are good enough for practical purposes in general.

Why the compositions of individual (deterministic) state complexities can be very different from the combined state complexities, but it appears not true for nondeterministic state complexities? Note that both (deterministic) state complexity and nondeterministic state complexity are worst-case complexities. One conjecture is that the (deterministic) state complexity of each individual operation can be far away from its corresponding average state complexity. However, this appears to be untrue in general for nondeterministic state complexities. Note that, unfortunately, average state complexity has not been studied except in [18] where several operations on unary automata, i.e., automata with the one-letter alphabet, have been studied. Here we talk about average state complexity only informally. The resulting finite automaton of an operation may fall into a proper subset of the finite automata in general setting, which may not include the worst cases of the second operation. However, for NFAs, it appears that the number of states in the worst cases after each of the operations, union, catenation, star, reversal, etc., is linear to their average case. Then the resulting NFAs from the first operation may not be very different from those worst-case NFAs for the second operation although they are restricted to only a proper subset of the general NFAs.

Using the same approach, i.e., through individual nondeterministic state complexities, we can give an upper bound for the (deterministic) state complexity of each of the following combined operations: reversal of union, reversal of intersection, reversal of catenation, and reversal of star.

Theorem 8. *Let A be an m-state DFA and B an n-state DFA, $m, n > 3$. Then*

(1) 2^{m+n+2} states are sufficient for a DFA to accept $(L(A) \cup L(B))^R$;
(2) 2^{mn+1} states are sufficient for a DFA to accept $(L(A) \cap L(B))^R$;
(3) 2^{m+n+1} states are sufficient for a DFA to accept $(L(A)L(B))^R$;
(4) 2^{n+2} states are sufficient for a DFA to accept $(L(B)^*)^R$.

Although several of the above estimates can be easily reduced, we predict that they are already very close to the accurate state complexities.

6   Conclusion and Open Problems

The state complexities of four different combinations of operations on regular languages have been considered: star of union, star of intersection, star of catenation, and star of reversal. In the first, third, and fourth cases, the state complexities of the combined operations are significantly smaller than the compositions of the state complexities of their participating individual operations. However, in the second case, they are very close. These results show that although the composition of the state complexities of individual operations gives an upper bound to the state complexity of the combined operation, this upper bound may or may not be close to the tight bound. The tight bound can be far from this bound. The state complexity of each combined operation has to be studied individually in order to know its result. There are many combinations of operations on regular languages that are worth studying. They are not restricted to combinations of two operations. Hopefully many new results on this topic will be obtained in the near future.

Consider the star operation on n-state DFA languages, $n > 0$, Clearly, there is only a subset of DFAs of n states such that the resulting minimal DFAs after the star operation on them have $2^{O(n)}$ states. We now call this set of DFAs the $2^{O(n)}$ group, for any $n \geq 1$. Clearly, the DFAs that accept the union of two regular languages and that are among the worst cases resulted from the union operation are not in the $2^{O(n)}$ group. Then there are at least the following two questions that may be interesting: (1) What are the properties of the $2^{O(n)}$ group for the star operation? (2) What are the properties of the DFAs that accept the union of two regular languages? Similar questions can be asked for many other operations and state complexities. It appears that many refined questions need to be solved in automata theory.

The estimates through individual nondeterministic state complexities for combined operations appear to be very close to the actual state complexities. One possible reason for this phenomenon is that the nondeterministic state complexity of an operation may be close to its average state complexity and this is not true for the (deterministic) state complexity of the same operation in general. Unfortunately, average state complexities in both deterministic case and nondeterministic case have not been studied except in [18]. Both deterministic and nondeterministic average state complexities, as well as their relations with the worst-case state complexities, are important future topics in this area of research.

References

1. J.-C. Birget, "Partial orders on words, minimal elements of regular languages, and state complexity", *Theoretical Computer Science* 119 (1993) 267-291.
2. C. Campeanu, K. Culik, K. Salomaa, S. Yu, "State Complexity of Basic Operations on Finite Languages", *Proceedings of the Fourth International Workshop on Implementing Automata* VIII 1-11, 1999. LNCS 2214, pp.60-70.
3. C. Campeanu, K. Salomaa, S. Yu, "Tight lower bound for the state complexity of shuffle of regular languages", *Journal of Automata, Languages and Combinatorics*, 7 (2002) 3, 303-310.
4. C. Campeanu, K. Salomaa, S. Yu, Chapter 5: "State Complexity of Regular Languages: Finite Versus Infinite", in *Finite vs Infinite – Contributions to an Eternal Dilemma*, edited by C. Calude and G. Paun, Springer 2000, pps. 53-73.
5. M. Domaratzki, "State complexity and proportional removals", *Journal of Automata, Languages and Combinatorics* 7 (2002) 455-468.
6. K. Ellul, B. Krawetz, J. Shallit, and M.-W. Wang, "Regular Expressions: New Results and Open Problems", *Journal of Automata, Languages and Combinatorics*, to appear.
7. Y. Gao, K. Salomaa, S. Yu, "State complexity of catenation and reversal combined with star", to appear at *Descriptional Complexity of Formal Systems* (DCFS 2006).
8. M. Holzer and M. Kutrib, "State complexity of basic operations on nondeterministic finite automata", *Proceedings of International Conference on Implementation and Application of Automata 2002* (CIAA 2002), Springer LNCS 2608, pp. 148-157.
9. M. Holzer and M. Kutrib, "Unary language operations and their nondeterministic state complexity", *Developments in Language Theory (DLT 2002)*, Springer LNCS 2450, pp. 162-172.
10. M. Holzer, K. Salomaa, S. Yu, "On the state complexity of k-entry deterministic finite automata", *Journal of Automata, Languages and Combinatorics* Vol. 6 (2001) 4, 453-466.
11. J.E. Hopcroft and J.D. Ullman, *Introduction to Automata Theory, Languages, and Computation*, Addison Wesley (1979), Reading, Mass.

12. K. Iwama, Y. Kambayashi, and K. Takaki, "Tight bounds on the number of states of DFAs that are equivalent to n-state NFAs", *Theoretical Computer Science* 237 (2000) 485-494.

13. G. Jirásková, "State complexity of some operations on regular languages", *Proceedings of 5th Workshop on Descriptional Complexity of Formal Systems* (2003) 114-125.

14. G. Jirásková, "State complexity of some operations on binary regular languages", *Theoretical Computer Science*, to appear.

15. J. Jirásek, G. Jirásková and A. Szabari, "State Complexity of Concatenation and Complementation of Regular Languages", *International Journal of Foundations of Computer Science* Vol. 16 (2005) 511–529.

16. G. Jirásková and A. Okhotin, "State complexity of cyclic shift" *Proceedings of DCFS 2005* (Como, Italy, June 30 - July 2, 2005) 182–193.

17. E. Leiss. Succinct representation of regular languages by boolean automata II. Theoretical Computer Science, 13 (1981), pp. 323–330.

18. C. Nicaud, "Average State Complexity of Operations on Unary Automata", *MFCS'99, LNCS* 1672 (1999) 231-240.

19. G. Pighizzini and J. Shallit, "Unary language operations, state complexity and Jacobsthal's function", *International Journal of Foundations of Computer Science* Vol. 13 No. 1 (2002) 145-159.

20. N. Rampersad, "The state complexity of L^2 and L^k", *Information Processing Letters* 98 (2006) 231-234.

21. A. Salomaa, *Theory of Automata*, Pergamon Press (1969), Oxford.

22. A. Salomaa, K. Salomaa, S. Yu, "State Complexity of Combined Operations", *Theoretical Computer Science*, to appear.

23. A. Salomaa, D. Wood, and S. Yu, "On the state complexity of reversals of regular languages", *Theoretical Computer Science* 320 (2004) 293-313.

24. K. Salomaa and S. Yu, "NFA to DFA Transformation for Finite Languages over Arbitrary Alphabets", *Journal of Automata, Languages and Combinatorics*, 2 (1997) 3, 177-186.

25. S. Yu, Regular languages. In: *Handbook of Formal Languages,* Vol. 1, (G. Rozenberg and A. Salomaa, Eds.), Springer-Verlag, 1997, pp. 41–110.

26. S. Yu, "State Complexity of Regular Languages", *Journal of Automata, Languages and Combinatorics*, 6 (2001) 2, 221-234.

27. S. Yu, "State Complexity: Recent Results and Open Problems", invited talk at ICALP 2004 Formal Language Workshop, also appears in *Fundamenta Informaticae* 64 (2005) 1-4, 471-480.

28. S. Yu, Q. Zhuang and K. Salomaa, The state complexities of some basic operations on regular languages, *Theoretical Computer Science* 125 (1994) 315–328.

Path-Equivalent Removals of ε-transitions in a Genomic Weighted Finite Automaton

Mathieu Giraud, Philippe Veber, and Dominique Lavenier

IRISA / CNRS / Université de Rennes 1
35042 Rennes Cedex, France
{mgiraud, pveber, lavenier}@irisa.fr

Abstract. Weighted finite automata (WFA) are used with accelerating hardware to scan large genomic banks. Hardwiring such automata raise surface area and clock frequency constraints, requiring efficient ε-transitions-removal techniques. In this paper, we present new bounds on the number of new transitions for several ε-transitions-removal problems. We study the case of acyclic WFA. We introduce a new problem, the partial removal of ε-transitions while accepting short chains of ε-transitions.

1 Introduction

Weighted Finite Automata (WFA) are used to find occurrences of biological patterns in genomic databases containing tens of gigabytes of data. Biological patterns can be seen as regular or weighted expressions over the 20-letter amino acid alphabet. They may represent the signature of a protein family, the features of a domain or the specific location of an active site. The usual length ranges of the patterns are from a few amino acids to a few tenth.

WFA can be efficiently hardwired onto reconfigurable architectures (namely FPGA components) to speed up the search of biological patterns, reducing computation time from hours to minutes [1]. Today, with the exponential growth of genomic data, the hardwire WFA alternative offers an interesting approach compared to pure software implementation.

Hardware speed comes from the ability to compute all WFA states simultaneously. Actually, genomic data (input string) are processed on-the-fly, and the performance of a hardwired WFA is mainly determined by the input data rate. Thus, the processing time becomes independent of the WFA size, and is only dictated by the time for accessing all the items of the database.

This scheme is valid as long as the WFA fits into FPGA components. Unfortunately, biological patterns may require consequent reconfigurable resources, particularly when insertion/deletion errors are considered. In that case, insertions are modeled by cyclic transitions and deletions by ε-transitions. Resulting WFA are thus much larger in terms of the number of transitions. From a hardware point of view, the resources are directly related to the number of transitions to hardwire. Hence, finding equivalent automata with less transitions is highly beneficial.

O.H. Ibarra and H.-C. Yen (Eds.): CIAA 2006, LNCS 4094, pp. 23–33, 2006.
© Springer-Verlag Berlin Heidelberg 2006

Beside the automaton size, a direct hardware implementation of ε-transitions is not realistic. Fig. 1 exemplifies the hardware mapping of a WFA with ε-transitions. Paths with ε-transitions are represented by dotted lines: they systematically bypass state registers. The main consequence is that a long *critical path* (dashed line) is created from the input to the output. The critical path is defined as the longest path between two registers, and determines the maximum clock frequency of the circuit. The longer the path, the lower the frequency. Hence, to keep a reasonable working frequency, the critical path needs to be broken into smaller parts by removing some ε-transitions.

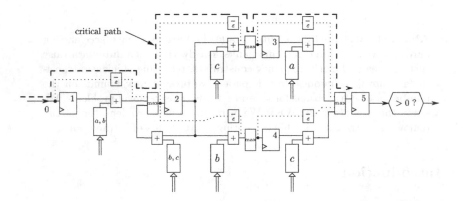

Fig. 1. Hardwiring a WFA with 5 regular transitions doubled with ε-transitions [2]. A critical path runs through the whole automaton.

The classical method removing ε-transitions in automata uses the ε-closure of every state [3,4]. Recently, for WFA, Mohri proposed a generic algorithm with a smallest distance method [5]. A certain condition must be checked to ensure that the weights are well-defined in cycles.

These algorithms can raise the number of transitions from n to $\mathcal{O}(n^2)$. The resulting automaton can be minimized [6], but for large automata, such a limit makes the hardware implementation impossible. As an example, in [7], we experienced an 80-state automaton for discovering olfactory receptor genes in the dog genome. On this automaton, the classical ε-transitions-removal algorithms produce more than 3100 new transitions. This number reaches the limit of today FPGA's technology and prevents larger automata from being hardwired.

Hromkovic proposed a study for ε-transitions in finite automata [8]. There are rational expressions of size $\mathcal{O}(n)$ such that every ε-free recognizing automaton has a size $\Omega(n \log n)$. Lifshits raised this bound to $\Omega(n \log^2 n / \log \log n)$ [9]. Other works optimized the creation time of those automata [10].

In this paper we study the *development* of WFA: we double every transition with an ε-transition, and we study the number of new transitions created when removing the ε-transitions. We previously proposed a first study for linear-shaped automata: in this case, we designed an optimal method that produces automata with $\Theta(n \log n)$ new transitions [2].

The rest of the paper is organized as follows. Section 2 provides WFA background. Then, in Section 3, we study the development of WFA for acyclic automata. Section 4 presents a new problem driven by the hardware constraints: the removal while accepting short ε-chains. The final section concludes with experimental results and perspectives.

2 Background

2.1 WFA and Pattern Matching

Definition 1. *A Weighted Finite Automaton (WFA) is a 5-tuple $\mathcal{A} = (Q, \Sigma, \Delta, I, F)$, where Q is a finite set of states, Σ a finite alphabet, $\Delta \subset Q \times Q \times (\delta : \Sigma \mapsto \mathbb{K})$ a finite transition table, $I \subseteq Q$ and $F \subseteq Q$ the sets of initial and final states.*

The number of transitions of the WFA is $|\Delta|$. For each transition $\tau = (q, q', \delta) \in \Delta$, we denote by $\mathsf{i}[\tau] = q$ its initial state, $\mathsf{f}[\tau] = q'$ its final state, and $\delta[\tau] = \delta$ its weight function. A WFA without ε-transitions is a WFA such that $\delta(\varepsilon) = -\infty$ for every transition (q, q', δ). Now we define paths as consecutive labeled transitions:

Definition 2. *A path $\pi = (\tau_1, \alpha_1) \ldots (\tau_k, \alpha_k) \in (\Delta \times (\Sigma))^*$ in a WFA $\mathcal{A}$ is a succession of pairs of transitions and characters where the transitions $\tau_1 \ldots \tau_k$ are consecutive transitions, that is $\mathsf{f}[\tau_i] = \mathsf{i}[\tau_{i+1}]$ for $i = 1 \ldots k-1$, and where the characters α_i are in Σ. The label of π is the word $\alpha_1 \ldots \alpha_k$.*

The weight function δ can be extended to paths: for a path $\pi = (\tau_1, \alpha_1) \ldots (\tau_k, \alpha_k)$, we define $\delta(\pi) = \delta[\tau_1](\alpha_1) + \ldots + \delta[\tau_k](\alpha_k)$. Weights on words used in pattern matching are computed as weights on paths between some initial and final states.

2.2 Path-Equivalence

Now we give a definition of our ε-transition-removal problem. We define it as finding a new automaton with a special kind of equivalence, the path-equivalence, which requires that some paths (the closed paths, see below) have a superior path in the corresponding automaton.

Definition 3. *One path π is superior to another one π' if both paths have the same label, the same initial state and the same final state, and if $\delta(\pi) \geq \delta(\pi')$.*

Definition 4. *A path $\pi = (\tau_1, \alpha_1) \ldots (\tau_k, \alpha_k)$ is left-closed if it begins with an initial state ($\mathsf{i}[\tau_1] \in I$) or if its first character α_1 is different than ε. Similarly, a path is right-closed if $\mathsf{f}[\tau_k] \in F$ or $\alpha_k \neq \varepsilon$. A path is closed if it is closed at both sides.*

Definition 5. *Two WFA $\mathcal{A} = (Q, \Sigma, \Delta, I, F)$ and $\mathcal{A}' = (Q, \Sigma, \Delta', I, F)$ are path-equivalent if every closed path in $\mathcal{A}$ labeled by a word $w \neq \varepsilon$ has a superior path in $\mathcal{A}'$ and reciprocally.*

Basically, the path-equivalence states that the two automata simulate each other through their paths. Usual algorithms that remove the ε-transitions such as [4] or [5] produce path-equivalent automata.

2.3   Development of an Automaton

Given a WFA without ε-transitions $\mathcal{A} = (Q, \Sigma, \Delta, I, F)$ and a deletion cost c_ε, we define $\mathcal{A}_\varepsilon$ as the WFA in which all transitions of $\mathcal{A}$ are doubled by ε-transitions. More precisely, every transition $(q, q', \delta) \in \Delta$ is extended with $\delta(\varepsilon) = c_\varepsilon$.

Definition 6. *Given a WFA $\mathcal{A}$, any WFA $\mathcal{A}'$ is a development of $\mathcal{A}$ if $\mathcal{A}'$ is path-equivalent to $\mathcal{A}_\varepsilon$ and if has no ε-transitions. We say that $\mathcal{A}'$ is developed from $\mathcal{A}$ if $\mathcal{A}'$ is a development of $\mathcal{A}$.*

To be efficiently harwired, a WFA needs to be developed with *as few new transitions as we can*. In the general case, the ε-transitions-removal from an automaton with n transitions gives an automaton with $\mathcal{O}(n^2)$ new transitions. In [2], we studied the case of linear-shaped automata. We designed an optimal method that produces automata with $\Theta(n \log n)$ new transitions.

3   Removal in Acyclic Automata

Here we use the results on linear-shaped WFA to analyze the number of new transitions in the developments of some more generic automata. To ensure that the weights are well defined, automata with cycles require special constraints [5]. The section 3.1 considers *acyclic automata* with n states : we give an upper bound to develop such automata. The section 3.2 extends the result to automata with cycles, but with no cycles on ε-transitions. Such automata are common in biological applications (Fig. 2).

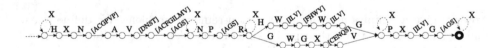

Fig. 2. Detail of a genomic automaton recognizing MIP membrane proteins [11]. The complete automaton has more than 300 transitions. Except for some insertion transitions (X), this automaton is acyclic.

3.1   Acyclic Automata

Definition 7. *A WFA $\mathcal{A} = (Q, \Sigma, \Delta, I, F)$ is acyclic if its graph has no cycle. The states of an acyclic WFA can be numbered $q_1, q_2, \ldots q_n$ such that there is no backward transition $(q_i, q_j, \delta_{i,j})$ with $i \geq j$.*

We call such a WFA a *numbered* automaton. The following algorithm develops a numbered automaton with n states from the development of two sub-automata obtained by cutting the automaton at a state q_z.

Algorithm 1. Development of a numbered WFA

Input: a numbered WFA with n states $\mathcal{A} = (Q, \Sigma, \Delta, I, F)$, an integer $z \in [2, n-1]$, a cost c_ε

> **Let** $\mathcal{C}$ be the set of all cut transitions $(q_i, q_j, \delta_{i,j})$ with $i < z < j$
> **Let** Z be a set of states touching $\mathcal{C}$
>
> **Let** $\mathcal{A}_1 = (Q_1 = \{q_1 \ldots q_z\} \cup Z, \Sigma, \Delta_1, I, \{q_z\} \cup Z)$
> and $\mathcal{A}_2 = (Q_2 = \{q_z \ldots q_n\} \cup Z, \Sigma, \Delta_2, \{q_z\} \cup Z, F)$
>   where the transition tables Δ_1 and Δ_2 are the restrictions of Δ on Q_1 and Q_2
>
> **Let** $\mathcal{A}'_1$ and $\mathcal{A}'_2$ recursively be two developments of $\mathcal{A}_1$ and $\mathcal{A}_2$
> **Let** $\mathcal{A}'$ be the concatenation of $\mathcal{A}'_1$ and $\mathcal{A}'_2$: $\mathcal{A}' = (Q, \Sigma, \Delta', I, F)$, $\Delta' = \Delta'_1 \cup \Delta'_2$
>
> **For** all q_i in Q_1
>   Add to Δ' the transition (q_i, q, δ'_i) for all final states $q \in F$
>   with $\delta'_i(\alpha) = \max_{i+1 \leq k \leq n} [(n-i-1)c_\varepsilon + \delta_k(\alpha)]$
>
> **For** all q_i in Q_2
>   Add to Δ' the transition (q, q_i, δ''_i) for all initial states $q \in I$
>   with $\delta''_i(\alpha) = \max_{1 \leq k \leq i} [(i-1)c_\varepsilon + \delta_k(\alpha)]$

Output: the WFA $\mathcal{A}' = (Q, \Sigma, \Delta', I, F)$

In the algorithm for linear-shaped WFA (Algorithm 1 in [2]), initial and final states of both sub-automata guarantee that the paths are closed. Here some transitions are *cut* over q_z (Fig. 3). All the paths are closed if one adds to each sub-automaton a set of states Z that *touches* the cut transitions, that is a set Z such that any cut transition starts or ends in Z. Each state in Z is a final state for the left sub-automaton and an initial state for the right one : the sub-automata are overlapping. We have the following property:

Property 1. *The algorithm 1 builds an automaton which is path-equivalent to the initial automaton.*

Proof. We just give the sketch of the proof, which is similar to the case of linear-shaped WFA (Lemma 3 in [2]). $\boxed{\mathcal{A} \mapsto \mathcal{A}'}$ Each closed path of $\mathcal{A}$ not labeled by ε and not completely included in $\mathcal{A}_1$ or in $\mathcal{A}_2$ can be written as $\pi_1\pi_2$, where π_1 and π_2 are closed paths in $\mathcal{A}_1$ and $\mathcal{A}_2$. Any such decomposition leads to a superior closed path in $\mathcal{A}'$. $\boxed{\mathcal{A}' \mapsto \mathcal{A}}$ Reciprocally, any closed path of $\mathcal{A}'$ either goes through a state $q \in \{q_z\} \cup Z$, or jumps over such a state. In both case a superior closed path of $\mathcal{A}$ can be reconstructed.

Each step of the algorithm adds no more than $|Q_1| \cdot |F| + |Q_2| \cdot |I|$ transitions. To bound this value, we need a bound on $|Z|$.

Definition 8. *Let be a numbered WFA with states $\{q_1, q_2 \ldots q_n\}$, and q_z a state. The* width κ_z *is the number of transitions (q_a, q_b, δ) with $a < z < b$.*

The *maximal width* is $\mathcal{K} = \max_i \kappa_i$: it can be seen as the maximal number of branches in the WFA, except the main branch. On the automaton depicted on

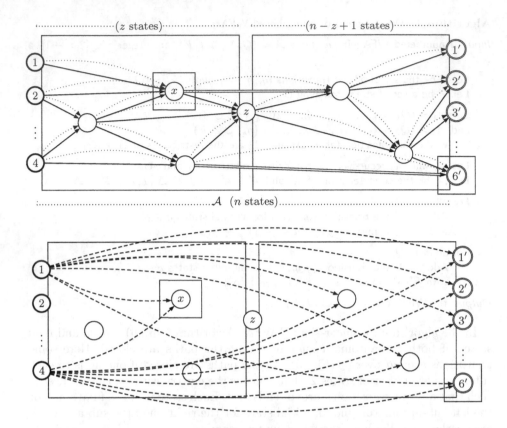

Fig. 3. Algorithm developing a numbered WFA with n states. A state q_z is chosen to split the automaton into two parts with z and $n - z + 1$ states. The two cut transitions are shown in double lines. The set $Z = \{x, 6'\}$ touches every cut transition. This set Z is added to the two parts to give the sub-automata $\mathcal{A}_1$ and $\mathcal{A}_2$. Final states of $\mathcal{A}_1$ (and initial states of $\mathcal{A}_2$) are $\{z\} \cup Z$. At the bottom, we add to the developments of the two sub-automata transitions from initial states of $\mathcal{A}_1$ to all states of $\mathcal{A}_2$. With the symmetrical operation, no more than $|Q_1| \cdot |F| + |Q_2| \cdot |I|$ transitions are created.

Fig. 2, we have $\mathcal{K} = 1$ for all numberings. In the general case, the widths depend on the chosen numbering.

At each step, the set Z has no more than $\mathcal{K}$ elements. When applying recursively algorithm 1, the sets I and F will always have no more than $\mathcal{K}+1$ elements. Then one step of the algorithm adds no more than $(|Q_1| + |Q_2|) \cdot (\mathcal{K} + 1) \leq (n + \mathcal{K}) \cdot (\mathcal{K} + 1)$ transitions. We thus have the following consequence of the property 1:

Property 2. *Any numbered WFA with a maximal width $\mathcal{K}$ can be developed with $\mathcal{O}((\mathcal{K} + 1) \cdot n \cdot (\log n + \mathcal{K}))$ transitions.*

This coarse bound guarantees that automata with a small maximum width are developed with very few new transitions (Fig. 6). This is sufficient for real-life genomic automata representing biological features. Such automata, hand-crafted or computed by state-merging techniques [11], are compounds of a few linear-shaped parts (Fig. 2).

For the *lower bound*, the generic argument on linear-shaped WFA can be applied to the longest path in the WFA. If this longest path has a size $\ell \leq n$, we have a bound of $\Omega(\ell \log \ell)$.

3.2 ε-acyclic Automata

To extend the previous bounds for automata *with cycles*, we can consider a slightly modified automaton. An *ε-acyclic automaton* is an automaton without cycles of ε-transitions (Fig. 4). As an ε-acyclic automaton has a numbering with no backward ε-transition, the algorithm 1 can still be used. The same bound of $\mathcal{O}((\mathcal{K}+1) \cdot n \cdot (\log n + \mathcal{K}))$ is obtained (each width κ_i is now the number of ε-transitions cut by the state q_i).

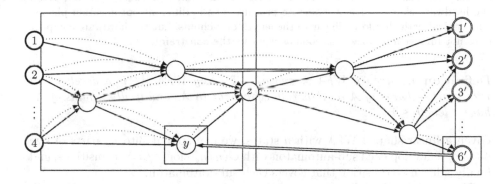

Fig. 4. Unlike the automaton on Fig. 3, this numbered automaton has a backward transition $(6', y, \delta)$. However, that transition is not doubled with an ε-transition.

In real applications, if we have an automaton $\mathcal{A}$ without ε-transitions, we add *some* ε-transitions while keeping the automaton ε-acyclic. This construction is justified when the automaton represents biological structures made of similar units. Those units are separated by sequences that cannot be deleted, as for instance in the case of exon recognition.

4   Removal with Short ε-chains

To further lower the number of new transitions, we can remark that short ε-chains (that is chains of successive ε-transitions) can be actually hardwired with a reasonable critical path (Fig. 5).

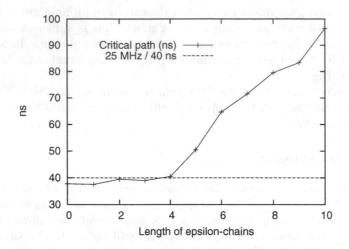

Fig. 5. Critical path for ε-chains with 8-bit weights and a 40 ns (25 MHz) constraint on a WFA with 20 regular transitions and different lengths of ε-chains. Chains of 3 ε-transitions can be hardwired. The FPGA being half-filled (between 48% and 51%), the hardware compiler has a moderate pressure on the different optimisation phases. The critical path should be linear to the length of ε-chains, but the hardware compiler does not further minimize it as soon as it meets the constraint.

Definition 9. *Given a WFA $\mathcal{A}$ and $n_\varepsilon \in \mathbb{N}$, any WFA $\mathcal{A}''$ is a development with short ε-chains of $\mathcal{A}$ if $\mathcal{A}''$ is path-equivalent to $\mathcal{A}_\varepsilon$ and if all ε-chains of $\mathcal{A}''$ have a length $\leq n_\varepsilon$.*

Given a linear-shaped WFA with n states, we can split it into n_ε parts of size $\mathcal{O}(n/n_\varepsilon)$, develop each sub-automaton with $\mathcal{O}(n/n_\varepsilon \cdot \log(n/n_\varepsilon))$ transitions, and finally add an ε-transition that covers each sub-automaton.

Thus we have the following property:

Property 3. *A linear-shaped WFA with n states can be developed with short ε-chains with $\mathcal{O}(n \log(n/n_\varepsilon))$ new transitions.*

Furthermore, if we restrict that all remaining ε-transitions are *original*, that is, they were present before the removal, the same bound is a lower bound:

Property 4. *Given n_ε, any development with short original ε-chains of a linear-shaped WFA with n states has $\Omega(n \log(n/n_\varepsilon))$ new transitions.*

The proof, which enumerates some sets in which at least one transition must appear in the automaton, is given in appendix. Although accepting short chains of ε-transitions is a local change, this technique lowers the actual number of new transitions (Fig. 6). The ε-chains can be used in (ε)-acyclic WFA to obtain $\mathcal{O}((\mathcal{K}+1) \cdot n \cdot (\log(n/n_\varepsilon) + \mathcal{K}))$ new transitions.

Number of states of the initial automaton	20	80	200
Quadratical ε-transitions-removal algorithms	190	3160	19900
Linear-shaped WFA [2]	69	433	1345
Linear-shaped WFA, development with short ε-chains (section 4)			
ε-chains of length $\leq n_\varepsilon = 3$	42	310	1022
ε-chains of length $\leq n_\varepsilon = 5$	30	250	890
(ε-)acyclic WFA (section 3)			
$\mathcal{K} = 1$, best-case	96	522	1555
$\mathcal{K} = 1$, worst-case	141	925	2835
$\mathcal{K} = 2$, best-case	124	612	1766
$\mathcal{K} = 2$, worst-case	176	1292	4096

Fig. 6. Number of new transitions produced while removing ε-transitions on various automata. For acyclic WFA, complexity range from best-case (only one additional branch through the whole WFA) to the worst-case (each cut has a maximal width: the automaton is constantly branching). Even in the worst-case situation, genomic WFA with 80 states and no more than $\mathcal{K} + 1 = 3$ branches can be efficiently hardwired with less than 1300 new transitions.

5 Conclusions and Perspectives

The removal techniques presented in sections 3 and 4 allow larger automata to be hardwired on a given FPGA. For acyclic automata, the best results for a strict application of algorithm 1 would require finding the numbering of the states that minimizes the maximal width $\mathcal{K}$. In fact, for real automata with a small number of branches as the one in Fig. 2, good solutions are found when cutting at the branching states.

Other studies could find more precise bounds. For acyclic automata, the initial number of transitions could be taken into account. Finally, we plan to study *approximated developments* of automata, in which the resulting automaton would not strictly be path-equivalent to the initial one. In real applications, the cost assigned to deletions prevents sequences with too many ε-transitions from being accepted.

References

1. Giraud, M., Lavenier, D.: Linear encoding scheme for weighted finite automata. In: Ninth International Conference on Implementation and Application of Automata (CIAA 2004), LNCS 3317. (2004)
2. Giraud, M., Lavenier, D.: Dealing with hardware space limits when removing epsilon-transitions in a genomic weighted finite automaton. Journal of Automata, Languages and Combinatorics **10** (2005)
3. Aho, A.V., Sethi, R., Ullman, J.D.: Compilers, Principles, Techniques and Tools. Addison Wesley (1986)
4. Thompson, K.: Regular expression search algorithm. Communications of the ACM **11** (1968) 419–422

5. Mohri, M.: Generic epsilon-removal and input epsilon-normalization algorithms for weighted transducers. International Journal of Foundations of Computer Science **13** (2002) 129–143
6. Mohri, M.: Finite-State Transducers in Language and Speech Processing. Computational Linguistics **23** (1997) 269–311
7. Quignon, P., Giraud, M., Rimbault, M., Lavigne, P., Tacher, S., Morin, E., Retout, E., Valin, A.S., Lindblad-Toh, K., Nicolas, J., Galibert, F.: The dog and rat olfactory receptor repertoires. Genome Biology **6** (2005) R83
8. Hromkovic, J., Seibert, S., Wilke, T.: Translating regular expressions into small epsilon-free nondeterministic finite automata. In: 14th Symposium on Theoretical Aspects of Computer Science (STACS 97), LNCS 1200. (1997) 55–66
9. Lifshits, Y.: A lower bound on the size of ε-free NFA corresponding to a regular expression. Information Processing Letters **85** (2003) 293–299
10. Hagenah, C., Muscholl, A.: Computing ε-free NFA from regular expressions in $\mathcal{O}(n \log^2(n))$ time. Mathematical Foundations of Computer Science (1998) 277–285
11. Kerbellec, G., Coste, F.: A similar fragments merging approach to learn automata on proteins. In: Machine Learning: ECML 2005. (2005)

Appendix

Proof of Property 4

This proof uses a similar technique than the proof of the Lemma 6 in [2], but additional work is done to handle the short ε-chains. The *span* of a transition (q_i, q_j, δ) is $|j - i|$.

Proof. Let $\mathcal{A}$ be a linear-shaped WFA with n states, and $\mathcal{A}''$ a development with short original ε-chains of $\mathcal{A}$. Let $\pi = (\tau_{a+1}, \alpha_A)(\tau_{a+2}, \varepsilon) \ldots (\tau_{b-1}, \varepsilon)(\tau_b, \alpha_B)$ be a closed path in $\mathcal{A}$, where α_A and α_B are two characters different from ε. This path has in $\mathcal{A}''$ a superior path π' that can be written as $\pi' = (\pi'_1, \varepsilon)\ (\tau_A, \alpha_A)\ (\pi'_2, \varepsilon)\ (\tau_B, \alpha_B)\ (\pi'_3, \varepsilon)$.

As the three paths π'_1, π'_2 are π'_3 are original ε-chains, any of them has a span not greater than n_ε transitions, that is $3n_\varepsilon$ globally. Therefore, at least one of the two transitions τ_A and τ_B has a span included in $\{\lceil \frac{k-3n_\varepsilon}{2} \rceil, \ldots, k-1\}$ with $k = b - a$ (Figure 7).

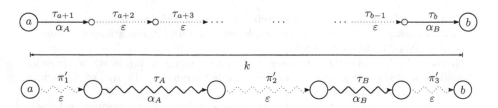

Fig. 7. Proof of the property 4. At least one of the transitions τ_A and τ_B has a span included in $\{\lceil \frac{k-3n_\varepsilon}{2} \rceil, \ldots, k-1\}$.

If we consider all $n-k+1$ pairs (a, b) with the same $k = b-a$, then the WFA $\mathcal{A}''$ has no less than $(n-k+1)/2$ transitions of span included in $\{ \lceil \frac{k-3n_\varepsilon}{2} \rceil, \ldots, k-1 \}$.

Let (k_i) the sequence defined by $k_{i+1} = 2k_i + 3n_\varepsilon$ and $k_0 = 1$. We have $k_i = 2^i(1 + 3n_\varepsilon) - 3n_\varepsilon$. We consider several ks taking the values of (k_i) from $i = 1$ to the last i such that $k_i \leq n$, that is $i_f = \left\lfloor \log \frac{n+3n_\varepsilon}{1+3n_\varepsilon} \right\rfloor = \Theta(\log(n/n_\varepsilon))$.

Then the WFA $\mathcal{A}''$ has not less than $\Sigma_{i=1}^{i_f}(n - k_i + 1)/2 = \Theta(n \log(n/n_\varepsilon))$ transitions.

Hybrid Extended Finite Automata

Henning Bordihn[1], Markus Holzer[2], and Martin Kutrib[3]

[1] Institut für Informatik, Universität Potsdam,
August-Bebel-Straße 89, D-14482 Potsdam, Germany
henning@cs.uni-potsdam.de
[2] Institut für Informatik, Technische Universität München,
Boltzmannstraße 3, D-85748 Garching bei München, Germany
holzer@informatik.tu-muenchen.de
[3] Institut für Informatik, Universität Giessen,
Arndtstraße 2, D-35392 Giessen, Germany
kutrib@informatik.uni-giessen.de

Abstract. Extended finite automata are finite state automata equipped
with the additional ability to apply an operation on the currently remaining input word, depending on the current state. *Hybrid* extended finite
automata can choose from a finite set of such operations. In this paper, five word operations are taken into consideration which always yield
letter-equivalent results, namely reversal and shift operations. The computational power of those machines is investigated, locating the corresponding families of languages in the Chomsky hierarchy. Furthermore,
different types of hybrid extended finite automata, defined by the set
of operations they are allowed to apply, are compared with each other,
demonstrating that there exist dependencies and independencies between
the input manipulating operations.

1 Introduction

Finite automata are probably best known for capturing the family of regular
languages. These machines have been intensively studied and moreover, have
been extended in various ways [4,5,7,9]. Recently, in a series of papers, so called
extended finite automata, which are finite state machines with the additional
ability to manipulate the unread part of the input by a formal language operation on words, were introduced and investigated. Typical formal language theoretical operations are, for instance, reversal, shift, or bio-inspired operations.
This led to the devices of flip-pushdown automata [13], the "flip-pushdown input-
reversal" theorem [10], input-reversal automata [1], revolving-input automata [2],
and hairpin finite automata [3]. It is worth mentioning that some of these devices
induce a hierarchy of languages based on the number of operations allowed during the computation. Loosely speaking, it was shown that $k + 1$ pushdown flips
are better than k for both deterministic and non-deterministic flip-pushdown automata [10]. A similar statement has been proved in the context of input-reversal
automata [1]. Moreover, input-reversal automata have been shown to be deeply
linked to controlled linear context-free languages [8], leading to an alternative

O.H. Ibarra and H.-C. Yen (Eds.): CIAA 2006, LNCS 4094, pp. 34–45, 2006.

characterization of the Khabbaz hierarchy of languages [11,12]. In the case of revolving-input finite automata and hairpin finite automata language families are obtained that are incomparable to classical classes like, e.g., the family of context-free languages.

Common to all of the above mentioned types of automata is that the machine is equipped with a *single* operation that can manipulate the remaining input during the computation. Here we restrict ourselves to the case of extended finite automata, that is, to finite state automata which can perform such an operation on the still unread part of the input. We further generalize the notion of extended finite automata to hybrid extended finite automata allowing the automaton to choose from a finite set $\mathcal{O}$ of operations during the computation. Obviously, with no further limitation on $\mathcal{O}$ one can define operations that provide computational power beyond that of Turing machines, for example, by defining an operation to be an oracle for the halting problem. So, there is an interest in natural operations that are somehow feasible. Therefore, we restrict ourselves to simple operations like those mentioned above such as input-reversal (ir), left- and right-revolving (lr and rr, respectively), circular-interchange (ci), and circular-shift (cs). Thus, we will have $\mathcal{O} = \{\text{ir}, \text{lr}, \text{rr}, \text{ci}, \text{cs}\}$ in this paper. Note that all these operations yield letter-equivalent results when being applied, i.e., they only change the ordering of the remaining input symbols.

At first glance we show that λ-moves, regardless whether they are used during ordinary transitions and/or non-ordinary transitions, do not increase the computational power of hybrid extended finite automata, whenever the operations are somehow "well-behaved." Here well-behaved means that applying an operation blindly and non-blindly at the same time gives the same result in both cases. For instance, the "blind" input-reversal mapping v to v^R and the "non-blind" input-reversal mapping av to $v^R a$, for all letters a, are well-behaved in the above sense. Observe that all operations from $\mathcal{O}$ are well-behaved. What concerns the relationships between the language families induced by hybrid extended finite automata with some set of operations $D \subseteq \mathcal{O}$ and the families of the Chomsky-hierarchy we find the following situation: (1) Obviously, if the number of operations applied is zero, the family of regular languages is characterized. We show that this remains true for every D as long as the number of operations is arbitrarily constant. (2) Moreover, it is shown that for every D the language accepted by any hybrid extended finite automaton with operations from D is context-sensitive. (3) In most cases, namely, whenever D contains at least one of the operations lr, rr, or cs, then the family of languages accepted by hybrid extended finite automata with D as set of operations is incomparable to the families of 2-linear (deterministic) context-free and (deterministic) context-free languages.

In the classical theory of automata and formal languages many results hold for a large variety of classes of automata, when appropriately abstracted. This led to the rich theory of abstract families of automata (AFA), which is the equivalent of the theory of abstract families of languages (AFL); for a general treatment of machines and languages we refer, e.g., to [6]. As a first step towards a similar theory for (hybrid) extended finite automata we study the dependencies of modes of operations. There it turns out that, hybrid extended finite automata without the circular-interchanging operation, but with at least *two* operations from the set $\{\text{ir}, \text{lr}, \text{rr}\}$ characterize the family of languages accepted by so called bi-revolving finite automata [2]. Observe, that a bi-revolving finite automaton is an $\{\text{lr}, \text{rr}\}$-NFA, i.e., a hybrid extended finite automaton with the operations lr and rr, in our terminology. Thus, this family of languages is the most general class that can be obtained by operations from the set $\mathcal{O} \setminus \{\text{ci}\}$. As the reader may have noticed, the circular-interchanging operation ci is excluded. Although extended finite automata with the ci operation characterize the family of regular languages, even in the case when the number of operations is unbounded [2], combining circular-interchange with some other operation may increase the computational power of the underlying device. For instance, we show that right-revolving and circular-interchanging is better than right-revolving, i.e., the family of languages accepted by $\{\text{rr}, \text{ci}\}$-NFA's is a strict superset of the family of languages accepted by rr-NFA's or in other words by right-revolving finite automata. On the other hand, when combining input-reversal with circular-interchanging, then no increase in computational power compared to input-reversal only is obtained. We have to leave open, whether the aforementioned most general language family of bi-revolving languages is "stable" under the circular-interchanging operation. Here stable means that every hybrid extended finite automaton with the operations lr, rr, and ci can be simulated by a bi-revolving finite automaton.

2   Preliminaries

We denote the cardinality of a set S by $|S|$ and its powerset by 2^S. The empty word is denoted by λ, the reversal of a word w by w^R, and for the length of w we write $|w|$. For the number of occurrences of a symbol a in w we use the notation $|w|_a$. Set inclusion and strict set inclusion are denoted by $\subseteq$ and $\subset$, respectively. If there is no danger of confusion, any singleton set may be identified with its element. By $\mathscr{L}(\text{CSL})$, $\mathscr{L}(\text{CFL})$, $\mathscr{L}(\text{DCFL})$, $\mathscr{L}(\text{2-LIN})$, $\mathscr{L}(\text{2-DLIN})$, $\mathscr{L}(\text{LIN})$, and $\mathscr{L}(\text{REG})$ the families of context-sensitive, context-free, deterministic context-free, 2-linear context-free, 2-linear deterministic context-free, linear context-free, and regular languages, respectively, are denoted.

A *(non-deterministic) finite state automaton*, NFA for short, is a 5-tuple $A = (Q, \Sigma, \delta, q_0, F)$, where Q is a finite set of states, Σ is the input alphabet, δ is a mapping from $Q \times (\Sigma \cup \{\lambda\})$ into 2^Q, called the transition function, $q_0 \in Q$ is the initial state, and $F \subseteq Q$ is the set of accepting states. A *configuration* of a finite state automaton is a couple (q, w), where $q \in Q$ is the current state and $w \in \Sigma^*$ is the still unread part of the input. For any a in $\Sigma \cup \{\lambda\}$ and w in Σ^*, we write $(q, aw) \vdash_A (p, w)$, if p is in $\delta(q, a)$.

In the following we consider finite state automata with the ability to apply additional operations to the unread input. We may start with a uniform definition which generalizes the one given in, e.g., [2].

Definition 1. *A (non-deterministic) hybrid extended finite (state) automaton is a 7-tuple $A = (Q, \Sigma, \delta, \Delta, \phi, q_0, F)$, where $A = (Q, \Sigma, \delta, q_0, F)$ is a finite state* *automaton,* Δ *is a finite set of mappings from* $Q \times (\Sigma \cup \{\lambda\})$ *into* 2^Q, *and* ϕ *is the interpretation of* Δ *which is a function from* Δ *into a set* $\mathcal{O}$ *of operation symbols.*

The configurations of a hybrid extended finite state automaton are defined as for finite state automata. The transitions according to δ will be referred to as *ordinary transitions* and denoted by $\vdash^o_A$. The operations which can be additionally applied to the unread part of the input are specified by the interpretation ϕ of Δ. In the present paper, we restrict ourselves to the set $\mathcal{O} = \{\mathrm{ir}, \mathrm{lr}, \mathrm{rr}, \mathrm{ci}, \mathrm{cs}\}$ of operation symbols. The corresponding transition relations are defined as follows: Let $p, q \in Q$, $a \in \Sigma \cup \{\lambda\}$, $b, c \in \Sigma$, and $v, w \in \Sigma^*$, then

- an *input-reversal* transition is defined by $(q, aw) \vdash^{\mathrm{ir}}_A (p, w^R a)$, if there is $\tau \in \Delta$ with $\phi(\tau) = \mathrm{ir}$ and $p \in \tau(q, a)$,
- a *left-revolving* transition is defined by $(q, a) \vdash^{\mathrm{lr}}_A (p, a)$ and $(q, awb) \vdash^{\mathrm{lr}}_A$ (p, baw), if there is $\tau \in \Delta$ with $\phi(\tau) = \mathrm{lr}$ and $p \in \tau(q, a)$,
- a *right-revolving* transition is defined by $(q, cw) \vdash^{\mathrm{rr}}_A (p, wc)$, if there is $\tau \in \Delta$ with $\phi(\tau) = \mathrm{rr}$ and $p \subset \tau(q, c)$ or $p \in \tau(q, \lambda)$, furthermore, $(q, \lambda) \vdash^{\mathrm{rr}}_A (p, \lambda)$, if $p \in \tau(q, \lambda)$,
- a *circular-interchanging* transition is defined by $(q, a) \vdash^{\mathrm{ci}}_A (p, a)$ and $(q, cwb) \vdash^{\mathrm{ci}}_A$ (p, bwc), if there is $\tau \in \Delta$ with $\phi(\tau) = \mathrm{ci}$ and $p \in \tau(q, a)$ and, respectively, $p \in \tau(q, c)$ or $p \in \tau(q, \lambda)$, and
- a *circular-shift* transition is defined by $(q, a) \vdash^{\mathrm{cs}}_A (p, a)$ and $(q, aw) \vdash^{\mathrm{cs}}_A$ (p, vau), for all u and v with $w = uv$, if there is $\tau \in \Delta$ with $\phi(\tau) = \mathrm{cs}$ and $p \in \tau(q, a)$.

Those transitions will also be referred to as *non-ordinary transitions.* Note that all these definitions include λ-transitions.

For any hybrid extended finite automaton, whenever there is a choice between an ordinary or another transition, the automaton non-deterministically chooses the next move. We write $(q, w) \vdash_A (p, v)$ for $(q, w) \vdash^f_A (p, v)$ with $f \in \{o, \mathrm{ir}, \mathrm{lr}, \mathrm{rr}, \mathrm{ci}, \mathrm{cs}\}$. As usual, the reflexive transitive closure of $\vdash_A$ is denoted by $\vdash^*_A$. The subscript A will be dropped from $\vdash_A$ and $\vdash^*_A$ whenever the meaning remains clear.

Let k be a non-negative integer. We define $T_k(A)$, the language *accepted with at most* k *non-ordinary steps* to be

$$T_k(A) = \{\, w \in \Sigma^* \mid (q_0, w) \vdash^*_A (q, \lambda)$$

with at most k non-ordinary steps and $q \in F \,\}$.

If the number of non-ordinary steps is not bounded, the language accepted is analogously defined as above and denoted by $T(A)$.

In order to clarify our notation we give an example. In what follows, when specifying an automaton we will list only those transitions which do not map to the empty set.

Example 1. The non-regular context-free language

$$L = \{\, wa \mid w \in \{a,b\}^*, \ |w|_a = |w|_b - 1 \,\} \cup \{\, wb \mid w \in \{a,b\}^*, \ |w|_a = 2|w|_b + 2 \,\}$$

is accepted by the hybrid extended finite automaton $A = (Q, \{a,b\}, \delta, \{\tau_r, \tau_c\}, \phi,$ $q_0, \{q_a, q_b\})$ with $\phi(\tau_r) = \mathrm{rr}$, $\phi(\tau_c) = \mathrm{ci}$, state set $Q = \{q_0, q_1, q_a, q_b, q_{a?}, q_{a??}, q_{b?}\}$, and

1. $\tau_c(q_0, a) = \tau_c(q_0, b) = \{q_1\}$
2. $\delta(q_1, a) = \delta(q_a, a) = \{q_{b?}\}$
3. $\delta(q_1, b) = \delta(q_b, b) = \{q_{a??}\}$
4. $\delta(q_{b?}, b) = \{q_a\}$
5. $\delta(q_{a??}, a) = \{q_{a?}\}$
6. $\delta(q_{a?}, a) = \{q_b\}$

7. $\tau_r(q_a, b) = \{q_a\}$
8. $\tau_r(q_b, a) = \{q_b\}$
9. $\tau_r(q_{a?}, b) = \{q_{a?}\}$
10. $\tau_r(q_{a??}, b) = \{q_{a??}\}$
11. $\tau_r(q_{b?}, a) = \{q_{b?}\}$

Automaton A accepts L as follows: When starting in state q_0 the first transition is a circular-interchange transition. Next, in state q_1, the (originally) last input symbol is read, yielding a decision of the kind of mode in which the input will be processed, either searching for one b after a symbol a has been read or searching for two as after a symbol b has been read. Note that A accepts the same language if $\phi(\tau_r) = \mathrm{lr}$ or $\phi(\tau_r) = \mathrm{cs}$.

Let D be any subset of the operation symbols forming the range $\mathcal{O}$ of the interpretation ϕ, that is, $D \subseteq \{\mathrm{ir}, \mathrm{lr}, \mathrm{rr}, \mathrm{ci}, \mathrm{cs}\}$ in our setting. A hybrid extended finite state automaton $A = (Q, \Sigma, \delta, \Delta, \phi, q_0, F)$ is referred to as D-NFA if and only if $\phi(\Delta) = D$, where ϕ is extended to sets of transition mappings in the natural way. The family of languages which can be accepted by some D-NFA (with an unbounded number of non-ordinary steps) is denoted by $\mathscr{L}(D\text{-NFA})$. The following lemma summarizes the relation between hybrid extended finite automata with different sets of operations. Since the proof is straight forward we omit the proof.

Lemma 1. *Let k be a non-negative integer and $D \subseteq \{\mathrm{ir}, \mathrm{lr}, \mathrm{rr}, \mathrm{ci}, \mathrm{cs}\}$. If $D' \subseteq D$, then, for any hybrid extended finite automaton $A = (Q, \Sigma, \delta, \Delta, \phi, q_0, F)$ with $\phi(\Delta) = D'$ there is a D-NFA B with $T_k(A) = T_k(B)$. The statement remains true if an unbounded number of non-ordinary moves is allowed. In conclusion, we have $\mathscr{L}(D'\text{-NFA}) \subseteq \mathscr{L}(D\text{-NFA})$.* □

The definition of hybrid extended finite automata allowed λ-transitions for ordinary moves, i.e., applications of the function δ, and non-ordinary moves, i.e., applications of functions from the set Δ. As usual, the aim of λ-transitions of δ is to allow changes of configurations without consuming input symbols. Since, basically, applications of functions from Δ do not consume input symbols, λ-transitions of Δ functions serve the purpose to apply operations independent of the current input symbol. This is why the corresponding transitions are called *blind operations*. Moreover, this intention implies that whenever an operation is applicable blindly and non-blindly at the same time, the effects of the applications are the same in both cases. Let us call computable operations, which meet this condition and lead to letter-equivalent results, *well-behaved*. Observe, that all operations in question are well-behaved.

We can show that λ-transitions do not increase the computational power of hybrid extended finite automata. We say that a hybrid extended finite automaton $A = (Q, \Sigma, \delta, \Delta, \phi, q_0, F)$ is λ-*free*, if δ is restricted to $Q \times \Sigma$. If all the mappings in Δ are restricted to $Q \times \Sigma$, then A is said to be *free of blind operations*. The construction proving the next lemma is omitted due to the page limitation.

Lemma 2. *Let k be a non-negative integer. For any hybrid extended finite automaton $A = (Q, \Sigma, \delta, \Delta, \phi, q_0, F)$ with $\phi(\Delta) = D$, one can construct a D-NFA B with $T_k(A) = T_k(B)$, which is both λ-free and free of blind operations. The statements remain true if an unbounded number of non-ordinary steps is allowed.*

3   Basic Results on Hybrid Extended Finite Automata

This section is devoted to some basic results on hybrid extended finite automata. We turn to prove the interesting fact that even a hybrid extended finite automaton which is allowed to apply all considered operations, cannot accept more languages than an ordinary deterministic finite state automaton, as long as the number of applied operations is bounded by an arbitrary constant. In order to prepare for the proof, we need an uncommon closure property of regular languages, which is shown in the following lemma—due to the lack of space the proof is omitted.

Lemma 3. *Let $A = (Q, \Sigma, \delta, q_0, F)$ be a deterministic finite state automaton and $a \in \Sigma$ be a distinguished input symbol. Then a deterministic finite state automaton A' can effectively be constructed which accepts the language $\{ vx \mid v, x \in \Sigma^* \text{ and } xav \in L(A) \}$.* $\square$

Now we are ready for the next theorem, which gives yet another characterization of the family of regular languages. The proof is based on induction on the number of non-ordinary moves k and is omitted here.

Theorem 1. *Let $D \subseteq \{\mathrm{ir}, \mathrm{lr}, \mathrm{rr}, \mathrm{ci}, \mathrm{cs}\}$ and k be a non-negative integer. A language L is accepted by a D-NFA A with at most k non-ordinary steps, that is, $T_k(A) = L$, if and only if L is regular.*

Whenever the number of non-ordinary moves is not restricted to be constant, then we find the following situation.

Theorem 2. *Let $D \subseteq \{\mathrm{ir}, \mathrm{lr}, \mathrm{rr}, \mathrm{ci}, \mathrm{cs}\}$. Then the family $\mathscr{L}(D\text{-NFA})$ is strictly included in $\mathscr{L}(\mathrm{CSL})$ and belongs to the complexity class NP.*

Proof. The inclusions in $\mathscr{L}(\mathrm{CSL})$ and NP are readily shown by construction of appropriate Turing machines. The strictness is seen as follows: Obviously, *unary* languages accepted by hybrid extended finite automata as considered in the present paper are regular since a non-ordinary transition does not change the remaining part of the input. Therefore, these non-ordinary transitions can be omitted. This shows that a unary language is accepted by a D-NFA if and only if it is regular. Thus, there is a context-sensitive language which cannot be accepted by any D-NFA, $D \subseteq \{\text{ir}, \text{lr}, \text{rr}, \text{ci}, \text{cs}\}$.   □

4   Hybrid Extended Finite Automata and Dependencies of the Modes

In this section we investigate the relation between D-NFA's with different sets of operations. First let us recall what is known from the literature. In case of the circular interchanging operation it was shown in [2] that this operation does not increase the computational power of (extended) finite automata, even if the number of circular interchanging operations is not bounded by a constant.

Theorem 3 ([2]). $\mathscr{L}(\text{ci-NFA}) = \mathscr{L}(\text{REG})$.

This is completely different to the remaining four operations we are interested in. Namely, for the input-reversal operation a precise characterization in terms of linear context-free languages was given in [1]. This result reads as follows:

Theorem 4 ([1]). $\mathscr{L}(\text{ir-NFA}) = \mathscr{L}(\text{LIN})$.

For the remaining revolving operations the following inclusions and comparability results were obtained in [2]:

Theorem 5 ([2]). *We have:*

1. $\mathscr{L}(\text{REG}) \subset \mathscr{L}(\text{rr-NFA}) \subset \mathscr{L}(\{\text{lr}, \text{rr}\}\text{-NFA}) \subset \mathscr{L}(\text{CSL})$.
2. $\mathscr{L}(\text{LIN}) \subset \mathscr{L}(\text{lr-NFA}) \subset \mathscr{L}(\{\text{lr}, \text{rr}\}\text{-NFA}) \subset \mathscr{L}(\text{CSL})$.
3. *The families* $\mathscr{L}(\text{lr-NFA})$, $\mathscr{L}(\text{rr-NFA})$ *are incomparable.*
4. *Each of the families* $\mathscr{L}(\text{lr-NFA})$, $\mathscr{L}(\text{rr-NFA})$, *and* $\mathscr{L}(\{\text{lr}, \text{rr}\}\text{-NFA})$ *are incomparable with each of* $\mathscr{L}(\text{2-LIN})$, $\mathscr{L}(\text{DCFL})$, *and* $\mathscr{L}(\text{CFL})$. *Furthermore,* $\mathscr{L}(\text{rr-NFA})$ *is incomparable with* $\mathscr{L}(\text{LIN})$.

By Theorems 4 and 5 we immediately obtain the following corollary.

Corollary 1. $\mathscr{L}(\text{ir-NFA}) \subset \mathscr{L}(\text{lr-NFA})$.   □

In Theorem 2 we have already seen that $\mathscr{L}(D\text{-NFA})$ is strictly included in $\mathscr{L}(\text{CSL})$ for any $D \subseteq \{\text{ir}, \text{lr}, \text{rr}, \text{ci}, \text{cs}\}$. The next theorem shows that $\mathscr{L}(D\text{-NFA})$ is incomparable to some standard families from the Chomsky hierarchy. The below given proof parallels the one given for bi-revolving finite automata in [2] and is omitted here. Note that a bi-revolving finite automaton is an $\{\text{lr}, \text{rr}\}$-NFA in our terminology.

Theorem 6. *For any* $D \subseteq \{\text{ir}, \text{lr}, \text{rr}, \text{ci}, \text{cs}\}$ *with* $|D \cap \{\text{lr}, \text{rr}, \text{cs}\}| > 0$, *the family* $\mathscr{L}(D\text{-NFA})$ *is incomparable with each of the families* $\mathscr{L}(\text{2-DLIN})$, $\mathscr{L}(\text{2-LIN})$, $\mathscr{L}(\text{DCFL})$, *and* $\mathscr{L}(\text{CFL})$.

The three lemmata given below show that the circular-interchanging operation when combined with other operations from $\mathcal{O}$ can or cannot increase the computational power of the underlying device. We start our investigation with an operation the computational power of which is not increased when combined with the circular-interchanging operation.

Lemma 4. $\mathscr{L}(\{\mathrm{ir},\mathrm{ci}\}\text{-NFA}) = \mathscr{L}(\mathrm{ir}\text{-NFA})$.

Proof (Sketch). Let $A = (Q, \Sigma, \delta, \Delta, \phi, q_0, F)$ be a λ-free $\{\mathrm{ir},\mathrm{ci}\}$-NFA which is free of blind operations with $\Delta = \{\tau_i, \tau_c\}$, $\phi(\tau_i) = \mathrm{ir}$, and $\phi(\tau_c) = \mathrm{ci}$. We construct an ir-NFA B the states of which are triples. Their first components mimic the states of A and the second and third component can store the first and the last symbol, respectively, of the remaining input. In order to store the first and the last symbol of the remaining input, these symbols are read from the input by ordinary transitions (and interposed input reversal transitions). Then the circular-interchange transition can be simulated by interchanging the symbols in the memory. If the stored symbols shall be read by A, they are deleted from the memory in B. The dash symbol $(-)$ as the second or third state component indicates that no symbol is currently stored as the first or last one, respectively, in the memory.

Formally, let $B = (Q', \Sigma, \delta', \{\tau\}, \phi', q_0', F')$ with $\phi'(\tau) = \mathrm{ir}$, $\overline{Q} = \{q, q', q'' \mid q \in Q\}$ and $\Sigma_- = \Sigma \cup \{-\}$; then set $Q' = \{f\} \cup (\overline{Q} \times \Sigma_- \times (\Sigma_- \cup \{?\}))$, $q_0' = (q_0, -, -)$ and $F' = \{f\} \cup (F \times \{-\} \times \{-\})$. The transition relations δ' and τ are specified as follows.

1. For all $p, q \in Q$, $a \in \Sigma$, $y \in \Sigma_-$, if $p \in \delta(q, a)$, let
   $(p, -, y) \in \delta'((q, -, y), a)$ and $(p, -, y) \in \delta'((q, a, y), \lambda)$.
2. For all $p, q \in Q$, $a \in \Sigma$, $y \in \Sigma_-$, if $p \in \tau_i(q, a)$, let
   $(p, y, -) \in \tau((q, -, y), a)$ and $(p, y, a) \in \tau((q, a, y), \lambda)$.
3. For all $p, q \in Q$, $a, b \in \Sigma$, if $p \in \tau_c(q, a)$, let
   (a) $(p, b, a) \in \delta'((q, a, b), \lambda)$ and $(p, b, a) \in \delta'((q, -, b), a)$,
   (b) $(q, a, ?) \in \tau((q, a, -), \lambda)$, $(q', a, b) \in \delta'((q, a, ?), b)$, and
       $(p, b, a) \in \tau((q', a, b), \lambda)$,
   (c) $(q', a, -) \in \delta'((q, -, -), a)$ and $(q, a, ?) \in \tau((q', a, -), \lambda)$.
4. For all $q \in Q$, $a \in \Sigma$, let
   $(q'', a, -) \in \delta'((q, a, -), \lambda) \cap \delta'((q, -, a), \lambda) \cap \delta'((q, -, -), a)$.
5. For all $p, q \in Q$, $a \in \Sigma$, if $p \in \tau_i(q, a)$ or $p \in \tau_c(q, a)$, let
   $(p'', a, -) \in \delta'((q'', a, -), \lambda)$.
6. For all $q \in Q$, $a \in \Sigma$, if $\delta(q, a) \cap F \neq \emptyset$, let
   $f \in \delta'((q'', a, -), \lambda)$.

This completes the description of the hybrid extended finite automaton B.

Ordinary moves of A are simulated by transitions of type (1). Here one has to distinguish two cases, namely whether the first symbol of the input is already memorized in the finite control or not. Transitions of type (2) switch the memorized first and last symbol of the input and simulate the input-reversal operation properly; as in the previous case one has to distinguish several cases. The transitions in (3) are for the simulation of the circular-interchanging operation. Again one has to cope with several cases: Type (3)a is used if both symbols or the last symbol is memorized in the finite control. If the last symbol is not yet known, type (3)b transitions are used to store it by making an input-reversal to transport the last symbol to the front, memorizing the last symbol by reading it, and finally turning the unread part of the input back by an input-reversal again. Similarly, one can treat the case if both symbols are not yet stored in the finite control; here transition from (3)c and then from (3)b are taken. Transitions (4) and (5) deal with the case if the remaining input consists of a single symbol (which may have been memorized in the state). Finally, type (6) transitions control the acceptance of the machine, if a transition of type (4) has been used.   □

In contrast to the above result, the circular-interchanging operation adds to the power of both rr-NFA's and cs-NFA's. These cases are treated in the two lemmata given below.

Lemma 5. $\mathscr{L}(\text{rr-NFA}) \subset \mathscr{L}(\{\text{rr}, \text{ci}\}\text{-NFA})$.

Proof. The inclusion holds by definition. For its strictness, we show that the language

$$L = \{\, wa \mid w \in \{a, b\}^*, \; |w|_a = |w|_b - 1 \,\} \cup \{\, wb \mid w \in \{a, b\}^*, \; |w|_a = 2|w|_b + 2 \,\}$$

from Example 1 cannot be accepted by any rr-NFA. Assume the contrary, and let $A = (Q, \Sigma, \delta, \Delta, \phi, q_0, F)$ be an rr-NFA accepting L and $|Q| = n$. Let us consider the word $w = b^{2n(n+1)+1} a^{2n(n+1)+1}$ as input. Note that $w \in L$. First we show that, in every accepting computation of w, the number of ordinary steps reading a sequence of b's between two consecutive revolving moves is bounded by n. This is obvious, because otherwise one state is repeated at least once due to the pigeon hole principle. Thus, cutting this loop leads to a valid computation. Therefore, whenever the original word is accepted, also the new word induced by the cut loop is also accepted. Since after the cutting the number of b's is not equal to the number of a's on the input the automaton accepts a word not of the appropriate form. Therefore, in the forthcoming we may assume that the automaton A fulfills the above mentioned property.

From this fact we deduce there are at least $2(n + 1)$ positions where a right-revolving move is started by reading a letter b. Because of the pigeon hole principle we find a state, say p, which appears at least twice during the first n of these positions. Thus, starting the computation in state q_0 with input w, the first appearance of state p is reached by i ordinary moves and j right-revolving moves (inter-winded), with $0 \leq j < n + 1$. Hence we have $(q_0, w) = (q_0, b^{2n(n+1)+1} a^{2n(n+1)+1}) \vdash_A^* (p, b^{2n(n+1)+1-i-j} a^{2n(n+1)+1} b^j)$. Then from the latter configuration state p is reached a second time by k ordinary moves and ℓ right-revolving moves (inter-winded) with $1 \leq \ell \leq (n + 1) - j$. Therefore we find $(p, b^{2n(n+1)+1-i-j} a^{2n(n+1)+1} a^j) \vdash_A^* (p, b^{2n(n+1)+1-i-j-k-\ell} a^{2n(n+1)+1} b^j b^\ell)$. Since we are considering an accepting computation, there is a state $q_f \in F$ such that $(p, b^{2n(n+1)+1-i-j-k-\ell} a^{2n(n+1)+1} b^{j+\ell}) \vdash_A^* (q_f, \lambda)$. Observe, that $\ell \geq 1$

and $i + j + k + \ell \leq n(n + 1)$, thus, $k < n(n + 1)$. Now we can fool the automaton A by constructing an accepting computation for the word $w' = b^{2n(n+1)+1-k-\ell}a^{2n(n+1)+1}b^{\ell}$ by cutting out the above considered loop in the computation. For this word we have the accepting computation

$$(q_0, w') = (q_0, b^{2n(n+1)+1-k-\ell}a^{2n(n+1)+1}b^{\ell}) \vdash^*_A$$
$$(p, b^{2n(n+1)+1-i-j-k-\ell}a^{2n(n+1)+1}b^{\ell}b^j) =$$
$$(p, b^{2n(n+1)+1-i-j-k-\ell}a^{2n(n+1)+1}b^{j+\ell}) \vdash^*_A (q_f, \lambda)$$

of A. We find $|w'|_b = 2n(n+1)+1-k > n(n+1)+1$, thus $2|w'|_b > 2n(n+1)+2 > |w'|_a$. Therefore, the constructed word w' is not a member of L, a contradiction. Thus no right-revolving finite automaton can accept the considered language L.   □

Next we compare the computational power of cs-NFA's and $\{cs, ci\}$-NFA's.

Lemma 6. $\mathscr{L}(\text{cs-NFA}) \subset \mathscr{L}(\{cs, ci\}\text{-NFA})$.

Proof. As the language L used in the previous proof is accepted by a $\{cs, ci\}$-NFA (see Example 1), it is sufficient to show that L cannot be accepted by some cs-NFA. Assume the contrary, then there is a cs-NFA A accepting L and an accepting computation for the input word $b^{n+2}a^{n+2}$, where n is the number of states of A. As in the previous proof, the number of consecutive ordinary transitions in such computation is bounded by n. Therefore, there is an integer i, $0 \leq i \leq n$ such that $(q_0, b^{n+2}a^{n+2}) \vdash^* (q, b^{n+2-i}a^{n+2}) \vdash^{cs} (p, w) \vdash^* (q_f, \lambda)$, for some $q, p \in Q$ and $q_f \in F$. Since the number of symbols moved in the circular-shift transition is not determined, then also the computation $(q_0, b^{n+1}a^{n+2}b) \vdash^* (q, b^{n+1-i}a^{n+2}b) \vdash^{cs} (p, w) \vdash^* (q_f, \lambda)$, is possible, accepting a word which is no member of L.   □

The next theorem locates the family $\mathscr{L}(\text{cs-NFA})$ in the hierarchy of languages which has been established so far.

Theorem 7. For $x \in \{lr, rr\}$, we have $\mathscr{L}(\text{REG}) \subset \mathscr{L}(\text{cs-NFA}) \subset \mathscr{L}(x\text{-NFA}) = \mathscr{L}(\{x, cs\}\text{-NFA})$.

Proof. The inclusions, including the equality, hold because of Lemma 1 and as a circular-shift transition can be simulated by a—non-deterministically chosen—number of revolving steps, either left or right. The first inclusion is strict due to Theorem 6. As $\mathscr{L}(lr\text{-NFA})$ and $\mathscr{L}(rr\text{-NFA})$ are incomparable [2], the latter inclusions are strict.   □

As a main result of this section we obtain that the family of languages accepted by $\{lr, rr\}$-NFA's is as powerful as at least seven other language families investigated in the present paper, namely as the families $\mathscr{L}(D\text{-NFA})$, where D contains at least two operations from the set $\{ir, lr, rr\}$, extended or not extended by the operation cs.

Theorem 8. *For any $D \subseteq \{\text{ir}, \text{lr}, \text{rr}, \text{cs}\}$ with $|D \cap \{\text{ir}, \text{lr}, \text{rr}\}| > 1$, we have*

$$\mathscr{L}(D\text{-NFA}) = \mathscr{L}(\{\text{lr}, \text{rr}\}\text{-NFA}).$$

Proof (Sketch). We argue as follows:

1. The inclusions of the language families $\mathscr{L}(\{\text{ir}, \text{lr}\}\text{-NFA})$, $\mathscr{L}(\{\text{ir}, \text{rr}\}\text{-NFA})$, and $\mathscr{L}(\{\text{lr}, \text{rr}\}\text{-NFA})$ in $\mathscr{L}(\{\text{ir}, \text{lr}, \text{rr}\}\text{-NFA})$ hold because of Lemma 1.

2. We show $\mathscr{L}(\{\text{ir}, \text{lr}, \text{rr}\}\text{-NFA}) \subseteq \mathscr{L}(\{\text{lr}, \text{rr}\}\text{-NFA})$. Given a hybrid extended finite automaton $A = (Q, \Sigma, \delta, \Delta, \phi, q_0, F)$ with $\Delta = \{\tau_i, \tau_l, \tau_r\}$ and $\phi(\tau_i) = \text{ir}$, $\phi(\tau_l) = \text{lr}$, $\phi(\tau_r) = \text{rr}$, which is λ-free and free of blind operations. The idea to construct an $\{\text{lr}, \text{rr}\}$-NFA B is as follows: Automaton B stores in the finite control whether the input is read from left-to-right or from right-to-left. With this information the input-reversal operation can be simulated by switching this information accordingly. Hence, an input-reversal is implemented virtually because the input cannot be mirrored anymore. Then we distinguish two cases: (1) The input is read from left-to-right. Then all transitions, i.e., ordinary and non-ordinary ones, can be simulated in a straight forward fashion. (2) The input is read from right-to-left. This means, that the first symbol of the actual input is on the right. Thus an ordinary transition must be simulated by a left-revolving operation which is followed by the appropriate read operation. Moreover, a right-revolving transition is in principle simulated by a left-revolving transition and *vice versa*. Here one has to be careful, because of the following obstacle: Before simulating a (non-blind) left- or right-revolving transition, one has to check its applicability to the current configuration, depending on the input symbol which is the first symbol of the actual input. Since this input symbol is on the right end of the word, a left-revolving followed by a right-revolving operation can be used. That is, for $a, b \in \Sigma$, $v \in \Sigma^*$ and appropriate states $\bar{q}, q', \bar{p}$, and p', one can simulate $(q, av^R b) \vdash_A^{\text{lr}} (p, bav^R)$ by $(\bar{q}, bva) \vdash_B^{\text{lr}} (q', abv) \vdash_B^{\text{rr}} (p', bva) \vdash_B^{\text{rr}} (\bar{p}, vab)$, where the first and the third transitions are performed as blind operations by B, and the second transition as a non-blind operation verifying that there is the symbol a. Symmetrically, one can simulate $(q, av^R) \vdash_A^{\text{rr}} (p, v^R a)$ by $(\bar{q}, va) \vdash_B^{\text{lr}} (q', av) \vdash_B^{\text{rr}} (p', va) \vdash_B^{\text{lr}} (\bar{p}, av)$. The tedious details are left to the reader.

3. The inclusion $\mathscr{L}(\{\text{ir}, \text{lr}, \text{rr}\}\text{-NFA}) \subseteq \mathscr{L}(\{\text{ir}, \text{lr}\}\text{-NFA})$ is seen as follows. Given an $\{\text{ir}, \text{lr}, \text{rr}\}$-NFA A which is—without loss of generality—free of blind operations, there is an equivalent $\{\text{ir}, \text{lr}\}$-NFA B performing ordinary, input-reversal, and left-revolving transitions as the automaton A does and simulating any right-revolving transition of the form $(q, av) \vdash_A^{\text{rr}} (p, va)$ with $a \in \Sigma$ and $v \in \Sigma^*$, by $(q, av) \vdash_B^{\text{ir}} (p', v^R a) \vdash_B^{\text{lr}} (p'', av^R) \vdash_B^{\text{ir}} (p, va)$, for some appropriate states p' and p''. The details of the construction are left to the reader.

4. Analogously, we find $\mathscr{L}(\{\text{ir}, \text{lr}, \text{rr}\}\text{-NFA}) \subseteq \mathscr{L}(\{\text{ir}, \text{rr}\}\text{-NFA})$ as the left-revolving $(q, avb) \vdash_A^{\text{lr}} (p, bav)$ with $a, b \in \Sigma$ and $v \in \Sigma^*$ can be simulated by $(q, avb) \vdash_B^{\text{ir}} (p', bv^R a) \vdash_B^{\text{rr}} (p'', v^R ab) \vdash_B^{\text{ir}} (p, bav)$; again, the details of the construction are left to the reader.

5. For $D \subseteq \{\mathrm{ir}, \mathrm{lr}, \mathrm{rr}\}$ with $|D| > 1$, we have $\mathscr{L}(D\text{-NFA}) \subseteq \mathscr{L}(D \cup \{\mathrm{cs}\}\text{-NFA})$ due to Lemma 1. The converse inclusions hold as a non-deterministically chosen number of both left- and right-revolving transitions simulates a circular-shift transition. □

Finally, we state the following result without proof.

Lemma 7. *There is a language accepted by an* lr-NFA *which can be accepted neither by an* $\{\mathrm{rr}, \mathrm{ci}\}$-NFA *nor by a* $\{\mathrm{cs}, \mathrm{ci}\}$-NFA.

There are a few questions in the context of this section which we have to leave open here. Mainly, these questions concern the power of hybrid extended finite automata which are allowed to perform, among others, the circular-interchanging operation, in particular in combination with the left-revolving transition.

References

1. H. Bordihn, M. Holzer, and M. Kutrib. Input reversals and iterated pushdown automata—a new characterization of Khabbaz geometric hierarchy of languages. In C. S. Calude, E. Calude, and M. J. Dinneen, editors, *Proceedings of the 8th International Conference on Developments in Language Theory*, number 3340 in LNCS, pages 102–113, Auckland, New Zealand, December 2004. Springer.
2. H. Bordihn, M. Holzer, and M. Kutrib. Revolving-input finite automata. In C. De Felice and A. Restivo, editors, *Proceedings of the 9th International Conference on Developments in Language Theory*, number 3572 in LNCS, pages 168–179, Palermo, Italy, July 2005. Springer.
3. H. Bordihn, M. Holzer, and M. Kutrib. Finite automata with bio-inspired operations: The hairpin inversion operation. Unpublished manuscript, February 2006.
4. N. Chomsky. *Handbook of Mathematic Psychology*, volume 2, chapter Formal Properties of Grammars, pages 323–418. Wiley & Sons, New York, 1962.
5. R. J. Evey. *The Theory and Applications of Pushdown Store Machines*. Ph.D thesis, Harvard University, Massachusetts, May 1963.
6. S. Ginsburg. *Algebraic and Automata-Theoretic Properties of Formal Languages*. North-Holland, Amsterdam, 1975.
7. S. Ginsburg, S. A. Greibach, and M. A. Harrison. One-way stack automata. *Journal of the ACM*, 14(2):389–418, April 1967.
8. S. Ginsburg and E. H. Spanier. Control sets on grammars. *Mathematical Systems Theory*, 2(2):159–177, 1968.
9. S. A. Greibach. An infinite hierarchy of context-free languages. *Journal of the ACM*, 16(1):91–106, January 1969.
10. M. Holzer and M. Kutrib. Flip-pushdown automata: $k + 1$ pushdown reversals are better than k. In J. C. M. Baeten, J. K. Lenstra, J. Parrow, and G. J. Woeginger, editors, *Proceedings of the 30th International Colloqium on Automata, Languages and Propgramming*, number 2719 in LNCS, pages 490–501, Eindhoven, The Netherlands, June–July 2003. Springer.
11. N. A. Khabbaz. Control sets and linear grammars. *Information and Control*, 25(3):206–221, July 1974.
12. N. A. Khabbaz. A geometric hierarchy of languages. *Journal of Computer and System Sciences*, 8(2):142–157, April 1974.
13. P. Sarkar. Pushdown automaton with the ability to flip its stack. Report TR01-081, Electronic Colloquium on Computational Complexity (ECCC), November 2001.

Refinement of Near Random Access Video Coding with Weighted Finite Automata

German Tischler

Universität Würzburg, Lehrstuhl für Informatik II, Am Hubland,
97074 Würzburg, Germany
tischler@informatik.uni-wuerzburg.de
http://www2.informatik.uni-wuerzburg.de/staff/tischler

Abstract. Random access video compression is mostly implemented without any reduction of temporal redundancy. Standard video compression systems like MPEG (1,2 and 4) are heavily based on motion compensation, which to some extent makes random access at single frame level impossible. We present a method for near random access video compression of low-motion video that is based on the discrete cosine transform and vector quantization and refine this system using weighted finite automata while keeping the random access property and using some reduction of temporal redundancy.

1 Introduction

Video compression standards like [1], [2] and [3] depend heavily on motion compensation for reduction of temporal redundancy. An introduction to this topic can be found e.g. in [4]. Motion compensation is usually implemented by the use of motion vectors. The most basic implementations of this concept are global motion compensation and block motion compensation. In block motion compensation each video frame is partitioned into some set of square blocks. For sake of simplicity we assume that global motion compensation is a special form of block motion compensation, where there is only one block that is the full frame. In the most simple case thus in a sequence of video frames $f_0, f_1, \ldots$ the blocks of f_{n+1} are displayed either as translated blocks of f_n, if a suitable block can be found in f_n, or as new pixel material that might have either not been present in frame f_n, or the corresponding object has been subject to a transformation that cannot be displayed by motion vectors, e.g. rotation or scaling. Reduction of spatial redundancy is in the majority of cases implemented in virtue of applying the discrete cosine transform (DCT [5]) on non-overlapping 8×8 pixel blocks in a fashion similar to still image compression in JPEG [6], [7]. An implementation of a video coder using MPEG like motion compensation but using weighted finite automata (WFA) for reduction of spatial redundancy was described in [8]. Algorithms for still image compression by WFA are presented in [9], [10] , [11] and [12].

The use of motion compensation in the described form, no matter how useful it is for the reduction of temporal redundancy, renders every system employing

O.H. Ibarra and H.-C. Yen (Eds.): CIAA 2006, LNCS 4094, pp. 46–57, 2006.

it unable to provide random access at single frame level. Applications for which random access is either required or highly desired, e.g. video editing or systems with high user interaction during video decoding, are usually working on uncompressed data or formats like Motion JPEG that do not make any use of temporal redundancy.

In section 2 of this paper we present a compression scheme for low motion video that is based on the DCT and vector quantization and allows near random access to each encoded frame. By *near random* we mean that random access is possible after some very short initialization time used to decode data efficiently storing per block position inter frame similarities. We then refine this approach further in section 3 by the use of WFA to improve the compression ratio relative to DCT coding while still keeping the random access property. The method works well for the example material shown in appendix B. It is not expected to work well for generic video material.

2 DCT Coding and Vector Quantization

Let $b(i, j)$ denote a real $n \times n$ matrix which we interpret as an image block. For b the discrete cosine transform (DCT) B of b is given by

$$B(i,j) = \alpha_i \alpha_j \sum_{k=0}^{n-1} \sum_{l=0}^{n-1} b(k,l) \cos\left(\frac{i\pi(2k+1)}{2n}\right) \cos\left(\frac{j\pi(2l+1)}{2n}\right) \quad (1)$$

and in turn is an $n \times n$ block of coefficients where

$$\alpha_m = \begin{cases} \frac{1}{\sqrt{2}} & \text{if } m = 0 \\ 1 & \text{otherwise} . \end{cases} \quad (2)$$

As n is finite we may also interpret b and B as vectors of dimension n^2 by following the raster scan order (left to right, top to bottom). The DCT decomposes the source block into a linear combination built from an orthogonal basis of $\mathbb{R}^{n^2}$ given by the functions

$$c_{i,j} = \cos(i2\pi x) \cos(j2\pi y) \quad (3)$$

which are sampled in the middle of the intervals

$$I_{l,m} = \left[\frac{il2\pi}{2n}, \frac{i(l+1)2\pi}{2n}\right] \times \left[\frac{jm2\pi}{2n}, \frac{j(m+1)2\pi}{2n}\right], \text{ for } 0 \leq l, m < n . \quad (4)$$

Figure 1 shows an example block in image and coefficient form as well as the transformed block matrix. Following the transformation the coefficients are quantized. Quantization is controlled by a matrix $q(i, j) \in \mathbb{N}_+^{n \times n}$. The matrix B is divided element-wise by q and each elementary result is rounded towards zero. This rounding process is the main cause of compression as well as distortion found in DCT based image coders like JPEG. The balance of compression and distortion is controlled by the elements of q. If all elements of q equal 1, distortion and compression rate are minimal. Higher compression is achieved by using values greater than 1 as elements of q, where coefficients corresponding to high frequency basis function are usually divided by greater numbers than those corresponding to low frequency basis functions, because high frequency errors are harder to perceive in the human visual system than low frequency errors. Figure 2 shows an example.

```
200 197 193 188 178 165 155 150          1264 143 -28 0 0 0 0 0
196 196 194 187 177 166 154 147           143   0   0  0 0 0 0 0
193 194 191 182 173 163 152 144           -28   0   0  0 0 0 0 0
188 187 184 176 166 156 145 138             0   0   0  0 5 0 0 0
178 176 173 168 158 145 134 128             0   0   0  0 0 0 0 0
167 164 161 156 147 133 122 117             0   0   4  0 0 0 0 0
156 154 151 144 134 122 112 107             0   0   0  0 0 0 0 0
148 148 146 138 128 117 106  98             0   0   0  0 0 0 0 0
```

Fig. 1. 8×8 pixel DCT example: source block matrix b *(left)*, image of source block *(middle, black at 0, white at 255)*, transformed block matrix B *(right)*

```
1264 143 -28 0  0 0 0 0     16 11 10 16  24  40  51  61     79 13 -2 0  0 0 0 0
 143   0   0 0  0 0 0 0     12 12 14 19  26  58  60  55     11  0  0 0  0 0 0 0
 -28   0   0 0  0 0 0 0     14 13 16 24  40  57  69  56     -2  0  0 0  0 0 0 0
   0   0   0 0 [5]0 0 0     14 17 22 29  51  87  80  62      0  0  0 0 [0]0 0 0
   0   0   0 0  0 0 0 0     18 22 37 56  68 109 103  77      0  0  0 0  0 0 0 0
   0   0  [4]0  0 0 0 0     24 35 55 64  81 104 113  92      0  0 [0]0  0 0 0 0
   0   0   0 0  0 0 0 0     49 64 78 87 103 121 120 101      0  0  0 0  0 0 0 0
   0   0   0 0  0 0 0 0     72 92 95 98 112 100 103  99      0  0  0 0  0 0 0 0
              B                           q                           B'
```

Fig. 2. The elements of the quantized matrix B' are obtained by dividing the transformed coefficients matrix B element-wise by the quantization matrix q and rounding the result in the direction of 0. Some elements of B might vanish after quantization.

Quantization with a non-trivial matrix q also implies that some similar blocks are equal after reconstruction. This allows a simple form of vector quantization, where only the first appearance of each reconstructed block needs to be stored and all subsequent appearances are only given as references to this first appearance. For compression of low-motion video we thus decompose each frame into a set of square image blocks and reorder the data so that for each position all occurring blocks are stored in a row as shown in figure 3. Let $B'_{x,y}(f')$ denote the sequence for spatial position (x, y) and $B''_{x,y}(f'')$ the f''th unique block in $B'_{x,y}$. We then compute the mapping $B'_{x,y}(f')$ to $B''_{x,y}(f'')$ (see figure 4) which is a function and is described for each position x, y by an integer sequence $i : f' \mapsto f''$.

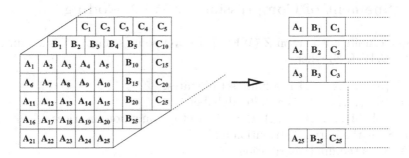

Fig. 3. Blocks are reordered according to block position

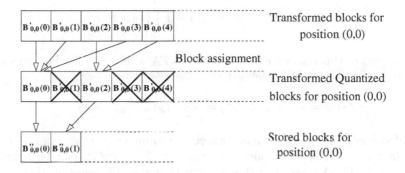

Transformed blocks for position (0,0)

Block assignment

Transformed Quantized blocks for position (0,0)

Stored blocks for position (0,0)

Fig. 4. The first occurrence of each block per position is stored

Thus the compressed file has the components

1. the number of stored blocks B'' per position,
2. the length of the coded blocks in B'',
3. the mapping i and
4. the coded blocks B''.

Points 1-3 are stored as meta-data to allow random access. Point 3 denotes for each frame and position, which block B'' is to decoded and the block length information in point 1 and 2 is used to compute for each frame which data is irrelevant and thus can be skipped.

Tests have shown that for real low-motion video the storage costs of the coded blocks in point 4 make up 90-98% of the total file size. Thus a better compression of the coded blocks promises the best chance to improve the compression ratio in a refined approach. An application of this compression method to low-motion video showing a page turn of a book filmed from above has yielded a compression rate 2 to 4 times higher than that reached my MJPEG. In the concrete case shown in appendix B the factor is about 2.45.

3   Refinement of Compression by WFA Coding

A weighted finite automaton Z (WFA, [13]) over some semiring S is a quintuple $Z = (Q, \Sigma, W, I, F)$ where

- $Q = \{0, 1, \ldots, n-1\}$ is a finite set of states,
- $\Sigma = \{0, 1, \ldots, l-1\}$ is a finite alphabet,
- $W = (A_0, A_1, \ldots, A_{l-1})$, $A_i \in S^{n \times n}$ are the transition matrices,
- $I \in S^n$ is the initial distribution and
- $F \in S^n$ is the final distribution.

The function computed by Z is defined as

$$f_Z(w = w_1 \ldots w_k \in \Sigma^*) = I \prod_{j=1}^{k} A_{w_j} F \ . \tag{5}$$

In the context of this paper we only consider WFA where $S = \mathbb{R}$. The extension of this function to ω-words is defined as

$$f_Z(w = w_1 w_2 \ldots \in \Sigma^\omega) = \lim_{n \to \infty} f_Z(w_1 w_2 \ldots w_n) \ . \tag{6}$$

A detailed study of these automata, where the input word $w = w_1 w_2 \ldots \in \Sigma^\omega$ is interpreted as the real number $0.w_1 w_2 \ldots = \sum_{i>0} w_i l^{-i}$, can be found in [14], [15] and [16]. One result of this study is that the only smooth (that means every derivative is continuous) functions computable by WFA are polynomials, implying that the basis functions of the DCT cannot be displayed at infinite precision by a WFA. As practical image compression is performed on images of finite precision, this is of no concern in applications. For images of dimension 2 we choose an alphabet size of 4, where the image is recursively partitioned into quadrants. This partitioning corresponds to a quadtree as shown in figure 5. For sake of simplicity we are limiting the scope of this paper to square images

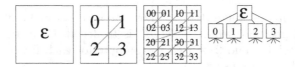

Fig. 5. Recursive partitioning of image into quadrants *(left for wordlength 0,1 and 2)* and quadtree *(right)*

of size $2^k \times 2^k$ for some $k \in \mathbb{N}$. We then identify the addresses of pixels in images with nodes of a quadtree of depth k. Each quadtree node is assigned the arithmetic average of the pixel values in the corresponding image block. This quadtree can be turned into a WFA displaying the image by the following steps, where quadtree nodes are transformed to WFA states:

1. Use the assigned arithmetic pixel averages as final weights for the states.
2. Each edge going from state w to wa is labeled with alphabet symbol a and weight 1.
3. Each quadtree leaf is assigned an edge back to itself with weight one for every alphabet symbol.
4. The state ϵ is assigned initial weight 1 and all other states initial weight 0.

The automaton produced in this construction is fully deterministic. Efficient WFA compression of natural images requires some amount of nondeterminism. Let for WFA Z denote $p_Z(j), j = 0, 1, \ldots, |Q| - 1$ the automaton produced from Z by changing its initial distribution to 1 at state j and 0 otherwise. We call $p_Z(j)$ the image of the automaton Z for state j. Now observe that

$$f_{p_Z(j)}(aw \in \Sigma^+) = \sum_{k=0}^{|Q|-1} A_a(j,k) f_{p_Z(k)}(w) \ . \tag{7}$$

This means that subquadrant a of state j is computed as a linear combination of state images of Z and the coefficients of this linear combination are given by row j of the transition matrix A_a. We thus can transform Z into an equivalent automaton Z' by substituting edges in a way that does not change the function f_Z the automaton computes. Algorithms for effectively computing minimal state WFA can be found for instance in [17] and [16]. The computed WFA is then a minimum state instance of all WFA computing exactly the function f_Z.

In image compression applications we are mostly not interested in exact (lossless) representations of images, but in such that give an approximation (lossy) that describes an image at a sufficient quality. Lossy image compression systems allow much higher compression rates, even in the case where the image quality is considered high enough so that the human visual system cannot tell any difference between the original image and the mathematically lossy reconstruction. The application of the minimization algorithm to WFA generated from quadtrees representing images does in general not reduce the automaton to a representation that would be small enough to compete with standard lossy compression systems. Thus it is necessary to transform the automaton in a way that does no longer exactly produce the original image but a sufficient approximation. The key to this can be found in equation 8, where we relax the equality constraint in equation 7 to

$$f_{p_Z(j)}(aw \in \Sigma^+) \approx \sum_{k=0}^{|Q|-1} A'_a(j,k) f_{p'_Z(k)}(w) \ . \tag{8}$$

For this approximation we also formulate a quality constraint in equation 9.

$$\left| \sum_{k=0}^{|Q|-1} A_a(j,k) f_{p_Z(k)}(w) - \sum_{k=0}^{|Q|-1} A'_a(j,k) f_{p'_Z(k)}(w) \right| < \epsilon(j) \ . \tag{9}$$

The distortion caused by the approximation we allow per state will in general depend on the image block that the corresponding state represents. Observe that changing the transition matrices changes at least some of the state images $p_Z(j)$. For this reason practical algorithms constructing WFA from images process the image in an order that avoids adding any edges to states that will have their state images changed in a later step of the algorithm. In practice it is also not necessary that each state image is produced by computations as given by equation 5. For the evaluation of a state image according to equation 7 at a certain resolution it is sufficient to have all referenced state images at half this resolution. The referenced state images do not have to be provided in WFA form.

This implies that we can use the DCT coded image blocks in section 2 as state images of finite resolution instead of a WFA generating the same image block. If the image blocks have size $2^k \times 2^k$, we can imagine them as quadrants referenced by WFA states representing image blocks of size $2^{k+1} \times 2^{k+1}$ as shown in figure 6. Due to the vector quantization process in section 2 each DCT

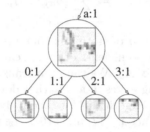

Fig. 6. DCT coded image blocks of size $2^k \times 2^k$ are used to describe the quadrants of a WFA state representing an image block of size $2^{k+1} \times 2^{k+1}$ that in turn is subquadrant a of some image block of size $2^{k+2} \times 2^{k+2}$. The image shows an example for $k = 3$.

coded block may be referenced multiple times. The goal of the refinement is to substitute edges ending in DCT coded blocks by linear combinations of other DCT coded blocks if the storage cost for a linear combination is lower than that of the DCT code and the quality of the approximation produced by the linear combination is at least as good as that of the DCT code. When choosing target states of edges used in these newly created linear combinations, it is important not to use states that themselves are displayed by linear combinations. If all edges of linear combinations end in DCT coded blocks, the decoding time of such a linear combination is bounded by some constant times the length of the linear combination. Otherwise the automaton could contain paths of arbitrary length depending on the image resolution until real pixel material is reached and random access would be lost.

Let $B_C(i)$ denote the sequence of DCT coded blocks resulting from the concatenation of the sequences $B''_{x,y}(f'')$ in raster scan order as it is appearing in the file produced in section 2 and $B_O(i)$ the corresponding sequence of original blocks. We are interested in approximating $B_O(m)$ by a short linear combination

$$B_O(m) \approx \sum_{k=1}^{e} \lambda_k B_C(t_k) \tag{10}$$

where

1. $t_k < m$ for $k \in \{1, \ldots, e\}$, which ensures that we do not use state images that we may change later in the algorithm,
2. none of the states denoted by the sequence t_k have been substituted by a linear combination of other states, so the decoding of the linear combination components is possible in constant time,
3. $e \leq e_{\max} \in \mathbb{N}_+$, to bound the decoding time of the approximation by about $e_{\max}$ times that of $B_C(m)$,
4.
$$\left| B_O(m) - \sum_{k=1}^{e} \lambda_k B_C(t_k) \right| < \left| B_O(m) - B_C(m) \right| \tag{11}$$

so the approximation does not decrease the quality of the reconstructed block and
5. the storage cost of the linear combination is not higher than that of the DCT code.

An example of the substitution of a single image block by a linear combination of other image blocks is shown in figure 7. The orthogonal matching pursuit

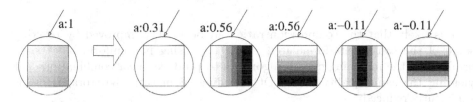

Fig. 7. Substitution of one image block by a linear combination of other blocks: the edge for label a ending in the state shown left is substituted by the linear combination of the states on the right

algorithm by Culik and Kari adapted for this application is shown in algorithm 1 in appendix A. The cost of a linear combination can for example be computed by encoding it in the components

1. length of the linear combination (e.g. Huffman coded),
2. target states of the edges (e.g. binary block code) and
3. weights of the edges (usually floating point numbers represented in sign, exponent and mantissa and then entropy coded).

Experiments have shown that non-adaptive Huffman coding is appropriate for entropy coding of the linear combinations in this application, where we expect a sufficient amount of data to reach stable probability distributions, so we can choose the better time performance of a Huffman coder over the marginally better compression performance of an arithmetic coder. Time performance of entropy coding is often one of the critical factors for the frame rate in video decoding.

The application of this refinement method to the test material mentioned in section 2 has shown that it is possible to improve the compression ratio by a factor of approximately 1.18 to 1.3, where up to 60% of the coded blocks can be substituted by WFA representations. The average length of the linear combinations was then around 3.4, meaning that on average decoding a WFA represented image block takes about 3.4 times as long as decoding a plain DCT coded block. In the concrete example shown in appendix B the compression rate is 3.15 times better than that of MJPEG. Table 1 shows a comparison with MJPEG and FFMPEGs MPEG4 codec for some group of picture (GOP) sizes. The method proposed in section 2 clearly outperforms the compression ratio of MPEG4 using only I-Frames.

Table 1. Performance comparison. Used methods: A: Uncompressed, B: MJPEG, C: Section 2, D: Section 3, E: MPEG4 GOP Size 1, F: MPEG4 GOP Size 4, G: MPEG4 GOP Size 12, H: MPEG4 GOP SIZE 80.

Method	A	B	C	D	E	F	G	H
Filesize/KB	62080	7552	3112	2404	4896	2076	1400	1248
Avg. Y-PSNR	∞	45.2625	45.3672	45.3411	45.3583	45.3511	45.3225	45.31

It is likely that the compression ratio can be further improved by relaxing some of the constraints formulated above, e.g. using non-uniform block sizes or allowing the matching pursuit algorithm to produce linear combinations not yielding the same quality as the DCT coding, if in turn the storage cost is sufficiently reduced.

4   Conclusion

We have presented a method for compressing low-motion video where near random access to the compressed frames is possible and have refined this approach by WFA coding. Experiments have shown that for some applications the proposed method yields a compression ratio up to 4 times higher than that of other compressed video formats allowing frame level random access.

References

1. ISO/IEC, ISO/IEC 11172-2:1993, Information technology – Coding of moving pictures and associated audio for digital storage media at up to about 1,5 Mbit/s – Part 2: Video (MPEG1-Video). ISO/IEC (1993)
2. ISO/IEC, ISO/IEC 13818-2:2000, Information technology – Generic coding of moving pictures and associated audio information: Video (MPEG2-Video). ISO/IEC (2000)
3. ISO/IEC, ISO/IEC 14496-2:2004. Information technology – Coding of audio-visual objects – Part 2: Visual (MPEG4-Video). ISO/IEC (2004)

4. Watkinson, J.: The MPEG Handbook. 2nd edn. Focal Press (2004)
5. Ahmed, N., Natarajan T., Rao, K. R.: Discrete cosine transform. IEEE Transactions on Computers **C-32** (1974) 90–93
6. Wallace, G. K.: The JPEG still picture compression standard: Communications of the ACM **34/4** (1991) 30–44
7. ISO/IEC: ISO/IEC IS 10918-1:1994, Information technology - Digital compression and coding of continuous-tone still images: Requirements and guidelines. ISO/IEC (1994)
8. Hafner, U.: Low Bit-Rate Image and Video Coding with Weighted Finite Automata. Mensch und Buch Verlag, Berlin (1999)
9. Culik II, K., Kari, J.: Image Compression Using Weighted Finite Automata. Computer and Graphics **17/3** (1993) 305–313
10. Culik II, K., Kari, J.: Image-data compression using edge-optimizing algorithm for WFA inference. Journal of Information Processing and Management **30** (1994) 829–838
11. Culik II, K., Kari, J.: Efficient inference algorithm for weighted finite automata. In: Y. Fisher (ed.): Fractal Image Encoding and Compression, Springer-Verlag (1995)
12. Culik II, K., Kari, K.: Inference Algorithms for WFA and Image Compression. In: Y. Fisher (ed.): Fractal Image Encoding and Compression, Springer-Verlag (1995)
13. Schützenberger, M. P.: On the definition of a family of automata. Information and Control **4/2-3** (1961) 245–270
14. Culik II, K., Karhumäki, J.: Finite automata computing real functions. SIAM Journal on Computing **23/4** (1994) 789–814
15. Derencourt, D., Karhumäki, J., Latteux, M., Terlutte, A.: On Computational Power of Weighted Finite Automata. Lecture Notes in Computer Science **629** (1992) 236–245
16. Droste, M., Kari, J., Steinby, P.: Observations on the smoothness properties of real functions computed by weighted finite automata. To appear in Fundamenta Informaticae.
17. Berstell, J., Reutenauer, C.: Rational Series and Their Languages. Springer-Verlag, Berlin (1988)

A   Orthogonal Matching Pursuit Algorithm

Input   : $b_O(i)$, $b_C(i)$,

  $cost_{b_C}(i)$ (storage cost of coded blocks), m (state to approximate)

Output: idx (highest used index in linear combination)

  $cost(i)$ (costs of prefixes of linear combination)

  $e(i)$ (errors of prefixes of linear combination)

  $t(i)$ target state vector, $c(i)$ weight vector

1 $idx \leftarrow 0$

2 **while** $idx < m$ and $idx < e_{\max}$ **do**

3   **for** $i \in \{0, 1, \ldots, m-1\}$ **do**

4          $\alpha(i) \leftarrow\ <b_o(m), b_c(i)> - \sum_{k=0}^{idx-1} \frac{<b_c(i),o(k)><b_o(m),o(k)>}{|o(k)|^2}$

5          $\beta(i) \leftarrow |b_c(i)|^2 - \sum_{k=0}^{idx-1} \frac{<b_c(i),o(k)>}{|o(k)|^2}$

6      $t(idx) \leftarrow \min\{i | \frac{\alpha(i)^2}{\beta(i)}$ maximal for $t(j) \neq i$ for $j < idx$

        and $b_C(i)$ was not replaced by a linear combination$\}$

7      $u(idx) \leftarrow b_C(t(idx))$

8      $o(idx) \leftarrow b_C(t(idx)) - \sum_{i=0}^{idx-1} \frac{<u(idx),o(i)>}{|o(i)|^2}o(i)$

9   **for** $i \in 0, 1, \ldots, idx$ **do**

10         $c(i) \leftarrow\ <b_o(m), o(i)>$

11   **for** $i = idx$ to 0 **do**

12   **for** $k \in \{0, 1, i-1\}$ **do**

13             $c(k) \leftarrow c(k) - c(i)\frac{<u(i),o(k)>}{|o(k)|^2}$

14     $e(idx) \leftarrow |b_o(m) - \sum_{i=0}^{idx} c(i)b_c(t(i))|$

15     $cost(idx) \leftarrow$ storage cost of linear combination up to index idx

16   **if** $cost(idx) > cost_{b_C}(m)$ **then** // cost too high ?

17   break

18   **if** $e(idx) < |b_o(m) - b_c(m)|$ **then** // error small enough ?

19   break

20     $idx \leftarrow idx + 1$

Algorithm 1. Orthogonal Matching Pursuit. Matching succeeds iff the algorithm aborts the while loop in line 19. $< \cdot, \cdot >$ denotes the scalar product of two vectors.

B   Example Material for Random Access Video Application

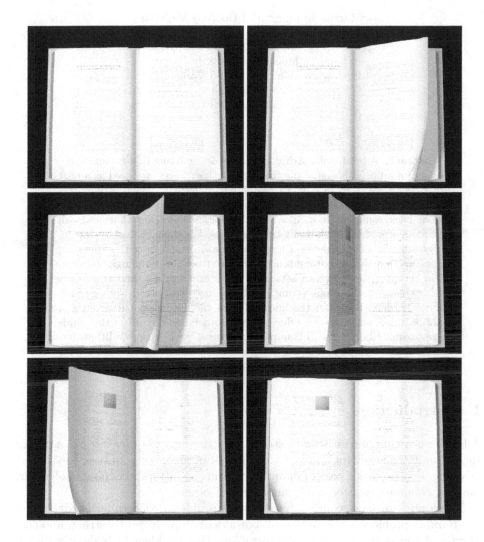

Fig. 8. Example material for random access video application: *Frames of a video showing a page flip.* The complete movie contains 80 frames.

Borders and Finite Automata*

Martin Šimůnek and Bořivoj Melichar

Department of Computer Science and Engineering
Czech Technical University in Prague
Karlovo nám. 13, 121 35 Praha 2,
Czech Republic
{simunem1, melichar}@fel.cvut.cz

Abstract. A border of a string is a prefix of the string that is simultaneously its suffix. It is one of the basic stringology keystones used as a part of many algorithms in pattern matching, molecular biology, computer-assisted music analysis and others. The paper discusses automata-theoretical background of Iliopoulos's ALL_BORDERS algorithm that finds all borders of a string with don't care symbols. We show that ALL_BORDERS algorithm is a simulator of a finite automaton together with explaining the function of the automaton. We show that the simulated automaton accepts intersection of sets of prefixes and suffixes (and thus a set of borders) of the input string. Last but not least we define approximate borders. Based on the knowledge of the automata background of ALL_BORDERS algorithm we offer an automata-based algorithm that finds approximate borders with Hamming distance. We discuss conditions under which the same principle can be used for other distance measures for which an approximate searching automaton can be constructed.

1 Introduction

A border is a kind of regularity in strings. A string has a border if it has a prefix that is simultaneously its suffix. An analysis of borders is one of basic keystones of stringology used as a part of many algorithms in pattern matching, molecular biology, computer-assisted music analysis and others.

There are two most commonly discussed problems concerning borders: the *All Borders* problem, i.e. is to find all borders of all prefixes of a string, and the *Border Array* problem. All Borders problem (see Problem 1) is dealt with in this paper. Border Array problem for string t, $n = |t|$, consists in computation of an array $\beta[1..n]$ where $\beta[i]$ is the length of the longest border of the prefix of t of lenght i. A border array is used in preprocessing of the Knuth-Morris-Pratt [MP70] pattern matching algorithm to compute failure function. It can be computed in linear time and stores all information needed to compute all borders of all prefixes of the string.

---

* This research has been partially supported by the Ministry of Education, Youth, and Sport of the Czech Republic under research program MSM6840770014 and by the Czech Science Foundation as project No. 201/06/1039.

O.H. Ibarra and H.-C. Yen (Eds.): CIAA 2006, LNCS 4094, pp. 58–68, 2006.

"Don't care" symbol is a special symbol that can be matched to any symbol including itself. Don't care symbol is a simple approach embracing errors and inaccuracy to the concepts of pattern matching and regularities searching. This approach originates from the field of DNA analysis. Pattern matching in strings with don't care symbols was first studied by Fischer and Paterson in [FP74]. They developed $\mathcal{O}(n.\log m \log |\Sigma|)$ time algorithm to search for a pattern of length m in a string of length n over alphabet $\Sigma \cup \{*\}$ based on convolutions. Algorithms that find borders, border array and covers (factors from which given string can be obtained by concatenations and overlaps) in string with don't care symbols were introduced by Iliopoulos et al. in [IMM+03].

Approximate regularities extend basic problems of searching for regularities by adding a measure of string similarity. This allows some level of errors and inaccuracy to be accepted. Similarity in this sense is more general than using don't care symbols as we do not need to specify the positions where errors can occur. We restrict only a total number of errors allowed.

In this paper we study both borders in strings with don't care symbols and approximate borders from the automata-oriented point of view. Our long-run goal is to create a scheme for finding regularities in strings based on automata-theoretical base. We hope that introduction of common theoretical base of existing algorithms can help to find analogies among problems and adapt existing algorithms to solve more specific variants of the problems.

In the area of pattern matching, Holub and Melichar have created a similar scheme in [Hol00] and [MHP05]. They have found interconnection between automata-oriented algorithms and algorithms based on dynamic programming and bit parallelism. We would like to follow that work and extend it to the area of searching for regularities.

This paper starts by reminding the reader of Iliopoulos's algorithm for finding all borders of all prefixes of string with don't care symbols. We show that the algorithm is in fact a simulator of a finite automaton. In accordance with the definition of a border, the appropriate finite automaton accepts the intersection of sets of prefixes and suffixes of the input string. Last but not least we define approximate border of a string and use the knowledge of the automata background of Iliopoulos's algorithm to generalise the algorithm for finding all approximate borders of all prefixes of the string.

2   Preliminaries

An *alphabet* Σ is a nonempty set of symbols. A *string* over alphabet Σ is a sequence of zero or more symbols from Σ. The set of all nonempty strings over alphabet Σ is denoted by Σ^+. Empty string is denoted by ε. We denote $\Sigma^* = \Sigma^+ \cup \{\varepsilon\}$.

If t_1 and t_2 are strings over Σ, their concatenation is denoted by $t_1 t_2$. We use exponents notation for repetition of strings: $t^0 = \varepsilon$, $t^1 = t$, $t^2 = tt, \ldots$ for any $t \in \Sigma^*$. Whenever $t = uwv$, $u, w, v \in \Sigma^*$, w is a *factor* of t. $t[i]$ denotes the i-th symbol of string t. $t[i \ldots j]$ denotes the factor of t beginning with i-th symbol and ending with j-th symbol of string t.

The length of string t is the number of symbols of t. We denote it by $|t|$. We use a convention that symbol n is used for the length of the analyzed string $n = |t|$. Whenever we use w for a factor of t etc., we use symbol m for its length: $m = |w|$. $|\varepsilon| = 0$.

String $w \in \Sigma^*$ is a prefix of string t if $t = wu$, $u \in \Sigma^*$. w is a *proper prefix* if $|w| < |t|$. Set of all prefixes of string t is denoted by $\text{Pref}(t)$. Similarly string $w \in \Sigma^*$ is a suffix of string t if $t = vw$, $v \in \Sigma^*$. w is a *proper suffix* if $|w| < |t|$. Set of all suffixes of string t is denoted by $\text{Suff}(t)$.

In many problems we need to check whether two strings are similar but not necessarily equal. One of possible approaches is to add a "don't care" symbol, i.e. a special universal symbol $* \notin \Sigma$ that can be *matched* to any symbol including itself. String with don't care symbols is a string over $\Sigma \cup \{*\}$. The relation of matching strings with don't care symbols is denoted by operator $\approx$. Another approach is to introduce a distance of strings. Distance is usually a metric, even though it is not necessary. (Metric is a function that satisfies conditions of positivity, symmetry and triangle inequality.)

In this paper we use Hamming distance metric. Hamming distance between two strings t_1 and t_2 is the minimum number of substitutions needed to convert string t_1 to t_2. Hamming distance is defined for strings of equal length.

Formal language L is a subset of set of all strings drawn from alphabet Σ: $L \subset \Sigma^*$.

A nondeterministic finite automaton M is a quintuple $(Q, \Sigma, \delta, I, F)$, where: Q is a finite set of states, Σ is an input alphabet, δ is a mapping $\delta: Q \times (\Sigma \cup \{\varepsilon\}) \to \mathcal{P}(Q)$ called a *state transition function*, $I \subset Q$ is a set of initial states, and $F \subset Q$ is a set of final states.

When reading a string with don't care symbols, automaton does a transition whenever read symbol matches (not necessarily equals to) the symbol for which the transition is defined.

A deterministic finite automaton M is a special case of nondeterministic finite automaton such that transition mapping is a function $\delta: Q \times \Sigma \to Q$ and there is only one initial state $q_0 \in Q$.

To describe transition function of finite automaton we often use transition diagrams. Let us use the following conventions:

- unuseful states (there is no word that can move automaton from such state to any final state) and transitions to unuseful states are omitted whenever it cannot cause a confusion,
- shortened form i or i^j is used to improve legibility instead of q_i or q_i^j, respectively, whenever it is unambiguous,
- if we label a transition in transition diagram by set of symbols, it represents a set of transitions each for one symbol from the set,
- notation $\bar{a}$ is used instead of longer $\Sigma \setminus \{a\}$ for any $a \in \Sigma$.

Definition 1. *Prefix searching automaton (SPOECO) for string w, $m = |w|$, with possible don't care symbols is a nondeterministic finite automaton $M_P = (Q, \Sigma, \delta, I, Q)$ such, that:*

$Q = \{q_0, q_1, \ldots, q_m\}$,

δ: *(match)* $q_{i+1} \in \delta(q_i, a)$, *for* $i \in \{0, 1, \ldots, m-1\}$, $a \approx w[i+1]$,

    (loop) $q_0 \in \delta(q_0, a)$, *for each* $a \in \Sigma$,

$I = \{q_0\}$.

Definition 2. *Approximate prefix searching automaton for string w, $m = |w|$, with Hamming distance at most k (SPORCO) is a nondeterministic finite automaton $M_P^{Ham} = (Q, \Sigma, \delta, I, Q)$ such, that:*

$$Q = \left\{ q_i^j \,:\, i \in \{0, 1, 2, \ldots, m\}, j \in \{0, 1, 2, \ldots, k\} \right\},$$

δ: *(match)* $q_{i+1}^j \in \delta\left(q_i^j, a\right)$, $i \in \{0, 1, \ldots, m-1\}$, $j \in \{0, 1, \ldots k\}$ *and* $a = w[i+1]$,

    (mismatch) $q_{i+1}^{j+1} \in \delta\left(q_i^j, a\right)$, $i \in \{0, 1, \ldots, m-1\}$, $j \in \{0, 1, \ldots, k-1\}$ *and* $a \neq w[i+1]$,

    (loop) $q_0^0 \in \delta(q_0^0, a)$, *for all* $a \in \Sigma$,

$I = \{q_0^0\}$.

Codes SPOECO and SPORCO are selected in compliance with taxonomy from [MHP05]. Both automata can be used in pattern matching. We construct the prefix searching automata for given pattern and read the input string. After reading any prefix of the pattern, automaton reaches a final state as the (approximate) prefix searching automaton for string w accepts any string t ending with an (respectively approximate) prefix of w (see [MHP05]). An example of an approximate prefix searching automaton for $t = \mathsf{abc} * \mathsf{b}$ with Hamming distance at most 2 is given in Figure 1.

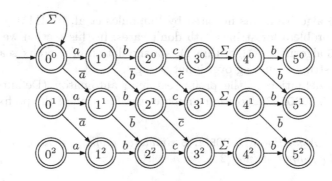

Fig. 1. Transition function of the approximate prefix searching automaton for $t = \mathsf{abc} * \mathsf{b}$ with Hamming distance at most 2

Note that a (eventually approximate) prefix automaton accepting (respectively approximate) prefixes of w can be obtained from (approximate) prefix searching automaton by removing the loop in the initial state.

3   Problem Statement

We are dealing with *All Borders* problem:

Definition 3. *A border w of string t over alphabet Σ is a proper prefix of t that is simultaneously a suffix of t: $w \in (\text{Pref}(t) \setminus \{t\}) \cap \text{Suff}(t)$. A set of all borders of t is denoted by* Bord (t).

Problem 1 (All Borders). Given string t, find all borders Bord (w) of each prefix $w \in \text{Pref}(t)$.

Note that a string of length n can have at most n borders. Thus number of all borders of all prefixes is at most $\sum_{i=1}^{n} i = \frac{1}{2}n(n+1)$. As an example consider string a^n that has n borders: ε, a, aa, ..., a^{n-1}. Each its prefix of length i has i borders.

Border array is an array storing for each prefix length $0, 1, \ldots n$ the length of the longest border of given prefix. Border array can be computed in linear time. Considering the "exact" version of the problem (neither don't care symbols nor approximation is allowed) a border w' of a border of string t is also a border of t ("border of a border is a border"). In this case a border array stores information about all borders of all prefixes of the string. On the other hand whenever we allow don't care symbols or approximate matching, border array cannot be used to find all borders of all prefixes any more. String matching under these circumstances is not transitive. As an example consider string $t = \text{aba} * \text{abaa}$. The longest border of t is abaa with length 4. The longest border of $t[1\ldots4]$ is ab. Still ab is not a border of t. An algorithm solving All Borders problem on a string with don't cares is discussed in the next section.

4   ALL_BORDERS Algorithm Simulates Finite Automaton

ALL_BORDERS algorithm was invented by Iliopoulos et al. in [IMM+03] to solve All Borders problem for strings with don't cares. In this section we show that ALL_BORDERS algorithm (Algorithm 1) is a simulation of a prefix searching automaton for string t running over input string t.

Using the definition of the prefix searching automaton (Definition 1), we show that ALL_BORDERS algorithm simulates the function of the prefix searching automaton.

Theorem 1. *Algorithm* ALL_BORDERS *simulates prefix searching automaton for string t reading input string $t[2\ldots n]$, $n = |t|$.*

Proof. Let us assume that array S_i stores indices of active states after reading a prefix $t[2\ldots i]$, $i \in \{2, 3, \ldots, n\}$. Note that the initial state q_0 is always included as there is a loop for all symbols of the alphabet in q_0.
Using induction according to i:
$i = 1$: Nothing is read yet and thus the only active state is the initial state q_0. S_1 is set during the initialisation.
Assume that the theorem holds for $i = k$. Let $i = k + 1$:

For each active state q_j, q_{j+1} will be active in the next step if $t[j + 1]$ can be matched to the read symbol $t[i]$. This is exactly what is done by the body of the cycle on lines 3–5.   □

Algorithm 1: Searching for all borders of all prefixes
Input: String t, $n = |t|$.
Output: Sets S_i, $i \in \{1, 2, \ldots, n\}$ such that S_i is a set of lengths of borders from Bord $(t[1 \ldots i])$.
Description: In each step we increase actual length of prefix and compute S_i based on S_{i-1} from the previous step. Note that in each step only sets S_i and S_{i-1} are used.
ALLBORDERS(t)
(1) $S_1 \leftarrow \{0\}$
(2)   **for** $i \leftarrow 2$ **to** n
(3) $S_i \leftarrow \{0\}$
(4)   **foreach** $j \in S_{i-1}$
(5)   **if** $t[i] \approx t[j + 1]$ **then** $S_i \leftarrow S_i \cup \{j + 1\}$;
(6)   output(Lengths of borders of $t[1 \ldots i]$: S_i);

Based on Theorem 1 we construct automata-based Algorithm 2 solving All Borders problem.

Algorithm 2: Searching for all borders (automata based)
Input: String t, $n = |t|$.
Output: Sets S_i, $i \in \{2, \ldots, n\}$ such that S_i is a set of lengths of borders from Bord $(t[1 \ldots i])$.
Description: Automata based equivalent of Algorithm 1.
ALLBORDERSFA(t)
(1)   Construct a prefix searching automaton
          $M_P = (Q, \Sigma, \delta, \{q_0\}, F)$ for string t.
(2)   Read $t[2 \ldots n]$ as an input string.
(3)   **for** $i \leftarrow 2$ **to** n
(4) $S_i = \delta^*(q_0, t[2 \ldots i]) \cap F$
(5)   output(Lengths of borders of $t[1 \ldots i]$: S_i);

4.1   ALL_BORDERS Algorithm and Intersection of Automata

Following the definition of border we can search for borders using automaton accepting intersection of languages of prefix automaton and suffix automaton. Algorithm based on this idea was published in [MHP05]. Efficient implementation of this algorithm has the same asymptotic complexity as ALL_BORDERS algorithm [ŠM06]. Let us show that ALL_BORDERS does the same.

Observation 1. Algorithm 2 finds lengths of prefixes of t that are equal to some proper suffix of t.

In the following text, please, take care to distinguish prefix *searching* automaton and accepts $L_P = \Sigma^*.\mathrm{Pref}\,(t)$ and prefix automaton accepting only $\mathrm{Pref}\,(t)$.

In ALL_BORDERS algorithm string $t[2\ldots n]$, $n = |t|$, is read by prefix searching automaton M_P for string t. As we know the length of the input string, we can expand the loop in the initial state and construct "expanded automaton" M_{Pe} by creating n "copies" "M_j", $j \in \{0, 1, \ldots, n-1\}$ of a prefix automaton. States of "M_j" are denoted by upper index j. State q_0^0 of "M_0" is the only initial state of M_{Pe}. States of subautomata "M_j", $j > 0$ are reached by "Σ-transitions" for all symbols of alphabet from states q_0^j of "M_j" to states q_0^{j+1} of "M_{j+1}" for each $j \in \{0, 1, \ldots, n-2\}$. M_{Pe} is equivalent to the prefix searching automaton for input strings shorter than n.

As an example consider string $t = \mathsf{abc} * \mathsf{b}$. Transition diagrams of automata M_P and M_{Pe} are depicted in Figure 2.

Note that a subautomaton "M_j" in the expanded automaton M_{Pe} reads suffix $t[j + 2 \ldots n]$ of input string $t[2 \ldots n]$, $j \in \{0, 1, \ldots, n-2\}$, "$M_{n-1}$" reads ε. The suffix is obtained after reading first j symbols of the input string in "Σ-transitions". Thus reading of $t[2 \ldots n]$ by expanded prefix searching automaton is equivalent to reading all proper suffixes of $t[2 \ldots n]$ by prefix automata. Lower index of accepting final state give then the lengths of borders (lengths of prefixes that equal to some proper suffix). See Figure 3 for example on $\mathsf{abc} * \mathsf{b}$. Similarly after reading $t[2 \ldots i]$, $i \in \{2, 3, \ldots, n\}$, we can detect borders of $t[1 \ldots i]$.

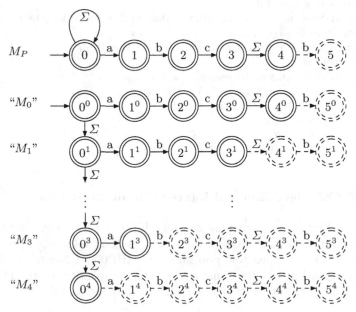

Fig. 2. Transition diagrams of both common and expanded version of prefix searching automaton for $\mathsf{abc} * \mathsf{b}$. Dashed states are never reached when reading $\mathsf{bc} * \mathsf{b}$.

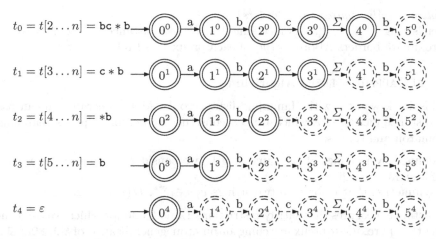

Fig. 3. Transition diagrams of prefix automata "M_j" for string abc $*$ b obtained by splitting expanded prefix searching automaton ("M_j" reads t_j as an input string)

4.2 Complexity of the Algorithm

Let us remind that ALL_BORDERS algorithm (Algorithm 1) is in fact direct implementation of Algorithm 2. Thus the complexity of both algorithms is the same. Complexity analysis of Algorithm 1 is given in [IMM+03]. The worst case time complexity is quadratic as the maximal number of borders on output is quadratic. Number of transitions performed is equal to the number of borders found. [IMM+03] shows that the algorithm is linear in average case for random strings.

5   Approximate Borders

We have shown that ALL_BORDERS algorithm simulates function of nondeterministic prefix searching automaton. Let us define *All Approximate Borders* problem and show a generalization of ALL_BORDERS algorithm solving this problem. We use the knowledge automata background of ALL_BORDERS algorithm.

Definition 4. *An approximate prefix (suffix) w of string t with a distance measure D and a distance bound k is $w \in \Sigma^*$: $D(w, p) \leq k$ for some $p \in \mathrm{Pref}(t)$ (or $p \in \mathrm{Suff}(t)$). The set of all approximate prefixes (suffixes) of string t with distance measure D and distance bound k is denoted by $\mathrm{APref}_{D,k}(t)$ (or $\mathrm{ASuff}_{D,k}(t)$ respectively).*

Approximate border w of string t is a proper prefix of t that is simultaneously its approximate suffix or an approximate prefix of t that is simultaneously its proper suffix.

Definition 5. *An approximate border of string t with distance measure D and distance bound k is $w \in \Sigma^*$: $w \in ((\mathrm{Pref}(t) \setminus \{t\}) \cap \mathrm{ASuff}_{D,k}(t)) \cup (\mathrm{APref}_{D,k}(t) \cap (\mathrm{Suff}(t) \setminus \{t\}))$. A set of all approximate borders of string t with distance measure D and distance bound k is denoted by $\mathrm{ABord}_{D,k}(t)$.*

Problem 2 (All Approximate Borders).
Given string t, $n = |t|$, distance function D and distance bound k, find all approximate borders $\text{ABord}_{D,k}(w)$ of each prefix $w \in \text{Pref}(t)$.

5.1   ALL_APPROX_BORDERS Algorithm

In this work we deal with Hamming distance only. More generally we can use any distance measure for which we can construct approximate prefix searching automaton and that is:

1. defined over strings of the same length (we consider distance to be infinite for strings of different length),
2. symmetric, that is for each two strings $u, v \in \Sigma^*$: $D(u, v) = D(v, u)$.

For distance measures that satisfy restrictions 1 and 2 and for which we can construct the approximate prefix searching automaton, generalisation of ALL_BORDERS algorithm to approximate borders can be done as shown in Algorithm 3. For Hamming distance we can use approximate prefix searching automaton SPORCO (Definition 2).

Algorithm 3: Searching for all approximate borders
Input: String t, distance bound k and distance measure D satisfying restrictions 1 and 2 for which we can construct the approximate prefix searching automaton.
Output: Set of all approximate borders of all prefixes of t with distance measure D and distance bound k.
Description: Generalisation of Algorithm 2. Computes sets S_i^l of approximate borders of $t[1 \ldots i]$ with distance l, $i \in \{0, 1, \ldots, n\}$, $l \in \{0, 1, \ldots, k\}$.
ALLAPPROXBORDERS(t)
(1)   Construct approximate prefix searching automaton $M_P^{Ham} = (Q, \Sigma, \delta, \{q_0^0\}, F)$ for string t with distance function D and distance bound k.
(2)   Use the longest proper suffix $t[2 \ldots n]$ as an input string.
(3)   **for** $i \leftarrow 2$ **to** n
(4) $S_i^l = \{j \colon q_j^l \in \delta^*(q_0^0, t[2 \ldots i]) \cap F\}$
(5)   output(Lengths of borders of $t[1 \ldots i]$: $\bigcup_{l \in \{0,1,\ldots,k\}} S_i^l$)

5.2   Correctness Analysis

An approximate border of a string is either a proper prefix and an approximate suffix or an approximate prefix and a proper suffix of the string. Intersection of these two sets contains exact borders of the string. Let D be a distance measure satisfying restrictions 1 and 2. Then these two sets are the same.

Lemma 1. *Given distance bound k and distance measure D satisfying restrictions 1 and 2: $u \in \text{Pref}(t)$ and $u \in \text{ASuff}_{D,k}(t)$ if and only if there exists $v \in \text{Suff}(t)$ such that $v \in \text{APref}_{D,k}(t)$ and $|u| = |v|$.*

Proof. Prefix u is in $\mathrm{ASuff}_{D,k}(t)$ if and only if there exists $v \in \mathrm{Suff}(t)$: $D(u,v) \leq k$. Using symmetry of D this is equivalent to $D(v,u) \leq k$ meaning that suffix v is in $\mathrm{APref}_{D,k}(t)$. Moreover lengths of u and v are the same because D is defined for strings of the same length only). $\qquad\square$

Lemma 2. *Algorithm 3 finds lengths of prefixes u such that there exists a proper suffix v, $D(u,v) \leq k$.*

Proof. A principle is the same as in Algorithm 2. In each step the nondeterministic automaton simultaneously tries to accept a proper suffix by an approximate prefix automaton and prepare one symbol shorter suffix by reading a symbol in the loop of the initial state. $\qquad\square$

Theorem 2. *Algorithm 3 finds all approximate borders.*

Proof. Lemma 1 tells that under given circumstances a set of approximate borders is equal to a set found by Algorithm 3 according to Lemma 2. $\qquad\square$

5.3   Complexity of the Algorithm

Let $n = |t|$. Algorithm ALL_APPROX_BORDERS does $n - 1$ steps to read $t[2 \ldots n]$. In each step one active state can be added as the initial state is reactivated by the loop in the initial state and each active state q_i, $i \in \{0, 1, \ldots n - 1\}$ can activate state q_{i+1}. Note that approximate prefix searching automaton for Hamming distance is acyclic and deterministic with exception of the initial state (that has a the loop). Thus the number of active states cannot be increased anywhere else.

There are $n - 1$ steps, in the i-th step we compute transition function for at most i states. Overall complexity is $\mathcal{O}(n^2)$.

6   Conclusion and Future Work

We have shown the automata theoretical background ALL_BORDERS algorithm developed by Iliopoulos et al. ALL_BORDERS algorithm solves All Borders problem on strings with don't cares. We have found that the algorithm is an implementation of intersection of prefix and suffix automaton.

By introducing the common theoretical base of algorithms from the field of regularities searching we try to improve consistency of algorithms. We hope we will be able to reuse ideas of algorithms solving similar problems to solve new variants of the problems. To test this attitude we have defined all approximate borders problem and generalised automata based version of ALL_BORDERS to solve all approximate borders problem for Hamming distance. Asymptotic complexity of the algorithm remained the same as that of ALL_BORDERS algorithm.

In future we would like to deal with generalisation of this attitude to other variants of All Borders problem based on the knowledge of appropriate searching automata. Namely we want to take under consideration approximate borders with Levenshtein distance, general approximate borders (i.e. strings, that are both approximate prefix and approximate suffix but do not need to be either prefix or suffix of string). Last but not least we would like to follow the idea of this paper and deal with other regularities searching problems like periods, covers etc.

References

[FP74]   M. J. Fischer and M. S. Paterson. String matching and other products. In R. M. Karp, editor, *Complexity of Computation. SIAM AMS Proceedings*, volume 7, pages 113–125. American Mathematical Society, 1974.

[Hol00]   Jan Holub. *Simulation of Nondeterministic Finite Automata in Pattern Matching*. PhD thesis, Czech Technical University in Prague, February 2000.

[IMM+03]   C. S. Iliopoulos, M. Mohamed, L. Mouchard, K. Perdikuri, W. F. Smyth, and A. Tsakalidis. String regularities with don't cares. *Nordic Journal of Computing*, 10(1):40–51, 2003.

[MHP05]   Bořivoj Melichar, Jan Holub, and Tomáš Polcar. *Text Searching Algorithms*, volume I. http://www.stringology.org/athens/, 2005.

[MP70]   J. H. Morris and V. R. Pratt. A Linear Pattern Matching Algorithm. Technical Report 40, Computing Center, University of California, Berkeley, 1970.

[ŠM06]   Martin Šimůnek and Bořivoj Melichar. Borders and finite automata. In *Proceedings of Workshop 2006*. Czech Technical University, Prague, February 2006.

Finding Common Motifs with Gaps Using Finite Automata*

Pavlos Antoniou[1], Jan Holub[2], Costas S. Iliopoulos[1], Bořivoj Melichar[2], and Pierre Peterlongo[3]

[1] Dept. of Computer Science, King's College London,
London WC2R 2LS, England, UK
{pavlos.antoniou, csi}@kcl.ac.uk
[2] Czech Technical University in Prague, Department of Computer Science and
Engineering, Karlovo nám. 13, 121 35, Prague 2, Czech Republic
{holub, melichar}@fel.cvut.cz
[3] Institut Gaspard-Monge, Université de Marne-la-Vallée, Cite Descartes,
Champs sur Marne, 77454 Marne-la-Vallée CEDEX 2, France
pierre.peterlongo@univ-mlv.fr

Abstract. We present an algorithm that uses finite automata to find
the common motifs with gaps occurring in all strings belonging to a
finite set $S = \{S_1, S_2, \ldots, S_r\}$. In order to find these common motifs we
must first identify the factors that exist in each string. Therefore the
algorithm begins by constructing a factor automaton for each string S_i.
To find the common factors of all the strings, the algorithm needs to
gather all the factors from the strings together in one data structure
and this is achieved by computing an automaton that accepts the union
of the above-mentioned automata. Using this automaton we are able
to create a new factor alphabet. Based on this factor alphabet a finite
automaton is created for each string S_i that accepts sequences of all non
overlapping factors residing in each string. The intersection of the latter
automata produces the finite automaton which accepts all the common
subsequences with gaps over the factor alphabet that are present in all
the strings of the set $S = \{S_1, S_2, \ldots, S_r\}$. These common subsequences
are the common motifs of the strings.

1 Introduction

The problem of finding common motifs in a set of strings has long been an area of
interest in the academic community. Given a set of strings, the problem of finding
common motifs in that set is the problem of finding similar substrings that lie in
all of these strings. In some particular applications, like in biology, this requirement is more flexible in the sense that motifs do not have to be identical but have
to share a certain degree of similarity. This degree is quantified using metrics

---

* This research has been partially supported by the Ministry of Education, Youth and
Sports under research program MSM 6840770014 and the Czech Science Foundation
as project No. 201/06/1039.

O.H. Ibarra and H.-C. Yen (Eds.): CIAA 2006, LNCS 4094, pp. 69–77, 2006.

such as Hamming and Levenshtein distances or by allowing don't care symbols to occur in the motifs. Don't care symbols are occurrences in the string that can match any symbol of the alphabet. In this paper, we are interested in finding common motifs in the strings that have don't care symbols concentrated in distinct parts of contiguous positions in the strings, i.e. common motifs with gaps.

This problem has engrossed biologists because of its applications in that area. It can be applied in understanding the fundamental process of gene expression [8]. Gene expression consists of two parts, transcription and translation. During transcription an mRNA molecule is created by copying a gene from the DNA and during translation the mRNA molecule is decoded to produce a protein. In order though for the transcription process to begin, one or more proteins, called transcription factors, have to bind to some specific regions of the gene called binding sites. These binding sites share common patterns which are the common motifs of the genes. If these common motifs are identified and extracted from the genes, they will give the opportunity to biologists to match these binding sites to their corresponding transcription factors in order to be able to fully understand the way gene expression works [8].

A classical approach to finding these motifs was by using artificial intelligence techniques [10] but these methods are inexact methods that used machine learning to discover the motifs by training the machines to recognize them. Recently, microarray technology has been used particularly in this application of the problem but this technology is inexact, it is based on probabilities and is limited by weak signal sequences [8].

In text algorithm applications, finding common motifs with gaps has been mainly handled using suffix trees [1,2,5,7] which provided exact results. In this paper we propose an algorithm using automata to index common gapped motifs. We believe that the use of automaton permit the indexation of bigger strings and allows more open definitions.

Section 2 formally introduces the general problem. Section 3 presents an algorithm in order to solve the question of finding common motifs with gaps. Moreover Section 4 presents a complete example following step by step the proposed algorithm. Eventually in Section 5 there is an analysis of the complexity of the proposed solution.

2   Definition of the Problem

Given a set of strings $S = \{S_1, S_2, \ldots, S_r\}$ and p, q, $1 \leq p \leq q \leq \min(|S_j| : j \in \langle 1, r \rangle)$. The problem of finding common motifs with gaps consists in finding words $B_1, B_2, \ldots, B_m$ such that:

1. $m > 1$.
2. $p \leq |B_i| \leq q$ for $i \in \langle 1, m \rangle$.
3. $B_1 \circ^{d_{i,1}} B_2 \circ^{d_{i,2}} \ldots \circ^{d_{i,m-1}} B_m$ occur in S_i for all $i \in \langle 1, r \rangle$, $m > 1$ and the size of the gap $d_{i,j}$ varies in each motif (Fig. 1), where $\circ$ denotes don't care symbol matching any symbol of alphabet and $\circ^j$ denotes concatenation of j don't care symbols.

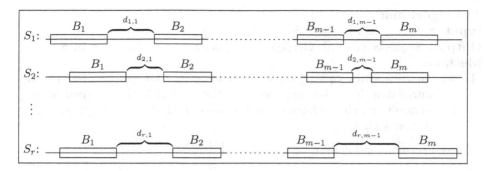

Fig. 1. An example of a motif with gaps that occurs in every string, where by $d_{i,j}$ we mean a size of a gap

3 Algorithm

The algorithm takes as input a set of strings $S = \{S_1, S_2, \ldots, S_r\}$ and two constants p, q, which will be the lower and upper bound respectively of the length each motif can have, and returns the common motifs with gaps found in all those strings. The algorithm begins with computing the set of all factors F of length between the constants p and q that appear in all strings belonging to the set $S = \{S_1, S_2, \ldots, S_r\}$.

In order to find all these factors in F that appear in all the strings, we begin by creating a factor automaton MF_i for each string $S_i \subset S$. Each factor automaton MF_i accepts all the factors of the particular string $S_i \in S$. Then, the algorithm joins all the MF_i automata together in one automaton. The resulting union automaton accepts the union of the languages accepted by each of the r automata. This automaton can either be deterministic or non-deterministic. If it is deterministic, then the algorithm finishes because this is a sign that there are no common symbols and therefore no common motifs are present in the strings from this set S. On the other hand, if the resulting union automaton is non-deterministic, the algorithm proceeds with transforming this non-deterministic automaton into a deterministic one.

From this deterministic union automaton we identify all factors having length between the two constants p and q that are repeating in all strings from the set S. These factors are subsequently used to create a repetition table RT, which is used to create a new factor alphabet containing only the symbols relevant to the factors extracted in the previous steps.

Based on the repetition table, we find the longest common subsequence over the factor alphabet of all the strings of S. To achieve this aim, we first create a finite automaton MS_i for each string $S_i \in S$ accepting sequences of non-overlapping factors using the factor alphabet as input alphabet. Then, we create the automaton MS by taking the intersection of these automata MS_i. The resulting automaton will accept the intersection of the languages accepted by each of the factor automata i.e. it accepts all sequences of factors occurring in all strings from the set S which are the common motifs of the strings with gaps.

The algorithm:
Input: Set of strings $S = \{S_1, S_2, \ldots, S_r\}$, p, q.
Output: Sequence of words $B_1, B_2, \ldots, B_m$ occurring in all strings in S.
Method:
1. (a) For each string $S_i \in S$ construct a factor automaton $M_{i\varepsilon}$ by creating automaton M_i, accepting string S_i (i.e. $L(M_i) = \{S_i\}$), then adding ε-transitions leading from the initial state to all states of M_i and making all states final.

   (b) Construct automaton M_ε, $L(M_\varepsilon) = \bigcup_{i=1}^{r} L(M_{i\varepsilon})$.

   (c) By eliminating ε-transitions in M_ε we get M_F.

   (d) If M_F is deterministic, then strings in S have no common symbol and thus they cannot have a common motif. Set $m = 0$ and exit the algorithm.

   (e) Using determinisation of M_F we construct M_{DF} while for each state q' of M_{DF} we preserve a set of states of M_F q' consists of. The set is called d-subset.

2. Find all states of M_{DF} representing factors of length between p and q and having at least one state from each automaton M_i in its d-subset. Construct a repetition table RT (the shortest path from the initial state to the state spells the repeated factor while members of d-subset identify locations).

3. Take all factors represented by states in the previous step and create a new "factor alphabet" FA.

4. For each string S_i in S construct a finite automaton MS_i accepting sequences of all non-overlapping factors from FA.

5. Construct automaton MS accepting all common subsequences of sequences accepted by automata MS_i for $i \in \langle 1, r \rangle$ using the following approach:

   (a) Add ε-transitions parallel to each transition in each finite automaton $MS_i, i \in \langle 1, r \rangle$. The resulting automata will be MS_i^ε.

   (b) By eliminating ε-transitions in MS_i^ε we get MS_i^N for each $i \in \langle 1, r \rangle$.

   (c) Construct the automaton MS, $L(MS) = \bigcap_{i=1}^{r} L(MS_i^N)$.

   (d) Finite automaton MS is accepting all sequences $B_1, B_2, \ldots, B_m$ which are sequences of factors occurring in all strings from set S.

4   An Example

As an example let's consider a set of strings $S = \{aabccddab, babbcdacd\}$. We will find common motifs in this set of strings bounded from parameters $p = 2, q = 3$.

First (step 1a of the algorithm) we construct finite automata $M_{1\varepsilon}$ and $M_{2\varepsilon}$ for both strings from S. See Fig. 2[1].

In the next step (step 1b of the algorithm) we construct automaton M_ε accepting the union of languages $L(M_{1\varepsilon})$ and $L(M_{2\varepsilon})$. See Fig. 3.

---

[1] All states in the automata presented in this paper are final.

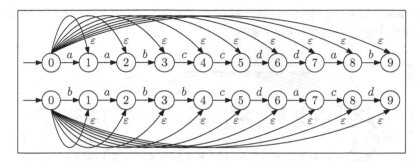

Fig. 2. Transition diagrams of finite automata $M_{1\varepsilon}$ and $M_{2\varepsilon}$ for the set of strings $S = \{aabccddab, babbcdacd\}$ from the example

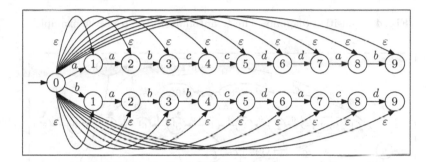

Fig. 3. Transition diagram of finite automaton M_ε from the example

According to step 1c of the algorithm, we construct automaton M_F by replacing the ε-transitions by non ε-transitions. The transition diagram of the resulting automaton is given in Fig. 4.

In this example, automaton M_F is nondeterministic. This means that there is a possibility that a common motif exists in set S. According to step 1e of the algorithm 3, we must construct its deterministic equivalent M_D. Its transition diagram is given in Fig. 5.

Table 1 is the repetition table RT of common factors created as described in step 2 of the algorithm. The factor alphabet (step 3 of the algorithm) is $FA = \{ab, bc, cd, da\}$. Subsequently we will construct, according to step 4 of the algorithm, finite automata MS_1 and MS_2 accepting all non-overlapping sequences of factors of the both strings. Their transition diagrams are depicted in Fig. 6.

The last step (step 5 of the algorithm involves the construction of an automaton which accepts all sequences of factors occurring in both strings of S. Transition diagrams of finite automata MS_1^ε and MS_2^ε are shown in Fig. 7 (step 5a).

Transition diagrams of finite automata MS_1^N and MS_2^N are shown in Fig. 8 (step 5b of the algorithm).

According to the step 5c of the algorithm, we need to construct a finite automaton accepting the language that corresponds to the intersection of the languages accepted by the two automata. The transition diagrams of the finite automaton accepting the intersection of the languages accepted by automaton MS_1^N and MS_2^N is depicted in Fig 9.

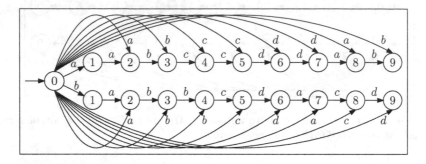

Fig. 4. Transition diagram of finite automaton M_F from the example

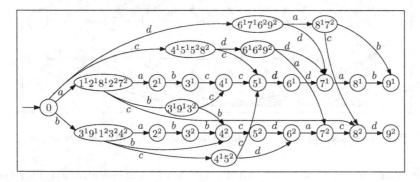

Fig. 5. Transition diagram of finite deterministic factor automaton M_D from the example

Table 1. Repetition table RT of common factors from the example (F – first occurrence, G – repetition with a gap)

Factor	d-subset	Repetitions
ab	$3^1 9^1 3^2$	$(3^1, F), (9^1, G), (3^2, F)$
bc	$4^1 5^2$	$(4^1, F), (5^2, F)$
cd	$6^1 6^2 9^2$	$(6^1, F), (6^2, F), (9^2, G)$
da	$8^1 7^2$	$(8^1, F), (7^2, F)$

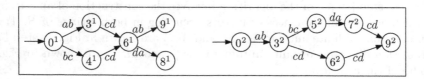

Fig. 6. Transition diagrams of finite automata MS_1 and MS_2 accepting sequences of non-overlapping factors of both strings from the example

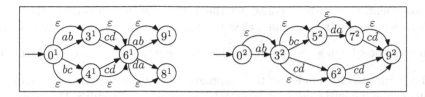

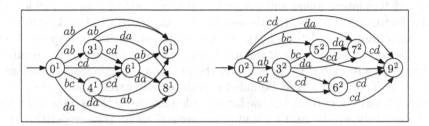

Fig. 7. Transition diagrams of finite automata MS_1^ε and MS_2^ε from the example

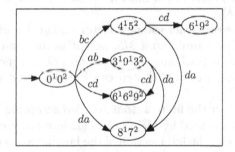

Fig. 8. Transition diagrams of finite automaton MS_1^N and MS_2^N from the example

Fig. 9. Transition diagram of finite automaton MS from the example

Finally, from the above computation we may conclude that in this particular set $S = \{aabccddab, babbcdacd\}$ and using parameters $p = 2, q = 3$ the following common motifs occur: $m_1 = \{ab, cd\}$, $m_2 = \{ab, da\}$, $m_3 = \{bc, cd\}$, $m_4 = \{bc, da\}$.

5 Time and Space Complexity of the Algorithm

We shall discuss the time and space complexity for each step of the algorithm. As described in Section 3 the algorithm requires five steps.

In Step 1 we fist construct r finite automata, one for each string S_i of the set of strings S. The time and space needed to construct each automaton depends on the length of each particular string S_i which is the language to be accepted by the automaton. Therefore this process requires linear time and space [4] with respect to the length of the strings.

Subsequently we wish to construct the automaton which accepts the union of these languages. If we assume that the value n is the cumulated size of the input sequences i.e. $n = \sum_{i=1}^{r} |S_i|$, then this step requires $\mathcal{O}(n)$ space and time for all the strings to be included in the automaton. Next, we wish to transform this union automaton into a deterministic factor automaton also called Direct Acyclic Word Graph (DAWG). In most cases the union automaton is non-deterministic. In order to create the deterministic factor automaton we need to transform the non-deterministic union automaton to a deterministic automaton which will be the factor automaton M_F. Generally, the construction of a deterministic automaton from a non-deterministic requires exponential time and space. In the case of factor automata though the maximum number of states of the resulting deterministic automaton is $2|n| - 1$ and the maximum number of transitions is $3|n| - 4$ [3]. Thus, this step is bounded overall by linear time and space.

In Step 2 we extract from M_F the factors belonging to all the strings and which have length between the values p and q, and we add them to the repetition table RT. In order to find all these factors we need to reach all the states at depth q. Let $\delta = q - p + 1$ the length of the last interval. As we are looking for all the factors between p and q there are at most $n \times \delta$ such factors. Thus the complexity of this step is $\mathcal{O}(n \times \delta)$.

In Steps 3 and 4 we construct the new factor alphabet and for each string S_i in S we construct a finite automaton MS_i accepting all non-overlapping factors from the factor alphabet. Each automaton requires $\mathcal{O}(n)$ time to be constructed and $\mathcal{O}(n)$ space. Thus, overall this step can be completed in linear time and requires linear space.

In Step 5 we construct the finite automaton MS accepting all common subsequences of the strings accepted by MS_i. This is achieved by creating the finite automaton MS that accepts the intersection of the languages accepted by automata MS_i taken from Step 4. The process of intersecting automata requires quadratic time and is usually done by cartesian product. In [6], Holub and Melichar present an algorithm for the intersection of factor automata which does not employ cartesian product but uses state marking. Using this algorithm we avoid the creation of all inaccessible states during the automaton construction.

Although the resulting automaton from the algorithm in [6] contains no inaccessible states as it would have if we had used cartesian product to construct it, nevertheless the time and space complexities of this step are still quadratic relative to the input. For the case of only two factor automata to be intersected, for example L_1 and L_2 having lengths n and m respectively then the state complexity of $L_1 \cap L_2$ is $\mathcal{O}(nm)$. When we transfer this into a problem with many automata the complexity will become $\mathcal{O}(n^k)$—polynomial with n size of texts and exponential with k the number of automata. This is a familiar situation relating to the problem of finding the longest common subsequences of many (> 3) strings using Dynamic Programming which is an NP-complete problem so no better exact algorithm is destined to appear [9].

Overall, looking over all the steps we can see that the algorithm's time and space complexity is exponential due to the last step that requires the intersection of many finite automata.

6   Conclusion

We have presented a complete automaton based algorithm to solve the problem of identifying and indexing the common motifs with gaps in a set of strings. The algorithm takes advantage of the fact that one can find common motifs of a set of strings by intersecting their corresponding factor automata which were created by the common factors residing in the strings. Other solutions of the problem require some limit of gaps (fixed gap, bounded gap, bounded sum of gaps). The presented algorithm allows any gaps while keeping the same time and space complexity. Moreover it offers a sound application of finite automata on the problem of finding common motifs with gaps in a set of strings.

References

1. C. Charras and T. Lecroq. *Exact string matching algorithms.* 2004.
2. T. Crawford, C. S. Iliopoulos, and R. Raman. String matching techniques for musical similarity and melodic recognition. *Computing in Musicology*, 11:73–100, 1998.
3. M. Crochemore and R. Vérin. Direct construction of compact directed acyclic word graphs. In A. Apostolico and J. Hein, editors, *Proceedings of the 8th Annual Symposium on Combinatorial Pattern Matching*, number 1264, pages 116–129, Aarhus, Denmark, 1997. Springer-Verlag, Berlin.
4. Maxime Crochemore and Christophe Hancart. Automata for matching patterns. In G. Rozenberg and A. Salomaa, editors, *Handbook of Formal Languages*, volume 2, Linear Modeling: Background and Application, chapter 9, pages 399–462. Springer-Verlag, 1997.
5. Maxime Crochemore and Wojciech Rytter. *Text algorithms.* Oxford University Press, Inc., New York, NY, USA, 1994.
6. Jan Holub and Bořivoj Melichar. Approximate string matching using factor automata. *Theor. Comput. Sci.*, 249(2):305–311, 2000.
7. C. S. Iliopoulos, J. McHugh, P. Peterlongo, N. Pisanti, W. Rytter, and M. Sagot. A first approach to finding common motifs with gaps. *International Journal of Foundations of Computer Science*, 2004.
8. Henry C.M. Leung. Finding motifs with insufficient number of strong binding sites. *Journal of Computational Biology*, 12(6):686–701, 2005.
9. Steven S. Skiena. *The algorithm design manual.* Springer-Verlag New York, Inc., New York, NY, USA, 1998.
10. Michael E. Baker Timothy L. Bailey and Charles P. Elkan. An artificial intelligence approach to motif discovery in protein sequences: Application to steroid dehydrogenases. *The Journal of Steroid Biochemistry and Molecular Biology*, 62(1):29–44, 1997.

Factor Oracles

Maxime Crochemore[1], Lucian Ilie[2,*,**], and Emine Seid-Hilmi[2]

[1] Institut Gaspard-Monge, Université de Marne-la-Vallée
F-77454 Marne-la-Vallée, Cedex 2, France
mac@univ-mlv.fr
[2] Department of Computer Science, University of Western Ontario
N6A 5B7, London, Ontario, Canada
{ilie, eseidhil}@csd.uwo.ca

Abstract. The factor oracle is a relatively new data structure for the set of factors of a string which has been introduced by Allauzen, Crochemore, and Raffinot in 1999. It may recognize non-factors (hence the name "oracle") but its implementational simplicity and experimental behaviour are stunning; factor oracle based string matching has been conjectured optimal on average. However, its structure is not well understood. We take important steps in clarifying its structure by explaining how it can be obtained as a quotient of the trie for the set of factors. When seen this way, all known properties of the factor oracle become simple observations. Also, we introduce a framework where various oracles can be compared. The factor oracle is better than several natural ones.

Keywords: factor oracle, string matching, suffix trie, suffix tree, graph quotient.

1 Introduction

The factor oracle is a relatively new data structure for the set of factors of a string which has been introduced by Allauzen, Crochemore, and Raffinot in [1,2]. The starting point was the notion of *weak factor recognition* which means constructing a NO-biased algorithm for detecting factors of a string. In the string matching algorithms based on reversed factors, identifying correctly non-factors is enough. Therefore, the factor oracle recognizes all factors of a string but may recognize some non-factors as well (hence the name "oracle"). On the other hand, the string matching algorithms based on it are as efficient as the best existing ones but far simpler to implement; they also require less memory. According to the experimental results, it has been conjectured in [1,2] that these algorithms are optimal on average. A number of other applications of the factor oracle to data compression, repetitions searching, and learning have been investigated in [3,7,8,9,10,11,12,13].

---

* Corresponding author.
** Research supported in part by NSERC.

O.H. Ibarra and H.-C. Yen (Eds.): CIAA 2006, LNCS 4094, pp. 78–89, 2006.

The structure of the factor oracle is however not well understood. Proving various properties of it was, so far, rather difficult and therefore solving the open problems concerning it difficult to attempt.

We present here a different way of looking at the factor oracle, namely as a quotient of the trie for the set of factors. Using our construction, all known properties of the factor oracle become simple observations. Moreover, we introduce the general notion of an oracle for the set of factors of a string – the factor oracle is a particular case here – and build a framework for comparing such oracles since, arguably, all of them have to include a quotient of the trie.

Several other natural oracles can be obtained in this way and the factor oracle proves to be the best among those. Particular examples exist when the factor oracle can be improved but whether there exists a general strategy for building better oracles remains open.

We hope that the new approach will be of help in solving various open problems concerning the factor oracle; see Section 9 for details.

The paper is structured as follows. We recall in the next section all basic concepts needed and then present in Section 3 a variant of Ukkonen's algorithm for building tries in which some additional information is computed; this information helps us later in constructing quotients of the trie. The very simple algorithm of [1,2] for constructing the factor oracles is described briefly in Section 4. Section 5 describes an oracle naturally obtained from the trie, called trie oracle. In Section 6 we show how the factor oracle can be obtained from the trie oracle and why it is better whereas Section 7 contains a direct construction of the factor oracle as a quotient of the trie[1], which makes it very simple to prove things about the factor oracle as done in Section 8. We conclude with a brief discussion concerning the main open problems in Section 9.

Some of the proofs had to be omitted due to limited space.

2   Basic Definitions

Let A be an alphabet; A^* is the free monoid generated by A, that is, the set of all finite strings over A. The empty string is ε. For a string $w \in A^*$, we denote by $|w|$ the length of w. If $w = xyz$, for $w, x, y, z \in A^*$, then x, y, z are a *prefix*, *factor*, and *suffix* of w, resp. When different from w they are called *proper*. The set of all factors of w is denoted $\mathsf{fact}(w)$. The same notation is used for a set of strings.

For a string w, we shall denote by $\mathsf{suf}(w)$ the longest proper suffix of w, that is the string obtained from w by removing its first letter; for the empty string we have $\mathsf{suf}(\varepsilon) = \mathsf{nil}$. The ith letter of w is $w[i]$ and, for $1 \leq i \leq j \leq |w|$, we denote $w[i..j] = w[i]w[i+1] \cdots w[j]$.

---

[1] Ways of obtaining the factor oracle as a quotient of the trie have been investigated in [4] and [5]; their automata may be different in some cases from the factor oracle; see the note on page 83.

A *finite automaton* is a directed graph[2] where the edges are labelled by letters from A; if we have an edge $i \xrightarrow{a} j$, then j is an *a-son* of i.

The automaton is *deterministic* if any node has at most one a-son, for any letter a and *nondeterministic* otherwise. To define the language recognized by an automaton, we need to identify an initial node and some final nodes. Then, the strings recognized are precisely those labelling paths from the initial node to a final node. The set of the strings recognized by an automaton M is denoted $L(M)$. In general, for a node i, the language $L(i)$ is the set of all labels of finite paths starting from i and ending in a final node. Unless otherwise specified, all our graphs, when seen as automata, have 0 or ε as initial node and all nodes are final.

The *quotient* of a graph G is any graph obtained from G by merging together the nodes according to a given equivalence relation $\equiv$. The edges are modified accordingly. The quotient is denoted $G|_{\equiv}$.

Inspired by the discussion of [1,2] on the properties the factor oracle should have, we introduce the notion of *oracle for the set of factors of a string* w; it is a deterministic automaton which:

(o_1) recognizes at least all factors of w;
(o_2) is acyclic (it recognizes a finite set of strings);
(o_3) has $|w| + 1$ states (lowest possible);
(o_4) has linearly many edges (independent of alphabet size);
(o_5) for each node, all incoming edges have the same label (for efficient implementation).

The criteria (o_1)-(o_4) appear in [1,2]; (o_5) is new but nevertheless satisfied by the factor oracle; it is very important for implementation because it makes the the memorization of the edge labels unnecessary. Notice the difference between an oracle for the set of factors of a string and *the* factor oracle of [1,2]. As we shall work with both finite automata and tries, we shall simply call them all graphs.

3   Ukkonen's Algorithm for Tries

The *trie* of a string $w \in A^*$, denoted trie(w), is the tree containing all factors of w. Formally, it is a directed graph having as nodes the factors of w and (labelled) edges $u \xrightarrow{a} ua$, where $u, ua \in \mathsf{fact}(w)$, $a \in A$. Each factor is the label of a path starting from the root. See Fig. 1 for an example. Whenever we discuss about tries, we shall identify each node with the corresponding path from the root.

The trie is, in some sense, the most basic data structure for strings as most of the other ones – suffix trees, DAWGs, suffix automata – can be obtained from it. As we show below, also the factor oracle can be obtained from it.

---

[2] In an automaton the nodes are usually called *states* and the labelled edges are called *transitions*.

Ukkonen [16] gave a linear time on-line algorithm for constructing suffix trees which are tries with all chains (paths of nodes of outdegree 1) compacted. However, his construction works also for the simpler case of tries. We describe it below as it is useful in constructing a number of oracles from the obtained trie.

We shall need *suffix links*, which are links from a node u to $\mathsf{suf}(u)$; we shall represent them as dotted arrows; the regular edges are represented as solid arrows. The suffix path from a node u is: $u, \mathsf{suf}(u), \mathsf{suf}^2(u), \ldots$, continuing as long as the suffix links are defined; we shall denote it by $\mathsf{suf}^*(u)$.

The algorithm works sequentially, considering all the letters of w one at a time. To add one letter a, we start from the deepest node in the current trie and follow the suffix links adding new a-sons with their suffix links; this is done until one node having an a-son is found or the value of the suffix link becomes nil; see [6] for more details.

Important for us later will be the time each node has been created, that is, the index of the letter in the string which caused the addition of that node. This will be denoted, for a node u, by $\mathsf{time}(u)$; we shall sometimes write the time as a subscript to the label of the node: $u_{\mathsf{time}(u)}$.

Here is the pseudocode for Ukkonen's algorithm. We also compute the time values and some S'-links which will be discussed later.

UKKONEN_TRIE(w)

- given a string $w = w[1]w[2]\cdots w[n]$, $w[i] \in A$, $1 \le i \le n$;
- return $\mathsf{trie}(w)$;

1. construct the two-node $\mathsf{trie}(w[1])$ with the suffix links
2. **for** i **from** 2 **to** n **do**
3. $v \leftarrow$ deepest leaf of $\mathsf{trie}(w[1..i-1])$
4. $k \leftarrow \min\{i \mid \mathsf{suf}^i(v)$ has a $w[i]$-son or it is nil$\}$
5.   **for** ℓ **from** 0 **to** $k-1$ **do**
6.   create $\mathsf{suf}^\ell(v) \xrightarrow{w[i]} x$
7.   create a suffix link for x [to $w[i]$-son of $\mathsf{suf}^{\ell+1}(v)$ (or ε if nil)]
8. $\mathsf{time}(x) \leftarrow i$
9.   **if** $\mathsf{suf}^k(v) = $ nil **then** $S'(i) \leftarrow 0$
10.   **else** $u \leftarrow w[i]$-son of $\mathsf{suf}^{k-1}(v)$
11. $S'(i) \leftarrow \mathsf{time}(u)$

The trie obtained for the string baababbabc is shown in Fig. 1. The string has been chosen to show the most important aspects of our constructions. It may seem a bit long but, probably, there is no shorter one which shows all situations that need to be analyzed.

Setting, by convention, $S'(0) = -1$, the values of S' for the example in Fig. 1 are:

i	0	1	2	3	4	5	6	7	8	9	10
$S'(i)$	-1	0	0	2	1	2	4	1	2	6	0

The following two remarks about Ukkonen's trie construction algorithm are very useful.

Remark 1. If v is the deepest node in the trie with $\text{time}(v) = i$, then all nodes in the trie with time equal to i are found on the suffix path $\text{suf}^*(v)$. The S'-link $S'(i)$ is the first node on the suffix path which has a time different from i.

Remark 2. Notice that, if u with $\text{time}(u) = j$ is a node on the suffix path $\text{suf}^*(v)$, then not all nodes with time equal with j need to be on the suffix path $\text{suf}^*(v)$. In our example we have the suffix path (the subscripts show the time values): $\text{baa}_3, \text{aa}_3, \text{a}_2$, but the node ba_2 is not on the suffix path of baa. The shallowest (closest to root) node with time value j must be on $\text{suf}^*(v)$. This gives also that $u \in \text{suf}^*(v)$ implies $\text{time}(u) \in S'^*(\text{time}(v))$, but the converse need not be true. (Here $S'^*(i)$ is the S'-path of i, that is, $i, S'(i), S'^2(i), \ldots$.)

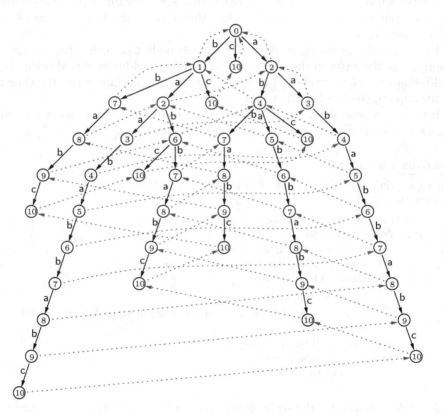

Fig. 1. The trie built by Ukkonen's algorithm for the string baababbabc

4   A Simple Algorithm for Factor Oracle

We recall in this section the sequential algorithm of Allauzen, Crochemore, and Raffinot (ACR, for short) for constructing factor oracles. However, we shall not assume we know that the obtained graph is the factor oracle. We shall show later that the same object can be obtained from the trie we described before and the most important properties we need about the factor oracle will follow from there.

ACR_FACTOR_ORACLE(w)

- given a string $w = w[1]w[2] \cdots w[n]$, $w[i] \in A$, $1 \leq i \leq n$;
- return factor_oracle(w);

1. $S(0) \leftarrow -1$
2.   **for** i from 1 **to** n **do**
3.   create $i - 1 \xrightarrow{w[i]} i$
4. $\ell \leftarrow S(i - 1)$
5.   **while** ($\ell \neq -1$) **and** (ℓ has no $w[i]$-son) **do**
6.   create $\ell \xrightarrow{w[i]} i$
7. $\ell \leftarrow S(\ell)$
8.   **if** $\ell = -1$ **then** $S(i) \leftarrow 0$
9.   **else** $S(i) \leftarrow$ the $w[i]$-son of ℓ

The factor oracle for the string baababbabc is shown in Fig. 2. Again, regular edges are solid arrows whereas the S-links are dotted. Notice the string baabc which is recognized but is not a factor. The S-links for the example are:

i	0	1	2	3	4	5	6	7	8	9	10
$S(i)$	-1	0	0	2	1	2	4	1	2	4	0

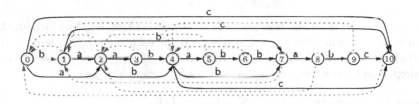

Fig. 2. factor_oracle(baababbabc)

5   Trie Oracle

We can obtain another oracle for fact(w) from the trie(w) in a natural way; we simply merge all nodes with the same time value to obtain trie(w)$|_{\text{time}}$. Obviously time gives an equivalence relation on the set of nodes. The nodes of trie(w)$|_{\text{time}}$ are the corresponding time values. The one for our string baababbabc is shown in Fig. 3. The edges are shown as continuous arrows and the S'-links are dotted. There are three differences with respect to the factor oracle – two edges and one S'-link; they are shown in bold.

We notice first that it is nondeterministic[3]; the node 2 has two b-sons. We make it deterministic in the following way: eliminate any edge $i \xrightarrow{a} j$ whenever we can find $i \xrightarrow{a} k$ with $k < j$. In our example the edge $2 \xrightarrow{b} 6$ is removed. Denote the obtained graph trie_oracle(w). The one for our example is shown in Fig. 4.

---

[3] It can be shown that the algorithm of [4] produces, in our notation, trie(w)$|_{\text{time}}$ whereas the (modified) version of [5] yields trie_oracle(w).

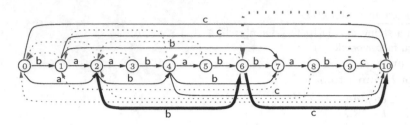

Fig. 3. trie(baababbbabc)$|_{\text{time}}$

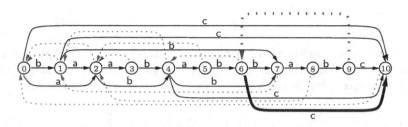

Fig. 4. trie_oracle(baababbbabc)

We prove below that the trie oracle is an oracle for fact(w). The trie oracle is deterministic, acyclic, has $|w| + 1$ states, and for each node all incoming edges are labelled the same. We prove next that it recognizes at least all factors of w. The next lemma concerns trie $|_{\text{time}}$ and is useful for our purpose.

Lemma 1. *In* trie(w)$|_{\text{time}}$, *if* $j \in S'^*(i)$, *then* $L(i) \subseteq L(j)$.

Proof. By induction on i from $|w|$ to 1. For $i = |w|$, we have $L(i) = \{\varepsilon\}$ and the property holds. Assume it true for $i+1, i+2, \ldots, |w|$ and prove it for i. For any edge $i \xrightarrow{a} i'$, there exists $v \xrightarrow{a} va$ in trie(w) with time(v) = i and time(va) = i'. We can also find a node $u \in$ suf$^*(v)$ such that time(u) = j and there exists an edge $u \xrightarrow{a} ua$; we can take for u the shallowest node with time value j. Now $ua \in$ suf$^*(va)$ and if we put $j' =$ time(ua), then $j' \in S'^*(i')$. By the inductive hypothesis, $L(i') \subseteq L(j')$. As this holds for every a-son of i, the claim follows. □

Corollary 1. *For any* w, trie_oracle(w) *recognizes at least all factors of* w.

Proof. It is clear that trie(w)$|_{\text{time}}$ recognizes at least all factors of w. But whenever an edge $j \xrightarrow{a} i$ is removed to create trie_oracle(w), there is another edge $j \xrightarrow{a} \ell$, with $\ell < i$. In such a case we have $\ell \in S'^*(i)$ and Lemma 1 says that eliminating the former edge does not affect the set of recognized strings. □

What is left to show is property (o_4) in the definition of an oracle.

Lemma 2. *For any* w, trie(w)$|_{\text{time}}$ *has at most* $2|w| - 1$ *edges.*

Proof. There are two types of edges in $\mathsf{trie}(w)|_{\mathsf{time}}$ and $\mathsf{trie}(w)$: (type 1) $i \xrightarrow{w[i]} i+1$ and (type 2) $i \longrightarrow j$, with $j \neq i+1$; for $\mathsf{trie}(w)$ we consider the time values of the ends of an edge. There are $|w|$ edges of type 1 in $\mathsf{trie}(w)|_{\mathsf{time}}$ so we need to count the other ones.

In $\mathsf{trie}(w)$, each internal node has exactly one outgoing edge of type 1. Therefore, the number of edges of type 1 is the same as the number of internal nodes. The total number of edges equals the number of nodes minus one (it is a tree). Therefore, the number of edges of type 2 is the number of leaves minus one. But the number of leaves is at most the number of non-empty suffixes of w, that is, $|w|$. So, there are at most $|w| - 1$ edges of type 2. The claim follows.   □

Corollary 2. *For any w, the set of strings recognized by $\mathsf{trie\_oracle}(w)$ is closed under taking factors.*

Proof. The sequence of S'-links starting from any node of $\mathsf{trie\_oracle}(w)$ ends in the initial node 0. Therefore, Lemma 1 implies that any string recognized starting from some i is also recognized starting from 0.   □

Proposition 1. *For any w, $\mathsf{trie\_oracle}(w)$ is an oracle for $\mathsf{fact}(w)$.*

Proof. It follows from the above results.   □

6   Factor Oracle from Trie Oracle

We shall see in this section how the factor oracle can be obtained from the trie oracle by removing certain edges. The differences between the two graphs in Figs. 2 and 4 are shown in bold in the latter. The factor oracle recognizes strictly less strings than the trie oracle in this case; for instance, baababc is recognized by the latter but not by the former.

Notice that we do not attempt to find a better algorithm for computing the factor oracle (the simplicity of the one in [1,2] we presented above seems almost impossible to beat) but to understand its tricky structure and properties. Here is the main result.

Theorem 1. *For any string w, we have*

(i) for any i there is $e_i \geq 1$ such that $S'^{e_i}(i) = S(i)$;

(ii) $\mathsf{factor\_oracle}(w)$ is obtained from $\mathsf{trie\_oracle}(w)$ by removing, for all i with $e_i \geq 2$, all edges $S'^k(i) \xrightarrow{w[i+1]} i+1$, $1 \leq k \leq e_i - 1$.

7   Factor Oracle from Trie

We describe two ways of obtaining the factor oracle directly from the trie, different from constructing the trie oracle and then performing the eliminations in Theorem 1(ii). Both constructions here are similar to the one above but they are independent of the factor oracle; in particular, they do not make reference to the S-links.

The first one uses the idea that the edges which the trie oracle has but the factor oracle does not appear from the fact that we may add an a-son to a node v even when there is already a node with the same time value as v which has an a-son. In our example, this happens when adding the edge $\mathsf{ba_2} \xrightarrow{b} \mathsf{bab_6}$ when there is already $\mathsf{a_2} \xrightarrow{b} \mathsf{ab_4}$ (subscripts show the time). Modifying Ukkonen's algorithm for tries so that such edges are not added would produce a graph whose quotient with respect to the time values produces precisely the factor oracle. For our example this new graph would look like the trie in Fig. 1 with the subtree rooted at bab removed. The new S'-links would be the same as the S-links in the factor oracle. However, the new suffix links would not be true suffix links but powers of those. Precisely, the new suffix link for a node u would link to the longest suffix of u that exists in the new graph. For instance, in our example, we would have the new (pseudo)suffix link of bbab pointing to $\mathsf{ab} = \mathrm{suf}^2(\mathsf{bbab})$ as the suffix bab is no longer in the new graph.

A better way to modify Ukkonen's algorithm is to add an a-son to a node v even if there exists another, say u, with the same time value and that has an a-son but the (new) time value of v will not be the index of the current letter in w but $\mathrm{time}(ua)$. This new version of the algorithm, say $\textsc{Ukkonen\_trie\_2}(w)$, would have line 8 replaced by the following pseudocode (for clarity, denote the new time values by $\mathsf{time\_2}$ and the new S'-links by S''):

8. $\mathsf{time\_2}(x) \leftarrow i$
8.1.   **if** $\mathrm{suf}^k(v) \neq \mathsf{nil}$ **then**
8.2. $t \leftarrow \mathsf{time\_2}(\mathrm{suf}^k(v)); \ t' \leftarrow \mathsf{time\_2}(\mathrm{suf}^k(v)w[i]); \ \ell \leftarrow k - 1$
8.3.   **while** $\mathsf{time\_2}(\mathrm{suf}^\ell(v)) = t$ **do**
8.4. $\mathsf{time\_2}(\mathrm{suf}^\ell(v)w[i]) \leftarrow t'; \ \ell \leftarrow \ell - 1$

Denote the graph constructed by this algorithm $\mathsf{trie\_2}(w)$ and let $\mathsf{trie\_oracle\_2}(w)$ be the quotient $\mathsf{trie\_2}(w)|_{\mathsf{time\_2}}$. From the construction it should be clear that a deterministic automaton is obtained.

Remarks 1 and 2 hold as well for $\mathsf{trie\_2}(w)$ with one exception. Not all nodes with a given $\mathsf{time\_2}$ are found on the suffix path from the deepest node with that $\mathsf{time\_2}$ value. The nodes with the same $\mathsf{time\_2}$ form a tree with the shallowest node as root. In our example, this happens for the nodes with $\mathsf{time\_2}$ value 4; the root is $\mathsf{ab_4}$.

The results in Lemma 1, Corollaries 1 and 2 and Proposition 1 hold also for $\mathsf{trie\_oracle\_2}(w)$. The proof of the next lemma is similar with the one of Lemma 1.

Lemma 3. *In* $\mathsf{trie\_oracle\_2}(w)$, *if* $j \in S''^*(i)$, *then* $L(i) \subseteq L(j)$.

The following results are now easy to prove.

Lemma 4. *For any w, we have:*
(i) $\mathsf{trie\_oracle\_2}(w)$ *recognizes at least all factors of w;*
(ii) the set of strings recognized by $\mathsf{trie\_oracle\_2}(w)$ *is closed under taking factors.*

Proposition 2. *For any w,* trie_oracle_2(w) *is an oracle for* fact(w).

For our string baababbabc, the differences between trie_2 and trie are: (i) time_2(bab) $= 4 \neq 6 =$ time(bab) and (ii) $S''(9) = 4 \neq 6 = S'(9)$. Therefore, the two graphs trie_oracle_2(baababbabc) and factor_oracle(baababbabc) are identical. The next theorem says that this is always the case.

Theorem 2. *For any string w, we have*

(i) for any i, $S''(i) = S(i)$;
(ii) factor_oracle(w) *and* trie_oracle_2(w) *are the same.*

8   Properties of the Factor Oracle

The properties of the factor oracle from [1,2] can be very easily deduced using Theorem 2. The first two are proved in Proposition 2 and Lemma 4.

1. factor_oracle(w) *is an oracle for the set of factors of w.*
2. *The set of strings recognized by* factor_oracle(w) *is closed under taking factors.*
   Denote, for u factor of w, poccur$(u, w) = \min\{|z| \mid z = xu, w = zy\}$.
3. *The shortest string recognized by* factor_oracle(w) *in i is a factor of w and is unique.* This is the string labelling the shallowest (closest to root) node with time_2 value i in trie_2(w). Denote it by min(i). The next property is also clear.
4. poccur$(\min(i), w) = i$.
5. min(i) *is a suffix of any string recognized by* factor_oracle(w) *in i.* The shallowest node with time_2 value i, corresponding to min(i), is on the suffix path of any node with time_2 i.
6. *Any factor u of w is recognized by* factor_oracle(w) *in $j \leq$* poccur(u, w). We have in trie_2(w), time_2$(u) \leq$ poccur(u, w).
7. *Any path in* factor_oracle(w) *whose label ends with* min(i) *leads to $j \geq i$.* Such a path in trie_2(w) leads to a node v such that the shallowest node of time_2 value i is on v's suffix path. It follows that $j =$ time_2$(v) \geq i$.
8. *Let v be a factor of w recognized by* factor_oracle(w) *in i. Then any suffix of v is recognized in $j \leq i$.* The suffix of v is in trie_2(w) on the suffix path of v and therefore has a lower, or equal, time_2 value.
9. factor_oracle(w) *has at most $2|w| - 1$ edges.* This follows from Lemma 2.
   Denote repet(w, i) the longest suffix of $w[1..i]$ that appears at least twice in $w[1..i]$.
10. *The reading of* repet(w, i) *in* factor_oracle(w) *ends in $S(i)$.* Starting from the deepest node of trie_2(w) with time_2 value i; it corresponds to the node $w[1..i]$. Moving up its suffix path, we encounter shorter suffixes until one which is already in trie_2(w) is found. That node has time_2 value $S(i)$ and its label is precisely repet(w, i).

9   Discussion and Open Problems

Our framework for discussing oracles for the set of factors of a string is provided by the following result.

Proposition 3. *Any oracle for the set of factors of a string* w *contains a quotient of* trie(w) *as a subgraph.*

Proof. Let O be an oracle and define a relation on the nodes of trie(w) by

$$u \equiv_O v \quad \text{iff} \quad \text{the paths labelled } u \text{ and } v \text{ in } O \text{ end in the same node .}$$

We claim that O must contain as a subgraph the quotient trie(w)$|_{\equiv_O}$.

First, it is clear that $\equiv_O$ is an equivalence relation with $|w| + 1$ classes. No two prefixes of w are in the same $\equiv_O$-class and denote the $\equiv_O$-class of the prefix of length i by i. Therefore, trie(w)$|_{\equiv_O}$ has the nodes $0, 1, \ldots, n$.

Consider an edge $i \xrightarrow{a} j$ of trie(w)$|_{\equiv_O}$. There must be then an edge $u \xrightarrow{a} ua$ in trie(w) such that $u \equiv_O w[1..i]$ and $ua \equiv_O w[1..j]$. Therefore, reading u in O from 0 leads to i whereas reading ua from 0 leads to j. As O is deterministic, there must be an edge $i \xrightarrow{a} j$ in O, proving the claim.   □

Remark 3. Notice that, in particular, for any oracle O, trie(w)$|_{\equiv_O}$ is deterministic. Also, all edges in O which are not in trie(w)$|_{\equiv_O}$ can be eliminated and it still remains an oracle.

Therefore, comparing oracles for the set of factors reduces to comparing quotients of the trie. Other natural oracles can be obtained from DAWGs, suffix automata, or factor automata; see [6]. It can be shown that the factor oracle is better than all of those.

There exist particular examples, such as the string abcacdace[4] from [4], for which the factor oracle is not the smallest possible oracle but finding a general (simple) strategy for building better oracles remains to be investigated. A discussion of this example using our trie quotients is omitted due to lack of space.

Finally, we recall briefly the most important open problems about the factor oracle; they apply to all oracles for the set of factors of a string:

1. Are factor oracle based string matching algorithms optimal on average, as conjectured by [1,2]?
2. Which is the number of errors (maximal and average), that is, non-factors that are recognized by the factor oracle? Examples are given in [14,15] where this is exponential but they are over an infinite alphabet. One can find examples over binary alphabet where it is still superpolynomial.
3. What is the average number of external transitions for the factor oracle or, put otherwise, what is its average size?

---

[4] The factor oracle for this example recognizes fewer non-factors than the smaller oracle of [4] but one can find examples for which smaller oracles which also "lie" less can be constructed.

4. Is there a simple strategy for building even better oracles, within our framework of quotients of the trie?
5. Characterize the set recognized by the factor oracle; not in terms of the factor oracle itself, like in [14,15].

References

1. C. Allauzen, M. Crochemore, and M. Raffinot, Factor oracle: a new structure for pattern matching, *SOFSEM'99: theory and practice of informatics (Milovy)*, Lecture Notes in Comput. Sci. **1725**, Springer, Berlin, 1999, 295 – 310.
2. C. Allauzen, M. Crochemore, and M. Raffinot, Efficient experimental string matching by weak factor recognition, *Combinatorial pattern matching (Jerusalem, 2001)*, Lecture Notes in Comput. Sci. **2089**, Springer, Berlin, 2001, 51 – 72.
3. G. Assayag and S. Dubnov, Using factor oracles for machine improvisation, *Soft Comput.* **8**(9) (2004) 604 – 610.
4. L. Cleophas, G. Zwaan, and B. Watson, Constructing factor oracles, *Proceedings of the Prague Stringology Conference 2003*, 37 – 50.
5. L. Cleophas, G. Zwaan, and B. Watson, Constructing factor oracles, *J. Autom. Lang. Comb.*, to appear.
6. M. Crochemore and W. Rytter, *Jewels of stringology*, World Scientific Publishing Co., Inc., River Edge, NJ, 2003.
7. R. Kato and O. Watanabe, Substring search and repeat search using factor oracles, *Inf. Process. Lett.* **93**(6) (2005) 269 – 274.
8. A. Lefebvre and T. Lecroq, Computing repeated factors with a factor oracle, *Proceedings of the 11th Australasian Workshop on Combinatorial Algorithms*, 2000, 145 – 158.
9. A. Lefebvre and T. Lecroq, Compror: compression with a factor oracle, *Data Compression Conference 2001*, 502.
10. A. Lefebvre and T. Lecroq, Compror: On-line lossless data compression with a factor oracle, *Inf. Process. Lett.* **83**(1) (2002) 1 – 6.
11. A. Lefebvre and T. Lecroq, A heuristic for computing repeats with a factor oracle: application to biological sequences, *Int. J. Comput. Math.* **79**(12) (2002) 1303 – 1315.
12. A. Lefebvre and T. Lecroq, Drastic improvements over repeats found with a factor oracle, *Proceedings of the 13th Australasian Workshop on Combinatorial Algorithms*, 2002, 253 – 265.
13. A. Lefebvre, T. Lecroq, and J. Alexandre, An improved algorithm for finding longest repeats with a modified factor oracle, *J. Autom. Lang. Comb.* **8**(4) (2003) 647 – 657.
14. A. Mancheron and C. Moan, Combinatorial characterization of the language recognized by factor and suffix oracles, *Proceedings of the Prague Stringology Conference 2004*, 139 – 154.
15. A. Mancheron and C. Moan, Combinatorial characterization of the language recognized by factor and suffix oracles, *Int. J. Found. Comput. Sci.* **16**(6) (2005) 1179 – 1191.
16. E. Ukkonen, Constructing suffix trees on-line in linear time, *Proc. Information Processing'92, Vol. 1, IFIP Transactions A-12*, Elsevier, 1992, 484 – 492.

Reducing Simple Grammars: Exponential Against Highly-Polynomial Time in Practice

Cédric Bastien[1], Jurek Czyzowicz[1], Wojciech Fraczak[1,2],
and Wojciech Rytter[3,*]

[1] Dépt d'informatique, Université du Québec en Outaouais, Gatineau PQ, Canada
[2] IDT Canada Inc., Ottawa ON, Canada
[3] Inst. of Informatics, Warsaw University, Warsaw, Poland

Abstract. The simple grammar reduction is an important component in the implementation of Concatenation State Machines (a hardware version of stateless pushdown automata designed for wire-speed network packet classification). We present a comparison and experimental analysis of the best-known algorithms for the grammar reduction. There are two approaches to this problem: one processing compressed strings without decompression and another one which processes strings explicitly. It turns out that the second approach is more efficient in the considered practical scenario despite having worst-case exponential time complexity (while the first one is polynomial). The study has been conducted in the context of network packet classification, where simple grammars are used for representing the classification policies.

1 Introduction

The simple grammar equivalence problem is a generalization of equality testing of two grammar-compressed strings. In the case of a simple grammar we have grammar-compressed sets of strings (languages). The theoretical background of the algorithms involved is an interesting mixture of string matching, text compression, algebraic theory of processes, and formal language theory.

The simple grammar equivalence problem is a classical question in formal language theory. It is a nontrivial problem, since the inclusion problem for simple languages is undecidable. A. Korenjak and J. Hopcroft, see [7,5], proved that the equivalence problem is decidable and they gave the first, doubly exponential time algorithm solving it. Their result was improved by D. Caucal to polynomial time in n and $v(G)$, see [3]. The parameter n is the size of the simple grammar and $v(G)$ is the length of a shortest string derived from a nonterminal, maximized over all nonterminals. Caucal's algorithm is exponential since $v(G)$ can be exponential with respect to n. Y. Hirshfeld, M. Jerrum, and F. Moller gave the first polynomial $O(n^{13})$ time algorithm for this problem in [6]. A recent paper [1] presented a variation of Caucal's algorithm using a technique developed in

* The research of the first three authors was supported by NSERC and the research of the fourth author was supported by the grants KBN 4T11C04425.

O.H. Ibarra and H.-C. Yen (Eds.): CIAA 2006, LNCS 4094, pp. 90–101, 2006.
© Springer-Verlag Berlin Heidelberg 2006

the context of pattern matching on compressed strings [8,9], improving the time complexity of the algorithm to $O(n^7 \log^2 n)$ and $O(n^5 \text{ polylog } v(G)))$. Interestingly, this seemingly theoretical problem, for which a polynomial-time algorithm was unknown for many years, turns out to have an important application in the domain of network packet processing. Moreover, in spite of their high worst-case complexities, the structure of these algorithms makes them potentially applicable in practical situations.

In this paper, we describe our experimental study comparing the performance of three implementations of simple grammar reduction in the context of the wire-speed network packet classification problem. These three implementations are variations of a general simple grammar reduction method but differ by using three different algorithms for deciding on simple grammar equivalence.

In the IDT solution for the wire-speed network packet classification problem, classes of network packets are represented using simple grammars, and their recognition is made by a so-called Concatenation State Machine [4], a hardware implementation of a stateless pushdown automaton. In order to store large sets of classification policies in memory, it is essential to reuse their common parts. A natural way to do this consists in decomposing simple languages into primes (languages not representable as concatenation of two simple languages), each of which is stored in memory only once. When a new classification policy is added to memory, we verify if its prime factors are already stored in the data base. Representation of finite automata by Concatenation State Machines can be seen as a compression technique. Indeed, the size of a finite state automaton is sometimes exponentially larger than the size of an equivalent Concatenation State Machine. However, certain problems which are easy for finite state machines, like language equivalence (by automata minimization) are much more complex for Concatenation State Machines, as witnessed by this paper. Despite the fact that a Concatenation State Machine is a compact representation of an automaton, in practical cases the sizes of Concatenation State Machines are still large (several tens of thousands of nodes). Hence, the complexities of the algorithms involved are of fundamental importance. Our experiments showed that despite a very large worst-case complexities of the considered algorithms, in practice some of them performed well.

2   Simple Grammar Equivalence Algorithms

A context-free grammar $G = (\Sigma, N, P)$ is composed of a finite set Σ of *terminals*, a finite set N of *nonterminals* disjoint from Σ, and a finite set $P \subset N \times (N \cup \Sigma)^*$ of *production rules*. For every $\beta, \gamma \in (N \cup \Sigma)^*$, if $(A, \alpha) \in P$, then $\beta A \gamma \to \beta \alpha \gamma$. A *derivation* $\beta \xrightarrow{*} \gamma$ is a finite sequence $(\alpha_0, \alpha_1, \ldots, \alpha_n)$ such that $\beta = \alpha_0$, $\gamma = \alpha_n$, and $\alpha_{i-1} \to \alpha_i$ for $i \in [1, n]$. For every sequence of nonterminals $\alpha \in N^*$ of a grammar $G = (\Sigma, N, P)$, the *language* derivable from α, denoted $L_G(\alpha)$, is the set of terminal strings derivable from α, i.e., $L_G(\alpha) \overset{\text{def}}{=} \{w \in \Sigma^* \mid \alpha \xrightarrow{*} w\}$. Often, if G is known from the context, we will write $L(\alpha)$ instead of $L_G(\alpha)$.

A grammar $G = (\Sigma, N, P)$ is in *Greibach Normal Form* if for every production rule $(A \rightarrow \alpha) \in P$, we have $\alpha \in \Sigma N^*$. A grammar $G = (\Sigma, N, P)$ is a *simple grammar* if G is a Greibach Normal Form grammar such that whenever $A \rightarrow a\,\alpha_1$ and $A \rightarrow a\,\alpha_2$, for a same $a \in \Sigma$, then $\alpha_1 = \alpha_2$. A language is a *simple language* if it can be derived from a simple grammar.

Let $G = (\Sigma, N, P)$ be a simple grammar and $\alpha, \beta \in N^*$ two strings of non-terminals. The equivalence problem consists in deciding whether $L(\alpha) = L(\beta)$ (also denoted by $\alpha \equiv \beta$). A function $H : N \rightarrow N^+$ is called a *decomposing morphism* if we can order the elements of N in such a way that for each $A \in N$, $H(A) = A$ or $A > B$ for each symbol B occurring in the string $H(A)$. We can extend this definition to the domain N^* by defining $H(A\alpha) = H(A) \cdot H(\alpha)$, with $\alpha \in N^*$. We denote $H^{|N|}$ by H^* since $H^{|N|+1} = H^{|N|}$. If H is a decomposing morphism, by $H_{[A \mapsto \alpha]}$ we denote a new mapping $N \rightarrow N^+$ which is identical on all nonterminals but A, and $H_{[A \mapsto \alpha]}(A) \overset{\text{def}}{=} \alpha$.

Let $G = (\Sigma, N, P)$ be a simple grammar. A decomposing morphism H is said to be self-proving in G if for each $A \in N$ we have:

- If $A \rightarrow a\alpha$, then $H(A) \rightarrow a\beta$ and $H^*(\alpha) = H^*(\beta)$, and
- If $H(A) \rightarrow a\beta$, then $A \rightarrow a\alpha$ and $H^*(\alpha) = H^*(\beta)$.

It has been proved (e.g., in [1]) that if H is an acyclic decomposing morphism self-proving in G, then for every $\alpha \in N^+$ we have $\alpha \equiv H(\alpha)$.

Therefore, if two strings α and $\beta \in N^*$ have the same decomposition, i.e. $H^*(\alpha) = H^*(\beta)$, and H is self-proving, then $\alpha \equiv \beta$. In order to prove that $\alpha \equiv \beta$ it is sufficient to find a self-proving decomposing morphism H, such that $H^*(\alpha) = H^*(\beta)$.

The quotient of A by B, denoted $\mathsf{quot}(A, B)$, is a word $\gamma \in N^*$, such that, if it exists, $L(A) = L(B)L(\gamma)$. As shown in [6], using the notion of $||A||$, the *norm* of A, i.e., the length of a shortest word of $L(A)$, it follows that there exists such a γ of length in $O(n^2)$, and it can be computed in time $O(n^2)$. The technique of calculating $\mathsf{quot}(A, B)$, was not originally considered in [3].

First Mismatch-Pair problem (First-MP) is defined as follows:

Input: decomposing morphism $H : N \mapsto N^+$ and strings $\alpha, \beta \in N^+$;
Output:
- *First-MP*$(\alpha, \beta, H) = nil$, if $H^*(\alpha) = H^*(\beta)$;
- *First-MP*$(\alpha, \beta, H) = failure$, if one of $H^*(\alpha)$, $H^*(\beta)$ is a proper prefix of the other;
- *First-MP*$(\alpha, \beta, H) = (A, B) \in N \times N$, where (A, B) is the *first mismatch pair*, i.e., the first symbols occurring at the same position in $H^*(\alpha)$ and in $H^*(\beta)$ which are different.

In the context of the simple grammar equivalence problem, the First-MP problem is important in the application of a process called *DecompositionProcess*.

Input: decomposing morphism $H : N \mapsto N^+$ and strings $\alpha, \beta \in N^+$;
Output:
- If $First\text{-}MP(\alpha, \beta, H) = nil$, then $DecompositionProcess(\alpha, \beta, H) = success$;
- If $First\text{-}MP(\alpha, \beta, H) = failure$, then $DecompositionProcess(\alpha, \beta, H) = failure$;
- If $First\text{-}MP(\alpha, \beta, H) = (A, B)$, then, assuming $||A|| >= ||B||$, the answer is given by a recursive call to $DecompositionProcess(\alpha, \beta, H_{[A \mapsto B \cdot \text{quot}(A,B)]})$.

Essentially, this process tries to make $H^*(\alpha)$ and $H^*(\beta)$ equal by updating H with a new decomposition whenever a mismatching pair (A, B) is found. The new decomposition is chosen by supposing that $L(B)$ is a left divider of $L(A)$, i.e. by setting $H_{[A \mapsto B \cdot \text{quot}(A,B)]}$, which eliminates the mismatch. This operation is done repeatedly until $First\text{-}MP$ returns $success$ or $failure$, which is bound to occur within n steps, where n is the size of N. The decomposition process is constructing a self-proving decomposing morphism, as implied by its definition, which would prove the equivalence of the two input strings.

3   Comparison of the Algorithms

We consider three simple grammar equivalence algorithms, which were presented in [3], [6], and [1]. Even though they all use a similar basic idea derived from [7], the manner in which this idea is applied differs significantly in two specific ways.

3.1   Two Basic Strategies in the Algorithms

The first difference resides in the way the self-proving decomposing morphism is created.

Incremental Algorithms: Both algorithms from [3] and [1] build the decomposing morphism as needed from the input pair of strings. Let S be a set of pairs of nonterminal strings. Initially, S contains only the input pair (α_1, β_1) and H is initialized to $H(A) = A$, for each $A \in N$. The decomposition process is applied to each pair contained in S. During this process, each time a nonterminal A is assigned a new decomposition in H, the algorithm verifies whether A and $H(A)$ have transitions over the same terminal symbols. If this is not the case, we have failed in building a self-proving decomposing morphism such that $H^*(\alpha_1) = H^*(\beta_1)$ and we conclude that the input strings are not equivalent. Otherwise, for each terminal symbol a for which $A \to a\alpha$ and $H(A) \to a\beta$, the pair (α, β) is added to the set S. When all elements in S have been processed, we conclude that H is self-proving and, since it has been applied successfully to the input pair of strings, that $\alpha_1 \equiv \beta_1$.

This method of constructing the self-proving decomposing morphism requires only $O(n)$ calls to First-MP, which is the only complex operation involved. However, this method does not directly perform grammar reduction, it only determines the equivalence between two nonterminals. In order to obtain a reduced grammar, we call the equivalence algorithm repeatedly over all pairs of nonterminals, increasing the overall complexity by a factor of $O(n^2)$.

Decremental Algorithm: The algorithm from [6] uses a different method to create the self-proving decomposing morphism. At first all possible decompositions are considered. That is, for every pair $(A, B) \in N \times N$ such that $||A|| >= ||B||$, we compute the pair $(A, B \cdot \texttt{quot}(A, B))$. All these potential decompositions are stored in a set S. The objective now is to transform S by removing invalid decompositions, until we have a maximal set of valid decompositions which permits the construction of any self-proving decomposing morphism. In order to do so, we consider every pair $(A, B \cdot \texttt{quot}(A, B)) \in S$ and we verify whether it respects the conditions of the definition of a self-proving decomposition. This is done as before by verifying that A and $B \cdot \texttt{quot}(A, B)$ have transitions for the same terminal symbols. If this is not the case, the pair is removed from S and we continue with the remaining elements in S. Otherwise, for each terminal symbol a for which $A \to a\alpha$ and $B\texttt{quot}(A, B) \to a\beta$, we apply the decomposition process to (α, β), each time with H initialized to $H(A) = A$, for every $A \in N$. Whenever a new decomposition needs to be set, that is whenever a mismatching pair (A', B') is found, we look for its corresponding decomposition $(A', B' \cdot \texttt{quot}(A', B'))$ in S. If a decomposition is found, we set $H_{[A' \to B' \cdot \texttt{quot}(A', B')]}$ and the decomposition process continues. Otherwise, we conclude that the pair $(A, B \cdot \texttt{quot}(A, B))$ cannot be part of a self-proving decomposing morphism and it is removed from S. If any pair is removed from S, we start a new iteration to test all the remaining pairs of S again. If no element can be removed from S then the process stops. At this point, for every pair $(A, \beta) \in S$ we have $A \equiv \beta$, and for every pair $(A, B) \in N^2$ such that $A \equiv B \cdot L$, for some language L, we have $(A, B \cdot \alpha) \in S$ and $L = L(\alpha)$. In order to check the equivalence of the input pair (α_1, β_1) we try to find a decomposing morphism H such that $H \subseteq S$ and $H^*(\alpha_1) = H^*(\beta_1)$. If we succeed in doing this, then $\alpha_1 \equiv \beta_1$.

3.2   Two Categories: Compressed or Uncompressed Representations

The second difference between the three algorithms resides in the way the First-MP operation is executed. The algorithm from [3] performs this operation directly on uncompressed strings, explicitly decomposing the strings and comparing them symbol by symbol. Since a decomposed string can have an exponential length with respect to the number of nonterminals, the algorithm has exponential complexity. However, if the lengths of decomposed strings are relatively small, which seems to be the case for all "real-life" examples we have considered, this approach may be acceptable in practice.

On the other side, the algorithms from [1] and [6] process the First-MP operation in polynomial time without a complete decompression of the strings by using a dynamic programming approach. This technique requires that we deal with morphism H in binary form, i.e., such that $H(A) = \alpha$ implies $|\alpha| \in \{1, 2\}$ for all $A \in N$. We can transform any morphism H into a binary one by introducing at most $O(n)$ new nonterminals per original nonterminal, thus increasing the number of nonterminals to $k = O(n^2)$, where n is the original number of nonterminals in the grammar. Let N' denote the new set of nonterminals. Then, the main task required by this approach is to compute a table $\mathcal{P}$ containing, for all $A, B, C \in N'$, the starting positions of a specific subset of the occurences of $H^*(A)$ in $H^*(B)H^*(C)$. The actual positions we need to find are those for which $H^*(A)$ is overlapping the first symbol of $H^*(C)$. Since, for each A, B, C, this set of positions forms an arithmetic progression, its representation takes constant memory space, thus the entire table $\mathcal{P}$ requires $O(k^3)$ (i.e., $O(n^6)$) memory space, which is the space complexity of algorithm from [6]. This space complexity can be improved to $O(k^2)$ as described in [8], leading to $O(n^4)$ space complexity of algorithm from [1]. For more details about calculating First-MP, see the appendix.

4   Implementation

We wrote three programs, SGR-1, SGR-2, and SGR-3, for simple grammar reduction which implement the algorithms from [3], [6], and [1], respectively, for checking on simple grammar equivalence.

The First Mismatch Problem was solved using techniques from the fully compressed string matching, [8]. Besides the First-MP problem, the three programs are relatively simple to implement. The extent to which the implementation can be improved depends on the structure and the internal mechanisms of the algorithm. Below we list the improvements made in comparison with a straightforward implementation.

Lazy Evaluation: Programs SGR-2 and SGR-3 compute the First-MP using dynamic programming. However, in case of SGR-3, we do not need to consult the set of all entries of the table at each call, but often only a small subset of it. Therefore, we implemented the dynamic programming section of the algorithm using "lazy evaluation", that is we compute any required value of the table only once, the first time it is needed, and store the result in the table for future references. Unnecessary values are never computed.

Reduced Number of Calls: When performing grammar reduction with SGR-1 or SGR-3, we can reduce the number of calls to function equivalence(A, B), which checks for equivalence of two nonterminals A and B, by sorting the nonterminals according to the length of the shortest word they generate. This permits to ignore all pairs for which the length of a shortest word derivable from each nonterminal differs.

Reduced Redundant Calculation of the Decomposing Morphism: In SGR-1 and SGR-3, whenever two nonterminals are found equivalent, the self-proving decomposing morphism H which was built during the verification of the equivalence, will be reused for subsequent calculations.

Reduced Redundant Calculation of Table $\mathcal{P}$: In SGR-3 the construction of the dynamic programming table $\mathcal{P}$ (see Section 3.2) depends only on the nonterminals of the grammar and the decomposing morphism used to decompose the symbols. Even though the algorithm introduces new temporary nonterminals before each regeneration of the table (which are needed to *compress* the compared strings of nonterminals before starting the computation of the first mismatch), the original nonterminals used in the morphism are always the same, and they do not depend on the temporary ones. Therefore, if two consecutive regenerations of table $\mathcal{P}$ use the same decomposing morphism, we can reuse the part of the table which is related to the original nonterminals. Whenever a call to `equivalence()` returns *false*, any changes to the table and the decomposing morphism made during that call should be rolled back, if we want to avoid the recalculation of them from scratch. We achieve this by *saving* table $\mathcal{P}$ and the decomposing morphism before each call to `equivalence()`.

5   Experimental Results

In this section we describe a performance comparison of the three programs SGR-1, SGR-2, and SGR-3. The benchmark of the test-cases on which the experiments were performed came from a real-life example of simple grammars used at IDT Canada for representing different policies of network packet filtering and classification. We have considered three different classes of simple grammars coming from three different applications. Namely:

(Class A) Every test-case from this class defines a valid HTTP packet over TCP with constraints correlating specific IP source and destination addresses, and HTTP headers defined by simple regular expressions.

(Class B) Test-cases from this class describe different policies for Sun content load balancing blades. Such a blade offers Layer 4 through Layer 7 load balancing. The parsing is based on IP protocol and TCP/UDP ports (Layer 4) or URLs, cookies, and CGI scripts (Layer 7).

(Class C) This class contains a set of policies demonstrating the capability of PAX.port (a programmable wire-speed packet classification co-processor) working as a firewall (Layer 3).

All test cases use a binary alphabet. Some other characteristics of the grammars in each class are as follows:

	Class A			Class B			Class C		
	Min	Avg	Max	Min	Avg	Max	Min	Avg	Max
Nb. of nonterminals	2878	11784	29520	1852	2568	3478	1122	4555	5765
Nb. of production rules	4972	19025	49735	2418	3415	4944	1707	5254	6789
Avg shortest word length	180	216	317	62	218	280	201	281	307
Max shortest word length	374	622	1064	624	773	824	680	680	680

We compare the performances of the programs by calling each of them over several examples of the three classes of input grammars and measure the time taken by each one to compute a reduced simple grammar, i.e., a simple grammar equivalent to the input grammar such that no two nonterminals are equivalent.

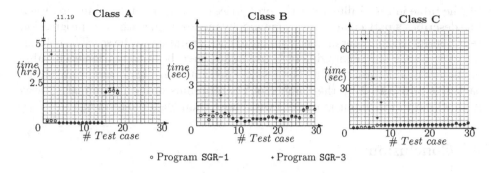

Fig. 1. Experimental results for grammar reduction. Each column represents a different test case, sorted from left to right by number of nonterminals.

Min	Step	Max	Times
10	10	90	10
100	50	950	10
1000	250	2000	3
2500	– – –	2500	1

Fig. 2. Execution time for SGR-2 on randomly generated simple grammars

The results, presented in Fig. 1, are compiled separately for each of the three classes of test-cases and sorted by number of nonterminals, each column representing one particular test-case.

Program SGR-1 performs well for all the test-cases. There is a very little variation in the time taken by this algorithm to perform the reduction of different grammars of similar sizes, making it a good practical solution to the problem of simple grammar reduction. Program SGR-1 gives the best results for most (but not all) test cases, although both programs, SGR-1 and SGR-3, have been able to handle all of them.

Program SGR-3 theoretically requires $O(n^4)$ memory space. However, the various improvements applied to the implementation of this algorithm, mainly the use of "lazy memory allocation", reduced the amount of memory needed to execute the algorithm over these test-cases.

Program SGR-2 is ineffective, since it could not compute a result within the allocated time frame, even for the smallest test-cases. In order to estimate the behavior of algorithm SGR-2, we generated several simple grammars, varying the number of nonterminals from 10 to 2500. It is important to remember that those simple grammars were randomly generated.

The table in Fig. 2 illustrates the properties of the generated grammars. Each line describes a particular set of grammars, by means of an arithmetic progression representing the number of nonterminals of each grammar in the set. The column *times* specifies how many different grammars have been tested for each value of the arithmetic progression. The results, presented in Fig. 2, are averaged for each size and sorted by the number of nonterminals of each grammar. It was impractical to test input grammars with more than 2500 nonterminals.

6   Conclusion

With a careful implementation, the algorithms for simple grammar equivalence checking from [1] and [3] can both be used to efficiently perform simple grammar reduction, even for large test-cases and in spite of their high worst-case complexities. The algorithm from [3] in particular has proved to be fast and to have stable performances when applied to different grammars of similar sizes. The good performance of the algorithm from [3] is due to the fact that in all analysed test-cases the length of the shortest word derivable from a nonterminal was never of exponential size with respect to the size of the grammar. Note, that it is easy to construct a simple grammar of size $O(n)$ generating a single word of length 2^n, for which the algorithm from [3] is impractical, while the algorithm from [1] runs instantaneously. Since such grammars do not occur in our test-cases, the exponential solution most often yields the best results. Therefore it is to be wondered whether the additional work needed to implement the polynomial solution to the problem of simple grammar reduction is really worth it, since a much simpler to implement solution based on [3] yields better performance in practice. Note that some part of good performance of algorithms from [1] and [3] is due to the applied practical improvements. From this perspective the algorithm from [6] was relatively harder to implement.

The algorithm from [6], has proven to be inefficient to solve the problem of simple grammar reduction. Even in the case of grammars of size of few hundreds of production rules this algorithm could not produce the result within the allocated timeframe. This is mainly due to the fact that, in average case, this algorithm performance is relatively close to its theoretical worst-case complexity. However, this algorithm was designed to answer a more general problem than simple grammar reduction, and as such, this result was to be expected. The purpose of [6] was to show that some language theoretical problem has a polynomial-time solution and the authors didnt't address the question of its optimality. In fact, the context-free processes considered in this algorithm correspond to Greibach Form grammars which are not necessarily deterministic.

It follows from our experiments that the worst-case exponential time algorithm performs in practice like a low-polynomial time algorithm, at the same time there is a point (which could be called the point of high sophistication of the input) from which the worst-case high-polynomial algorithm substantially beats the exponential algorithm. However in practical situations the input for our problem does not reach such a high point of sophistication. The practical situations which we considered appear genuinely in the network packet processing applications, and are of great importance in the context of the IDT solution. This analysis made us believe that the two approaches based on algorithms from [3] and [1], may represent a valid practical solution to the problem of simple grammar reduction.

The future work is to implement a *hybrid* algorithm which would combine two categories of algorithms. We can precompute in $O(n \log n)$ time the lengths of the shortest words derivable from all grammar nonterminals. Then, depending on the maximal shortest word v, for example when $v = O(n^2)$, we can run the direct algorithm with explicit decompression of involved strings, otherwise the algorithm using sophisticated compressed matching techniques is called. The practical efficiency of the *hybrid* algorithm would depend on the careful selection of the choice criteria. This requires further work.

Acknowledgments. We would like to thank Feliks Welfeld, Senior Architect at IDT Canada Inc., for providing us with the real-life test examples which made this experimental research possible.

References

1. Cédric Bastien, Jurek Czyzowicz, Wojciech Fraczak, and Wojciech Rytter. Prime normal form and equivalence of simple grammars. In I. Litovsky J. Farré and S. Schmitz, editors, *CIAA 2005*, volume 3845 of *LNCS*, pages 78–89. Springer, 2006.
2. Cédric Bastien, Jurek Czyzowicz, Wojciech Fraczak, and Wojciech Rytter. Equivalence of Functions Represented by Simple Context-Free Grammars with Output. In Developments in Language Theory, DLT 2006, volume 4036 of LNCS, pages 71–82. Springer, 2006.
3. Didier Caucal. A fast algorithm to decide on simple grammars equivalence. In *Optimal Algorithms*, volume 401 of *LNCS*, pages 66–85. Springer, 1989.
4. Wojciech Debski and Wojciech Fraczak. Concatenation state machines and simple functions. In *Implementation and Application of Automata, CIAA 2004*, volume 3317 of *LNCS*, pages 113–124. Springer, 2004.
5. M.A. Harrison. *Introduction to formal language theory*. Addison Wesley, 1978.
6. Yoram Hirshfeld, Mark Jerrum, and Faron Moller. A polynomial algorithm for deciding bisimilarity of normed context-free processes. *Theoretical Computer Science*, 158(1–2):143–159, 1996.
7. A. J. Korenjak and J. E. Hopcroft. Simple deterministic languages. In *Proc. IEEE 7th Annual Symposium on Switching and Automata Theory*, IEEE Symposium on Foundations of Computer Science, pages 36–46, 1966.
8. Masamichi Miyazaki, Ayumi Shinohara, and Masayuki Takeda. An improved pattern matching for strings in terms of straight-line programs. *Journal of Discrete Algorithms*, 1(1):187–204, 2000.
9. Wojciech Rytter. Grammar Compression, LZ-Encodings, and String Algorithms with Implicit Input. In *ICALP 2004*, volume 3142 of *LNCS*, pages 15–27. Springer, 2004.

Appendix: Solving the First-Mismatch Problem

The First Mismatch Problem can be solved using techniques from the fully compressed string matching, where compression is in terms of *grammar compression*, as proposed in [8]. Hence, for technical reasons, we change terminology of morphisms to grammar compression. Each morphism can be treated as a context-free grammar generating a single word $H^*(\alpha)$. The symbols X such that $H^*(X) = X$ are terminal symbols of the grammar and other symbols are its nonterminals. The fact that $H(A) = BC$ can be treated as a production (in a context-free grammar) $A \rightarrow BC$. Therefore we assume that we have a context-free grammar G in Chomsky normal form which generates exactly one terminal word. The size n of the grammar is the number of nonterminals.

As mentioned is Section 3.2, in order to convert our grammar to a binary (Chomsky) form we may increase the number of its non-terminals to $k = O(n^2)$. Since the best algorithm for fully compressed matching with k nonterminals works in $O(k^4)$ time, First-Mismatch would work in $O(n^8)$ time. To reduce it to $O(n^6)$we introduce another parameter of grammars — the height.

The height of the morphism H, denoted by $height(H)$ is $\min\{k \geq 0 \mid H^k = H^{k+1}\}$. The height of a context-free grammar G generating a single word, denoted by $height(G)$, is the length of the longest path in the derivation tree.

Lemma 1. *Assume H is an acyclic morphism over N, where $n = |N|$ such that $|H(A)| \leq n$ for each A. Then we can construct a binary H_b such that $H_b^* = H^*$, over the set of at most n^2 nonterminals and with height $O(n \log n)$.*

Denote by $val(A)$ the terminal string derived from A. When it creates no ambiguity we identify the names of variables with their values. In terms of the morphism $val(A) = H^*(A)$. Denote by $First\text{-}GMP(A, B)$ the first position in $val(A)$ which contains a symbol different than the corresponding symbol in $val(B)$. The basic data structure needed to compute $First\text{-}GMP$ is the table of *overlapping occurrences*, where by an occurrence of a string we mean its starting position. Assume we have a rule $X \rightarrow BC$. The *splitting point* of X is the position between B and C in X. We define the overlap-occurrences table $\mathcal{P}$, where for each two variables X, Y, $\mathcal{P}(Y, X)$ is the set of occurrences of Y in X overlapping the splitting point of X.

The following key property of the sets $\mathcal{P}(Y, X)$ follows from the so called *periodicity-lemma*.

Property A: Each set $\mathcal{P}(Y, X)$ is a single arithmetic progression.

Hence the set $\mathcal{P}(Y, X)$ can be of exponential size but it has a small representation (starting point, period, continuation) and membership query in this set can be answered in constant time. There is another important property of table $\mathcal{P}$. Let $Y = BC$, denote by $\mathcal{P}_{left}(Y, X)$ the set of overlap occurrences of Y in X in which B overlaps the splitting point of X and by $\mathcal{P}_{right}(Y, X)$ the set of overlap occurrences of Y in X in which C overlaps the splitting point of X. Note that the constant-size representation of $\mathcal{P}(Y, X)$ can be easily constructed from representations of $\mathcal{P}(B,X)$ and $\mathcal{P}(C,X)$. We have the following nontrivial facts which are the basis for efficient computation of table $\mathcal{P}$:

Property B:
1. $\mathcal{P}(Y,X) = \mathcal{P}_{left}(Y,X) \cup \mathcal{P}_{right}(Y,X)$;
2. $\mathcal{P}_{left}(Y,X)$ is a prefix segment of the arithmetic progression $\mathcal{P}(B,X)$ or $|\mathcal{P}_{left}(Y,X)| \leq 1$;
3. $\mathcal{P}_{right}(Y,X)$ is a suffix segment of the arithmetic progression $\mathcal{P}(C,X)$ or $|\mathcal{P}_{right}(Y,X)| \leq 1$.

For nonterminals $A \neq B$ we write $B \prec A$ iff B is in a derivation tree starting with A, in other words to compute $val(A)$ first $val(B)$ should be computed. The relation $\prec$ corresponds to an acyclic graph. Assume that the variables are topologically sorted $X_1, X_2, \ldots X_n$, this means that $X_i \prec X_j \Rightarrow i < j$.

Lemma 2. *Assume that the table $\mathcal{P}(X_k, X_r)$ is computed for all $k < j, r \leq i$, then*

Equality-Testing: *For any $k < j$ we can check if there is a full occurrence of X_k in X_i starting at a given position t in time $O(height(G))$.*

First-Mismatch Computation: *We can check where is the first mismatch in a full occurrence of X_j in X_i starting at a given position in time $O(height^2(G))$.*

Proof. We start with the proof of the first point. In the derivation tree for X_i we go down to the deepest node X_r containing the interval corresponding to potential occurrence of X_k starting at t. Then this potential occurrence overlaps the splitting point of X_r, we simply check if $t \in \mathcal{P}(X_k, X_r)$. This takes constant time since $\mathcal{P}(X_k, X_r)$ is an arithmetic progression. The traversal down to the node X_r takes $O(height(G))$ time. The second point follows from the first one. We need only $O(height(G))$ calls to the equality testing.

The structure of the algorithm for computing table $\mathcal{P}$ is as follows:

> **for** $i = 1$ **to** n **do**
> **for** $i = j$ **to** n **do**
>   compute $\mathcal{P}(X_j, X_i)$ in time $O(height^2(G))$, using Properties A and B;
> $O(1)$ applications of the algorithm from Lemma 2.b are sufficient.

In this way we described informally algorithmic construction which proves the following fact.

Lemma 3. *Assume that given acyclic morphism H is binary, then we can solve the First-MP problem in time $O(k^2 \cdot h^2)$, where k is the number of nonterminals and $h = height(H)$ is the height of the morphism.*

The last lemma together with Lemma 1 implies the following:

Corollary 1. *The First-Mismatch problem for an acyclic morphism can be computed in $O(n^6)$ time.*

Tiburon: A Weighted Tree Automata Toolkit*

Jonathan May and Kevin Knight

Information Sciences Institute
University of Southern California
Marina Del Rey, CA 90292
{jonmay, knight}@isi.edu

Abstract. The availability of weighted finite-state string automata toolkits made possible great advances in natural language processing. However, recent advances in syntax-based NLP model design are unsuitable for these toolkits. To combat this problem, we introduce a weighted finite-state *tree* automata toolkit, which incorporates recent developments in weighted tree automata theory and is useful for natural language applications such as machine translation, sentence compression, question answering, and many more.

1 Introduction

The development of well-founded models of natural language processing applications has been greatly accelerated by the availability of toolkits for finite-state automata. The influential observation of Kaplan & Kay, that cascades of phonological rewrite rules could be expressed as regular relations (equivalent to finite-state transducers) [1], was exploited by Koskenniemi in his development of the two-level morphology and accompanying system for its representation [2]. This system, which was a general program for analysis and generation of languages, pioneered the field of finite-state toolkits [3].

Successive versions of the two-level compiler, such as that written by Karttunen and others at Xerox [4], were used for large-scale analysis applications in many languages [3]. Continued advances, such as work by Karttunen in intersecting composition [5] and replacement [6,7], eventually led to the development of the Xerox finite-state toolkit, which superseded the functionality and use of the two-level tools [3].

Meanwhile, interest in adding uncertainty to finite-state models grew alongside increased availability of large datasets and increased computational power. Ad-hoc methods and individual implementations were developed for integrating uncertainty into finite-state representations [8,9], but the need for a general-purpose weighted finite-state toolkit was clear [10]. Researchers at AT&T led the way with their FSM Library [11] which represented weighted finite-state automata by incorporating the theory of semirings over rational power series cleanly into the existing automata theory. Other toolkits, such as van Noord's FSA utilities [12], the RWTH toolkit [13], and the USC/ISI Carmel toolkit [14], provided additional interfaces and utilities for working with weighted finite-state automata. As in the unweighted case, the availability of

* The authors wish to thank Steve DeNeefe, Jonathan Graehl, Mark Hopkins, Liang Huang, Daniel Marcu, and Magnus Steinby for their advice and comments. This work was partially supported by NSF grant IIS-0428020 and by GALE-DARPA Contract HR0011-06-C-0022.

O.H. Ibarra and H.-C. Yen (Eds.): CIAA 2006, LNCS 4094, pp. 102–113, 2006.
© Springer-Verlag Berlin Heidelberg 2006

this software led to many research projects that took advantage of pre-existing implementations [15,16,17] and the development of the software led to the invention of new algorithms and theory [18,19].

While these toolkits are very robust and capable of development of a wide array of useful applications in NLP and beyond, they all suffer from the limitation that they can only operate on string-based regular languages. In the 1990s, this was begrudgingly accepted as sufficient — the power of computers and the relatively limited availability of data prevented any serious consideration of weighted automata of greater complexity, even though more complex automata models that better captured the syntactic nature of language had long been proposed [20]. As NLP research progressed and computing power and available data increased, researchers started creating serious probabilistic tree-based models for such natural language tasks as translation [21,22,23], summarization [24], paraphrasing [25], language modeling [26], and others. And once again, software implementations of these models were individual, one-off efforts that took entire PhD theses' worth of work to create [27]. GRM, an extension of the AT&T toolkit that uses approximation theory to represent higher-complexity structure such as context-free grammars in the weighted finite-state string automata framework, was useful for handling certain representations [28], but a tree automata framework is required to truly capture tree models.

Knight and Graehl [29] put forward the case for the top-down tree automata theory of Rounds [20] and Thatcher [30] as a logical sequel to weighted string automata for NLP. All of the previously mentioned tree-based models fit nicely into this theory. Additionally, as Knight and Graehl mention [29], most of the desired general operations in a general weighted finite-state toolkit are applicable to top-down tree automata.

We thus propose and present a toolkit designed in the spirit of its predecessors but with the tree, not the string, as its basic data structure. Tiburon is a toolkit for manipulation of weighted top-down tree automata. It is designed to be easy to construct automata and work with them — after reading this article a linguist with no computer science background or a computer scientist with only the vaguest notions of tree automata should be able to write basic acceptors and transducers. To achieve these goals we have maintained simplicity in data format design, such that acceptors and transducers are very close to the way they appear in tree automata literature. We also provide a small set of generic but powerful operations that allow robust manipulation of data structures with simple commands. In subsequent sections we present an introduction to the formats and operations in the Tiburon toolkit and demonstrate the powerful applications that can be easily built.

2 Related Work

The rich history of finite-state string automata toolkits was described in the previous section. Tree automata theory is extensively covered in [31,32]. Timbuk [33] is a toolkit for unweighted finite state tree automata that has been used for cryptographic analysis. It is based on ELAN [34], a term rewriting computational system. MONA [35] is an unweighted tree automata tool aimed at the logic community. Probabilistic tree automata were first proposed by Magidor and Moran [36]. Weighted tree transducers were first described by Fülöp and Vogler [37] as an operational representation of tree series transducers, first introduced by Kuich [38].

3   Trees

Tree automata represent sets of trees and tree relations. Formally, a tree is constructed from a ranked alphabet Σ. Each member of the alphabet is assigned one or more non-negative integers, called a *rank*, and Σ_m refers to all $x \in \Sigma$ with rank m. A tree over Σ is thus defined as:

- x, where $x \in \Sigma_0$, or
- $x(t_1, ...t_m)$, where $x \in \Sigma_m$ and $t_1, ..., t_m$ are trees over Σ.

Figure 1 shows a typical tree and its representation in Tiburon. In this example, NP has rank 2, DT and NN have rank 1, and "the" and "boy" have rank 0.

```
        NP
      /    \
    DT     NN          NP(DT("the") NN("boy"))
     |      |
   "the"  "boy"

     (a)                      (b)
```

Fig. 1. (a) A typical syntax tree, and (b), its Tiburon representation

4   Regular Tree Grammars

As finite-state string acceptors recognize the same family of string languages as regular string grammars, so do finite-state tree acceptors recognize the same family of tree languages as regular tree grammars (RTG) [39]. For simplicity we favor the grammar representation, as tree acceptors must be written as hypergraphs, and this can be confusing. RTGs look very similar to context-free grammars (CFG) (in fact, a CFG is a special case of an RTG) and thus tend to be a very comfortable formalism. Analogous to their string counterpart, a weighted regular tree grammar (wRTG) recognizes a weighted, possibly infinite set of trees. Formally, a wRTG over Σ and under semiring $(\mathbb{K}, \oplus, \otimes, \bar{0}, \bar{1})$ consists of a finite set N of *nonterminal symbols* disjoint from Σ, a start symbol $s \in N$, and a set P of *productions* of the form $a \rightarrow r, \delta$, where $a \in N$, r is a tree

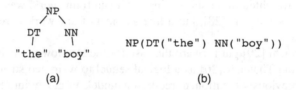

```
q -> A(q r)  # 0.8              A
q -> B(r E)  # 0.2            /   \
r -> C(r)                   B      C
r -> D                     / \      \
                          D   E      D

        (a)                   (b)
```

Fig. 2. (a) A regular tree grammar, and (b), a tree in the grammar's language

over $\Sigma \cup N$, and $\delta \in \mathbb{K}$ is an associated weight. Informally, a wRTG "works" similar to a CFG in that from the start symbol, a sequence of rewrites is performed, replacing nonterminals with trees as specified by the productions, until the generated/recognized tree has no nonterminals remaining. To calculate the weight w of the resulting tree, start with $w = \bar{1}$ and for each production $p = a \rightarrow r, \delta$ used, let $w = w \otimes \delta$. Figure 2(a) shows a typical wRTG in Tiburon format. When weights are omitted on productions, a weight of $\bar{1}$ is assumed. Figure 2(b) shows one of the trees that this grammar recognizes. If we use the probability semiring, the tree has an associated weight of 0.16.

4.1 Generation

One fundamental operation on a wRTG is the generation of trees that are in the grammar's language. Naturally, one might want to know the tree of highest weight in a grammar. Knuth's extension [40] of Dijkstra's classic best-path algorithm [41] to the hypergraph case efficiently finds the best path in the tree recognizer equivalent of a wRTG. However, in many cases it is desirable to obtain a *list* of trees, ordered by weight. A machine translation application may output a wRTG encoding billions of partial translations, and we may want to list the top scoring 25,000 trees for a subsequent re-ranking operation. The $-k$ operation in Tiburon adapts the k-best paths algorithm of Huang and Chiang [42] to wRTGs. For example, given the grammar even.rtg depicted in Fig. 3(a), we issue this command:

```
java -jar tiburon.jar -k 5 even.rtg
```

The five derivations with highest weight in the grammar are returned, as depicted in Fig. 3(b).

```
qe
qe -> A(qe qo) # .1          B(C): 0.0100
qe -> A(qo qe) # .8          A(C B(C)): 0.0008
qe -> B(qo) # .1             B(A(C C)): 0.0006
qo -> A(qo qo) # .6          A(B(C) C): 0.0001
qo -> A(qe qe) # .2          B(B(B(C))): 0.0001
qo -> B(qe) # .1
qo -> C # .1
```

            (a)   (b)

Fig. 3. (a) even.rtg, and (b) its top 5 derivations

Another operation, $-g$, stochastically generates trees from a grammar, probabilistically choosing states to expand until a tree is obtained or a threshold of expansion is reached. This operation is useful for diagnosis — designers of wRTGs may wish to verify that their wRTGs generate trees according to the distribution they have in mind. Given the grammar vic.rtg, depicted in Fig. 4(a), we issue the following command, obtaining five random derivations, as seen in Fig. 4(b):

```
java -jar tiburon.jar -g 5 vic.rtg
```

```
q
q -> S(np vp)
np -> NP(dt nn)
np -> NP(dt jj nn)
dt -> the
dt -> a
jj -> funny
jj -> blue
jj -> strange
nn -> fish
nn -> carrot
vp -> VP(v np)
v -> ate
v -> created
```

```
S(NP(the carrot) VP(ate NP(a fish))): 1.0000
S(NP(the fish) VP(created NP(a carrot))): 1.0000
S(NP(a carrot) VP(created NP(the funny fish))): 1.0000
S(NP(the fish) VP(created NP(a carrot))): 1.0000
S(NP(a fish) VP(created NP(a fish))): 1.0000
```

(a)   (b)

Fig. 4. (a) `vic.rtg`, and (b) five random derivations

4.2   Intersection

Weighted intersection of wRTGs is useful for subdividing large problems into smaller ones. As noted in [31], RTGs (and by extension wRTGs) are closed under intersection. Thus, a wRTG representing machine translation candidate sentences can be intersected with another wRTG representing an English syntax language model to produce re-weighted translations. As a simpler example, consider the grammar `even.rtg` depicted in Fig. 3(a), which produces trees with an even number of labels. The grammar `three.rtg` depicted in Fig. 5(a) produces trees with a number of labels divisible by three. We obtain a grammar which produces trees with a number of labels divisible by six, by using the following command. The grammar is partly shown in Fig. 5(b).

```
java -jar tiburon.jar even.rtg three.rtg
```

```
q3                              qe_q3
q3 -> A(q1 q1) # .25            qe_q3 -> A(qo_q1 qe_q1) # 0.2000
q3 -> A(q3 q2) # .25            qe_q3 -> A(qo_q3 qe_q2) # 0.2000
q3 -> A(q2 q3) # .25            qe_q3 -> A(qo_q2 qe_q3) # 0.2000
q3 -> B(q2)   # .25            qe_q3 -> B(qo_q2) # 0.0250
q2 -> A(q2 q2) # .25            qe_q3 -> A(qe_q1 qo_q1) # 0.0250
q2 -> A(q1 q3) # .25            qe_q3 -> A(qe_q3 qo_q2) # 0.0250
q2 -> A(q3 q1) # .25            qe_q3 -> A(qe_q2 qo_q3) # 0.0250
q2 -> B(q1)   # .25            qe_q2 -> A(qe_q3 qo_q1) # 0.0250
q1 -> A(q3 q3) # .025           qe_q2 -> A(qe_q1 qo_q3) # 0.0250
q1 -> A(q1 q2) # .025           qe_q2 -> A(qe_q2 qo_q2) # 0.0250
q1 -> A(q2 q1) # .025           qe_q2 -> A(qo_q3 qe_q1) # 0.2000
q1 -> B(q3)   # .025           qe_q2 -> A(qo_q1 qe_q3) # 0.2000
q1 -> C       # .9             qe_q2 -> A(qo_q2 qe_q2) # 0.2000
                                qe_q2 -> B(qo_q1) # 0.0250
```

(a)   (b)

Fig. 5. (a) `three.rtg`, and (b) a portion of the intersection of `even.rtg` (see Fig. 3) and `three.rtg`. The complete grammar has 43 productions.

4.3   Weighted Determinization

wRTGs produced by automated systems such as those used to perform machine translation [43] or parsing [44] frequently contain multiple derivations for the same tree with different weight. This is due to the systems' representation of their result space in terms of weighted partial results of various sizes that may be assembled in multiple ways. This property is undesirable if we wish to know the total probability of a particular tree in a language. It is also frequently undesirable to have repeated results in a k-best list. The -d operation invokes May and Knight's weighted determinization algorithm for tree automata [45]. As an example, consider the grammar undet.rtg, depicted in Fig. 6(a). This grammar has two differently-weighted derivations of the tree D(A B), as we see when the top three derivations are obtained, depicted in Fig. 6(b). The following command determinizes the grammar and attempts to return the top three derivations in the resulting grammar:

```
java -jar tiburon.jar -d 5 -k 3 undet.rtg
```

Of course, since there are now only two derivations, only two trees are returned, as seen in Fig. 6(c). The -d 5 argument signifies the maximum time allowed for determinization, in minutes. Determinization is, in the worst case, an exponential-time operation, so it is helpful in practical matters to prevent overly lengthy operations.

```
t
t -> D(q r) # 0.2
t -> D(q s) # 0.3                         Warning: returning fewer
q -> A # 0.3        D(A B): 0.0540        trees than requested
r -> B # 0.2        D(A C): 0.0360        D(A B): 0.0660
s -> B # 0.6        D(A B): 0.0120        D(A C): 0.0360
s -> C # 0.4

     (a)                (b)                    (c)
```

Fig. 6. (a) Undeterminized grammar undet.rtg, (b) k-best list without determinization, and (c) k best list with determinization

4.4 Pruning

In real systems using large grammars to represent complex tree languages, memory and cpu time are very real issues. Even as computers increase in power, the added complexity of tree automata forces practitioners to combat computationally intensive processes. One way of avoiding long running times is to prune weighted automata before operating on them. One technique for pruning finite-state (string) automata is to use the forward-backward algorithm to calculate the highest-scoring path each arc in the automaton is involved in, and then prune the arcs that are only in relatively low-scoring paths [46].

We apply this technique for tree automata by using an adaptation [47] of the inside-outside algorithm [48]. The -p option with argument x removes productions from a tree grammar that are involved in paths x times or more worse than the best path. The -c option provides an overview of a grammar, and we can use this to demonstrate the effects of pruning. The file cls4.determ.rtg represents a language of possible translations of a particular Chinese sentence. We inspect the grammar as follows:

```
java -jar tiburon.jar -m tropical -c cls4.determ.rtg
Check info:
        113 states
        168 rules
        28 unique terminal symbols
        2340 derivations
```

Note that the -m tropical flag is used because this grammar is weighted in the tropical semiring. We prune the grammar and then inspect it as follows:

```
java -jar tiburon.jar -m tropical -p 8 -c c1s4.determ.rtg
Check info:
        111 states
        158 rules
        28 unique terminal symbols
        780 derivations
```

Since we are in the tropical semiring, this command means "Prune all productions that are involved in derivations scoring worse than the best derivation plus 8". This roughly corresponds to derivations with probability 2980 times worse than the best derivation. Note that the pruned grammar has fewer than half the derivations of the unpruned grammar. A quick check of the top derivations after the pruning (using -k) shows that the pruned and unpruned grammars do not differ in their sorted derivation lists until the 455th-highest derivation.

5   Tree Transducers

Top-down tree transducers in Tiburon come in two varieties: *tree-to-tree* [20,30] and *tree-to-string* [49]. They represent the weighted transformation of a tree language into either a tree language or a string language, respectively. One can also think of transducers as representing a language of weighted tree/tree or tree/string pairs [50,51]. We omit a formal definition of top-down tree transducers here; we refer the reader to [31] for a thorough treatment.

Figure 7(a) shows a sample tree-to-tree transducer in Tiburon format. Like a tree grammar, it has a start symbol and a set of optionally weighted productions. A transduction operation walks down an input tree, transforming it and recursively processing its branches. For example, the first production in Fig. 7(a) means: "When in state q, facing an input subtree with root symbol A and two children about which we know nothing, replace it with an output subtree rooted at R with two children. To compute the output subtree's left child, recursively process the input subtree's right child beginning in state r. To compute the output subtree's right child, recursively process the input subtree's left child beginning in state r." Figure 7(b) shows one transduction licensed by this transducer. The format for tree-to-string transducers in Tiburon is similar to that for tree-to-tree transducers; the sole differences are the right side of productions are strings, not trees, and the special symbol *e* representing the empty string may be used.

```
q
q.A(x0: x1:) -> R(r.x1 r.x0) # 0.4
q.A(x0: x1:) -> R(r.x0 s.x1) # 0.6
q.C(x0:) -> L(q.x0)
r.C(x0:) -> T # 0.8
r.C(x0:) -> S # 0.2
r.C(x0: B(D x1:)) -> R(q.x0 r.x1)
r.B(x0: x1:E) -> Q
s.B -> X            (a)
```

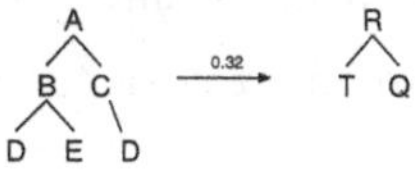

Fig. 7. (a) A tree-to-tree transducer, and (b), a weighted transduction licensed by the transducer

Knight and Graehl [29] describe a wide hierarchy of transducer classes. Transducers in Tiburon are specifically *top-down transducers with extended left-hand sides*, also known as **xR** in Knight and Graehl's hierarchy, where "R" denotes "root-to-frontier" (i.e. top-down) and the "x" denotes the extended left-hand sides. By extended, we mean that the left side of productions can be trees of arbitrary depth. The sixth and seventh productions in Fig. 7(a) show an example of extended left-hand side productions. Strictly speaking, the class xR refers to only tree-to-tree transducers; tree-to-string transducers with the same characteristics are in the class **xRs**. There are no restrictions on copying or deleting of variable children in xR or xRs; the seventh production shows an example of a deleted child. The xR and xRs class of transducers were selected for Tiburon because of their good fit with natural language applications [20,29].

5.1   Forward and Backward Application

Application is the operation of passing a tree or grammar onto a transducer and obtaining the resultant image. Tiburon supports forward application of a tree onto a tree-to-tree or tree-to-string transducer with the -1 operation (for "left-side" transduction). If the transducer in Fig. 7(a) is in a file xr1.trans the transduction performed in Fig. 7(b) can be accomplished as follows:

```
echo "A(B(D E) C(D))" | java -jar tiburon.jar -1 -s xr1.trans
q2
q2 -> R(q0 q1) # 0.4000
q1 -> Q # 1.0000
q0 -> S # 0.2000
q0 -> T # 0.8000
```

The -s flag tells Tiburon to expect the input tree from *stdin* instead of a file. As seen above, the image of a tree onto a tree-to-tree transducer is a wRTG. The image of a tree onto a tree-to-string transducer is a wCFG, currently represented in Tiburon as a one-state wRTG. The image of a wRTG onto the transducers supported in Tiburon is not a wRTG [31] and as such is currently not supported. However, limited versions of the transducers supported, such as transducers that do not copy their variables, do produce wRTG images [31]. We will soon release the next version of Tiburon, which will support the -r operation for backward application (the inverse image of a tree or wRTG onto a transducer is a wRTG) and forward application of wRTGs onto limited classes of transducers.

5.2   Composition

We often want to build a cascade of several small transducers and then programmatically combine them into one. Unlike string transducers, general top-down tree transducers are not closed under composition, that is, a transduction carried out by a sequence of two transducers may not be possible with a single transducer. Engelfriet showed that top-down tree transducers that do not allow deletion or copying of variables (known as RLN transducers; the L signifies "linear" and the "N" signifies "non-deleting") are closed under composition [52]. Tiburon, however, allows composition of tree-to-tree transducers without checking if the transducers to be composed are composable. For example, consider the transducer below, which is in a file xr2.trans:

```
q
q.R(x0: x1:) -> R(R q.x1 R q.x0)
q.T -> B # 0.6
q.T -> D # 0.4
q.Q -> C
q.S -> E
q.X -> A
```

The following command composes xr1.trans with xr2.trans and passes a tree through them, returning the top three output derivations:

```
echo "A(B(D E) C(D))" | java -jar tiburon.jar -ls -k 3 \
    xr1.trans xr2.trans
R(R C R B): 0.1920
R(R C R D): 0.1280
R(R C R E): 0.0800
```

xr1.trans is not RLN, it is xRL (i.e. it has an extended left side and deletes variables but does not copy), but in this case the two transducers are composable. We believe that many of the xR transducers used in natural language applications will not suffer from the general noncomposability of their class.

5.3 Training

A common task in building tree transducer models is the assignment of appropriate weights to productions. We can use Expectation-Maximization training [53] to set the weights of an unweighted tree transducer such that they maximize the likelihood of a training corpus of tree/tree or tree/string pairs. Tiburon provides the -t operation, which implements the technique described by Graehl and Knight for training tree transducers using EM [54].

As an example, consider training a machine translation model using bilingual input/output pairs. Given the 261-production unweighted tree-to-string transducer depicted in Fig. 8(a) in file y1.ts, and the 15 tree/string pairs in Fig. 8(b) in file y1.train, we run this command to produce the transducer in Fig. 8(c):

```
java -jar tiburon.jar -t 20 y1.train y1.trans
```

6   Applications Using Tiburon

The translation model of Yamada and Knight [22] is a specialized model for predicting a Japanese string given an English tree. The custom implementation of this model, built by Yamada as part of his PhD thesis [27], took more than one year to complete. Graehl and Knight [54] showed how this model could be represented as a four-state tree-to-string transducer. We built an untrained transducer from Yamada's model and trained it on the same data used by Yamada and Knight to produce their alignment sentence pairs [22]. The complete process took only 2 days. For details we refer the reader to [55].

Knight and Graehl [56] describe a cascade of finite-state string transducers that perform English-Japanese transliteration. Of course, a weighted string transducer toolkit

```
q                                    X(Garcia X(and associates))
q.X(x0: x1:) -> q.x0 q.x1            Garcia y asociados
q.X(x0: x1:) -> q.x1 q.x0            X(X(Carlos Garcia) X(has X(three associates)))
q.a -> *e*                           Carlos Garcia tiene tres asociados
q.a -> empresa                       X(X(his associates) X(X(are not) strong))
q.a -> Garcia                        sus asociados no son fuertes
q.also -> asociados                  X(Garcia X(X(has X(a company)) also))
q.also -> *e*                        Garcia tambien tiene una empresa
q.also -> empresa                    X(X(its clients) X(are angry))
q.also -> enfadados                  sus clientes estan enfadados
q.also -> estan                      X(X(the associates) X(X(are also) angry))
q.also -> Garcia                     los asociados tambien estan enfadados
q.also -> los                        X(X(X(the clients) X(and X(the associates))) X(are enemies))
q.also -> tambien                    los clientes y los asociados son enemigos
q.also -> tiene                      X(X(the company) X(has X(three groups)))
q.also -> una                        la empresa tiene tres grupos
q.and -> asociados                   X(X(its groups) X(are X(in Europe)))
q.and -> clientes                    sus grupos estan en Europa
q.and -> *e*                         X(X(the X(modern groups)) X(sell X(strong pharmaceuticals)))
q.and -> enemigos                    los grupos modernos venden medicinas fuertes
...                                  X(X(the groups) X(X(do not) X(sell zanzanine)))
                                     los grupos no venden zanzanina
                                     X(X(the X(small groups)) X(X(are not) modern))
                                     los grupos pequenos no son modernos
```

```
q
q.X(x0: x1:) -> q.x0 q.x1 # 0.8571
q.X(x0: x1:) -> q.x1 q.x0 # 0.1429
q.are -> son # 0.5
q.are -> estan # 0.5
q.the -> los # 0.8571428571428571
q.the -> la # 0.14285714285714288
q.not -> no # 1.0
q.do -> *e* # 1.0
q.Garcia -> Garcia # 1.0
q.enemies -> enemigos # 1.0
q.angry -> enfadados # 1.0
q.has -> tiene # 1.0
q.zanzanine -> zanzanina # 1.0
```

(a)   (b)   (c)

Fig. 8. (a) Portion of a 261-production unweighted tree-to-string transducer. (b) 15 (tree, string) training pairs. (c) Portion of the 31-production weighted tree-to-string transducer produced after 20 iterations of EM training (all other productions had probability 0).

such as Carmel is well suited for this task, but Tiburon is suited for the job as well. By converting string transducers into monadic (non-branching) tree transducers, we obtain equivalent results. We used simple scripts to transform the string transliteration transducers into these monadic trees, and reproduced the transliteration operations. Thus, we see how Tiburon may be used for string-based as well as tree-based applications.

7 Conclusion

We have described Tiburon, a general weighted tree automata toolkit, and described some of its functions and their use in constructing natural language applications. Tiburon can be downloaded at http://www.isi.edu/licensed-sw/tiburon/

References

1. Kaplan, R.M., Kay, M.: Phonological rules and finite-state transducers. In: Linguistic Society of America Meeting Handbook, Fifty-Sixth Annual Meeting. (1981) Abstract.
2. Koskenniemi, K.: Two-level morphology: A general computational model for word-form recognition and production. Publication 11, University of Helsinki, Department of General Linguistics, Helsinki (1983)
3. Karttunen, L., Beesley, K.R.: A short history of two-level morphology. Presented at the ESSLLI-2001 Special Event titled "Twenty Years of Finite-State Morphology" (2001) Helsinki, Finland.
4. Karttunen, L., Beesley, K.R.: Two-level rule compiler. Technical Report ISTL-92-2, Xerox Palo Alto Research Center, Palo Alto, CA (1992)
5. Karttunen, L., Kaplan, R.M., Zaenen, A.: Two-level morphology with composition. In: COLING Proceedings. (1992)
6. Karttunen, L.: The replace operator. In: ACL Proceedings. (1995)

7. Karttunen, L.: Directed replacement. In: ACL Proceedings. (1996)
8. Riccardi, G., Pieraccini, R., Bocchieri, E.: Stochastic automata for language modeling. Computer Speech & Language 10(4) (1996)
9. Ljolje, A., Riley, M.D.: Optimal speech recognition using phone recognition and lexical access. In: ICSLP Proceedings. (1992)
10. Mohri, M., Pereira, F.C.N., Riley, M.: The design principles of a weighted finite-state transducer library. Theoretical Computer Science 231 (2000)
11. Mohri, M., Pereira, F.C.N., Riley, M.: A rational design for a weighted finite-state transducer library. In: Proceedings of the 7th Annual AT&T Software Symposium. (1997)
12. van Noord, G., Gerdemann, D.: An extendible regular expression compiler for finite-state approaches in natural language processing. In: 4th International Workshop on Implementing Automata. (2000)
13. Kanthak, S., Ney, H.: Fsa: An efficient and flexible c++ toolkit for finite state automata using on-demand computation. In: ACL Proceedings. (2004)
14. Graehl, J.: Carmel finite-state toolkit. http://www.isi.edu/licensed-sw/carmel (1997)
15. Kaiser, E., Schalkwyk, J.: Building a robust, skipping parser within the AT&T FSM toolkit. Technical report, Center for Human Computer Communication, Oregon Graduate Institute of Science and Technology (2001)
16. van Noord, G.: Treatment of epsilon moves in subset construction. Comput. Linguist. 26(1) (2000)
17. Koehn, P., Knight, K.: Feature-rich statistical translation of noun phrases. In: ACL Proceedings. (2003)
18. Pereira, F., Riley, M.: Speech recognition by composition of weighted finite automata. In Roche, E., Schabes, Y., eds.: Finite-State Language Processing. MIT Press, Cambridge, MA (1997)
19. Mohri, M.: Finite-state transducers in language and speech processing. Comput. Linguist. 23(2) (1997)
20. Rounds, W.C.: Mappings and grammars on trees. Mathematical Systems Theory 4 (1970)
21. Och, F.J., Tillmann, C., Ney, H.: Improved alignment models for statistical machine translation. In: EMNLP/VLC Proceedings. (1999)
22. Yamada, K., Knight, K.: A syntax-based statistical translation model. In: ACL Proceedings. (2001)
23. Eisner, J.: Learning non-isomorphic tree mappings for machine translation. In: ACL Proceedings (companion volume). (2003)
24. Knight, K., Marcu, D.: Summarization beyond sentence extraction: A probabilistic approach to sentence compression. Artificial Intelligence 139 (2002)
25. Pang, B., Knight, K., Marcu, D.: Syntax-based alignment of multiple translations extracting paraphrases and generating new sentences. In: NAACL Proceedings. (2003)
26. Charniak, E.: Immediate-head parsing for language models. In: ACL Proceedings. (2001)
27. Yamada, K.: A Syntax-Based Translation Model. PhD thesis, University of Southern California (2002)
28. Allauzen, C., Mohri, M., Roark, B.: A general weighted grammar library. In: CIAA Proceedings. (2004)
29. Knight, K., Graehl, J.: An overview of probabilistic tree transducers for natural language processing. In: CICLing Proceedings. (2005)
30. Thatcher, J.W.: Generalized^2 sequential machines. J. Comput. System Sci. 4 (1970)
31. Gécseg, F., Steinby, M.: Tree Automata. Akadémiai Kiadó, Budapest (1984)
32. Comon, H., Dauchet, M., Gilleron, R., Jacquemard, F., Lugiez, D., Tison, S., Tommasi, M.: Tree automata techniques and applications. Available on: http://www.grappa.univ-lille3.fr/tata (1997) release October 1 2002.

33. Genet, T., Tong, V.V.T.: Reachability analysis of term rewriting systems with timbuk. In: LPAR Proceedings. (2001)
34. Borovansky, P., Kirchner, C., Kirchner, H., Moreau, P., Vittek, M.: Elan: A logical framework based on computational systems. In: Proceedings of the first international workshop on rewriting logic. (1996)
35. Henriksen, J., Jensen, J., Jørgensen, M., Klarlund, N., Paige, B., Rauhe, T., Sandholm, A.: Mona: Monadic second-order logic in practice. In: TACAS Proceedings. (1995)
36. Magidor, M., Moran, G.: Probabilistic tree automata. Israel Journal of Mathematics **8** (1969)
37. Fülöp, Z., Vogler, H.: Weighted tree transducers. J. Autom. Lang. Comb. **9**(1) (2004)
38. Kuich, W.: Tree transducers and formal tree series. Acta Cybernet. **14** (1999)
39. Brainerd, W.S.: Tree generating regular systems. Inform. and Control **14** (1969)
40. Knuth, D.: A generalization of Dijkstra's algorithm. Inform. Process. Lett. **6**(1) (1977)
41. Dijkstra, E.W.: A note on two problems in connexion with graphs. Numerische Mathematik **1** (1959)
42. Huang, L., Chiang, D.: Better k-best parsing. In: IWPT Proceedings. (2005)
43. Galley, M., Hopkins, M., Knight, K., Marcu, D.: What's in a translation rule? In: HLT-NAACL Proceedings. (2004)
44. Bod, R.: An efficient implementation of a new DOP model. In: EACL Proceedings. (2003)
45. May, J., Knight, K.: A better n-best list: Practical determinization of weighted finite tree automata. In: NAACL Proceedings. (2006)
46. Siztus, A., Ortmanns, S.: High quality word graphs using forward-backward pruning. In: Proceedings of the IEEE Conference on Acoustic, Speech and Signal Processing. (1999)
47. Graehl, J.: Context-free algorithms. Unpublished handout (2005)
48. Lari, K., Young, S.J.: The estimation of stochastic context-free grammars using the inside-outside algorithm. Computer Speech and Language **4** (1990)
49. Aho, A.V., Ullman, J.D.: Translations of a context-free grammar. Inform. and Control **19** (1971)
50. Shieber, S.M.: Synchronous grammars as tree transducers. In: TAG+7 Proceedings. (2004)
51. Schabes, Y.: Mathematical and Computational Aspects of Lexicalized Grammars. PhD thesis, Univ. of Pennsylvania, Phila., PA (1990)
52. Engelfriet, J.: Bottom-up and top-down tree transformations. a comparison. Mathematical Systems Theory **9** (1976)
53. Dempster, A.P., Laird, N.M., Rubin, D.B.: Maximum likelihood from incomplete data via the EM algorithm. Journal of the Royal Statistical Society, Series B **39**(1) (1977)
54. Graehl, J., Knight, K.: Training tree transducers. In: HLT-NAACL Proceedings. (2004)
55. Graehl, J., Knight, K., May, J.: Training tree transducers. Comput. Linguist. (Submitted)
56. Knight, K., Graehl, J.: Machine transliteration. Comput. Linguist. **24**(4) (1998)

Around Hopcroft's Algorithm

Manuel Baclet[1] and Claire Pagetti[2]

[1] LSV - ENS de Cachan & CNRS - Cachan, France
IRIT - UPS & CNRS - Toulouse, France
baclet@lsv.ens-cachan.fr
[2] ONERA / Cert - Toulouse, France
claire.pagetti@cert.fr

Abstract. In this paper, a reflection is made on an indeterminism inherent to Hopcroft's minimization algorithm: the *splitter* choice. We have implemented two natural policies (FIFO and FILO) for managing the set of splitters for which we obtain the following practical results: the FILO strategy performs better than the FIFO strategy, in the case of a one letter alphabet, the practical complexity in the FILO case never exceeds a linear one and our implementation is more efficient than the minimization algorithm of the FSM tool. This implementation is being integrated in a finite automata library, the Dash library. Thus, we present an efficient manner to manipulate automata by using *canonical* minimal automata.

Keywords: Finite automata, minimization, Hopcroft's algorithm.

1 Introduction

The problem of minimizing a deterministic finite automaton has been widely studied. Finite automata libraries, such as FSM [MPR00], Mona [KM01], etc., include a minimization procedure. State of the art implementations of minimization algorithm is then an important issue for practical efficiency.

Minimization Algorithms. For a detailed presentation of the currently known minimization algorithms, the reader is referred to Watson's taxonomy [Wat95].

For a given automaton labeled by the alphabet Σ where Q is the states set and F the final states set, most of minimization algorithms have a $O(|Q|^2)$ complexity and use one of the following two fix point strategies:

(S1) Consider the coarsest partition $\{F, Q/F\}$ and refine this partition until it satisfies some congruence properties;

(S2) Consider the finest partition and gather the equivalent classes.

Among the algorithms using other strategies, the Brzozowski algorithm [Brz62] allows to compute the minimal automaton from a non deterministic automaton in an exponential time. A linear algorithm exists for complete deterministic automata over a one letter alphabet [PTB85]. Indeed, the problem is equivalent to determining the *coarsest partition* of the states set stable with respect to the transition relation function. Thus, the authors of [PTB85] use the second strategy (S2): the starting partition

O.H. Ibarra and H.-C. Yen (Eds.): CIAA 2006, LNCS 4094, pp. 114–125, 2006.

is the partition with singleton classes and the output is built via a sequence of steps in which two or more classes are merged. An incremental algorithm has been proposed in [WD03, Wat01]. Unlike the other iterative algorithms, the intermediate results can be used since they consist in partially minimized automata. The Hopcroft's algorithm proposed in [Hop71] has a theoretical $O(|\Sigma|.|Q|.\log|Q|)$ complexity which is currently the best for a minimization algorithm.

Contribution. We propose a new implementation of the Hopcroft algorithm in the OCaml[1] language. We describe this implementation and some heuristics that significantly improve the speed of the practical state-of-the-art Hopcroft's minimization algorithm.

In the Hopcroft's algorithm, at each step a splitter is chosen among a set of classes in order to refine the partition. Every complexity computation leans on the worst case choice. It is the case in [BC04] where the authors exhibit an automata family over a one letter alphabet and a bad strategy that lead to the $O(|Q|.\log|Q|)$ complexity with the Hopcroft's algorithm. This means that there exists a bad strategy in the splitter choice while applying the Hopcroft's algorithm.

Our point of view is that there exists a good strategy in the splitter choice that allows a fast implementation of the Hopcroft's algorithm. This heuristic consists in a FILO strategy in which the most recent class is chosen as the splitter. In practice, this heuristic is powerful. In the case of a one letter alphabet, the practical complexity seems linear, even on the "bad" automata depicted in [BC04].

This implementation is being included in the Dash library (currently developed at the LSV[2]) which is a finite automata library designed to share common connected components between automata. The sharing of common components imposes that two equivalent automata are represented with the same minimal automaton. We thus propose an extension of our implementation, based on the work of [Cou04], to automatically compute a canonical representative.

Outline. Section 2 recalls basic definitions and results concerning minimization. We present the Hopcroft's algorithm in section 3. We discuss its complexity and present an open question. In the section 4, the implementation is precisely depicted and the two strategies, FILO and FIFO are detailed. These implementations are then experimented on benchmarks and compared to other softwares in section 5. Finally, in section 6, we detail the efficient representation of automata in the Dash library using *canonical minimal automata*.

2   Minimal Automaton

In this section, we recall some basic notions and terminology on finite automata and regular languages. For a complete theory, one can refer to [BBC92, HU79]. In the sequel, Σ is a non empty finite alphabet.

---

[1] http://caml.inria.fr/index.en.html
[2] http://www.lsv.ens-cachan.fr

Definition 1. *A deterministic, complete and* finite automaton[3] *over Σ is a tuple (Q, q_0, T, F) where:*

- *Q is a finite set of states;*
- *$q_0 \in Q$ is the initial state;*
- *$T : Q \times \Sigma \to Q$ is the* transition function*;*
- *$F \subseteq Q$ is the set of final states.*

A rational language is associated to any finite automaton: it consists in the set of letter sequences which label paths from the initial state to a final state. We suppose that every considered automaton is *reachable*, i.e. any state of the automaton is reachable from the initial state. The automata theory ensures [Ner58, BBC92] that any rational language is recognized by a unique finite automaton (up to an isomorphism) with a minimal number of states. This automaton is the *minimal automaton* associated with the language.

For a given deterministic, complete and finite automaton, the equivalent (in term of language recognized) minimal automaton can be obtained by defining a congruence relation on the initial automaton's states, i.e. an equivalence relation which is stable with the transition function:

$$q \sim q' \implies \forall a \in \Sigma, \; T(q, a) \sim T(q', a)$$

If $\sim_m$ is the coarsest congruence such that

$$q \sim_m q' \implies (q, q') \in F^2 \text{ or } (q, q') \in (Q/F)^2,$$

we have the following result:

Proposition 1. *The finite automaton $(Q/\sim_m, \overline{q_0}, T', F')$ where*

- *$\overline{q_0}$ is the q_0 class up to $\sim_m$;*
- *$T'(a, \overline{q}) = \overline{T(a, q)}$;*
- *$\overline{q} \in F' \Leftrightarrow q \in F$;*

is the minimal automaton associated to the automaton (Q, q_0, T, F).

Given a finite automaton, this proposition allows to compute the associated minimal automaton by simply computing the equivalence relation. In the next section, we introduce an efficient algorithm for computing this equivalence.

3   Hopcroft's Algorithm

The Hopcroft's algorithm [Hop71] is detailled in Algorithm 1. It has a theoretical $O(|\Sigma|.|Q|.\log|Q|)$ complexity. The main principle consists in refining the coarsest partition until finding a stable partition (strategy S1). The initial partition is $\{F, Q \setminus F\}$ and each step of the algorithm consists in splitting the classes for which the stability constraint is not satisfied.

$\mathcal{P}$ is the current partition and L contains the elements of the partition to be treated. The set C is called the *splitter*.

---

[3] Since we only consider deterministic, complete and finite automata, we use the shortcut finite automaton.

$L := \emptyset$
if $|F| < |Q/F|$ **then**
   $C_0 := Q/F; C_1 := F; \text{ADD}(C_1, L)$
else
   $C_1 := Q/F; C_0 := F; \text{ADD}(C_1, L)$
end if
$\mathcal{P} := \{C_0, C_1\};$
while $L \neq \emptyset$ {The while loop corresponds to the Cut procedure} **do**
  let $C = \text{EXTRACT}(L)$ in
  for all $a \in \Sigma$ **do**
    for all $B \in \mathcal{P}$ {The forall loop corresponds to $\text{split}\ (C, a)$ procedure} **do**
      let $(B', B'') = \text{SPLIT}(B, C, a)$
      if $|B'| < |B''|$ **then**
        $B := B''; \text{ADD}(B', \mathcal{P}); \text{ADD}(B', L)$
      else
        $B := B'; \text{ADD}(B'', \mathcal{P}); \text{ADD}(B'', L);$
      end if
    end for
  end for
end while

Algorithm 1. Hopcroft's Algorithm

1. The function split covers all the classes in $\mathcal{P}$ whose image by the transition function meets the splitter and determines the refined classes. Its implementation will be precise latter.
2. SPLIT has three arguments and decomposes the second argument (a subset) into two subsets depending on the splitter (the first argument) and the transitions labeled by the third argument. More precisely:

$$(B \cap T^{-1}(C, a), B \cap^c T^{-1}(C, a)) = \text{SPLIT}(B, C, a);$$

3. ADD has two arguments and adds a new subset in a set of subsets;
4. EXTRACT is the choice function on which we act to define the strategies we studied.

In the next section, we detail our implementation.

4 Implementation

4.1 Automata Representation

In our implementation, automata states are represented by integers: the states of an automaton $\mathcal{A}$ are numbered from 0 to $|Q| - 1$ and the following data structures will be used:

- the initial state is represented by an integer,
- the final states are represented by a boolean array of size $|Q|$,
- the transition function is represented by an array of integer array:

$$transition.(i).(a) = j \Leftrightarrow T(i, a) = j$$

4.2 Data Structures

The current partition is represented by an integer array *partition* of size $|Q|$ and an integer couple array *class_indices*.

To each class B of the current partition, the array *class_indices* maps the integer couple (l, h) so that elements of class B are the elements of the array *partition* whose indices are between l and h. During the execution of our implementation, elements in a class always have consecutive indices in the array *partition*.

When a class B is split in B' and B'', the elements in *partition* with indices between l and h are permuted so that elements of class B' have indices between l and h' and elements of B'' have indices between $l' = (h' + 1)$ and h. An integer array *class* is used to quickly find the class of an element.

In order to find efficiently the index of an element, an integer array $partition^{-1}$ is held up to date. It has the following property:

$$partition.(i) = j \Leftrightarrow partition^{-1}.(j) = i.$$

The *partition* array represents a one-to-one mapping over the integers between 0 and $|Q| - 1$ and the array $partition^{-1}$ represents the inverse mapping.

In order to realize the split operation efficiently, an integer list array $transition^{-1}$ is used to decide which classes have to be (possibly) split. It represents the inverse of the transition function:

$$i \in transition^{-1}.(a).(j) \Leftrightarrow T(i, a) = j$$

A *pointer_array* is used to decide whether a class needs to be split: if B is a class with indices h and l in *class_indices* and if $pointer\_array.(B) \neq (h - 1)$, then B needs to be split in B' and B'', with respective indices (l, h') and $(h' + 1, h)$, where $h' = pointer\_array.(B)$. At the beginning of each iteration of the algorithm, *pointer_array* associates to each class B the upper index h associated to B, if $class\_indices.(B) = (l, h)$.

In our implementation, the two initial classes are numbered 0 and 1. Then, the created classes during the algorithm execution are numbered with increasing indices above 2.

4.3 L's Implementation

There are two natural choices for implementing the L object. By natural, we mean that there is no other simple choice that allows to carry out the ADD and EXTRACT operations in constant time [Knu01]. For instance, always choosing the class of L with the smallest size needs important resources and leads to a loss of performance in practice.

FIFO Strategy. For this strategy, the classes are treated in their appearance order. If *classes_number* refers to the number of known classes and *next_class* indicates the next splitter, the algorithm 1 while loop, where the function incr increments an integer pointer, becomes Algorithm 2.

```
while next_class ⩽ classes_number do
  let C =next_class
  for all a ∈ Σ do
    split (C, a)
  end for
  incr next_class
end while
```

Algorithm 2. FIFO Cut Procedure

FILO Strategy. For this strategy, the chosen splitter is the most recent class of the splitter set. The L object is then represented by a list: additions and deletions then occur on the top of the list. The Algorithm 1 while loop becomes Algorithm 3.

```
while L ≠ ∅ do
  let C = head(L) in remove_head(L);
  for all a ∈ Σ do
    split (C, a)
  end for
end while
```

Algorithm 3. FILO Cut Procedure

4.4 split **Function Implementation**

Let C be the splitter and a a letter, the split function acts in two steps:

1. First, the set $T^{-1}(C, a)$ is considered and the elements of the array *partition* are permuted so that each class B is transformed into:

$$\boxed{B \cap T^{-1}(C, a) \,\big|\, B \cap {}^{\mathsf{C}}(T^{-1}(C, a))}$$

   where ${}^{\mathsf{C}}A$ denotes the complementary of A in Q.
   Moreover, a list *visited_classes* which stores the encountered classes is also computed. A particular care must be taken when $C \cap T^{-1}(C, a) \neq \emptyset$.

2. For every B in *visited_classes*, we determine if B is refined by C: B is refined if, and only if $B \cap {}^{\mathsf{C}}(T^{-1}(C, a)) \neq \emptyset$. (Since B was encountered in the first step, $B \cap T^{-1}(C, a) \neq \emptyset$.) If it is the case, a new class with the smaller part of B is created and added to L, otherwise nothing is done.

Due to a lack of space, the details of the split procedure can be found in [BP06].

We have presented the implementation, thus the contiguous question is its complexity and its efficiency. We only have actually partial results that we present in the following.

4.5 Complexity

We do not go into the details of the Hopcroft's algorithm complexity computation. The reader is referred to [BBC92, Knu01] for instance.

Theoretical Upper Bound. The computation of the time complexity preponderant term is realized by bounding the sum, denoted by S, of the lists size of T^{-1} covered during the execution. It can be shown that $S \leqslant |\Sigma|.(\log_2 |Q|).|Q|$.

Reachability of the Upper Bound. For the case of one letter alphabet, the authors of [BC04] construct an automata family and a splitter choice so that the bound $O(|Q| \log |Q|)$ is reached. Their strategy consists in choosing at each step a splitter that does not refine classes in L (if possible).

Conjecture. There are open questions: does there exists a static strategy such that for every automaton the complexity is linear? And if it does, is it the case of the FILO strategy?

We have not found yet any way to compute this complexity. We only have practical results that we develop in the next section. For each automaton, a tree derivation can be constructed as proposed in [Knu01] for representing the program execution. It is a binary tree such that a node is a set of states and each son is a subset of the root such that the two sons form a partition. We add three colors: black when a set belongs to L and has never been modified, blue when a set belongs to L and has been refined, green when the set does not belong to L. A cost function can be associated to each node to compute the complexity. The idea is that the smaller the splitter is the smaller the cost function is locally, but this does not ensure that the minimum is global.

In order to obtain precise practical results of our two implementations behavior, our programs also compute the value of S.

5 Experiments

We realized many experiments on different automata families and we implemented several automata generators: a random automata family over a one letter alphabet with a number of states between 40 and 4.10^6; the automata family over a one letter alphabet constructed from the de Bruijn words given in [BC04]; a random automata family over a two letters alphabet with a number of states between 40 and 4.10^6 and a particular automata family over a four letters alphabet developped in previous works [BPP04] to model hardware signal processing components.

These experimentations allowed to compare the practical performances of our program with those of the Finite-State Machine Library FSM [MPR00].

Random One Letter. The random automata generation over a one letter alphabet is a simple problem since the topology of a reachable finite automaton over this particular alphabet has the particular structure of a *frying pan*.

The diagram given on the left of Figure 1 depicts our experimentations results: for any fixed size minimized automaton, we represent $max\{S/(|Q|.|\Sigma|)\}$ in function of

$|Q|$, which corresponds to the worst case. The scale of the abscissa axis is logarithmic. We notice that the FIFO strategy is a linear function and it means that we obtain a bad complexity around $|Q| \log |Q|$.

On the opposite, the curve associated to the FILO strategy is always below the constant 3 and seems to converge towards the constant 2. This suggests a linear complexity for the one letter case.

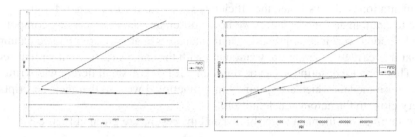

Fig. 1. One letter and two letters alphabet experimental results

De Bruijn's Words Automata. A n-de Bruijn's word w over Σ is a word of minimal size such that for every word v of size n, v is a contiguous sub-word of w^2: $\forall v$, $|v| = n$, $\exists u_1, u_2$ such that $w = u_1.v.u_2$. For instance, the word $\omega = 11101000$ is 3-de Bruijn's word.

In [BC04], the authors use these words to construct one letter automata with a circular shape: if 1 and 0 are the letters, if $w = w_0.w_2...w_{n-1}$ is the de Bruijn's word, the associated automaton has n states $\{0, \cdots, n-1\}$, the transition function is $T : i \mapsto (i+1)$ mod n and a state i is final if, and only if $w_i = 1$.

For the word $\omega = 11101000$, the automaton is depicted in Figure 2.

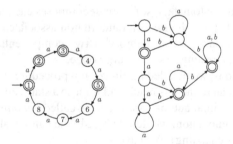

Fig. 2. Automaton for $\omega = 11101000$ and a two letter automaton

The experiments are made over automata associated to de Bruijn's word of size between 3 and 21. The results are identical to those of the previous subsection.

Random Two Letters. The topology of a two letters alphabet is more complex than the case of one letter. We thus have chosen a particular family with the shape of a binary tree given in Figure 2.

Such automata with various number of states, which are final with a probability p, were minimized and the worst case results are given on the right side of Figure 1.

FSM Minimization Comparison. FSM [MPR00] is a powerful and performant finite-state machine library. It is able to manipulate large size automata and transducers. In particular, it holds a minimization implementation whose code is not known. We compared the library with our implementations on the benchmarks previously depicted. Our implementation is always faster, the efficiency varies from 4 to 15 times faster.

The test automata for four letters we have chosen are signal processing components studied in some verification process. Their interest is that they are realistic examples and that it is easy to generate many automata with the same structure but with different sizes. Their precise description can be found in [BPP04]. A small library was written to handle these models which are specified in a functional way, so that their descriptions are very close to the automaton definition.

Two families of automata were studied and the results are given in Figure 3.

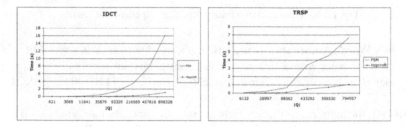

Fig. 3. Comparison with FSM

6   Canonical Minimal Automaton

When manipulating huge automata, a software decomposes each automaton in its connected components and stores the minimal automaton associated to each component. In order to reduce the resources and memory, if two components recognize the same language, it would be interesting to store it only once.

In the previous sections, we detailed minimization procedures that compute two isomorphic automata. We can refine this result and impose a states encoding so that we can compute an identical minimal automaton, which is called *canonical minimal automaton*. Thus, let $\mathcal{A}$ be an automaton, we denote by $\mathcal{A}_c$ the canonical minimal automaton (w.r.t. a particular states encoding). We have:

$$\forall \mathcal{A}, \mathcal{B}, \mathcal{L}(\mathcal{A}) = \mathcal{L}(\mathcal{B}) \implies \mathcal{A}_c = \mathcal{B}_c.$$

Finding the canonical minimal automaton is rather straightforward: once the classical Hopcroft's algorithm has been applied, the states are renamed by a procedure of complexity $O(|\Sigma|.|Q|)$ with numbers in $\{0, \cdots, n-1\}$. The idea is roughly the following:

- the letters are ordered,
- the initial state has the number 0,

- if the state reached from 0 by a is not the initial state, then it is denoted 1 and is stored in a stack. Every successor of 0 is treated in the same way,
- every successor of the state in the top of the stack is numbered like the successors of 0 (note that if a state is already visited, nothing is done),
- the procedure ends when the stack is empty.

The previous solution can be applied when there is an initial state which is not the case when dealing with connected components. The author of [Cou04] proposes two techniques, which he did not prove formally, to find a canonical representative:

- a *sorted* Hopcroft's algorithm that needs to be executed twice;
- a *sorted* Hopcroft's algorithm with a static storage policy that computes directly the solution.

We prove in this paper that these solutions are correct. We included them in our FILO implementation so that we could experiment this approach on different automata families. Due to a lack of space, proves of propositions 2 and 3 can be found in [BP06].

Two-Pass Solution. In this case, the idea is to sort the encountered classes list *visited_classes* handled in the split procedure. Thus, this procedure is modified by adding a sorting algorithm:

```
visited_classes:=sort(visited_classes).
```

With this modification, the canonical minimal automaton is obtained by applying twice the FILO strategy. Let us denote by $\min_2$ this new implementation.

Proposition 2. *Let $\mathcal{A}$ and $\mathcal{B}$ two automata such that $\mathcal{L}(\mathcal{A}) = \mathcal{L}(\mathcal{B})$, then*

$$\min_2 \circ \min_2(\mathcal{A}) = \min_2 \circ \min_2(\mathcal{B}).$$

The complexity is not easy to estimate. Nevertheless, on practical analyses, the sorting does not increase that much the execution time: the number of classes is often small.

One-Pass Solution. The sorted Hopcroft's algorithm can be improved in the following way:

- when a class B is split in $\{B \cap T^{-1}(C, a), B \cap {}^{\complement}(T^{-1}(C, a))\}$, we add to L either $B \cap T^{-1}(C, a)$, or $B \cap {}^{\complement}(T^{-1}(C, a)$. The author of [Cou04] proposes to impose statically that one of these sets is always chosen. In our experiments, we found that the set $B \cap T^{-1}(C, a)$ is more profitable,
- during the initialization of L, again a static choice of the final set or the non-final states is done.

Note that the modifications do not act on the correction but only on the complexity which could be increased and that there does not exist a good static strategy for the initialization step: indeed, if for $\mathcal{A} = (Q, q_0, T, F)$ it is more efficient to choose F, then for $\mathcal{A}' = (Q, q_0, T, Q \setminus F)$ the choice of $Q \setminus F$ is more advantageous.

Let us denote this new algorithm $\min_1$. It computes a canonical minimal automaton:

Proposition 3. *Let $\mathcal{A}$ and $\mathcal{B}$ be two automata such that $\mathcal{L}(\mathcal{A}) = \mathcal{L}(\mathcal{B})$, then*

$$\min_1(\mathcal{A}) = \min_1(\mathcal{B}).$$

Practical Results. We apply the two sorted Hopcroft's algorithm on the automata families depicted in the section 5. The two-pass solution goes practically twice slower than

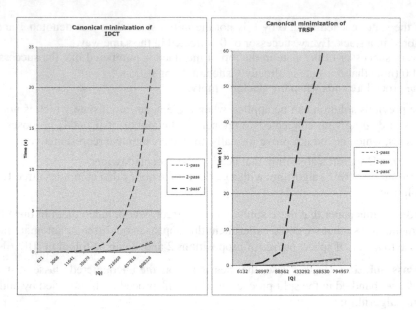

Fig. 4. Canonical Minimization

the one-pass solution if the initialization step is good. At the opposite, if the initialization is badly realized, the complexity of the one-pass solution increases a lot. These practical results are presented in Figure 4. Since the initialization step of the one-pass algorithm is too sensitive, the two-pass algorithm is included in the Dash library.

7 Conclusion

We have presented a detailed implementation of the Hopcroft's algorithm which is very efficient in practice. This implementation is being included in the Dash library. The way the set of splitters is handled is a crucial point for the efficiency and we studied two natural implementations. On very large scale experiments, we discover that the FILO strategy performs better and could lead to a minimization procedure that could be linear in the size of the automaton in the case of a one letter alphabet. In future works, we plan to find a proof of this belief.

In the second part of the paper, we investigate how the original algorithm can be modified in order to obtain a canonical minimal automaton associated to a rational language. Two solutions are proved correct and experimental results are depicted that show that, most of the time, one solution is better than the other.

References

[BBC92]   D. Beauquier, J. Berstel, and P. Chrétienne. *Éléments d'Algorithmique*. Masson, 1992.
[BC04]   J. Berstel and O. Carton.   On the complexity of Hopcroft's state minimization algorithm.   In *Proc. 9th Conference on Implementation and Application of Automata (CIAA'04)*, volume 3317 of *Lecture Notes in Computer Science*, pages 35–44. Springer, 2004.

[BP06]   M. Baclet and C. Pagetti. Around Hopcroft's Algorithm. Technical Report LSV-06-12, Laboratoire Spécification et Vérification, ENS de Cachan, France, 2006.

[BPP04]   M. Baclet, R. Pacalet, and A. Petit. Register transfer level simulation. Technical Report LSV-04-10, Laboratoire Spécification et Vérification, ENS de Cachan, France, 2004.

[Brz62]   J. A. Brzozowski. Canonical regular expressions and minimal state graphs for definite events. In *Mathematical Theory of Automata*, volume 12 of *MRI Symposia Series*, pages 529–561. Polytechnic Press, 1962.

[Cou04]   J.-M. Couvreur. A BDD-like implementation of an automata package. In *Proc. 9th International Conference on Implementation and Application of Automata (CIAA'04)*, volume 3317 of *Lecture Notes in Computer Science*, pages 310–311. Springer, 2004.

[Hop71]   J. E. Hopcroft. An $n \log n$ algorithm for minimizing the states in a finite automaton. In Z. Kohavi, editor, *The Theory of Machines and Computations*, pages 189–196. Academic Press, 1971.

[HU79]   J. E. Hopcroft and J. D. Ullman. *Introduction to Automata Theory, Languages, and Computation*. Addison-Wesley, 1979.

[KM01]   N. Klarlund and A. Møller. *MONA Version 1.4 User Manual*. BRICS Notes Series NS-01-1, Department of Computer Science, University of Aarhus, January 2001.

[Knu01]   T. Knuutila. Re-describing an algorithm by Hopcroft. *Theoretical Computer Science*, 250(1-2):333–363, 2001.

[MPR00]   M. Mohri, F. Pereira, and M. Riley. The design principles of a weighted finite-state transducer library. *Theoretical Computer Science*, 231(1):17–32, 2000.

[Ner58]   A. Nerode. Linear automaton transformation. In *Proc. American Mathematical Society*, volume 9, pages 541–544, 1958.

[PTB85]   R. Paige, R. E. Tarjan, and R. Bonic. A linear time solution to the single function coarsest partition problem. *Theoretical Computer Science*, 40:67–84, 1985.

[Wat95]   B. W. Watson. *Taxonomies and Toolkits of Regular Language Algorithms*. PhD thesis, Eindhoven University of Technology, the Netherlands, 1995.

[Wat01]   B. W. Watson. An incremental DFA minimization algorithm. In *Proc. 3rd International Workshop on Finite-State Methods and Natural Language Processing (FSMNLP'01)*, 2001.

[WD03]   B. W. Watson and J. Daciuk. An efficient incremental DFA minimization algorithm. *Natural Language Engineering*, 9(1):49–64, 2003.

Multi-tape Automata with Symbol Classes

F. Nicart[1,2], J.-M. Champarnaud[2], T. Csáki[3,4,*], T. Gaál[3], and A. Kempe[3]

[1] LLI–IRISA, ENSSAT, 6 rue de Kérampont, 22305 Lannion Cedex – France
nicart@enssat.fr
[2] LITIS (Université de Rouen), Avenue de l'Université,
76800 Saint Etienne du Rouvray – France
Jean-Marc.Champarnaud@univ-rouen.fr
[3] Xerox Research Centre Europe – Grenoble Laboratory, 6 chemin de Maupertuis,
38240 Meylan – France
{gaal, kempe}@xrce.xerox.com
[4] Department of Computer Science, Institute of Mathematics and Informatics
University of Debrecen, H-4010, Debrecen – Hungary
csakit@inf.unideb.hu

Abstract. We propose a new model of finite state machine: multi-tape automata with symbol classes and identity and non-identity constraints (in short *MASCIN*). This model generalizes both classical single or multi-tape machines, and machines with extended alphabet. We define this model in terms of a *constraint satisfaction problem* and discuss a problem occurring when projection is used on the model. Finally, we describe its implementation and results of a performance test.

1 Introduction

In this paper, we focus on various extensions of the transition labelling of finite state automata. The transitions of an automaton are usually labelled by the symbols of an alphabet. However, other possibilities have been investigated. For example, transitions are labelled by words in the generalized automata introduced by Eilenberg [2] or in the block automata [5], and by rational expressions in the expression automata [6]. The main interest of these types of labelling is essentially their compactness.

Labelling techniques of a different nature have been introduced in the eighties in order to take into account arbitrarily wide alphabets. This is of particular interest in computational linguistics, where it is common to use alphabets of words; this makes it necessary to efficiently handle large alphabets. The emergence of UniCode, bringing the coding of characters up to 21 bits, increases this need. The first solutions that appeared to handle large alphabets are based on the use of special transitions, called default transitions, or, in an equivalent way, on the introduction of a generic symbol inducing a default processing or a failure function [12].

---

* Supported by grant T049409 from the Hungarian Scientific Research Fund, OTKA and by UAC grant 1478-2004, Xerox Foundation, U.S.A.

O.H. Ibarra and H.-C. Yen (Eds.): CIAA 2006, LNCS 4094, pp. 126–136, 2006.
© Springer-Verlag Berlin Heidelberg 2006

The model of automata and transducers with extended alphabet [9,1], originally implemented [8] at Xerox PARC, is based on this notion of a generic symbol that allows the interpretation of the machine behaviour with respect to the (infinite) universal alphabet (the alphabet that contains all the possible symbols). The modeling and efficiency problems that this model can solve, in particular the introduction of identity and non-identity relations in the case of transducers (at XRCE), are described in [4]. This model has induced other generalizations, such as the model of automata and transducers with predicates [14].

The model that we are presenting here is a generalization of the labelling of automata and transducers with extended alphabet. It is based on the notion of symbol class and supports the use of any subset of the alphabet of the machine (or of the complement of such a subset with respect to the universal alphabet) as a label or as a component of a label. Moreover, it supports machines with n tapes and extends, in the case where $n \geq 2$, identity and non-identity handling introduced in transducers with extended alphabet, by augmenting each label with a set of binary identities or non-identities (applying to two classes that are components of the label). We show that the formalism of Constraint Satisfaction Problems (CSP) is suitable for describing such labels.

The next section gives some details of n-ary relations and multi-tape automata. Section 3 introduces symbol classes and multi-tape machines with symbol classes. Section 4 deals with identities and non-identities in the scope of multi-tape machines with symbol classes; the formalism of CSPs is introduced and the operation of projection is studied. Finally, the implementation of this model inside WFSC (Weighted Finite State Compiler [10]) as an extension of its weighted multi-tape machine model [11] and experimental results are described in Section 5.

2 Preliminaries

An *alphabet* Σ is a non-empty and, usually, finite set of symbols. A *word* of *length* m over an alphabet Σ is a sequence of m symbols of Σ, for example $u = \sigma_1 \sigma_2 \ldots \sigma_m$, $\sigma_i \in \Sigma$. We denote by $|u|$ the length of the word u. We call *empty word* the word of length 0, denoted by ε. A language is a subset of Σ^*. We denote by $\emptyset$ the empty language and by Σ_ε the set $\Sigma \cup \{\varepsilon\}$.

A n-*ary relation* R over the alphabets $\Sigma_1, \ldots, \Sigma_n$ is a subset of $\Sigma_1^* \times \cdots \times \Sigma_n^*$. The set of n-tuples $\langle u_1, \ldots, u_n \rangle$ belonging to R is the *graph* of the relation R. In the sequel, we will consider, without loss of generality, n-ary relations over a single alphabet Σ.

A n-ary relation is *rational* if it can be obtained by combining atomic relations, that is n-tuples of the set $\{\langle s_1, \ldots, s_n \rangle \in (\Sigma^*)^n \mid |s_i| \leq 1\}$, via the classical operations of union, concatenation and iteration. The n-ary rational relations are realized by finite state automata with n tapes.

Definition 1. *A finite state multi-tape machine of arity n is a 5-tuple $\mathcal{M} = \langle \Sigma, Q, E, I, F \rangle$ where Σ is a finite alphabet, Q is the finite set of states, $E \subseteq$*

$Q \times \Sigma_\varepsilon{}^n \times Q$ is the set of transitions, $I \subseteq Q$ is the set of initial states, and $F \subseteq Q$ is the set of final states.

Multi-tape machines generalize classical automata ($n=1$) and transducers ($n=2$). Let $e = \langle p, \ell, d \rangle$ be a transition of $\mathcal{M}$. The label $l(e)$ of e is a n-tuple of $\Sigma_\varepsilon{}^n$. A *path* γ from a state q to a state q' in $\mathcal{M}$ is a sequence $\gamma = e_1 e_2 \ldots e_k$ of transitions such that $p(e_1) = q$, $d(e_k) = q'$ and $\forall i \in [\![1, k-1]\!]$, $d(e_i) = p(e_{i+1})$. A path γ is *successful* if and only if $q \in I$ and $q' \in F$. The *label* $l(\gamma)$ of the path γ is the n-tuple $l(\gamma) = l(e_1)l(e_2)\ldots l(e_k)$ of $(\Sigma^*)^n$. A n-tuple $w \in (\Sigma^*)^n$ is *recognized* by the machine $\mathcal{M}$ if there exists a path labelled by w in $\mathcal{M}$.

3   Machines with Symbol Classes

Machines with extended alphabet have been designed in the 1980s at the Xerox Palo Alto Research Center (PARC) [8] with the purpose of developing applications supporting arbitrarily large alphabets. Such a machine defines a language or a relation over a (possibly infinite) super-alphabet Ω. Its alphabet Σ is finite and contains a special symbol called $OTHER$ (denoted by ?) that represents the set of symbols $\Omega \setminus \Sigma$. Transitions are labelled as usual. However, in the case of transducers, two special labels have been added to allow the representation of the identity relation $\langle ?_i, ?_i \rangle$ and the non-identity relation $\langle ?, ? \rangle$, with regard to ? [3]. The language (resp. relation) over Ω can be obtained from the language (resp. relation) over the alphabet Σ of an automaton (resp. transducer) with extended alphabet thanks to a morphism. A formal definition of these machines has been given in [4].

We present here a model that leads to a generalization of the labelling of automata and transducers with extended alphabet [13]. This model is based on the notion of *symbol class*, close to the notion of *character class* in UNIX's, and makes it possible to use any subset of the alphabet, or its complement, as a label or label component. This model also generalizes multi-tape machines. We look into the properties of this type of labelling, and then deduce the definition of a machine with symbol classes.

3.1   Symbol Classes

Definition 2. *Let Ω be the universal alphabet. We call symbol class any finite or cofinite subset C_i of Ω. Let Σ be a finite subset of Ω. The set $\mathcal{C}_\Sigma$ of symbol classes over Σ is defined by*

$$\mathcal{C}_\Sigma = \{ C_i \subseteq \Omega \mid C_i \subseteq \Sigma \vee \overline{C_i} \subseteq \Sigma \} \tag{1}$$

where $\overline{C_i}$ is the complement of C_i with respect to Ω.

Property 1. *For every finite subset $\Sigma \subset \Omega$, the set $\mathcal{C}_\Sigma$ of symbol classes over Σ is finite: $|\mathcal{C}_\Sigma| = 2^{|\Sigma|+1}$.*

Proposition 1. *The set C_Σ of symbol classes defined over a subset Σ of Ω is closed by union, intersection and complementation and by every operation (such as difference) that can be expressed as a combination of these operations.*

Proof. By definition, the complement (with respect to Ω) of a finite class is cofinite. In addition, a cofinite class C_i over Σ can be described under the form $C_i = C_i' \cup \overline{\Sigma}$ where C_i' is the finite class $\Sigma \setminus \overline{C_i}$.

Let C_1 and C_2 be two classes over Σ. The finite case is obvious: $C_1 \cup C_2$ and $C_1 \cap C_2$ are two finite classes. Let us assume that C_1 and C_2 are cofinite. Then we have $C_1 = C_1' \cup \overline{\Sigma}$ and $C_2 = C_2' \cup \overline{\Sigma}$, where C_1' and C_2' are two finite classes over Σ. We get

$$C_1 \cup C_2 = (C_1' \cup C_2') \cup \overline{\Sigma} \text{ and } C_1 \cap C_2 = (C_1' \cap C_2') \cup \overline{\Sigma}$$

thus $C_1 \cup C_2$ and $C_1 \cap C_2$ are two cofinite classes.

Let us assume now that C_1 is finite and C_2 is cofinite, with $C_2 = C_2' \cup \overline{\Sigma}$. We have

$$C_1 \cup C_2 = (C_1 \cup C_2') \cup \overline{\Sigma} \text{ and } C_1 \cap C_2 = (C_1 \cap C_2')$$

As a consequence, $C_1 \cup C_2$ is a cofinite class and $C_1 \cap C_2$ is a finite class.   □

Let $\langle C_\Sigma^*, \cdot, \varepsilon \rangle$ be the free monoid[1] defined over C_Σ. We call a *word of classes* any finite sequence $C_1 C_2 \ldots C_n$ with $\forall i \in [\![1, n]\!], C_i \in C_\Sigma$ and we call a *language of classes* any subset of C_Σ^*. The evaluation over Ω of a word of classes is a subset of Ω^* calculated according to the morphism of monoids $\lambda : \langle C_\Sigma^*, \cdot, \varepsilon \rangle \to \langle 2^{\Omega^*}, \cdot, \{\varepsilon\} \rangle$ defined by:

$$\lambda(\varepsilon) = \{\varepsilon\}; \forall C_i, C_j \in C_\Sigma, \ \lambda(C_i) = C_i, \lambda(C_i \cdot C_j) = \lambda(C_i) \cdot \lambda(C_j)$$

The evaluation over Ω of the language of classes L is defined by:

$$\forall L \subseteq C_\Sigma^*, \ \lambda(L) = \bigcup_{u \in L} \lambda(u) \tag{2}$$

Property 2. *The evaluation over Ω of a word of classes u is either the empty set or a language made of words having the same length as u: $\forall u \in C_\Sigma^*, \lambda(u) \neq \emptyset \Rightarrow \forall v \in \lambda(u), |v| = |u|$.*

The cardinality of the language generated over Ω by a word of classes is equal to the product of the cardinalities of the classes it is made of: $\forall u = C_1 C_2 \ldots C_n \in C_\Sigma, |\lambda(u)| = \prod_{i=1}^{n} |C_i|$. The cardinality $|\lambda(u)|$ is infinite if at least one of the classes is cofinite, and zero if at least one of the classes is the empty set.

3.2 Multi-tape Automata with Symbol Classes

Definition 3. *A multi-tape automaton with symbol classes (MASC) $\mathcal{A}^{(n)}$, with arity n, is an automaton whose transitions are labelled with n-tuples of symbol classes. It is a 6-tuple $\mathcal{A} = \langle \Sigma, C, Q, E, I, F \rangle$ where Σ is a finite alphabet, $C \subset C_\Sigma$ is a finite set of symbol classes over Σ, and $E \subset Q \times (C \cup \{\varepsilon\})^n \times Q$ is the set of transitions.*

---

[1] The empty set is assumed to be a symbol with no particular properties.

Figure 1 illustrates the efficiency of modeling by an automaton with symbol classes with respect to an automaton with extended alphabet.

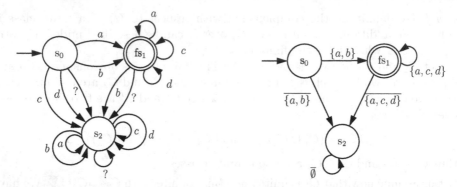

(a) A complete automaton with extended alphabet $\mathcal{A}$ (The ? means $\Omega \backslash \Sigma = \overline{\{a, b, c, d\}}$)

(b) A complete automaton with symbol classes $\mathcal{A}'$ equivalent to $\mathcal{A}$

Fig. 1. Illustration of the efficiency of modeling by automata with symbol classes

4   Machines with Symbol Classes, Identities and Non–identities

We now propose an extension to the identity and non–identity labels of the transducers with extended alphabet, and we define multi-tape automata with symbol classes, identities and non–identities ($MASCIN$). In order to make the implementation more efficient, we use binary relations that are either an identity relation between two classes, denoted by id_{C_i, C_j}, or a non–identity relation, denoted by nid_{C_i, C_j}.

The formalism of Constraint Satisfaction Problems (CSP) [7] is very convenient for the description of labels of a $MASCIN$. Indeed, a CSP is given by a set X of variables each defined over a discrete (and usually finite) domain, and by a set T of constraints, each applying on a subset of variables. Thus, the label of any transition of a $MASCIN$ is a CSP whose set of solutions is the evaluation over Ω of the label.

We recall some definitions concerning CSPs in order to enlighten the link with the labelling of $MASCIN$s. In particular, we express the elementary properties of the labelling based on identities and non–identities in terms of a CSP problem. Finally, we investigate the properties of the projection operation.

4.1   Constraint Satisfaction Problems

Definition 4. *A Constraint Satisfaction Problem (CSP), $\mathcal{P} = \langle X, \mathcal{D}, T \rangle$, is defined by a set of n variables $X = \{x_1, \ldots, x_n\}$, the set $\mathcal{D} = \{C_1, \ldots, C_n\}$ of their domains and a set of constraints $T = \{t_1, \ldots, t_m\}$ that each apply over a subset of variables.*

The subset of variables involved by a constraint t is denoted by $var(t)$. We also denote by $var(U)$ the subset of variables concerned by the constraints of U, with $U \subseteq T$. Each constraint defines a subset of the cross-product of the concerned variable domains.

A *total assignment* is obtained by instantiating every variable by a value of its domain. We denote it by $A = \{\langle x_1, v_1 \rangle, \ldots \langle x_n, v_n \rangle\}$, or more simply by $A = \langle v_1, \ldots, v_n \rangle$. A *partial* assignment instantiates a subset of variables.

Let t be a constraint and A be an assignment that instantiates every variable of $var(t)$. We say that $t(A)$ is true if A satisfies the constraint t. An assignment is *consistent* if $t(A)$ is true for every $t \in T$. A total and consistent assignment is a *solution* of the CSP. The set of solutions, denoted by $CSP(X, \mathcal{D}, T)$, is the graph of the n-ary relation $\mathcal{R}$ defined over the sets $C_1, C_2, \ldots, C_n$ by the set of constraints T and denoted $\langle \mathcal{D}, T \rangle$. Two CSPs are equivalent if they admit the same set of solutions.

A *binary* constraint applies over a subset of two variables. Among the binary constraints, we distinguish the *equality constraints*, of the form $(x_i = x_j)$, and the *disequality constraints*, of the form $(x_i \neq x_j)$. Theses two types of binary constraints are referred to as *equi-constraints*. We call $ECSP$ a CSP having only equi-constraints and we call *equi-constraint relation* the relation defined by a $ECSP$. A CSP without any constraint is a particular case of $ECSP$.

Proposition 2. *Let* $\mathcal{P} = \langle X, \mathcal{D}, T \rangle$ *be a* $ECSP$.

1. *We set* $T_1 = T \cup \{(x_j = x_k) \mid \exists i, (x_i = x_j) \in T \wedge (x_i = x_k) \in T\}$ *and* $\mathcal{P}_1 = \langle X, \mathcal{D}, T_1 \rangle$. *The* $ECSP$ $\mathcal{P}$ *and* $\mathcal{P}_1$ *are equivalent.*
2. *Let us set* $T_2 = T_1 \cup \{(x_j \neq x_k) \mid \exists i, (x_i = x_j) \in T_1 \wedge (x_i \neq x_k) \in T_1\}$ *and* $\mathcal{P}_2 = \langle X, \mathcal{D}, T_2 \rangle$. *The* $ECSP$ $\mathcal{P}$ *and* $\mathcal{P}_2$ *are equivalent.*
3. *The equality relation in* X *determines a partition of* X. *Let* $[x_i]$ *be the class of* x_i. *Let us set* $C_i' = \bigcap_{x_k \in [x_i]} C_k$ *and let* $\mathcal{D}'$ *be the set of domains* C_i'. *Let us consider the problem* $\mathcal{P}' = \langle X, \mathcal{D}', T \rangle$. *The* $ECSP$ $\mathcal{P}$ *and* $\mathcal{P}'$ *are equivalent.*

Proof. The proof is straightforward: 1. is directly deduced from the transitivity of the equality in X; 2. comes from the fact that $(x_i = x_j \wedge x_i \neq x_k) \Rightarrow x_j \neq x_k$; 3. is a consequence of the fact that every variable of a same class is involved in the same set of constraints.   □

In the sequel, we will say that $\mathcal{P}_2$ is the *normalized* form of $\mathcal{P}$ and that $\mathcal{P}'$ is the *reduced* form of $\mathcal{P}$. Proposition 2 can be illustrated over the undirected graph $\mathcal{G} = \langle X, E \cup D \rangle$ associated to $\mathcal{P}$. Every edge represents a constraint of T:

$$(x_i, x_j) \in E \Leftrightarrow (x_i = x_j) \in T \tag{3}$$
$$(x_i, x_j) \in D \Leftrightarrow (x_i \neq x_j) \in T$$

Figure 2 shows the graph $\mathcal{G}$ of a problem $\mathcal{P}$ that is partitioned into two classes and the graph $\mathcal{G}_1$ of the equivalent problem $\mathcal{P}_1$. The graph $\mathcal{G}_1$ is the transitive closure of $\mathcal{G}$. Each component of $\mathcal{G}$ is transformed into a clique in $\mathcal{G}'$. Figure 3(a) represents the graph of a problem $\mathcal{P}$ partitioned into four classes. Figure 3(b) represents the graph of the problem $\mathcal{P}_2$ equivalent to $\mathcal{P}$.

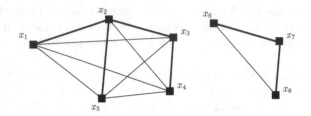

Fig. 2. The graph of a $ECSP$ (bold edges) and the graph of its transitive closure (all edges)

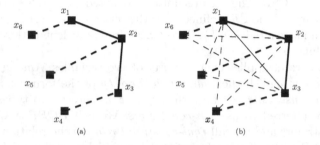

Fig. 3. The graph of a $ECSP$ (equality edges in bold, disequality edges in dashed bold) and its normalized graph (equality edges in solid, disequality edges in dashed)

4.2 Multi-tape Automata with Symbol Classes, Identities and Non–identities

Let $\mathcal{A}$ be a $MASC$ with n tapes. Let e be a transition of $\mathcal{A}$ and $l(e)$ be its label. We have: $l(e) = \langle C_1, \ldots, C_n \rangle$, with, for all $i \in [\![1, n]\!]$, $C_i \in \mathcal{C}_{\Sigma} \cup \{\varepsilon\}$. For all $i \in [\![1, n]\!]$ we consider a variable x_i whose domain is C_i. Let X be the set of variables and $\mathcal{D}$ be the set of domains. It is clear that the label $l(e) = \langle C_1, \ldots, C_n \rangle$ is equivalent to the problem $ECSP$ $\langle X, \mathcal{D}, \emptyset \rangle$. In addition, the evaluation $\lambda(l(e))$ of $l(e)$ over Ω is equal to the set of solutions of this $ECSP$.

In the case where there exist some disequality binary constraints between the variables, the number of transitions can be decreased by turning $\mathcal{A}$ into an automaton with identities and non-identities. This can be achieved by equipping each label with a set T of identity or non–identity relations over the classes involved by the label.

An identity id_{C_i,C_j} (resp. a non-identity nid_{C_i,C_j}) is a binary equality constraint $x_i = x_j$ (resp. a binary disequality constraint $x_i \neq x_j$). As a consequence, for all transitions e of a $MASCIN$, the label $l(e) = \langle \langle C_1, \ldots, C_n \rangle, T \rangle$ is equal to the $ECSP$ $\langle X, \mathcal{D}, T \rangle$. In addition the evaluation $\lambda(l(e))$ of $l(e)$ over Ω is equal to the set of solutions of this $ECSP$.

Definition 5. *A multi-tape automaton with symbol classes, identities and non–identities is an automaton in which every transition is labelled by a CSP having only equality or disequality binary constraints.*

4.3   Projection of an Equi-constrained n-ary Relation

Let $\mathcal{R}$ be an n-ary relation over the sets $C_1, \ldots, C_n$. We consider the case of the projection of $\mathcal{R}$ with the suppression of one tape (called *single* projection in the following). In order to simplify notation, and without any loss of generality, we assume that the tape that is removed is the n-th tape and we denote this projection by $\pi(\mathcal{R})$.

By definition:

$$\pi(\mathcal{R}) = \{\langle x_1, \ldots, x_{n-1} \rangle \mid \exists x_n \in C_n, \ \langle x_1, \ldots, x_n \rangle \in \mathcal{R}\} \tag{4}$$

Let us suppose that $\mathcal{R}$ is an equi-constrained relation, i.e. $\mathcal{R} = \langle \mathcal{D}, T \rangle$ where T is a set of equality or disequality constraints. The projection $\pi(\mathcal{R})$ is a relation over the domains $C_1, \ldots, C_{n-1}$; let $\mathcal{D}'$ be the set of these domains.

We show that $\pi(\mathcal{R})$ is not necessarily an equi-constrained relation over $\mathcal{D}'$ and we investigate a set of sufficient conditions such that this property holds. In the following, we assume that the $ECSP$ associated to $\mathcal{R}$ is in normalized and reduced form.

Proposition 3. *Let us consider the equi-constrained relation* $\mathcal{R}' = \langle \mathcal{D}', T \setminus T_n \rangle$, *where* T_n *is the set of constraints of* T *that involve the tape* n. *Then we have:*

1. $\pi(\mathcal{R}) \subseteq \mathcal{R}'$,
2. *A necessary and sufficient condition for* $\pi(\mathcal{R})$ *to be strictly included in* $\mathcal{R}'$ *is that there exists a partial assignment* $\langle x_1, \ldots, x_{n-1} \rangle$ *that satisfies every constraint of* $T \setminus T_n$ *and such that, for all* $x_n \in C_n$, *there exists at least one constraint of* T_n *that is not satisfied by the assignment* $\langle x_1, \ldots, x_n \rangle$.

Proof. Let $T' = T \setminus T_n$. We have $var(T') = X \setminus \{x_n\}$. Since $T' \subseteq T$ we have $\mathcal{R} = \langle \mathcal{D}, T \rangle \subseteq \langle \mathcal{D}, T' \rangle$. In addition, as $var(T') = X \setminus \{x_n\}$, we have $\pi(\langle \mathcal{D}, T' \rangle) = \langle \mathcal{D}', T' \rangle = \mathcal{R}'$. Finally, we have $\pi(\mathcal{R}) \subseteq \mathcal{R}'$.

Proposition 3.2 comes directly from the equivalence $\langle x_1, \ldots, x_{n-1} \rangle \notin \pi(\mathcal{R}) \Leftrightarrow \forall x_n \in C_n, \langle x_1, \ldots, x_n \rangle \notin \mathcal{R}$. □

Corollary 4. *If* T *contains an equality relation* $x_i = x_n$, *then* $\pi(\mathcal{R}) = \mathcal{R}'$.

Proof. Let us recall that the $ECSP$ associated to $\mathcal{R}$ is under normalized form. Due to Proposition 2, for every constraint involving the tapes k and n there exists a constraint of the same type between the tapes i and n. As a consequence, every assignment $\langle x_1, \ldots, x_n \rangle$ such that $\langle x_1, \ldots, x_{n-1} \rangle$ satisfies the constraints of $T \setminus T_n$ satisfies the constraints of T. □

Thus, in the following, we will consider only disequality constraints.

Example 1. *This example illustrates the fact that* $\pi(\mathcal{R})$ *is not necessarily equi-constrained. We take* $C_1 = \{a, b, c\}$, $C_2 = \{a, b, d\}$, $C_3 = \{a, b\}$ *and* $T = \{(x_1 \neq x_3), (x_2 \neq x_3)\}$. *Thus we have:* $\pi(\mathcal{R}) = (C_1 \times C_2) \setminus \{\langle a, b \rangle, \langle b, a \rangle\}$. *It is clear that* $\pi(\mathcal{R})$ *is equal to none of the three equi-constrained relations on* C_1 *and* C_2: $C_1 \times C_2$, id_{C_1, C_2} *and* nid_{C_1, C_2}.

When $\pi(\mathcal{R}) = \mathcal{R}'$, it is possible to merely delete the tape n, which provides an efficient implementation of the projection. Among the simple criteria that allow one to determine that $\pi(\mathcal{R}) = \mathcal{R}'$, let us cite:

1. There exists an equality relation $(x_i = x_n)$ in T.
2. The condition $|C_n| > |T_n|$ is satisfied.
3. The condition $D = C_n \setminus \bigcup_{(x_j \neq x_n) \in T} C_j \neq \emptyset$ is verified.

5   Implementation and Experimental Results

5.1   Implementation

In the regular expression notation of WFSC [10], classes are written as sequences of atoms and ranges. For example, the class [ac-hn-p'VERB''NOUN'], consists of the atoms a, c to h, n to p, VERB, and NOUN. The complement of this class is written as [^ac-hn-p'VERB''NOUN']. A tuple of classes with constraints is written in the following style: for example, the triple [a-p]:[^b-e]:m{1=2,1~3} consists of a class [a-p] on tape 1, a class [^b-e] on tape 2, and the atomic symbol m on tape 3. There is an identity constraint between tapes 1 and 2, and a non-identity constraint between tapes 1 and 3.

In the internal encoding of WFSC, each transition of a machine carries a symbolic identifier, ID in the following, referring to its label. Labels and their components are referred to by an ID and are defined in a symbol table. An atomic label is stored in the symbol table with its ID and its value (e.g., $\langle 70201, "VERB"\rangle$). A complex label is stored with its own ID and the vector of the IDs of its n components: $\langle \text{ID}, \langle \text{ID}_1, \dots \text{ID}_n\rangle\rangle$. For a symbol class, each ID_i (with $i \in [\![1, n]\!]$) defines a range, such as a-h, or an atom, such as g or VERB; in addition, we need to store whether the class is the union of all its components, or the complement of this union. For a tuple of classes, each ID_i (with $i \in [\![1, n]\!]$) defines a symbol class; if there are constraints between these classes, then those are defined in a $(n \times n)$-matrix M which is appended to the tuple definition in the symbol table. Each element of M defines the constraint between two classes and can have the values *identity*, *non-identity*, or *unconstrained*.

In order to avoid multiple definition and to allow fast label comparison, a canonization is performed on any label added into the table by constructing the transitive closure among its constraints and removing from its classes all letters that, due to constraints, cannot occur. For example, the canonical form of [a-p]:[^b-e]{1=2} is [af-p]:[af-p]{1=2} and the canonical form of [a-p]:[^b-e]:m{1=2,1~3} is [af-ln-p]:[^af-ln-p]:m{1=2}.

5.2   Experimental Results

The use of symbol classes is advantageaus regarding memory usage and running time. We tested some cases[2] where an ordinary transducer was trans-

---

[2] Due to space limitation, we are reporting a composition test only here. Composition allows the creation of cascades of filters; this is customary in NLP. Moreover, composition is in membership tests, too.

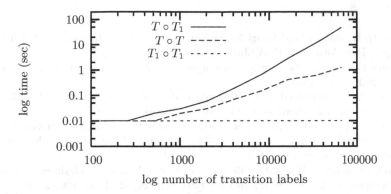

Fig. 4. Time of composition with (T_1) or without (T) symbol classes. The number of transitions of T is on the x axis whereas it is just *one* in T_1—but it represents exactly the corresponding labels (and transitions) of T!

formed into an equivalent $MASCIN$. In this composition test 128, 256, ..., 65536 labels in T were replaced, successively, by equivalent symbol classes in T_1. The relative storage gain is obvious: in the last case, the basic UniCode range (BMP, Basic Multilingual plane), represented on 65536 transitions (as a:a, b:b etc.) in T, was represented by a *single* transition in T_1, labelled by [\u0000-\uffff]:[\u0000-\uffff]{1=2}. The relative *time* of $T \circ T$, $T \circ T_1$ and $T_1 \circ T_1$ was measured (see Figure 4). The time complexity of the operation reduces to a (small) constant in the $T_1 \circ T_1$ case.

In our experiments, we noted efficiency improvement when symbol classes were applicable. We identified some classes of tasks where $MASCIN$s can be used successfully. We consider the enhanced modelling power even more important.

6   Conclusion

The model of multi-tape automata with symbol classes, identities and non–identities is a generic model for a wide class of finite state machines: a 1-tape automaton is a single tape $MASC$ labelled with singletons, a n-tape automaton ($n \geq 2$) is a n-tape $MASC$ labeled by CSPs of arity n whose domains are singletons, an automaton with extended alphabet is a single-tape $MASC$ labelled with singletons or with the class that is the complement of the alphabet, and a transducer with extended alphabet is a two-tape $MASCIN$ labelled with CSPs of arity 2. Moreover, this model generalizes the model of automata and transducers with extended alphabet in two ways: on the one hand, it supports n-tape machines, and on the other hand, it makes it possible to use any subset of the alphabet Σ, or its complement, as a label or as a label component. Thanks to this property, this model is a very good candidate for the development of algorithms in a very general framework: finite or infinite alphabet, 1, 2 or n tapes, handling of identities and non–identities. In applications, $MASCIN$s may yield efficiency improvements.

References

1. Kenneth R. Beesley and Lauri Karttunen. *Finite State Morphology*. CSLI Publications, Palo Alto, CA, USA, June 2003.
2. Samuel Eilenberg. *Automata, Languages, and Machines*, volume A. Academic Press, San Diego, 1974.
3. Tamás Gaál. Extended sequentializaton of transducers. pages 569–585, 1999. Publicationes Mathematicae Debrecen, Supplement 60 (2002).
4. Tamás Gaál, Franck Guingne, and Florent Nicart. *OTHER* extension to finite state automata. volume 65, pages 535–552, 2002. Publicationes Mathematicae Debrecen, Supplement 65 (2005).
5. Dora Giammarresi, Rosa Montalbano, and Derick Wood. Block-deterministic regular languages. *Lecture Notes in Computer Science*, 2202:184–196, 2001.
6. Yo-Sub Han and Derick Wood. The generalization of generalized automata: Expression automata. *Lecture Notes in Computer Science*, 3317:156–166, 2004.
7. Pascal Van Hentenryck. *Constraint satisfaction in logic programming*. MIT Press, Cambridge, MA, USA, 1989.
8. Ronald M. Kaplan and Martin Kay. Regular models of phonological rule systems. *Computational Linguistics*, 20(3):331–378, 1994.
9. Lauri Karttunen. The replace operator. In *Proceedings of the 33rd Annual Meeting of the Association for Computational Linguistics*, pages 16–23, Boston, Massachusetts, 1995.
10. André Kempe, Christof Baeijs, Tamás Gaál, Franck Guingne, and Florent Nicart. WFSC - a new weighted finite state compiler. *Lecture Notes in Computer Science*, 2759:108–119, 2003.
11. André Kempe, Jean-Marc Champarnaud, Jason Eisner, Franck Guingne, and Florent Nicart. A class of rational n-wfsm auto-intersections. *Lecture Notes in Computer Science*, 3845:188–198, 2005.
12. Kimmo Koskenniemi. *Two-level Morphology: A General Computational Model for Word-Form Recognition and Production*. 1983. PhD thesis at the University of Helsinki, Department of General Linguistics.
13. Florent Nicart. *Conception de modèles génériques pour les machines à états finis*. 2005. Thèse de doctorat de l'Université de Rouen.
14. Gertjan van Noord and Dale Gerdemann. Finite state transducers with predicates and identities. *Grammars*, 4(3):263–286, 2001.

On the Computation of Some Standard Distances Between Probabilistic Automata

Corinna Cortes[1], Mehryar Mohri[1,2,*], and Ashish Rastogi[2]

[1] Google Research,
1440 Broadway, New York, NY 10018
[2] Courant Institute of Mathematical Sciences,
251 Mercer Street, New York, NY 10012

Abstract. The problem of the computation of a distance between two probabilistic automata arises in a variety of statistical learning problems. This paper presents an exhaustive analysis of the problem of computing the L_p distance between two automata. We give efficient exact and approximate algorithms for computing these distances for p even and prove the problem to be NP-hard for all odd values of p, thereby completing previously known hardness results. We also give an efficient algorithm for computing the Hellinger distance between unambiguous probabilistic automata. Our results include a general algorithm for the computation of the norm of an unambiguous probabilistic automaton based on a monoid morphism and efficient algorithms for the specific case of the computation of the L_p norm. Finally, we also describe an efficient algorithm for testing the equivalence of two arbitrary probabilistic automata A_1 and A_2 based on Schützenberger's standardization with a running time complexity of $O(|\Sigma|\,(|A_1| + |A_2|)^3)$, a significant improvement over the previously best algorithm reported for this problem.

1 Introduction

A probabilistic automaton is a finite automaton with transition probabilities. It represents a probability distribution over the set of all strings [14]. Probabilistic automata are used extensively in a variety of areas, including text and speech processing [11], image processing [5], and computational biology [6].

These automata are typically derived from large data sets using statistical learning algorithms. The convergence of these algorithms is often tested by measuring the distance between the probabilistic automata obtained after consecutive iterations. The computation of the distance between probabilistic automata is also needed in other learning problems such as clustering when the objects to cluster, e.g., documents, images, biosequences, are modeled as Hidden Markov Models (HMMs) or probabilistic automata.

This motivates our study of the computation of various distances between probabilistic automata. We have previously shown that the relative entropy,

---

* This work was partially funded by the New York State Office of Science Technology and Academic Research (NYSTAR).

O.H. Ibarra and H.-C. Yen (Eds.): CIAA 2006, LNCS 4094, pp. 137–149, 2006.

or Kullback-Leibler divergence, of unambiguous probabilistic automata can be computed efficiently [4] and that, in the general case of arbitrary probabilistic automata, the computational cost is at least $O(c^{\sqrt{n/\log n}})$, where c is a constant and n the size of the automaton [3].

Here, we present an exhaustive analysis of the problem of computing the L_p distance between two automata. We give efficient exact and approximate algorithms for computing these distances for p even and prove that the problem is NP-hard for all odd values of p using a reduction from the Max-clique problem by [15]. These latter results complete those given by [15] who showed the problem to be NP-hard for L_1 and L_∞. We also give an algorithm for computing the Hellinger distance between unambiguous probabilistic automata. In addition, we present a general algorithm for the computation of the norm of an unambiguous probabilistic automaton using a monoid morphism and give efficient algorithms for the specific case of the computation of the L_p norm.

A problem closely related to that of computing a distance between two probabilistic automata is to test for their equivalence. Our algorithm for computing the L_2 distance of two arbitrary probabilistic automata A_1 and A_2 provides in fact a polynomial-time method for testing their equivalence since A_1 and A_2 are equivalent iff their L_2 distance is null. However, we will describe a more efficient algorithm based on Schützenberger's standardization technique [17,1] with a running-time complexity of $O(|\Sigma|\,(|A_1| + |A_2|)^3)$, a significant improvement over the previously best algorithm reported for this problem whose complexity is $O(|\Sigma|\,(|A_1| + |A_2|)^4))$ [19].

The remainder of the paper is organized as follows. Section 2 introduces some basic algebraic definitions and notation related to probabilistic automata needed for the description of our algorithms. Section 3 presents several algorithms for the computation of the norm of a probabilistic automaton, including an approximate solution. The problem of the computation of the L_p distance and Hellinger distance is examined in detail in Section 4.

2   Preliminaries

Definition 1. *Let* $(\mathbb{K}, \otimes, \overline{1})$ *be a monoid. A function* $\Phi : (\mathbb{R}_+, \cdot, 1) \to (\mathbb{K}, \otimes, \overline{1})$ *is said to be a* monoid morphism *if* $\Phi(1) = \overline{1}$, $\Phi(0) = \overline{0}$, *and* $\Phi(x \cdot y) = \Phi(x) \otimes \Phi(y)$ *for all* $x, y, \in \mathbb{R}_+$.

Definition 2 ([10]). *A semiring is a system* $(\mathbb{K}, \oplus, \otimes, \overline{0}, \overline{1})$ *such that:* $(\mathbb{K}, \oplus, \overline{0})$ *is a commutative monoid with* $\overline{0}$ *as the identity element for* $\oplus$; $(\mathbb{K}, \otimes, \overline{1})$ *is a monoid with* $\overline{1}$ *as the identity element for* $\otimes$; $\otimes$ *distributes over* $\oplus$: *for all* a, b, c *in* $\mathbb{K}$: $(a \oplus b) \otimes c = (a \otimes c) \oplus (b \otimes c)$ *and* $c \otimes (a \oplus b) = (c \otimes a) \oplus (c \otimes b)$, *and* $\overline{0}$ *is an annihilator for* $\otimes$: $\forall a \in \mathbb{K}, a \otimes \overline{0} = \overline{0} \otimes a = \overline{0}$.

A semiring $\mathbb{K}$ is said to be *closed* if for all $a \in \mathbb{K}$, the infinite sum $\bigoplus_{n=0}^{\infty} a^n$ is well-defined and in $\mathbb{K}$, and if associativity, commutativity, and distributivity apply to countable sums [13]. $\mathbb{K}$ is said to be k-*closed* if for all $a \in \mathbb{K}$, $\bigoplus_{n=0}^{k+1} a^n = \bigoplus_{n=0}^{k} a^n$. More generally, we will say that $\mathbb{K}$ is *closed (k-closed) for an automaton*

A, if the closedness (resp. k-closedness) axioms hold for all cycle weights of A. In some semirings, e.g., the probability semiring $(\mathbb{R}_+, +, \cdot, 0, 1)$, the equality $\bigoplus_{n=0}^{k+1} a^n = \bigoplus_{n=0}^{k} a^n$ may hold for the cycle weights of A only approximately, modulo $\epsilon > 0$. A is then said to be ϵ-k-*closed* for that semiring.

Definition 3 ([7,16,1]). *A weighted automaton $A = (\Sigma, Q, I, F, E, \lambda, \rho)$ over a semiring $(\mathbb{K}, \oplus, \otimes, \overline{0}, \overline{1})$ is a 7-tuple where: Σ is the finite alphabet of the automaton, Q is a finite set of states, $I \subseteq Q$ the set of initial states, $F \subseteq Q$ the set of final states, $E \subseteq Q \times \Sigma \cup \{\epsilon\} \times \mathbb{K} \times Q$ a finite set of transitions, $\lambda : I \to \mathbb{K}$ the initial weight function mapping I to $\mathbb{K}$, and $\rho : F \to \mathbb{K}$ the final weight function mapping F to $\mathbb{K}$.*

Stochastic automata are probabilistic automata such that at each state the weights of the outgoing transitions and the final weight sum to one.

We denote by $|A| = |E| + |Q|$ the size of an automaton $A = (\Sigma, Q, I, F, E, \lambda, \rho)$, that is the sum of the number of states and transitions of A. Given a transition $e \in E$, we denote by $i[e]$ its input label, $p[e]$ its origin or previous state and $n[e]$ its destination state or next state, $w[e]$ its weight (weighted automata case). Given a state $q \in Q$, we denote by $E[q]$ the set of transitions leaving q.

A *path* $\pi = e_1 \cdots e_k$ in A is an element of E^* with consecutive transitions: $n[e_{i-1}] = p[e_i]$, $i = 2, \ldots, k$. We extend n and p to paths by setting: $n[\pi] = n[e_k]$ and $p[\pi] = p[e_1]$. We denote by $P(q, q')$ the set of paths from q to q' and by $P(q, x, q')$ the set of paths from q to q' with input label $x \in \Sigma^*$. The labeling functions i and the weight function w can also be extended to paths by defining the label of a path as the concatenation of the labels of its constituent transitions, and the weight of a path as the $\otimes$-product of the weights of its constituent transitions: $i[\pi] = i[e_1] \cdots i[e_k]$, $w[\pi] = w[e_1] \otimes \cdots \otimes w[e_k]$.

The output weight associated by an automaton A to an input string $x \in \Sigma^*$ is defined by:

$$[\![A]\!](x) = \bigoplus_{\pi \in P(I, x, F)} \lambda[p[\pi]] \otimes w[\pi] \otimes \rho[n[\pi]]. \tag{1}$$

Definition 4. *A weighted automaton A defined over the probability semiring $(\mathbb{R}_+, +, \cdot, 0, 1)$ is said to be* probabilistic *if for any state $q \in Q$, $\sum_{\pi \in P(q,q)} w[\pi]$, the sum of the weights of all cycles at q, is well-defined and in $\mathbb{R}$, and the weights assigned to the all strings sums to one: $\sum_{x \in \Sigma^*} [\![A]\!](x) = 1$.*

A weighted automaton is said to be *unambiguous* if for any string $x \in \Sigma^*$ it admits at most one accepting path labeled with x. It is said to be *deterministic* or *subsequential* if it has a unique initial state and if no two transitions leaving the same state share the same input label.

3 Computation of the Norm of a Probabilistic Automaton

The computation of single-source shortest-distances is needed in many of the algorithms presented in this section and the following ones. We denote by $s[A]$

the $\oplus$-sum of the weights of all successful paths of a weighted automaton A when it is defined and in $\mathbb{K}$. $s[A]$ can be viewed as the *shortest-distance* from the initial states to the final states.

When the semiring $\mathbb{K}$ is closed, or when A is closed for $\mathbb{K}$, $s[A]$ can be computed exactly using a generalization of the Floyd-Warshall algorithm in time $O(|A|^3)$ and space $\Omega(|A|^2)$, assuming a constant cost for the semiring operations [13].

3.1 Case of Unambiguous Automata

In previous work, we gave a general algorithm for computing the entropy of a probabilistic automaton by relating this problem to a shortest-distance one [4]. Here, we generalize these results by considering an arbitrary monoid morphism.

Let $(\mathbb{K}, \oplus, \otimes, \overline{0}, \overline{1})$ be a closed, or ϵ-k-closed semiring. Let $\Phi : (\mathbb{R}_+, \cdot, 1) \to (\mathbb{K}, \otimes, \overline{1})$ be a monoid morphism. We will say that Φ *preserves closedness*, if for all x, $0 \leq x < 1$, $\bigoplus_{n=0}^{\infty} \Phi(x^n)$ is well-defined and in $\mathbb{K}$. For a such a morphism, we can define the Φ-norm *of a probabilistic automaton* as:

$$\|A\|_{\Phi} = \bigoplus_{x \in \Sigma^*} \Phi(\llbracket A \rrbracket(x)). \tag{2}$$

Theorem 1. *Let* $(\mathbb{K}, \oplus, \otimes, \overline{0}, \overline{1})$ *be a closed or ϵ-k-closed semiring and let $\Phi :$ $(\mathbb{R}_+, \cdot, 1) \to (\mathbb{K}, \otimes, \overline{1})$ be a monoid morphism preserving closedness. Then, for any unambiguous probabilistic automaton A, $\|A\|_{\Phi}$ can be computed exactly in time $O(|A|^3)$.*

Proof. The automaton $\Phi(A)$ derived from A by replacing each weight x by $\Phi(x)$ is a weighted automaton over the semiring $\mathbb{K}$. Since A is unambiguous, at most one path in A, $\pi = e_1 \cdots e_k$, is labeled with any string $x \in \Sigma^*$. Since Φ is a monoid morphism, $\Phi(\llbracket A \rrbracket(x)) = \bigotimes_{j=1}^{k} \Phi(i[e_j])$, that is the weight of the path labeled with x in $\Phi(A)$. This shows that $\|A\|_{\Phi} = s(A)$ and proves the theorem. $\square$

Theorem 1 provides an algorithm for computing the Φ-norm of unambiguous probabilistic automata for arbitrary monoid morphisms preserving closedness. We will briefly illustrate two applications of the theorem.

(a) Entropy of a Probabilistic Automaton.

Let $\mathbb{K}$ denote $(\mathbb{R} \cup \{+\infty, -\infty\}) \times (\mathbb{R} \cup \{+\infty, -\infty\})$. For pairs (x_1, y_1) and (x_2, y_2) in $\mathbb{K}$, define the following :

$$(x_1, y_1) \oplus (x_2, y_2) = (x_1 + x_2, y_1 + y_2) \tag{3}$$

$$(x_1, y_1) \otimes (x_2, y_2) = (x_1 x_2, x_1 y_2 + x_2 y_1) \tag{4}$$

Then, the system $(\mathbb{K}, \oplus, \otimes, (0,0), (1,0))$ defines a commutative semiring [2,8,4], called the *entropy semiring*. It can be shown [4] that the function $\Phi : (\mathbb{R}_+, +, \cdot, 0, 1) \to (\mathbb{K}, \oplus, \otimes, (0,0), (1,0))$ defined by: $\forall x \in \mathbb{R}_+, \Phi(x) = (x, -x \log x)$, is a monoid morphism preserving closedness. Thus, the norm-Φ of an unambiguous probabilistic automaton can be computed efficiently using a single-source shortest-distance algorithm. Its second component is exactly the entropy of A, thus this provides an efficient and simple algorithm for computing the entropy of A.

(b) Norm L_α of a Probabilistic Automaton, $\alpha \in \mathbb{R}_+$.

   The function $\Phi : (\mathbb{R}_+, +, \cdot, 0, 1) \to (\mathbb{R}_+, +, \cdot, 0, 1)$ defined by $\Phi(x) = x^\alpha$ is clearly a monoid morphism. Since for $0 \leq x < 1$, $0 \leq x^\alpha < 1$, it also preserves closedness. Thus, the L_α-norm of an unambiguous probabilistic automaton A can be computed efficiently using a shortest-distance algorithm. In particular, the Bhattacharya norm, i.e., $L_{\frac{1}{2}}$-norm, of A can be computed efficiently.

3.2   General Case

In general, a probabilistic automaton may not be unambiguous. But, the L_p norm can still be computed in polynomial time for any integer $p \geq 1$.

Theorem 2. *The L_p-norm of a probabilistic automaton A can be computed exactly in time $O(|A|^{3p})$ time and $\Theta(|A|^{2p})$ space.*

Proof. Let $A^{(p)}$ denote the automaton obtained by intersecting A with itself $p-1$ times. Then, by definition of intersection, $(s[A^{(p)}])^{1/p}$ represents the L_p norm of A. The cost of intersection to create $A^{(p)}$ is in $O(|A|^p)$.   □

3.3   Approximate Computation

Here we consider the specific case of the computation of the L_p norm of a probabilistic automaton. Our results can be generalized to cover more general cases, in particular in the case of unambiguous automata.

Since for any $\epsilon > 0$, a probabilistic automaton is ϵ-k-closed for the probability semiring, instead of the (generalized) Floyd-Warshall algorithm, we can use a single-source shortest-distance algorithm to compute $s[A]$ [13]. This algorithm works with any queue discipline, its space complexity is linear which is significantly more efficient than the Floyd-Warshall algorithm.

The time complexity of the algorithm depends on the queue discipline used. With a breadth-first queue discipline (as in the Bellman-Ford shortest-distance algorithm), an analysis similar to [4] can be used to show that the overall complexity of this approximate algorithm is:

$$O(|Q| + (|E| + |Q|)\frac{\log(1/\epsilon)}{\log(1/|\lambda_2|)}). \tag{5}$$

For ϵ exponentially smaller than $|\lambda_2|$ ($\epsilon = |\lambda_2|^d$), the cost in complexity is only linear: $O(|Q| + d(|E| + |Q|))$. Other queue disciplines may lead to more efficient algorithms, depending on the probabilistic automaton considered.

4   Computation of Distances Between Probabilistic Automata

There are several standard distances used to compare distributions which can be used in particular to compare probabilistic automata. Here are the definitions of some of the most commonly used ones, the *relative entropy* or *Kullback-Leibler divergence*, and the L_p *distance* between two distributions q_1, q_2 over a discrete set $\mathcal{X}$:

$$D(q_1 \| q_2) \qquad = \sum_{x \in \mathcal{X}} q_1(x) \log \frac{q_1(x)}{q_2(x)}$$

$$L_p(q_1, q_2) \qquad = \left(\sum_{x \in \mathcal{X}} (q_1(x) - q_2(x))^p \right)^{1/p} \qquad (6)$$

$$\text{Hellinger}(q_1, q_2) = \left(\sum_{x \in \mathcal{X}} (\sqrt{q_1(x)} - \sqrt{q_2(x)})^2 \right)^{1/2}.$$

Since we have previously specifically studied the problem of the computation of the relative entropy [4,3], in what follows, we will focus on the computation of the L_p distance and the Hellinger distance.

4.1 L_{2p} Distance of Probabilistic Automata

In [15], the authors give an approximate algorithm to compute the L_2 distance between two HMMs. Their algorithm applies to the specific cases of HMMs in which each state belongs to at most one cycle.[1] This section presents a simple and general algorithm for the computation of the L_{2p} distance of two arbitrary probabilistic automata, for $p \in \mathbb{N}$.

Our algorithm computes $(L_{2p}(A_1, A_2))^{2p}$. The L_{2p} distance between A_1, A_2 can then be obtained straightforwardly by taking the $2p$th root. $(L_{2p}(A_1, A_2))^{2p}$ can be rewritten as:

$$(L_{2p}(A_1, A_2))^{2p} = \sum_{x \in \Sigma^*} |[\![A_1]\!](x) - [\![A_2]\!](x)|^{2p} = \sum_{x \in \Sigma^*} ([\![A_1]\!](x) - [\![A_2]\!](x))^{2p}$$

$$= \sum_{x \in \Sigma^*} \sum_{i=0}^{2p} \binom{2p}{i} ([\![A_1]\!](x))^i (-[\![A_2]\!](x))^{2p-i} \qquad (7)$$

$$= \sum_{i=0}^{2p} \binom{2p}{i} (-1)^i \sum_{x \in \Sigma^*} ([\![A_1]\!](x))^i ([\![A_2]\!](x))^{2p-i}. \qquad (8)$$

Let $T(i, 2p - i)$ denote $\sum_{x \in \Sigma^*} ([\![A_1]\!](x))^i ([\![A_2]\!](x))^{2p-i}$. Note that if A_1, A_2 are acyclic, then one can compute $T(i, 2p - i)$ exactly using a generalization of the

---

[1] For more general HMMs, they claim without proof that an iterative version of their method yields an approximate algorithm that works in time $O((|A_1|+|A_2|)^{6p})$, where A_1 and A_2 are the HMMs considered. The approximation does not appear explicitly in this complexity term however.

single-source shortest-distance algorithm [13] that works for arbitrary semirings, in linear time $O(|A_1| + |A_2|)$.

Next, let us consider the case of unambiguous automata A_1, A_2. If $A_i = (\Sigma, Q_i, I_i, F_i, E_i, \lambda_i, \rho_i)$, $i = 1, 2$, then the transitions in the intersection automaton $A = A_1 \cap A_2$ are defined according to the following rule:

$$(q_1, a, w_1, q_1') \in E_1 \text{ and } (q_2, a, w_2, q_2') \in E_2 \Rightarrow ((q_1, q_2), a, w_1 w_2, (q_1', q_2')) \in E.$$

Since we are dealing with unambiguous automata, we can avoid the re-computation of the intersection automaton for different is. During intersection, instead of multiplying w_1 and w_2, we can keep instead the pair (w_1, w_2). Then, we only need to intersect A_1 and A_2 once, and modify the weight of each transition in the intersection automaton for different is in the computation of $T(i, 2p - i)$ as $((q_1, q_2), a, (w_1^i (w_2)^{2p-i}), (q_1', q_2'))$. Running the shortest-distance algorithm over the intersection automaton with weights modified as described above yields $T(i, 2p - i)$. Computing the intersection automaton takes $O(|A_1||A_2|)$ time.

Thus, if we use the exact algorithm to compute the shortest-distance, then for each i, computing $T(i, 2p - i)$ costs $O(|A_1 \cap A_2|^3)$ time and $\Theta(|A_1 \cap A_2|^2)$. Therefore, the time complexity of computing the $2p$-distance between A_1, A_2 is $O((2p)|A_1 \cap A_2|^3)$ and the space complexity $\Theta(|A_1 \cap A_2|^2)$.

Theorem 3. *The L_{2p} distance of unambiguous probabilistic automata can be computed exactly in time $O(2p|A_1|^3|A_2|^3)$.*

Note that this theorem significantly improves the result of [15], which is exponential in p. Thus, for unambiguous automata, our algorithms are, to the best of our knowledge, the only polynomial time algorithms for computing the $2p$ norm exactly.

For the computation of the L_{2p}-distance of arbitrary automata, we can no longer intersect A_1, A_2 just once. Since there may be multiple paths in $A_i, i = 1, 2$ with the same label, cross terms appear in $T(i, 2p-i)$. This makes it necessary to perform $2p$ separate intersections for each i. The computational cost and space complexity of intersection to compute $T(i, 2p - i)$ is in $O(|A_1|^i|A_2|^{2p-i})$. Thus, the exact shortest-distance algorithm has complexity $O((|A_1|^i|A_2|^{2p-i})^3)$. This leads us to the following result.

Theorem 4. *The L_{2p} distance of two arbitrary probabilistic automata A_1 and A_2 can be computed in time $\sum_{i=0}^{2p} O((|A_1|^i|A_2|^{2p-i})^3) = O((|A_1| + |A_2|)^{6p})$.*

Note that our algorithm for computing the L_{2p} distance of two arbitrary probabilistic automata A_1 and A_2 clearly also provides an efficient method for testing their equivalence since A_1 and A_2 are equivalent iff their L_p distance is null. For $p = 1$, our exact algorithm can be used to test for equivalence in time $O((|A_1||A_2|)^3)$. However, the standardization algorithm of Schützenberger [17] can be used to derive a more efficient algorithm.

Theorem 5. *The equivalence of two arbitrary probabilistic automata A_1 and A_2 can be computed in time $O(|\Sigma| (|A_1| + |A_2|)^3)$.*

Proof. The standardization algorithm of Schützenberger [17,1] applies to any weighted automaton defined over a field. It leads to a representation of a weighted automaton with the smallest number of states. The algorithm requires the construction of bases for vectorial spaces for which spanning sets are known. Using LUP decompositions, the complexity of the standardization algorithm applied to a weighted automaton A is in $O(|\Sigma||A|^3)$.

For the purpose of equivalence, we may view a probabilistic automaton as an automaton over the field $(\mathbb{R}, +, \cdot, 0, 1)$. Since negation is allowed over this field, we can construct the automaton $A = A_1 - A_2$, which can be done in linear time, and apply standardization. A_1 and A_2 are equivalent iff A is equivalent to the null weighted machine, that is iff after standardization A has no state. Thus, this leads to an algorithm for testing the equivalence of two probabilistic automata A_1 and A_2 with overall complexity $O(|\Sigma||A|^3) = O(|\Sigma| (|A_1| + |A_2|)^3)$. $\qquad\square$

To our knowledge, this is the most efficient algorithm for testing the equivalence of probabilistic automata. The best algorithm previously reported in the literature was that of Wen-Guey Tzeng whose complexity is $O(|\Sigma| (|A_1| + |A_2|)^4))$ [19]. The alphabet factor does not appear in the expression of the complexity reported by the author most likely because the proof is restricted to a binary alphabet. The technique described by Wen-Guey Tzeng is in fact closely related to the standardization algorithm of Schützenberger [17], which the author was apparently not aware of.

4.2 L_{2p+1} and L_∞ Distance of Probabilistic Automata

It was shown by [15] that the problem of computing the L_1 or L_∞ distance of two probabilistic automata is NP-hard, even for acyclic automata. Here, we extend these results to the case of arbitrary L_{2p+1} distances, where $p \in \mathbb{N}$.

Our proof of the hardness of computing the L_{2p+1} distance between two acyclic probabilistic automata is by reduction from the Max-clique problem and is based on a technique used by [15].

Given a graph $G = (V, E)$, one can construct an acyclic weighted automaton A_G over the probability semiring of size polynomial in $|V| + |E|$ such that $[\![A]\!](x) = k$ for some string x iff G has a clique of size k. A_G is constructed as follows. It has a single initial state q_s and a single final state q_t. For each $i \in V$, it admits the following transitions:

(a) a transition from q_s to $q_{i,0}$ with label ϵ and weight 1;
(b) a transition from $q_{i,n}$ to the final state q_t with label ϵ and weight 1;
(c) a transition from $q_{i,i-1}$ to $q_{i,i}$ with label i and weight 1;
(d) a transition from $q_{i,j-1}$ to $q_{i,j}$ with label ϵ and weight 1 for each $j \neq i$; and
(e) if $(i, j) \in E$, a transition from $q_{i,j-1}$ to $q_{i,j}$ with label j and weight 1.

The size of A_G is clearly polynomial in $|V| + |E|$. Given a set $S \subseteq V$, let $[S]$ denote the ordered tuple with elements of S. For example, if $S = \{1, 2, 5, 3\}$, then $[S] = (1, 2, 3, 5)$. By construction, for any clique S, A_G contains a distinct path labeled with $[S]$ starting at the initial state and going through $q_{i,0}$ for each $i \in S$. Since all accepting paths have the same weight 1, this proves the property that $[\![A]\!](x) = k$ for some string x iff G has a clique of size k.

The automaton A_G is not probabilistic. But, an equivalent probabilistic automaton without ϵ-transitions can be computed from A_G by using the weighted ϵ-removal algorithm [12], and a weight-pushing algorithm can be used to normalize the sum of its weights to one [11]. For the sake of the simplicity of the presentation, we will continue to work with A_G. Our results can be generalized to the case of a probabilistic automaton without ϵ-transitions without difficulty.

Theorem 6. *The problem of computing the L_{2p+1} distance of two probabilistic automata is NP-hard.*

Proof. Using the notation used in [15], let a_k denote the number of strings accepted by A_G with weight exactly k. a_k is in fact exactly the number of cliques of size k in the original graph G. Thus determining the maximum k such that $a_k \neq 0$ is equivalent to determining the size of the largest clique.

For each $i \in \{0, 1, \ldots, n\}$, let C_i denote the constant weighted automaton assigning the same weight i to all subsequences of $\{1, \ldots, n\}$ and weight 0 to all other strings. By definition of the L_{2p+1} norm,

$$\forall i \geq 0, \quad [L_{2p+1}(C_i, A_G)]^{2p+1} = \sum_{j=0}^{n} a_j |i - j|^{2p+1} \tag{9}$$

This defines a system of linear equation with unknown variables $a_j, j = 0, \ldots, n$. Let $M \in \mathbb{R}^{(n+1)\times(n+1)}$ be the matrix defined by $M_{i,j} = |i-j|^{2p+1}, i \in \{0, 1, \ldots, n\}$. If M is invertible, then all a_js can be defined with respect the L_{2p+1} distance of the automata C_i and A_G, which will prove the statement of the theorem.

This matrix is a specific Toeplitz matrix, but it is not straightforward to compute its determinant [15]. Instead, we can do our reasoning in $\mathbb{Z}_3$. Indeed, in $\mathbb{Z}_3$, the coefficients of M are either 0, 1, or -1, regardless of the value of p. The determinant of M in $\mathbb{Z}_3$ is given by:

$$\det(M) = \begin{cases} -1 & \text{if } n+1 = 2 \mod 3 \\ 1 & \text{if } n+1 = 0 \mod 3 \\ 0 & \text{if } n+1 = 1 \mod 3. \end{cases} \tag{10}$$

We delay the proof of this fact to Lemma 1.

This implies that for all $n \in \mathbb{N}$ such that n is of the form $n \equiv \pm 1 \mod 3$, the matrix M of size $(n+1) \times (n+1)$ defined by $M_{i,j} = |i - j|^{2p+1}, i \in \{0, 1, \ldots, n\}$ is invertible in $\mathbb{R}$. Therefore, for $n \equiv \pm 1 \mod 3$, one can compute the matrix A and determine the size of the largest clique in the original graph G. This leaves us only with the case where $n \equiv 0 \mod 3$ in the original graph $G = (V, E)$. But, in this case, one can add a *dummy vertex* to G that is connected to all other vertices of V. Doing so increases the size of the largest clique by exactly one, and yields a graph $G' = (V', E')$ with $|V'| \equiv 1 \mod 3$. Since the size of the largest clique in G is one less than the size of the largest clique in G', the reduction is complete. Thus, the problem of determining the computing $2p+1$ distance between two probabilistic automata is NP-hard.   □

We conjecture that the problem of computing the L_{2p+1} distance, or L_∞, is in fact undecidable. Note that it was shown by [15] that, in view of the hardness of approximation results for cliques of [18,9], even a polynomial approximation of the L_∞ distance within a factor of $n^{\frac{1}{4}-\epsilon}$ is impossible unless NP = P.

Lemma 1. *The determinant of M in $\mathbb{Z}_3$ is given by*

$$\det(M) = \begin{cases} -1 & \text{if } n+1 = 2 \mod 3 \\ 1 & \text{if } n+1 = 0 \mod 3 \\ 0 & \text{if } n+1 = 1 \mod 3. \end{cases} \tag{11}$$

Proof. Let $M[n] \in \mathbb{R}^{n \times n}$ be the matrix defined by $M_{i,j} = |i-j|^{2p+1} \mod 3$. Note that in $\mathbb{Z}_3$, $|i-j|^{2p+1} \mod 3 = |i-j|$ for all $p \in \mathbb{N}$. Let R_i, C_j denote the ith row and the jth column of M respectively. Consider n such that $n+1 = 1 \mod 3$, i.e. let $n+1 = 3k+1$ for some $k \in \mathbb{N}$. For all $j \in \{1, \ldots, 3k+1\}$,

$$M_{3k+1,j} = |3k+1-j|^{2p+1} \mod 3 = (1-j)^{2p+1} \mod 3 \tag{12}$$
$$= -|1-j|^{2p+1} \mod 3 = -M_{1,j} \tag{13}$$

Since the last row is a scalar multiple of the first row, $\det(M) = 0$ for $n+1 = 1 \mod 3$.

Next, suppose $n+1 = 2 \mod 3$. Let $n+1 = 3k+2$ for some $k \in \mathbb{N}$. In this case, we show that $\det(M[3k+2]) = -\det(M[3k])$. Given $M[3k+2]$, we perform the following row and column operations:

$$R_1 \leftarrow R_1 + R_{3k+1} \qquad C_1 \leftarrow C_1 + C_{3k+2}. \tag{14}$$

The resulting matrix has zeros everywhere in the first row and column except at $M_{1,1} = 1, M_{1,3k+2} = M_{3k+2,1} = -1$. Developing the determinant of M along R_1, it is not hard to see that $\det(M[3k+2]) = \det(M[3k+1]) - \det(M[3k])$. Since $\det(M[3k+1]) = 0$, we obtain

$$\det(M[3k+2]) = -\det(M[3k]). \tag{15}$$

Finally, suppose $n+1 = 0 \mod 3$. Let $n+1 = 3k$ for $k \in \mathbb{N}$. We show that $\det(D[3k]) = \det(D[3k-4]) - \det(D[3(k-1)])$. Given $M[3k]$, we perform the following operations

$$\begin{array}{llll} R_1 & \leftarrow R_1 + R_{3k-2} & C_1 & \leftarrow C_1 + C_{3k-2} \\ R_{3k} & \leftarrow R_{3k} + R_3 & C_{3k} & \leftarrow C_{3k} + C_3 \\ R_2 & \leftarrow R_2 + R_1 & C_2 & \leftarrow C_2 + C_1 \\ R_{3k-1} & \leftarrow R_{3k} + R_{3k-1} & C_{3k-1} & \leftarrow C_{3k} + C_{3k-1} \\ R_2 & \leftarrow R_2 + R_{3k-1} & C_2 & \leftarrow C_2 + C_{3k-1} \end{array} \tag{16}$$

The resulting matrix has zeros everywhere in the first and last row and column, except for $M_{1,3k} = 1, M_{3k,1} = 1$. Furthermore, the submatrix defined by

R_i, C_j for $i, j \in \{2, \ldots 3k - 1\}$ is the same as $M[3k - 2]$ except for $M_{2,2} = 1$ and $M_{2,3k-1} = M_{3k-1,2} = -1$. Developing the determinant along the following sequence of rows and columns: R_1, C_1, R_2, C_2 yields

$$\det(M[3k]) = \det(M[3k - 4]) - \det(M[3(k - 1)]), \qquad (17)$$

and ends the proof.   □

4.3 Hellinger Distance of Probabilistic Automata

The ideas presented in the previous section can be used in a straightforward manner to compute the Hellinger distance of two unambiguous probabilistic automata. The Hellinger distance $\text{Hellinger}(A_1, A_2)$ of two probabilistic automata A_1, A_2 is given by:

$$\text{Hellinger}(A_1, A_2) = \Big(\sum_{x \in \Sigma^*} (\sqrt{[\![A_1]\!](x)} - \sqrt{[\![A_2]\!](x)})^2 \Big)^{1/2}. \qquad (18)$$

Thus,

$$[\text{Hellinger}(A_1, A_2)]^2 = \sum_{x \in \Sigma^*} (\sqrt{[\![A_1]\!](x)} - \sqrt{[\![A_2]\!](x)})^2 \qquad (19)$$

$$= \sum_{x \in \Sigma^*} [\![A_1]\!](x) + \sum_{x \in \Sigma^*} [\![A_2]\!](x) - 2 \sum_{x \subseteq \Sigma^*} \sqrt{[\![A_1]\!](x)[\![A_2]\!](x)}$$

$$= 2(1 - \sum_{x \in \Sigma^*} \sqrt{[\![A_1]\!](x)[\![A_2]\!](x)}) \qquad (20)$$

The problem of computing the Hellinger distance between A_1, A_2 therefore reduces to efficiently computing $\sum_{x \in \Sigma^*} \sqrt{[\![A_1]\!](x)[\![A_2]\!](x)}$. Once again, as long as A_1 and A_2 are unambiguous there is at most one accepting string with label x in $A_1 \cap A_2$. Intersecting A_1 and A_2 over the probability semiring, the weight of the transition corresponding to the intersection of the transitions $e_1 = (q_1, a, w_1, q_1')$ and $e_2 = (q_2, a, w_2, q_2')$ is given by $w_1 w_2$.

The function $\Phi : (\mathbb{R}_+, +, \cdot, 0, 1) \to (\mathbb{R}_+, +, \cdot, 0, 1)$ defined by $\Phi(x) = \sqrt{x}$ is clearly a monoid morphism. Since $0 \leq x < 1$, $0 \leq \sqrt{x} < 1$, it also preserves closedness. Since the Φ norm of the intersection automaton is precisely the quantity we are interested in, we obtain an efficient algorithm to compute the Hellinger distance. The complexity of this computation is the same as the complexity of the shortest distance algorithm on the intersection automaton $A_1 \cap A_2$. If A_1, A_2 are acyclic, then the shortest-distance computation can be done in linear time, i.e. $O(|A_1 \cap A_2|)$. For A_1, A_2 unambiguous, one could compute the Hellinger distance exactly in time that is cubic in the size of the intersection automaton and space that is quadratic using a generalization of the classical Floyd-Warshall all-pairs shortest-distance algorithm that works for arbitrary closed semirings. However, a more efficient approximate solution can be obtained using the general single-source shortest-distance algorithm [13] that uses only linear space.

5 Conclusion

We examined the problem of the computation of several standard distances between probabilistic automata. We showed that in each case, the problem can be viewed as a shortest-distance computation over an appropriate semiring. In each case, we either gave an efficient algorithm for the computation of the norm of a probabilistic automaton or the distance between two probabilistic automata, or showed the intractability of the problem.

Our algorithms can be used to compute distances between very large probabilistic automata. Some of our results could perhaps be extended to the case of finitely ambiguous probabilistic automata. Many of our results can be straightforwardly extended to the case of weighted tree automata.

References

1. Jean Berstel and Christophe Reutenauer. *Rational Series and Their Languages.* Springer-Verlag: Berlin-New York, 1988.
2. Stephen Bloom and Zoltan Ésik. *Iteration Theories.* Springer-Verlag, Berlin, 1991.
3. Corinna Cortes, Mehryar Mohri, Ashish Rastogi, and Michael Riley. Distances between Probabilistic Automata. In preparation, journal version, 2006.
4. Corinna Cortes, Mehryar Mohri, Ashish Rastogi, and Michael Riley. Efficient Computation of the Relative Entropy of Probabilistic Automata. In *Proceedings of LATIN 2006*, volume 3887 of *LNCS*, pages 323–336. Springer-Verlag, 2006.
5. Karel Culik II and Jarkko Kari. Digital Images and Formal Languages. In Grzegorz Rozenberg and Arto Salomaa, editors, *Handbook of Formal Languages*, volume 3, pages 599–616. Springer, 1997.
6. R. Durbin, S.R. Eddy, A. Krogh, and G.J. Mitchison. *Biological Sequence Analysis: Probabilistic Models of Proteins and Nucleic Acids.* Cambridge University Press, Cambridge UK, 1998.
7. Samuel Eilenberg. *Automata, Languages and Machines*, volume A–B. Academic Press, 1974–1976.
8. Jason Eisner. Expectation Semirings: Flexible EM for Finite-State Transducers. In *Proceedings of the ESSLLI Workshop on Finite-State Methods in NLP*, 2001.
9. Lars Engebretsen and Jonas Holmerin. Clique is hard to approximate within $n^{1-o(1)}$. In *Proceedings of the 27th International Colloquium on Automata, Languages and Programming (ICALP 2000)*, pages 2–12, London, UK, 2000. Springer-Verlag.
10. Werner Kuich and Arto Salomaa. *Semirings, Automata, Languages.* Number 5 in EATCS Monographs on Theoretical Computer Science. Springer-Verlag, Berlin, Germany, 1986.
11. Mehryar Mohri. Finite-State Transducers in Language and Speech Processing. *Computational Linguistics*, 23(2), 1997.
12. Mehryar Mohri. Generic Epsilon-Removal and Input Epsilon-Normalization Algorithms for Weighted Transducers. *International Journal of Foundations of Computer Science*, 13(1):129–143, 2002.
13. Mehryar Mohri. Semiring Frameworks and Algorithms for Shortest-Distance Problems. *Journal of Automata, Languages and Combinatorics*, 7(3):321–350, 2002.
14. Azaria Paz. *Introduction to probabilistic automata.* Academic Press, New York, 1971.

15. Rune B. Lyngsø and Christian N. S. Pederson. The Consensus String Problem and the Complexity of Comparing Hidden Markov Models. *Journal of Computer and System Sciences*, 65(3):545–569, 2002.
16. Arto Salomaa and Matti Soittola. *Automata-Theoretic Aspects of Formal Power Series*. Springer-Verlag, 1978.
17. Marcel-Paul Schützenberger. On the definition of a family of automata. *Information and Control*, 4, 1961.
18. J. Håstad. Clique is hard to approximate within $n^{1-\epsilon}$. In *FOCS '96: Proceedings of the 37th Annual Symposium on Foundations of Computer Science*, page 627, Washington, DC, USA, 1996. IEEE Computer Society.
19. Wen-Guey Tzeng. A Polynomial-Time Algorithm for the Equivalence of Probabilistic Automata. *Foundations of Computer Science (FOCS)*, pages 216–227, 1992.

Does o-Substitution Preserve Recognizability?

Andreas Maletti

Technische Universität Dresden
Department of Computer Science
01062 Dresden, Germany
maletti@tcs.inf.tu-dresden.de

Abstract. Substitution operations on tree series are at the basis of systems of equations (over tree series) and tree series transducers. Tree series transducers seem to be an interesting transformation device in syntactic pattern matching. In this contribution, it is shown that o-substitution preserves recognizable tree series provided that the target tree series is linear and the semiring is idempotent, commutative, and continuous. This result is applied to prove that the range of the o-t-ts transformation computed by a linear recognizable tree series transducer is pointwise recognizable.

1   Introduction

Tree series transducers [1] were introduced as a joint generalization of tree transducers [2,3] and weighted tree automata [4,5]. They thereby serve as the transducing devices corresponding to weighted tree automata. Both historical predecessors of tree series transducers have successfully been motivated from and applied in practice. Specifically, tree transducers are motivated from syntax-directed translations in compilers [6], and they are applied in, *e. g.*, computational linguistics [7] and query languages of XML databases [8]. Weighted tree automata have been applied to code selection in compilers [9] and tree pattern matching [10].

In [11] a tree-based syntactic pattern matching approach is presented and shown to be competetive. The approach is tailored to digit recognition. Using a training procedure for regular tree grammars a tree automaton is trained. To accomodate for training errors, usually a refined model using probabilities is applied. Essentially this corresponds to a weighted tree automaton. A common observation is that the recognized digit is invariant under small translations of the input image (such as, *e. g.*, small tiltings). Finitely presentable transformations (also respecting the probabilities) on the input tree can be realised by tree series transducers. Another application of tree series transducers (using the semiring of probabilities) is demonstrated in [12], where tree series transducers are trained to perform machine translation. Yet another application of tree series transducers is presented in [13], where tree series transducer are applied to code selection.

Let us illustrate one application of tree series transducers in the setting of natural language processing. Imagine a statistical channel model that is applied to a channel that translates Japanese text into English text [14]. Statistical models

O.H. Ibarra and H.-C. Yen (Eds.): CIAA 2006, LNCS 4094, pp. 150–161, 2006.

are built from a large corpus of hand-annotated and translated input sentences. Any such channel model gives rise to an automatically generated (statistical) translation system, which may assist translators by providing suitable candidate translations. In [14] the simple IBM model 1 [15,16] is displayed. This model consists of several stages: reordering, insertion, and word translation. The first stage just reorders parse subtrees to accomodate for different word order (English: Subject-Verb-Object and Japanese: Subject-Object-Verb); the second stage inserts words that have no direct translation; and the final stage just perform word-to-word translation. All operations are probabilistic, so with a certain probability, the reordering TO NN $\rightarrow$ NN TO takes place. In fact, all stages are simple weighted tree to weighted tree (where the weight is a probability) transformations, which can easily be modelled by a tree series transducer. We depict the working of a tree series transducer for the reordering stage in Figure 1.

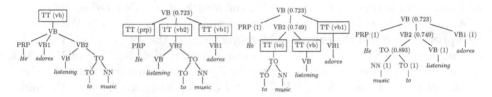

Fig. 1. Reordering performed by a tree series transducer

Tree substitution is at the core of the semantics of tree transducers, and tree series substitution fulfills this purpose for tree series transducers. In this paper we investigate o-substitution [17]. A tree series is a mapping from a set of output trees into some semiring. Let us illustrate o-substitution using the semiring of probabilities. The probability (e. g., reliability), that is associated with an output tree, is taken to the nth power, if the output tree is used in n copies (is copied n times into some other tree). In this approach, an output tree stands for a composite, and the probability associated with the output tree reflects, e. g., the reliability of this particular composite. When we combine composites into a new composite, then we obtain the reliability of the composite by a simple multiplication of the reliabilities of its components; each component taken as often as needed to assemble the composite (under the assumption that each component is critical for the correct functioning of the composite).

Tree series substitutions have also been studied in relation with recognizable tree series [4]. Substitution is a standard operation on tree series, and in particular, OI-substitution [18] was studied with respect to preservation of recognizability [19]. A tree series is called recognizable, if there exists a finite state automaton that computes this tree series. Recognizable tree series are of particular interest, because they are finitely representable. It is known that the result of certain substitutions is not recognizable. We study the limit of recognizability under o-substitution. Which o-substitutions will lead to recognizable tree series? Thus we aim towards classes of transformations that preserve the ability to finitely represent tree series.

Our main result states that o-substitution preserves recognizable tree series in semirings that are commutative, idempotent, and continuous [20], whenever the participating tree series are linear (*i. e.*, each variable may occur at most once in the trees in the support).

We apply this result to show that the o-t-ts transformation computed by a linear recognizable tree series transducer over a commutative, idempotent, and continuous semiring is pointwise recognizable.

2   Preliminaries

We use $\mathbb{N}$ and $\mathbb{N}_+$ to represent the nonnegative and positive integers, respectively. Further let $[k]$ be an abbreviation for $\{n \in \mathbb{N} \mid 1 \leqslant n \leqslant k\}$. A set Σ which is nonempty and finite is also called an *alphabet*. As usual, Σ^* denotes the set of all (finite) words over Σ. Given $w \in \Sigma^*$, the *length of w* is denoted by $|w|$.

A *ranked alphabet* is an alphabet Σ with a mapping $\mathrm{rk}_\Sigma \colon \Sigma \longrightarrow \mathbb{N}$. We use Σ_k to represent $\{\sigma \in \Sigma \mid \mathrm{rk}_\Sigma(\sigma) = k\}$. Moreover, we use the set $X = \{x_i \mid i \in \mathbb{N}_+\}$ of *variables* and $X_k = \{x_i \mid i \in [k]\}$. Given a ranked alphabet Σ and $V \subseteq X$, the set of *Σ-trees indexed by V*, denoted by $T_\Sigma(V)$, is inductively defined to be the smallest set T such that (i) $V \subseteq T$ and (ii) for every $k \in \mathbb{N}$, $\sigma \in \Sigma_k$, and $t_1, \dots, t_k \in T$ also $\sigma(t_1, \dots, t_k) \in T$. Since we generally assume that $\Sigma \cap X = \emptyset$, we write α instead of $\alpha()$ whenever $\alpha \in \Sigma_0$. Moreover, we also write T_Σ to denote $T_\Sigma(\emptyset)$.

For every $t \in T_\Sigma(X)$, we denote by $|t|_x$ the number of occurrences of $x \in X$ in t. Let $I \subseteq \mathbb{N}_+$ be finite, $u \in T_\Sigma(X)$ and $u_i \in T_\Sigma(X)$ for every $i \in I$. By $u[u_i]_{i \in I}$ we denote the tree obtained from u by replacing every occurrence of a variable x_i with $i \in I$ by u_i. We write $u[u_1, \dots, u_n]$ for $u[u_i]_{i \in I}$ if $I = [n]$. Let $V \subseteq X$. We say that $u \in T_\Sigma(X)$ is *linear* and *nondeleting* in V, if every $x \in V$ occurs at most once and at least once in t, respectively. Moreover, we use $\mathrm{var}(u)$ to represent the set of variables that occur in u.

A *(commutative) semiring* is an algebraic structure $\mathcal{A} = (A, +, \cdot, 0, 1)$ consisting of two commutative monoids $(A, +, 0)$ and $(A, \cdot, 1)$ such that $\cdot$ distributes over $+$ and 0 is absorbing with respect to $\cdot$. As usual we use $\sum_{i \in I} a_i$ for sums of families $(a_i)_{i \in I}$ of $a_i \in A$ where for only finitely many $i \in I$ we have $a_i \neq 0$. A semiring $\mathcal{A} = (A, +, \cdot, 0, 1)$ is called *idempotent*, if $1 + 1 = 1$, and $\mathcal{A}$ is called *complete*, if it is possible to define an infinitary sum operation such that for arbitrary index sets I and $(a_i)_{i \in I}$ of $a_i \in A$ we have

- $\sum_{i \in \{j_1, j_2\}} a_i = a_{j_1} + a_{j_2}$ with $j_1 \neq j_2$;
- $\sum_{i \in I} a_i = \sum_{j \in J}(\sum_{i \in I_j} a_i)$ for all $(I_j)_{j \in J}$ such that $\bigcup_{j \in J} I_j = I$ and for every $j_1 \neq j_2$ we have $I_{j_1} \cap I_{j_2} = \emptyset$; and
- $a \cdot (\sum_{i \in I} a_i) = \sum_{i \in I}(a \cdot a_i)$ for all $a \in A$.

Whenever we speak of a complete semiring, we silently assume that the infinitary sum operation is given. A semiring is *naturally ordered*, whenever $\sqsubseteq \subseteq A^2$, defined by $a \sqsubseteq b$ iff there exists a $c \in A$ such that $a + c = b$, constitutes a partial order on A. Let $\mathcal{A}$ be complete and naturally ordered. We say that $\mathcal{A}$ is *continuous*, if for every index set I and $(a_i)_{i \in I}$ of $a_i \in A$ the following supremum exists and $\sum_{i \in I} a_i = \sup\{\sum_{i \in F} a_i \mid F \subseteq I \text{ with } F \text{ finite}\}$ where the supremum is taken with respect to the natural order $\sqsubseteq$. Examples of continuous semirings are

- the Boolean semiring $\mathbb{B} = (\{0,1\}, \vee, \wedge, 0, 1)$,
- the natural number semiring $\mathbb{N} = (\mathbb{N} \cup \{\infty\}, +, \cdot, 0, 1)$, and
- the arctic semiring $\mathbb{A} = (\mathbb{N} \cup \{\infty, -\infty\}, \max, +, -\infty, 0)$.

Let S be a set and $\mathcal{A} = (A, +, \cdot, 0, 1)$ be a semiring. A *(formal) power series* ψ is a mapping $\psi \colon S \longrightarrow A$. Given $s \in S$, we denote $\psi(s)$ also by (ψ, s) and write the series as $\sum_{s \in S} (\psi, s)\, s$. The *support* of ψ is $\mathrm{supp}(\psi) = \{s \in S \mid (\psi, s) \neq 0\}$. Power series with finite support are called *polynomials*. We denote the set of all power series by $\mathcal{A}\langle\!\langle S \rangle\!\rangle$ and the set of polynomials by $\mathcal{A}\langle S \rangle$. The polynomial with empty support is denoted by $\widetilde{0}$. Power series $(\psi_i)_{i \in I} \in \mathcal{A}\langle\!\langle S \rangle\!\rangle$ are added componentwise; i. e., $(\sum_{i \in I} \psi_i, s) = \sum_{i \in I}(\psi_i, s)$ for every $s \in S$, and we multiply $\psi \in \mathcal{A}\langle\!\langle S \rangle\!\rangle$ with a coefficient $a \in A$ componentwise; i. e., $(a \cdot \psi, s) = a \cdot (\psi, s)$ for every $s \in S$.

In this paper, we only consider power series in which the set S is a set of trees. Such power series are also called *tree series*. Let Δ be a ranked alphabet. A tree series $\psi \in \mathcal{A}\langle\!\langle T_\Delta(X) \rangle\!\rangle$ is said to be *linear* and *nondeleting* in $V \subseteq X$, if every $t \in \mathrm{supp}(\psi)$ is linear and nondeleting in V, respectively. We also use $\mathrm{var}(\psi) = \bigcup_{u \in \mathrm{supp}(\psi)} \mathrm{var}(u)$.

Now let $\mathcal{A}$ be a complete semiring and $\psi \in \mathcal{A}\langle\!\langle T_\Delta(X) \rangle\!\rangle$ and let $I \subseteq \mathbb{N}_+$ be finite and $\psi_i \in \mathcal{A}\langle\!\langle T_\Delta(X) \rangle\!\rangle$ for every $i \in I$. The o-*substitution* of $(\psi_i)_{i \in I}$ *into* ψ, denoted by $\psi \xleftarrow{\;\;}_{o} (\psi_i)_{i \in I}$, is defined by

$$\psi \xleftarrow{\;\;}_{o} (\psi_i)_{i \in I} = \sum_{\substack{u \in \mathrm{supp}(\psi), \\ (\forall i \in I)\colon u_i \in \mathrm{supp}(\psi_i)}} \left((\psi, u) \cdot \prod_{i \in I} (\psi_i, u_i)^{|u|_{x_i}} \right) u[u_i]_{i \in I} \;.$$

If we suppose that $I = [n]$, then we also write $\psi \xleftarrow{\;\;}_{o} (\psi_1, \ldots, \psi_n)$ instead of $\psi \xleftarrow{\;\;}_{o} (\psi_i)_{i \in I}$. In an expression $\psi \xleftarrow{\;\;}_{o} (\psi_1, \ldots, \psi_n)$ the series ψ is called the *target* and every ψ_i is called a *source*.

Let us recall the notion of recognizable tree series [4,5,18,21]. Let Σ be a ranked alphabet and $\mathcal{A} = (A, +, \cdot, 0, 1)$ be a semiring. A *(bottom-up) weighted tree automaton M (over Σ and $\mathcal{A}$)*, abbreviated to wta, is a tuple $(Q, \Sigma, \mathcal{A}, F, \mu)$ where Q is an alphabet of *states*, $F \colon Q \longrightarrow A$ is a *final weight distribution* and $\mu = (\mu_k)_{k \in \mathbb{N}}$ with $\mu_k \colon \Sigma_k \longrightarrow A^{Q \times Q^k}$ is a *tree representation*. The *initial algebra semantics* of M is determined by the mapping $h_\mu \colon T_\Sigma \longrightarrow A^Q$ given by

$$h_\mu(\sigma(t_1, \ldots, t_k))_q = \sum_{q_1, \ldots, q_k \in Q} \mu_k(\sigma)_{q, q_1, \ldots, q_k} \cdot h_\mu(t_1)_{q_1} \cdot \ldots \cdot h_\mu(t_k)_{q_k}$$

for every $k \in \mathbb{N}$, $\sigma \in \Sigma_k$, $q \in Q$, and $t_1, \ldots, t_k \in T_\Sigma$. The tree series *recognized* by M, denoted by $\|M\|$, is defined by $(\|M\|, t) = \sum_{q \in Q} F_q \cdot h_\mu(t)_q$ for every $t \in T_\Sigma$.

We use the method of [22,21] to graphically represent wta. Note that we write $\mu_0(\alpha)_q$ instead of $\mu_0(\alpha)_{q,()}$ for every $\alpha \in \Sigma_0$ and $q \in Q$. A tree series $\psi \in \mathcal{A}\langle\langle T_\Sigma \rangle\rangle$ is termed *recognizable*, if there exists a wta M over Σ and $\mathcal{A}$ such that $\psi = \|M\|$. The class of all recognizable tree series over Σ and $\mathcal{A}$ is denoted by $\mathcal{A}^{\mathrm{rec}}\langle\langle T_\Sigma \rangle\rangle$.

Let Q be an alphabet. We write $Q(V)$ for $\{q(v) \mid q \in Q, v \in V\}$. Now let $\mathcal{A} = (A, +, \cdot, 0, 1)$ be a semiring and Σ and Δ be ranked alphabets. A *tree representation* μ (over Q, Σ, Δ, and $\mathcal{A}$) [1] is a family $(\mu(\sigma))_{\sigma \in \Sigma}$ of matrices $\mu(\sigma) \in \mathcal{A}\langle\langle T_\Delta(\mathrm{X}) \rangle\rangle^{Q \times Q(\mathrm{X}_k)^*}$ where $k = \mathrm{rk}_\Sigma(\sigma)$ such that for every $q \in Q$ and $w \in Q(\mathrm{X}_k)^*$ it holds that $\mu(\sigma)_{q,w} \in \mathcal{A}\langle\langle T_\Delta(\mathrm{X}_n) \rangle\rangle$ with $n = |w|$, and $\mu(\sigma)_{q,w} \neq \widetilde{0}$ for only finitely many $(q, w) \in Q \times Q(\mathrm{X}_k)^*$. A tree representation μ is said to be *recognizable* and *linear*, if $\mu(\sigma)_{q,w}$ is recognizable and linear for every $k \in \mathbb{N}$, $\sigma \in \Sigma_k$, and $(q, w) \in Q \times Q(\mathrm{X}_k)^*$, respectively. A *tree series transducer* [1,20], in the sequel abbreviated to tst, is a sixtuple $M = (Q, \Sigma, \Delta, \mathcal{A}, F, \mu)$ consisting of

- an alphabet Q of *states*,
- ranked alphabets Σ and Δ, also called *input* and *output ranked alphabet*, respectively,
- a complete semiring $\mathcal{A} = (A, +, \cdot, 0, 1)$,
- a vector $F \in \mathcal{A}\langle\langle T_\Delta(\mathrm{X}_1) \rangle\rangle^Q$, called *top-most output*, such that for all $q \in Q$: F_q is nondeleting and linear in X_1, and
- a tree representation μ over Q, Σ, Δ, and $\mathcal{A}$.

Tst inherit the properties *recognizable* and *linear* from their tree representation. Let $M = (Q, \Sigma, \Delta, \mathcal{A}, F, \mu)$ be a tst. Then M induces a mapping $\|M\|^{\mathrm{o}}: T_\Sigma \longrightarrow \mathcal{A}\langle\langle T_\Delta \rangle\rangle$ as follows. For every $k \in \mathbb{N}$, $\sigma \in \Sigma_k$, and $t_1, \ldots, t_k \in T_\Sigma$ we define the mapping $h_\mu^{\mathrm{o}}: T_\Sigma \longrightarrow \mathcal{A}\langle\langle T_\Delta \rangle\rangle^Q$ inductively for every $q \in Q$ by

$$h_\mu^{\mathrm{o}}(\sigma(t_1, \ldots, t_k))_q = \sum_{\substack{w \in Q(\mathrm{X}_k)^*, \\ w = q_1(\mathrm{x}_{i_1}) \cdots q_n(\mathrm{x}_{i_n})}} \mu_k(\sigma)_{q,w} \overset{}{\underset{\mathrm{o}}{\longleftarrow}} (h_\mu^{\mathrm{o}}(t_{i_1})_{q_1}, \ldots, h_\mu^{\mathrm{o}}(t_{i_n})_{q_n}) \ .$$

For every $t \in T_\Sigma$ the *o-tree-to-tree-series (for short: o-t-ts) transformation* computed by M is $\|M\|^{\mathrm{o}}(t) = \sum_{q \in Q} F_q \overset{}{\underset{\mathrm{o}}{\longleftarrow}} (h_\mu^{\mathrm{o}}(t)_q)$.

3   Preservation of Recognizability

In this section we consider the question whether o-substitution preserves recognizability. Let Σ be a ranked alphabet. It is known that IO substitution does not, in general, preserve recognizability. However, IO substitution on linear tree languages preserves recognizability [23].

In [24] a first result on tree series is presented for OI substitution. For every $k \in \mathbb{N}$, $\sigma \in \Sigma_k$, and $\psi_1, \ldots, \psi_k \in \mathcal{A}\langle\langle T_\Sigma(\mathrm{X}) \rangle\rangle$, we define

$$\sigma(\psi_1, \ldots, \psi_k) = \sum_{t_1, \ldots, t_k \in T_\Sigma(\mathrm{X})} \left((\psi_1, t_1) \cdot \ldots \cdot (\psi_k, t_k) \right) \sigma(t_1, \ldots, t_k) \ .$$

Note that this sum is always well-defined. Let $t \in T_\Sigma(X)$ be a tree, $n \in \mathbb{N}$, and $\psi_1, \ldots, \psi_n \in \mathcal{A}\langle\langle T_\Sigma(X)\rangle\rangle$. For every $j \in [n]$, $\ell \in \mathbb{N}_+ \setminus [n]$ let

$$\mathrm{x}_j \overleftarrow{\mathrm{OI}} (\psi_1, \ldots, \psi_n) = \psi_j \quad \text{and} \quad \mathrm{x}_\ell \overleftarrow{\mathrm{OI}} (\psi_1, \ldots, \psi_n) = 1\,\mathrm{x}_\ell$$

and for every $k \in \mathbb{N}$, $\sigma \in \Sigma_k$, and $t_1, \ldots, t_k \in T_\Sigma(X)$ let

$$t \overleftarrow{\mathrm{OI}} (\psi_1, \ldots, \psi_n) = \sigma(t_1 \overleftarrow{\mathrm{OI}} (\psi_1, \ldots, \psi_n), \ldots, t_k \overleftarrow{\mathrm{OI}} (\psi_1, \ldots, \psi_n)) \ ,$$

where $t = \sigma(t_1, \ldots, t_k)$. Now let $\psi \in \mathcal{A}\langle\langle T_\Sigma(X)\rangle\rangle$. We define $\psi \overleftarrow{\mathrm{OI}} (\psi_1, \ldots, \psi_n)$ by

$$\psi \overleftarrow{\mathrm{OI}} (\psi_1, \ldots, \psi_n) = \sum_{t \in T_\Sigma(X)} (\psi, t) \cdot \left(t \overleftarrow{\mathrm{OI}} (\psi_1, \ldots, \psi_n)\right) \ .$$

Note that also this sum is always well-defined. With the help of [24] we can easily relate o-substitution and OI substitution. Recall that our semirings are always commutative.

Proposition 1. *Let $n \in \mathbb{N}$, $\psi \in \mathcal{A}\langle\langle T_\Sigma(X_n)\rangle\rangle$ be nondeleting and linear in X_n, and $\psi_1, \ldots, \psi_n \in \mathcal{A}\langle\langle T_\Sigma(X)\rangle\rangle$.*

$$\psi \overleftarrow{\mathrm{o}} (\psi_1, \ldots, \psi_n) = \psi \overleftarrow{\mathrm{OI}} (\psi_1, \ldots, \psi_n)$$

Proof. Clearly, $t \overleftarrow{\mathrm{OI}} (1\,t_i)_{i \in I} = 1\,t[t_i]_{i \in I}$ for every $t \in T_\Sigma(X_I)$ and family $(t_i)_{i \in I} \in T_\Sigma(X)^I$.

$$\psi \overleftarrow{\mathrm{o}} (\psi_i)_{i \in I} = \sum_{\substack{t \in T_\Sigma(X_I), \\ (\forall i \in I)\,:\, t_i \in T_\Sigma(X)}} \left((\psi, t) \cdot \prod_{i \in I} (\psi_i, t_i)\right) \cdot (1\,t[t_i]_{i \in I})$$

$$= \quad (\text{by } t \overleftarrow{\mathrm{OI}} (1\,t_i)_{i \in I} = 1\,t[t_i]_{i \in I})$$

$$\sum_{\substack{t \in T_\Sigma(X_I), \\ (\forall i \in I)\,:\, t_i \in T_\Sigma(X)}} \left((\psi, t) \cdot \prod_{i \in I} (\psi_i, t_i)\right) \cdot \left(t \overleftarrow{\mathrm{OI}} (1\,t_i)_{i \in I}\right)$$

$$= \quad (\text{by [24, Theorem 6] and definition of } \overleftarrow{\mathrm{OI}})$$

$$\sum_{t \in T_\Sigma(X_I)} (\psi, t) \cdot \left(t \overleftarrow{\mathrm{OI}} (\psi_i)_{i \in I}\right) = \psi \overleftarrow{\mathrm{OI}} (\psi_i)_{i \in I}$$

Theorem 2 (cf. [24]). *For every $n \in \mathbb{N}$, $\psi \in \mathcal{A}^{\mathrm{rec}}\langle\langle T_\Sigma(X_n)\rangle\rangle$ such that ψ is nondeleting and linear in X_n, and every $\psi_1, \ldots, \psi_n \in \mathcal{A}^{\mathrm{rec}}\langle\langle T_\Sigma\rangle\rangle$ we have that $\psi \overleftarrow{\mathrm{o}} (\psi_1, \ldots, \psi_n) \in \mathcal{A}^{\mathrm{rec}}\langle\langle T_\Sigma\rangle\rangle$.*

Proof. The statement is proved for OI-substitution in [24, Corollary 14]. Since OI-substitution coincides with o-substitution on nondeleting and linear target tree series (see Proposition 1), we obtain the statement.

We would like to achieve a result which does not depend on nondeletion of ψ (see Theorem 2). Let us show the main idea in a simple setting. Let $\psi \in \mathcal{A}^{\mathrm{rec}}\langle\langle T_\Sigma(X_1)\rangle\rangle$

be linear in X_1 and $\psi_1 \in \mathcal{A}^{\mathrm{rec}}\langle\!\langle T_\Sigma \rangle\!\rangle$. Our goal is to show that $\psi \leftarrow_{\mathrm{o}} (\psi_1)$ is recognizable, thus we need to present a wta $M' = (Q', \Sigma, \mathcal{A}, F', \mu')$ that recognizes $\psi \leftarrow_{\mathrm{o}} (\psi_1)$. Let $M = (Q, \Delta, \mathcal{A}, F, \mu)$ and $M_1 = (Q_1, \Sigma, \mathcal{A}, F_1, \mu_1)$ be wta that recognize ψ and ψ_1, respectively. We employ a standard idea for the construction of M'. Roughly speaking, we take the disjoint union of M and M_1 and add transitions that nondeterministically change from M_1 to M. More precisely, for every $k \in \mathbb{N}_+$, $\sigma \in \Sigma_k$, $q \in Q$, and $q_1, \ldots, q_k \in Q_1$ we set

$$\mu'_k(\sigma)_{q,q_1,\ldots,q_k} = \sum_{p \in Q_1} \mu_0(x_1)_q \cdot (F_1)_p \cdot (\mu_1)_k(\sigma)_{p,q_1,\ldots,q_k} .$$

Roughly, for each state p of M_1 we take $(\mu_1)_k(\sigma)_{p,q_1\cdots q_k}$ of M_1, multiply $(F_1)_p$, and multiply $\mu_0(x_1)_q$ for entering M (via x_1) in state q. Nullary symbols σ are treated similarly. We employ a proof method, which requires us to make the input alphabets Σ and Δ disjoint. This simplifies the proof because each tree then admits a unique decomposition into (at most one) part that needs to be processed by M_1 and a part that needs to be processed by M.

Proposition 3. *Let $\mathcal{A}$ be idempotent and continuous. Let $J \subseteq I \subseteq \mathbb{N}_+$ be finite, $\psi \in \mathcal{A}\langle\!\langle T_\Delta(X) \rangle\!\rangle$ such that $J \cap \mathrm{var}(\psi) = I \cap \mathrm{var}(\psi)$, and for every $i \in I$ let $\psi_i \in \mathcal{A}\langle\!\langle T_\Delta(X) \rangle\!\rangle$ such that $\psi_i \neq \widetilde{0}$ for every $i \in I \setminus J$.*

$$\psi \leftarrow_{\mathrm{o}} (\psi_i)_{i \in I} = \psi \leftarrow_{\mathrm{o}} (\psi_j)_{j \in J}$$

Theorem 4. *Let $\mathcal{A}$ be a continuous and idempotent semiring. Let $n \in \mathbb{N}$, $\psi \in \mathcal{A}^{\mathrm{rec}}\langle\!\langle T_\Sigma(X_n) \rangle\!\rangle$ be linear in X_n, and $\psi_1, \ldots, \psi_n \in \mathcal{A}^{\mathrm{rec}}\langle\!\langle T_\Sigma \rangle\!\rangle$.*

$$\psi \leftarrow_{\mathrm{o}} (\psi_1, \ldots, \psi_n) \in \mathcal{A}^{\mathrm{rec}}\langle\!\langle T_\Sigma \rangle\!\rangle$$

Proof. Let $\psi_i = \widetilde{0}$ for some $i \in [n]$. Then $\psi \leftarrow_{\mathrm{o}} (\psi_1, \ldots, \psi_n) = \widetilde{0}$, which is recognizable. Thus let $\psi_i \neq \widetilde{0}$ for all $i \in [n]$. For every $k \in \mathbb{N}_+$ let $\Delta_k = \Sigma_k$ and $\Delta_0 = \Sigma_0 \cup X_n$. Since $\psi \in \mathcal{A}^{\mathrm{rec}}\langle\!\langle T_\Sigma(X_n) \rangle\!\rangle$ and $\psi_1, \ldots, \psi_n \in \mathcal{A}^{\mathrm{rec}}\langle\!\langle T_\Sigma \rangle\!\rangle$, there exist wta $M = (Q, \Delta, \mathcal{A}, F, \mu)$ and $M_i = (Q_i, \Sigma, \mathcal{A}, F_i, \mu_i)$ such that $\|M\| = \psi$ and $\|M_i\| = \psi_i$ for every $i \in [n]$.

For every $i \in [n]$ and $k \in \mathbb{N}$ let $\overline{\Sigma}^i$ be $\overline{\Sigma}_k^i = \{\overline{\sigma}^i \mid \sigma \in \Sigma_k\}$. We define $\mathrm{bar}_i \colon T_\Sigma \longrightarrow T_{\overline{\Sigma}^i}$ by $\mathrm{bar}_i(\sigma(t_1, \ldots, t_k)) = \overline{\sigma}^i(\mathrm{bar}_i(t_1), \ldots, \mathrm{bar}_i(t_k))$ for every $k \in \mathbb{N}$, $\sigma \in \Sigma_k$, and $t_1, \ldots, t_k \in T_\Sigma$. Moreover, we define the mapping $\mathrm{bar}_i \colon \mathcal{A}\langle\!\langle T_\Sigma \rangle\!\rangle \longrightarrow \mathcal{A}\langle\!\langle T_{\overline{\Sigma}^i} \rangle\!\rangle$ for every $\varphi \in \mathcal{A}\langle\!\langle T_\Sigma \rangle\!\rangle$ by

$$\mathrm{bar}_i(\varphi) = \sum_{t \in T_\Sigma} (\varphi, t)\, \mathrm{bar}_i(t) .$$

Without loss of generality, we assume that for every $i \in [n]$ we have that (i) Σ and $\overline{\Sigma}^i$ are disjoint and (ii) Q and Q_i are disjoint. Let $\Sigma'_k = \Sigma_k \cup \bigcup_{1 \leq i \leq n} \overline{\Sigma}_k^i$ for every $k \in \mathbb{N}$, and $Q' = Q \cup \bigcup_{1 \leq i \leq n} Q_i$. We construct a wta M' recognizing $\psi \leftarrow_{\mathrm{o}} (\mathrm{bar}_1(\psi_1), \ldots, \mathrm{bar}_n(\psi_n))$ as follows. Let $M' = (Q', \Sigma', \mathcal{A}, F', \mu')$ where for every $i \in [n]$, $k \in \mathbb{N}$, $\sigma \in \Sigma_k$:

- $F'_q = F_q$ for every $q \in Q$ and $F'_p = 0$ for every $p \in \bigcup_{1 \leq i \leq n} Q_i$;
- $\mu'_k(\overline{\sigma}^i)_{p,w} = (\mu_i)_k(\sigma)_{p,w}$ for every $p \in Q_i$ and $w \in (Q_i)^k$;
- $\mu'_k(\sigma)_{q,w} = \mu_k(\sigma)_{q,w}$ for every $q \in Q$ and $w \in Q^k$; and
- $\mu'_k(\overline{\sigma}^i)_{q,w} = \sum_{p \in Q_i} \mu_0(\mathrm{x}_i)_q \cdot (F_i)_p \cdot (\mu_i)_k(\sigma)_{p,w}$ for every $q \in Q$ and $w \in (Q_i)^k$.

All the remaining entries in μ' are set to 0.

We claim that $\psi' = \psi \overleftarrow{\leftarrow}_{\mathrm{o}} (\mathrm{bar}_1(\psi_1), \ldots, \mathrm{bar}_n(\psi_n))$ is recognizable. In fact, M' recognizes ψ'. Clearly, $h_{\mu'}(\mathrm{bar}_i(t))_p = h_{\mu_i}(t)_p$ for every $i \in [n]$, $t \in T_\Sigma$, and $p \in Q_i$. Next we prove that for every $q \in Q$ and $t \in T_\Sigma(X_n)$, which is linear in X_n, and family $(u_i)_{i \in \mathrm{var}(t)} \in T_\Sigma^{\mathrm{var}(t)}$ we have

$$h_{\mu'}(t[\mathrm{bar}_i(u_i)]_{i \in \mathrm{var}(t)})_q = h_\mu(t)_q \cdot \prod_{i \in \mathrm{var}(t)} (\|M_i\|, u_i) .$$

We prove this statement inductively, so let $t = \mathrm{x}_j$ for some $j \in [n]$. Moreover, let $u_j = \sigma(t_1, \ldots, t_k)$ for some $k \in \mathbb{N}$, $\sigma \in \Sigma_k$, and $t_1, \ldots, t_k \in T_\Sigma$.

$$h_{\mu'}(\mathrm{x}_j[\mathrm{bar}_i(u_i)]_{i \in \mathrm{var}(\mathrm{x}_j)})_q$$

$=$ (by substitution and definition of bar_j)

$$h_{\mu'}(\overline{\sigma}^j(\mathrm{bar}_j(t_1), \ldots, \mathrm{bar}_j(t_k)))_q$$

$$= \sum_{q_1, \ldots, q_k \in Q'} \mu'_k(\overline{\sigma}^j)_{q, q_1 \cdots q_k} \cdot \prod_{i \in [k]} h_{\mu'}(\mathrm{bar}_j(t_i))_{q_i}$$

$=$ (by definition of μ' and $h_{\mu'}(\mathrm{bar}_j(t_i))_{q_i} = h_{\mu_j}(t_i)_{q_i}$)

$$= \sum_{q_1, \ldots, q_k \in Q_j} \sum_{p \in Q_j} \mu_0(\mathrm{x}_j)_q \cdot (F_j)_p \cdot (\mu_j)_k(\sigma)_{p, q_1 \cdots q_k} \cdot \prod_{i \in [k]} h_{\mu_j}(t_i)_{q_i}$$

$$= \sum_{p \in Q_j} \mu_0(\mathrm{x}_j)_q \cdot (F_j)_p \cdot h_{\mu_j}(\sigma(t_1, \ldots, t_k))_p$$

$$= \mu_0(\mathrm{x}_j)_q \cdot (\|M_j\|, \sigma(t_1, \ldots, t_k))$$

$$= h_\mu(\mathrm{x}_j)_q \cdot \prod_{i \in \mathrm{var}(\mathrm{x}_j)} (\|M_i\|, u_i)$$

Let $t = \sigma(t_1, \ldots, t_k)$ for some $k \in \mathbb{N}$, $\sigma \in \Sigma_k$, and $t_1, \ldots, t_k \in T_\Sigma(X_n)$.

$$h_{\mu'}(\sigma(t_1, \ldots, t_k)[\mathrm{bar}_i(u_i)]_{i \in \mathrm{var}(t)})_q$$

$=$ (by substitution)

$$h_{\mu'}(\sigma(t_1[\mathrm{bar}_i(u_i)]_{i \in \mathrm{var}(t_1)}, \ldots, t_k[\mathrm{bar}_i(u_i)]_{i \in \mathrm{var}(t_k)}))_q$$

$$= \sum_{q_1, \ldots, q_k \in Q'} \mu'_k(\sigma)_{q, q_1 \cdots q_k} \cdot \prod_{j \in [k]} h_{\mu'}(t_j[\mathrm{bar}_i(u_i)]_{i \in \mathrm{var}(t_j)})_{q_j}$$

$$= \quad \text{(by induction hypothesis and definition of } \mu')$$

$$\sum_{q_1,\dots,q_k \in Q} \mu_k(\sigma)_{q,q_1 \cdots q_k} \cdot \prod_{j \in [k]} \left(h_\mu(t_j)_{q_j} \cdot \prod_{i \in \mathrm{var}(t_j)} (\|M_i\|, u_i) \right)$$

$$= h_\mu(\sigma(t_1,\dots,t_k))_q \cdot \prod_{j \in [k], i \in \mathrm{var}(t_j)} (\|M_i\|, u_i)$$

$$= \quad \text{(because } t \text{ is linear in } X_n)$$

$$h_\mu(\sigma(t_1,\dots,t_k))_q \cdot \prod_{i \in \mathrm{var}(t)} (\|M_i\|, u_i)$$

This completes the proof of the auxiliary statement. Consequently,

$$(\|M'\|, t[\mathrm{bar}_i(u_i)]_{i \in \mathrm{var}(t)}) = (\|M\|, t) \cdot \prod_{i \in \mathrm{var}(t)} (\|M_i\|, u_i)$$

$$= (\psi, t) \cdot \prod_{i \in \mathrm{var}(t)} (\psi_i, u_i) \ . \tag{1}$$

Using this result, we can show that $\psi' = \psi \leftarrow_\circ (\mathrm{bar}_i(\psi_i))_{i \in I}$ is recognizable. In fact, this is the tree series that is recognized by M'.

$$\psi \leftarrow_\circ (\mathrm{bar}_1(\psi_1),\dots,\mathrm{bar}_n(\psi_n))$$

$$= \quad \text{(by distributivity)}$$

$$\sum_{t \in \mathrm{supp}(\psi)} (\psi, t) \cdot \left((1 \, t) \leftarrow_\circ (\mathrm{bar}_1(\psi_1),\dots,\mathrm{bar}_n(\psi_n)) \right)$$

$$= \quad \text{(by Proposition 3)}$$

$$\sum_{t \in \mathrm{supp}(\psi)} (\psi, t) \cdot \left((1 \, t) \leftarrow_\circ (\mathrm{bar}_i(\psi_i))_{i \in \mathrm{var}(t)} \right)$$

$$= \quad \text{(by definition of } \leftarrow_\circ \text{ because } t \text{ is linear)}$$

$$\sum_{\substack{t \in \mathrm{supp}(\psi), \\ (\forall i \in \mathrm{var}(t)) \colon u_i \in \mathrm{supp}(\mathrm{bar}_i(\psi_i))}} \left((\psi, t) \cdot \prod_{i \in \mathrm{var}(t)} (\mathrm{bar}_i(\psi_i), u_i) \right) t[u_i]_{i \in \mathrm{var}(t)}$$

$$= \quad \text{(by definition of } \mathrm{bar}_i)$$

$$\sum_{\substack{t \in T_\Sigma(X_n), \\ (\forall i \in \mathrm{var}(t)) \colon u_i \in T_\Sigma}} \left((\psi, t) \cdot \prod_{i \in \mathrm{var}(t)} (\psi_i, u_i) \right) t[\mathrm{bar}_i(u_i)]_{i \in \mathrm{var}(t)}$$

$$= \quad \text{(by (1))}$$

$$\sum_{\substack{t \in T_\Sigma(X_n), \\ (\forall i \in \mathrm{var}(t)) \colon u_i \in T_\Sigma}} \left(\|M\|, t[\mathrm{bar}_i(u_i)]_{i \in \mathrm{var}(t)} \right) t[\mathrm{bar}_i(u_i)]_{i \in \mathrm{var}(t)}$$

$$= \sum_{\substack{u \in T_{\Sigma'} }} \left(\sum_{\substack{t \in T_\Sigma(X_n), \\ (\forall i \in \mathrm{var}(t)):\, u_i \in T_\Sigma}} \left(\|M\|, t[\mathrm{bar}_i(u_i)]_{i \in \mathrm{var}(t)} \right) t[\mathrm{bar}_i(u_i)]_{i \in \mathrm{var}(t)} \,,\, u \right) u$$

$$= \qquad \text{(because } t \text{ and } u_i \text{ are uniquely determined by } u \text{)}$$

$$\sum_{u \in T_{\Sigma'}} \left(\|M\|, u \right) u \;=\; \|M\|$$

Finally, we need to remove the annotation. To this end we define the mapping unbar: $T_{\Sigma'}(X) \longrightarrow T_\Sigma(X)$ for every $x \in X$, $k \in \mathbb{N}$, $i \in [n]$, $\sigma \in \Sigma_k$, and $t_1, \dots, t_k \in T_{\Sigma'}(X)$ by

$$\mathrm{unbar}(x) = x$$
$$\mathrm{unbar}(\sigma(t_1, \dots, t_k)) = \sigma(\mathrm{unbar}(t_1), \dots, \mathrm{unbar}(t_k))$$
$$\mathrm{unbar}(\overline{\sigma}^i(t_1, \dots, t_k)) = \sigma(\mathrm{unbar}(t_1), \dots, \mathrm{unbar}(t_k)) \ .$$

Finally, let unbar: $\mathcal{A}\langle\!\langle T_{\Sigma'}(X) \rangle\!\rangle \longrightarrow \mathcal{A}\langle\!\langle T_\Sigma(X) \rangle\!\rangle$ be defined by

$$\mathrm{unbar}(\varphi) = \sum_{t \in T_{\Sigma'}(X)} (\varphi, t)\, \mathrm{unbar}(t)$$

for every $\varphi \in \mathcal{A}\langle\!\langle T_{\Sigma'}(X) \rangle\!\rangle$. Clearly, $\mathrm{unbar}(\psi') = \psi \xleftarrow{\ \ }_{\mathrm{o}} (\psi_1, \dots, \psi_n)$. Moreover, unbar can be realized by a nondeleting, linear tree transducer (with one state) of [24] (which uses OI substitution). Since ψ' is a recognizable tree series and nondeleting, linear tree transducers of [24] preserve recognizability, also $\mathrm{unbar}(\psi')$ is recognizable, which proves the statement.

Let us illustrate the previous theorem on an example.

Example 5. Let $\Sigma = \{\gamma^{(1)}, \alpha^{(0)}\}$ and consider the arctic semiring. Let

$$\psi = \max_{u \in T_\Sigma(X_1)} \mathrm{height}(u)\, u \quad \text{and} \quad \psi' = \max_{u \in T_\Sigma} \mathrm{height}(u)\, u \ .$$

Then $\psi \xleftarrow{\ \ }_{\mathrm{o}} (\psi')$ is recognizable. In fact, $\psi \xleftarrow{\ \ }_{\mathrm{o}} (\psi') = \psi'$. We show the wta that recognize ψ and $\psi \xleftarrow{\ \ }_{\mathrm{o}} (\psi')$ [the automaton that is constructed in Theorem 4] in Fig. 2.

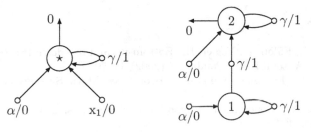

Fig. 2. Wta recognizing ψ [left] and $\psi \xleftarrow{\ \ }_{\mathrm{o}} (\psi')$ [right] over $\mathbb{A}$

4   Application to Tree Series Transducers

In Theorem 4 we showed that o-substitution preserves recognizability under certain conditions. We now apply this theorem to tst. In fact this means that theorems about wta can be applied. We demonstrate such an application after the theorem.

Theorem 6. *Let $\mathcal{A}$ be an idempotent and continuous semiring. Moreover, let $M = (Q, \Sigma, \Delta, \mathcal{A}, F, \mu)$ be a linear recognizable tst. Then $\|M\|^\circ(t)$ is recognizable for every $t \in T_\Sigma$.*

Proof. We first prove that $h_\mu^\circ(t)_q$ is recognizable for every $t \in T_\Sigma$ and $q \in Q$ by induction on t. Let $t = \sigma(t_1, \ldots, t_k)$ for some $k \in \mathbb{N}$, $\sigma \in \Sigma_k$, and $t_1, \ldots, t_k \in T_\Sigma$.

$$h_\mu^\circ(\sigma(t_1, \ldots, t_k))_q = \sum_{\substack{w \in Q(X_k)^*, \\ w = q_1(x_{i_1}) \cdots q_n(x_{i_n})}} \mu_k(\sigma)_{q,w} \xleftarrow{\;\;\circ\;\;} (h_\mu^\circ(t_{i_1})_{q_1}, \ldots, h_\mu^\circ(t_{i_n})_{q_n}) \ .$$

By induction hypothesis $h_\mu^\circ(t_{i_j})_{q_j}$ is recognizable for every $j \in [n]$. Since M is recognizable, $\mu_k(\sigma)_{q,w}$ is recognizable. By Theorem 4 also

$$\mu_k(\sigma)_{q,w} \xleftarrow{\;\;\circ\;\;} (h_\mu^\circ(t_{i_1})_{q_1}, \ldots, h_\mu^\circ(t_{i_n})_{q_n})$$

is recognizable because $\mu_k(\sigma)_{q,w}$ is linear in X_n. Since recognizable tree series are closed under finite sums [4] we obtain that $h_\mu^\circ(t)_q$ is recognizable.

For every $t \in T_\Sigma$ we have $\|M\|^\circ(t) = \sum_{q \in Q} F_q \xleftarrow{\;\;\circ\;\;} (h_\mu^\circ(t)_q)$. We showed that $h_\mu^\circ(t)_q$ is recognizable. Moreover, $F_q \xleftarrow{\;\;\circ\;\;} (h_\mu^\circ(t)_q)$ is recognizable due to Theorem 4. Thus, also $\|M\|^\circ(t)$ is recognizable.

Since idempotent semirings are zero-sum free [25], we obtain the following corollary. Other results on recognizable tree series can be applied similarly.

Corollary 7. *Let $\mathcal{A}$ be an idempotent and continuous semiring with recursive operations. Moreover, let $M = (Q, \Sigma, \Delta, \mathcal{A}, F, \mu)$ be a linear recognizable tst. Then for every $t \in T_\Sigma$ it is decidable whether $\|M\|^\circ(t) = \widetilde{0}$ or not.*

Proof. By Theorem 6 we have that $\psi = \|M\|^\circ(t)$ is recognizable and by [26] we can decide whether $\psi = \widetilde{0}$.

References

1. Engelfriet, J., Fülöp, Z., Vogler, H.: Bottom-up and top-down tree series transformations. J. Autom. Lang. Combin. **7** (2002) 11–70
2. Rounds, W.C.: Mappings and grammars on trees. Math. Systems Theory **4** (1970) 257–287
3. Thatcher, J.W.: Generalized² sequential machine maps. J. Comput. System Sci. **4** (1970) 339–367
4. Berstel, J., Reutenauer, C.: Recognizable formal power series on trees. Theoret. Comput. Sci. **18** (1982) 115–148

5. Kuich, W.: Formal power series over trees. In Bozapalidis, S., ed.: Proc. 3rd Int. Conf. Develop. in Lang. Theory, Aristotle University of Thessaloniki (1998) 61–101
6. Irons, E.T.: A syntax directed compiler for ALGOL 60. Commun. ACM **4** (1961) 51–55
7. Morawietz, F., Cornell, T.: The MSO logic-automation connection in linguistics. In Lecomte, A., Lamarche, F., Perrier, G., eds.: Proc. 2nd Int. Conf. Logical Aspects of Comput. Linguist. Volume 1582 of LNCS. (1999) 112–131
8. Bex, G.J., Maneth, S., Neven, F.: A formal model for an expressive fragment of XSLT. Inform. Systems **27** (2002) 21–39
9. Ferdinand, C., Seidl, H., Wilhelm, R.: Tree automata for code selection. Acta Inform. **31** (1994) 741–760
10. Seidl, H.: Finite tree automata with cost functions. Theoret. Comput. Sci. **126** (1994) 113–142
11. López, D., Piñaga, I.: Syntactic pattern recognition by error correcting analysis on tree automata. In Ferri, F.J., Quereda, J.M.I., Amin, A., Pudil, P., eds.: Proc. Joint IAPR Int. Workshops Advances in Pattern Recognition. Volume 1876 of LNCS., Springer (2000) 133–142
12. Graehl, J., Knight, K.: Training tree transducers. In: HLT-NAACL. (2004) 105–112
13. Borchardt, B.: Code selection by tree series transducers. In Domaratzki, M., Okhotin, A., Salomaa, K., Yu, S., eds.: Proc. 9th Int. Conf. Implementation and Application of Automata. Volume 3317 of LNCS., Springer (2004) 57–67
14. Yamada, K., Knight, K.: A syntax-based statistical translation model. In: Proc. 39th Annual Meeting Assoc. Comput. Ling., Morgan Kaufmann (2001) 523–530
15. Brown, P.F., Cocke, J., Della Pietra, S., Della Pietra, V.J., Jelinek, F., Mercer, R.L., Roossin, P.S.: A statistical approach to language translation. In: Proc. 12th Int. Conf. Comput. Ling. (1988) 71–76
16. Brown, P.F., Della Pietra, S., Della Pietra, V.J., Mercer, R.L.: The mathematics of statistical machine translation: Parameter estimation. Comput. Linguist. **19** (1993) 263–311
17. Fülöp, Z., Vogler, H.: Tree series transformations that respect copying. Theory Comput. Systems **36** (2003) 247–293
18. Bozapalidis, S.: Equational elements in additive algebras. Theory Comput. Systems **32** (1999) 1–33
19. Kuich, W.: Full abstract families of tree series I. In Karhumäki, J., Maurer, H.A., Paun, G., Rozenberg, G., eds.: Jewels Are Forever. Springer (1999) 145–156
20. Ésik, Z., Kuich, W.: Formal tree series. J. Autom. Lang. Combin. **8** (2003) 219–285
21. Borchardt, B.: The Theory of Recognizable Tree Series. PhD thesis, Technische Universität Dresden (2005)
22. Pech, C.: Kleene-Type Results for Weighted Tree-Automata. PhD thesis, Technische Universität Dresden (2003)
23. Engelfriet, J.: Tree automata and tree grammars. Technical Report DAIMI FN-10, Aarhus University (1975)
24. Kuich, W.: Tree transducers and formal tree series. Acta Cybernet. **14** (1999) 135–149
25. Golan, J.S.: Semirings and their Applications. Kluwer Academic, Dordrecht (1999)
26. Maletti, A.: Relating tree series transducers and weighted tree automata. Int. J. Found. Comput. Sci. **16** (2005) 723–741

Correctness Preservation and Complexity of Simple RL-Automata*

H. Messerschmidt[1], F. Mráz[2], F. Otto[1], and M. Plátek[2]

[1] Fachbereich Mathematik/Informatik, Universität Kassel
34109 Kassel, Germany
{hardy, otto}@theory.informatik.uni-kassel.de
[2] Charles University, Faculty of Mathematics and Physics
Department of Computer Science, Malostranské nám. 25
118 00 Praha 1, Czech Republic
mraz@ksvi.ms.mff.cuni.cz, Martin.Platek@mff.cuni.cz

Abstract. *Analysis by reduction* is a method used in linguistics for checking the correctness of sentences of natural languages. This method can be modelled by *restarting automata*. Here we study a new type of restarting automaton, the so-called *t-sRL-automaton*, which is an RL-automaton that is rather restricted in that it has a window of size 1 only, and that it works under a *minimal acceptance condition*. On the other hand, it is allowed to perform up to *t* rewrite (that is, delete) steps per cycle. We study the *correctness preservation* of these automata on the one hand, and the *complexity* of these automata on the other hand, establishing a *complexity measure* that is based on the description of *t*-sRL-automata in terms of so-called *meta-instructions*. We present a hierarchy result and we show that the correctness preserving nondeterministic *t*-sRL-automata are not stronger than the deterministic *t*-sRL-automata.

1 Introduction

The original motivation for introducing the restarting automaton was the desire to model the so-called *analysis by reduction* of natural languages. Analysis by reduction is usually presented by finite samples of sentences of a natural language and by sequences of their correct reductions (see, e.g., [6]). An important property of the analysis by reduction is the so-called *correctness preserving property*. Restarting automata with this property form a useful tool for robust parsing with the syntactic error detection and error recovery capabilities [5,11]. Similarly they form a basis for the linguistic task of rule-based disambiguation (see, e.g., [2]).

* F. Mráz and M. Plátek were partially supported by the Grant Agency of the Czech Republic under Grant-No. 201/04/2102 and by the program 'Information Society' under project 1ET100300517. F. Mráz was also partially supported by the Grant Agency of Charles University in Prague under Grant-No. 358/2006/A-INF/MFF.

O.H. Ibarra and H.-C. Yen (Eds.): CIAA 2006, LNCS 4094, pp. 162–172, 2006.
© Springer-Verlag Berlin Heidelberg 2006

Here we continue the study of a new variant of the restarting automaton, the so-called *simple* RL-*automaton* (sRL-automaton) [10], that is rather restricted in various aspects. However, by admitting that t (≥ 1) delete operations may be performed in each cycle, the expressive power of this model of the restarting automaton is parametrized by t, which yields an infinite hierarchy of automata and language classes. In [10] we studied the number of gaps generated during a reduction as a dynamic complexity measure for t-sRL-automata. A bounded number of gaps implies that only feasible languages are accepted, that is, languages that are recognizable in polynomial time, while with an unbounded number of gaps these automata accept NP-complete languages.

Here we concentrate on the correctness preserving property of sRL-automata and their descriptional complexity. A (nondeterministic) sRL-automaton M can be seen as a reduction system which defines a 'simplification' relation $\vdash^c_M$ on the set of its input words. For two words u and v, the relation $u \vdash^c_M v$ expresses the fact that M can reduce u to v in a single cycle of a computation. A nondeterministic sRL-automaton M is called *strongly correctness preserving* if, for each cycle $u \vdash^c_M v$ of M, the word v produced belongs to the language $L(M)$ accepted by M if the word u belongs to the language $L(M)$ (see Section 2 for the definitions). Thus, if $u \in L(M)$, then each reduction that M may apply to u produces an element of $L(M)$. While nondeterministic sRL-automata are clearly more expressive than their deterministic counterparts, we will see that this in not true anymore when we restrict our attention to nondeterministic sRL-automata that are strongly correctness preserving.

In [3] a complexity measure is defined for restarting automata that is based on the length of their description in terms of elementary instructions, and exponential trade-offs are established between nondeterministic and deterministic finite-state acceptors and deterministic 1-sRR-automata (that is 1-sRL-automata which do not use move-left instructions). Working with elementary instructions of restarting automata is very cumbersome. More conveniently a t-sRL-automaton can be described by a finite set of reduction rules called 'meta-instructions.' Accordingly, we introduce a new descriptional complexity measure for sRL-automata — the number of meta-instructions — and we establish an infinite hierarchy with respect to this measure.

The paper is structured as follows. After introducing the simple RL-automaton in Section 2 and restating some of its basic properties, we present the announced result on correctness preserving sRL-automata. The complexity measure is then introduced and studied in Section 3. Another complexity measure for sRL-automata is briefly mentioned in the concluding section.

2   The t-sRL-Automaton

Here we describe in short the type of restarting automaton we will be dealing with. More details on restarting automata in general can be found in [12].

An sRL-*automaton* (*simple* RL-*automaton*) M is a (in general) nondeterministic machine with a finite-state control Q, a finite input alphabet Σ, and a head (window of size 1) that works on a flexible tape delimited by the left sentinel ¢ and the right sentinel \$. For an input $w \in \Sigma^*$, the initial tape inscription is ¢w\$. To process this input M starts in its initial state q_0 with its window over the left end of the tape, scanning the left sentinel ¢. According to its transition relation, M performs *move-right steps* and *move-left steps*, which change the state of M and shift the window one position to the right or to the left, respectively, and *delete steps*, which delete the content of the window, thus shortening the tape, change the state, and shift the window to the right neighbour of the symbol deleted. Of course, neither the left sentinel ¢ nor the right sentinel \$ may be deleted. At the right end of the tape M either halts and accepts, or it halts and rejects, or it *restarts*, that is, it places its window over the left end of the tape and reenters the initial state. It is required that before the first restart step and also between any two restart steps, M executes at least one delete operation.

A *configuration* of M is a string $\alpha q \beta$ where $q \in Q$, and either $\alpha = \lambda$ and $\beta \in \{¢\} \cdot \Sigma^* \cdot \{\$\}$ or $\alpha \in \{¢\} \cdot \Sigma^*$ and $\beta \in \Sigma^* \cdot \{\$\}$; here q represents the current state, $\alpha\beta$ is the current content of the tape, and it is understood that the window contains the first symbol of β. A configuration of the form q_0¢w\$ is called a *restarting configuration*.

We observe that each computation of an sRL-automaton M consists of certain phases. Each part of a computation of M from a restarting configuration to the next restarting configuration is called a *cycle*. The part after the last restart operation is called the *tail*. We use the notation $u \vdash^c_M v$ to denote a cycle of M that begins with the restarting configuration q_0¢u\$ and ends with the restarting configuration q_0¢v\$; the relation $\vdash^{c^*}_M$ is the reflexive and transitive closure of $\vdash^c_M$. We require that no delete operation is executed in a tail computation. Observe that this does not influence the expressive power of (nondeterministic) sRL-automata.

An input $w \in \Sigma^*$ is *accepted* by M, if there is an accepting computation which starts with the (initial) configuration q_0¢w\$. By $L(M)$ we denote the language consisting of all words accepted by M; we say that M *recognizes (accepts) the language* $L(M)$. By $S(M)$ we denote the *simple language* accepted by M, which consists of all words that M accepts by tail computations. Obviously, $S(M)$ is a regular sublanguage of $L(M)$. By $RS(M)$ we denote the *reduction system* $RS(M) := (\Sigma^*, \vdash^c_M, S(M))$ that is induced by M. Observe that, for each $w \in \Sigma^*$, we have $w \in L(M)$ if and only if $w \vdash^{c^*}_M v$ holds for some word $v \in S(M)$.

We say that M is an sRR-automaton if M does not use any move-left steps. By sRL (sRR) we denote the class of all sRL-automata (sRR-automata). A t-sRL-automaton ($t \geq 1$) is an sRL-automaton which uses at most t delete operations in a cycle, and similarly we obtain the t-sRR-automaton. By $\mathcal{L}(A)$ we denote the class of languages that are accepted by automata of type A (A-automata), and by $\mathcal{L}_{\leq n}(A)$ we denote the class of finite languages that are accepted by automata of type A and that do not contain any words of length exceeding the number n.

On the set of words Σ^*, we consider the well-founded partial ordering $\leq$ that is defined by $u \leq v$ if and only if u is a scattered subword of v. By $<$ we denote the proper part of $\leq$.

For $L \subseteq \Sigma^*$, let $L_{\min} := \{ w \in L \mid u < w$ does not hold for any $u \in L \}$, that is, $L_{\min}$ is the set of minimal words of L. It is well-known that $L_{\min}$ is finite for each language L (see, e.g., [7]). We say that an sRL-automaton M accepting the language L works with *minimal acceptance* if it accepts in tail computations exactly the words of the language $L_{\min}$, that is, $S(M) = L_{\min}$. Thus, each word $w \in L \setminus L_{\min}$ is reduced to a word $w' \in L_{\min}$ by a sequence of cycles of M. We will use the prefix min- to denote sRL-automata that work with minimal acceptance.

An sRL-automaton working with minimal acceptance is forced to perform sequences of cycles even for accepting a regular language. In fact, this is even true for most finite languages.

Example 1. Let $t \geq 1$, and let $L^{<t>} := \{a^t, \lambda\}$. Then $L^{<t>}_{\min} = \{\lambda\}$. Hence, an sRL-automaton for the language $L^{<t>}$ that works with minimal acceptance must execute the cycle $a^t \vdash^c \lambda$, which means that it must execute t delete operations during this cycle. Hence, it is a t-sRL-automaton.

Concerning the relationship between sRR- and sRL-automata, we have the following important result, which generalizes a corresponding result for RLWW-automata from [14].

Theorem 1. [10] *For each integer $t \geq 1$ and each t-sRL-automaton M, there exists a t-sRR-automaton M' such that the reduction systems $\mathrm{RS}(M)$ and $\mathrm{RS}(M')$ coincide.*

Observe that, in each cycle, M' executes its up to t delete operations strictly from left to right, while M may execute them in arbitrary order.

Based on Theorem 1 we can describe a t-sRL-automaton by meta-instructions of the form $(\mathfrak{c} \cdot E_0, a_1, E_1, a_2, E_2, \ldots, E_{s-1}, a_s, E_s \cdot \$)$, where $1 \leq s \leq t$, $E_0, E_1, \ldots, E_s$ are regular languages (often represented by regular expressions), called the *regular constraints* of this instruction, and $a_1, a_2, \ldots, a_s \in \Sigma$ correspond to letters that are deleted by M during one cycle. On trying to execute this meta-instruction starting from a configuration $q_0 \mathfrak{c} w \$$, M will get stuck (and so reject), if w does not admit a factorization of the form $w = v_0 a_1 v_1 a_2 \cdots v_{s-1} a_s v_s$ such that $v_i \in E_i$ for all $i = 0, \ldots, s$. On the other hand, if w admits factorizations of this form, then one of them is chosen nondeterministically, and $q_0 \mathfrak{c} w \$$ is transformed into $q_0 \mathfrak{c} v_0 v_1 \cdots v_{s-1} v_s \$$. In order to also describe the tails of accepting computations, we use accepting meta-instructions of the form $(\mathfrak{c} \cdot E \cdot \$, \mathsf{Accept})$, where E is a regular language. Actually we can require that there is only a single accepting meta-instruction for M. If M works with minimal acceptance, then this accepting meta-instruction is of the form $(\mathfrak{c} \cdot L(M)_{\min} \cdot \$, \mathsf{Accept})$.

Example 2. Let $t \geq 1$, and let $LR_t := \{ c_0 w c_1 w c_2 \cdots c_{t-1} w \mid w \in \{a, b\}^* \}$, where $\Sigma_0 := \{a, b\}$ and $\Sigma_t := \{c_0, c_1, \ldots, c_{t-1}\} \cup \Sigma_0$. We obtain a t-sRR-automaton M_t for the language LR_t through the following sequence of meta-instructions:

(1) $(\mathfrak{c} c_0, a, \Sigma_0^* \cdot c_1, a, \Sigma_0^* \cdot c_2, \ldots, \Sigma_0^* \cdot c_{t-1}, a, \Sigma_0^* \cdot \$)$,
(2) $(\mathfrak{c} c_0, b, \Sigma_0^* \cdot c_1, b, \Sigma_0^* \cdot c_2, \ldots, \Sigma_0^* \cdot c_{t-1}, b, \Sigma_0^* \cdot \$)$,
(3) $(\mathfrak{c} c_0 c_1 \cdots c_{t-1} \$, \mathsf{Accept})$.

It follows easily that $L(M_t) = LR_t$ holds, and that M_t works with minimal acceptance. Actually, the automaton M_t is even deterministic.

For each $n \in \mathbb{N}_+$, we consider the finite approximation of order $(n + 1) \cdot t$ of the language LR_t which is defined as follows:

$$LR_t^{(n)} := \{ c_0 w c_1 w c_2 \cdots c_{t-1} w \mid w \in \{a, b\}^*, |w| \leq n \}.$$

A t-sRR-automaton $M_t^{(n)}$ for $LR_t^{(n)}$, also working with minimal acceptance, is easily obtained from M_t by taking the following sequence of meta-instructions, where $\Sigma_0^{\leq n-1} := \{ w \in \Sigma_0^* \mid |w| \leq n - 1 \}$:

(1) $(\text{¢}c_0, a, \Sigma_0^{\leq n-1} \cdot c_1, a, \Sigma_0^{\leq n-1} \cdot c_2, \ldots, \Sigma_0^{\leq n-1} \cdot c_{t-1}, a, \Sigma_0^{\leq n-1} \cdot \$)$,
(2) $(\text{¢}c_0, b, \Sigma_0^{\leq n-1} \cdot c_1, b, \Sigma_0^{\leq n-1} \cdot c_2, \ldots, \Sigma_0^{\leq n-1} \cdot c_{t-1}, b, \Sigma_0^{\leq n-1} \cdot \$)$,
(3) $(\text{¢}c_0 c_1 \cdots c_{t-1}\$, \text{Accept})$.

We emphasize the following properties of restarting automata, which are used implicitly in proofs. They play an important role in linguistic applications of restarting automata (e.g., for the analysis by reduction, grammar-checking, and morphological disambiguation).

Definition 1. (Correctness Preserving Property)
A t-sRL-automaton M is (strongly) correctness preserving if $u \in L(M)$ and $u \vdash_M^{c*} v$ imply that $v \in L(M)$.

Definition 2. (Error Preserving Property)
A t-sRL-automaton M is error preserving if $u \notin L(M)$ and $u \vdash_M^{c*} v$ imply that $v \notin L(M)$.

It is rather obvious that each t-sRL-automaton is error preserving, and that all deterministic t-sRL-automata are correctness preserving. On the other hand, one can easily construct examples of nondeterministic t-sRL-automata that are not correctness preserving.

Concerning the parameter t and the relation of t-sRL-automata to other language classes the following results have been obtained.

Theorem 2. [10] *For each suffix $Y \in \{\text{sRR}, \text{sRL}\}$, and each integer $t \geq 2$,*
(a) $\mathcal{L}(\text{det-}(t-1)\text{-Y}) \subset \mathcal{L}(\text{det-}t\text{-Y})$ *and*
    $\mathcal{L}((t-1)\text{-Y}) \subset \mathcal{L}(t\text{-Y})$.
(b) $\mathcal{L}(\text{min-det-}(t-1)\text{-Y}) \subset \mathcal{L}(\text{min-det-}t\text{-Y})$ *and*
    $\mathcal{L}(\text{min-}(t-1)\text{-Y}) \subset \mathcal{L}(\text{min-}t\text{-Y})$.
(c) $\mathcal{L}_{\leq n}(\text{min-det-}(t-1)\text{-Y}) \subset \mathcal{L}_{\leq n}(\text{min-det-}t\text{-Y})$ *and*
    $\mathcal{L}_{\leq n}(\text{min-}(t-1)\text{-Y}) \subset \mathcal{L}_{\leq n}(\text{min-}t\text{-Y})$ *for each $n \geq t$.*

Theorem 3. [10]
(a) $\text{DCFL} \subset \bigcup_{t \in \mathbb{N}_+} \mathcal{L}(\text{min-det-}t\text{-sRL}) \subset \bigcup_{t \in \mathbb{N}_+} \mathcal{L}(\text{min-}t\text{-sRL})$.
(b) *The language classes $\bigcup_{t \in \mathbb{N}_+} \mathcal{L}(\text{min-}t\text{-sRL})$ and $\bigcup_{t \in \mathbb{N}_+} \mathcal{L}(t\text{-sRL})$ are incomparable under inclusion to the class CFL of context-free languages and to the class GCSL of growing context-sensitive languages.*

Correctness preserving nondeterministic t-sRR-automata are strictly more expressive than deterministic t-sRR-automata. For example, the language $L :=$ $\{\, a^n b^n c, a^n b^{2n} d \mid n \geq 0 \,\}$ is accepted by the 3-sRR-automaton M that is given through the following meta-instructions:

$$(1)\ (\mathfrak{c}, a, a^*, b, b^* \cdot c \cdot \$),$$
$$(2)\ (\mathfrak{c}, a, a^*, b, \{\lambda\}, b, b^* \cdot d \cdot \$),$$
$$(3)\ (\mathfrak{c} \cdot (c + d) \cdot \$, \mathsf{Accept}).$$

If M should select the wrong meta-instruction, then this is recognized at the right sentinel, and then M simply halts and rejects. Thus, M is correctness preserving. On the other hand, it is easily shown that L cannot be accepted by a deterministic sRR-automaton. Surprisingly, however, we have the following equivalence for sRL-automata.

Theorem 4. *For each correctness preserving t-sRL-automaton M, there exists a deterministic t-sRL-automaton M' such that $L(M') = L(M)$.*

Proof. Let M be a correctness preserving t-sRL-automaton that is given through meta-instructions $I_1, \ldots, I_i$. We will describe a deterministic t-sRL-automaton M' that recognizes the same language as M. First, for each $j = 1, \ldots, i$, we construct a finite-state acceptor A_j for the set of words to which meta-instruction I_j is applicable. The automaton M' will then proceed as follows:

1. M' scans the current word w on its tape from left to right simulating all the acceptors $A_1, \ldots, A_i$ in parallel. At the right sentinel M' knows which meta-instructions of M are applicable to the current word. If none is applicable, then M' halts and rejects; if one of the applicable meta-instructions is accepting, then M' halts and accepts. Otherwise, any correct application of any of the applicable meta-instructions will yield a word w' such that $w' \in L(M)$ if and only if $w \in L(M)$, as M is correctness preserving. Thus, M' simply chooses one of the applicable meta-instructions, e.g., the one with the smallest index. By I we denote this meta-instruction.
2. M' simulates an application of I to its current tape content.

It remains to show how M' can simulate an application of I to the configuration $q_0 \mathfrak{c} w \$$. Let $w = y_1 \cdots y_n$, where $y_1, \ldots, y_n \in \Sigma$, and assume that $I = (\mathfrak{c} \cdot E_0, x_1, E_1, x_2, E_2, \ldots, E_{s-1}, x_s, E_s \cdot \$)$, where $1 \leq s \leq t$, $E_0, E_1, \ldots, E_s$ are regular languages, and $x_1, x_2, \ldots, x_s \in \Sigma$ correspond to letters that are deleted by M during one cycle. M' must determine a factorization of the form $w = v_0 x_1 v_1 x_2 \cdots v_{s-1} x_s v_s$ such that $v_i \in E_i$ for all $i = 0, \ldots, s$, and remove the symbols $x_1, x_2, \ldots, x_s$. As w may have many such factorizations, M' must choose one of them deterministically. For this task M' will use finite-state acceptors $M_1, \ldots, M_s$ and $M_1^R, \ldots, M_s^R$, which accept the following regular languages:

$$
\begin{aligned}
L(M_1) &= E_0 \cdot x_1, & (E_1 \cdot x_2 \cdot E_2 \cdot x_3 \cdots E_{s-1} \cdot x_s \cdot E_s)^R &= L(M_1^R), \\
L(M_2) &= E_1 \cdot x_2, & (E_2 \cdot x_3 \cdots E_{s-1} \cdot x_s \cdot E_s)^R &= L(M_2^R), \\
&\ \ \vdots & &\ \ \vdots \\
L(M_{s-1}) &= E_{s-2} \cdot x_{s-1}, & (E_{s-1} \cdot x_s \cdot E_s)^R &= L(M_{s-1}^R), \\
L(M_s) &= E_{s-1} \cdot x_s, & (E_s)^R &= L(M_s^R).
\end{aligned}
$$

After step (1) above (that is, when choosing the meta-instruction I), M' is at the right sentinel. Now it scans its tape again, this time from right to left, thereby simulating the finite-state acceptors $M_1^R, \ldots, M_s^R$ in parallel. For each $0 \le j \le s$ and $1 \le \ell \le n$, let $q(j, \ell)$ denote the state of M_j^R after reading the word $y_n \ldots y_{\ell+1}$. When reaching the left sentinel, M' changes direction again. Now, while moving to the right, M' simulates the finite-state acceptor M_1. Simultaneously, it recomputes the internal states of all the acceptors $M_1^R, \ldots, M_s^R$ on the respective tape symbol, that is, it runs these acceptors in reverse. This it can do due to the following technical result from [1] (pages 212–213).

Lemma 1. *Let A be a deterministic finite-state acceptor. For each word x and each integer i, $1 \le i \le |x|$, let $q_A(x, i)$ be the internal state of A after processing the prefix of length i of x. Then there exists a deterministic two-way finite-state acceptor A' such that, for each input x and each $i \in \{2, 3, \ldots, |x|\}$, if A' starts its computation on x in state $q_A(x, i)$ with its head on the i-th symbol of x, then A' finishes its computation in state $q_A(x, i-1)$ with its head on the $(i-1)$-th symbol of x. During this computation A' only visits (a part of) the prefix of length i of x.*

As meta-instruction I is applicable to the configuration $q_0 \text{¢} w \$$, w belongs to the set $E_0 \cdot x_1 \cdot E_1 \cdot x_2 \cdot E_2 \cdot x_3 \cdots E_{s-1} \cdot x_s \cdot E_s$. Hence, there is a smallest index ℓ_1 such that $y_1 \cdots y_{\ell_1} \in L(M_1)$ and $y_{\ell_1+1} \cdots y_n \in [L(M_1^R)]^R$. That is, after scanning $y_1 \cdots y_{\ell_1}$, the finite-state acceptor M_1 is in an accepting state, and simultaneously $q(1, \ell_1)$ is an accepting state of M_1^R. On reaching this position, M' deletes $y_{\ell_1} = x_1$, aborts the simulations of M_1 and M_1^R, and starts to simulate M_2 from its initial state. Now M' looks for an index $\ell_2 > \ell_1$ such that M_2 is in an accepting state after processing $y_{\ell_1+1} \cdots y_{\ell_2}$, and $q(2, \ell_2)$ is an accepting state of M_2^R. Once this position is reached, M' deletes the symbol $y_{\ell_2} = x_2$, aborts the simulations of M_2 and M_2^R, and starts to simulate M_3. This process is then continued for $i = 3, 4, \ldots, s$. In this way, M' deletes s symbols $y_{\ell_1}, \ldots, y_{\ell_s}$ such that $y_1 \cdots y_{\ell_1-1} \in E_0$, $y_{\ell_1} = x_1$, $y_{\ell_1+1} \cdots y_{\ell_2-1} \in E_1$, $y_{\ell_2} = x_2$, $\ldots, y_{\ell_s} = x_s$, and $y_{\ell_s+1} \cdots y_n \in E_s$.

It is easy to see that the t-sRL-automaton M' constructed in the way described above is deterministic, and that it accepts the same language as the given t-sRL-automaton M. □

3 A Complexity Measure for sRL-Automata

A t-sRL-automaton M can be interpreted as a description of the language $L(M)$. Hence, the question about the succinctness of this description in comparison to other descriptions of the same language arises. Thus, we need to introduce a measure for the size of a t-sRL-automaton.

In [3] the descriptional complexity of various types of deterministic restarting automata is investigated. There the number of instructions in the transition relation of a restarting automaton is taken as the size of that automaton, that is, for an sRL-automaton M this would yield the number

$$\text{size}_\delta(M) := |Q| \cdot (|\Sigma| + 2) \cdot \mu,$$

where μ denotes the maximal degree of nondeterminism that M has in any situation. However, the description of sRL-automata in terms of transition relations is rather cumbersome. Therefore we prefer to consider measures that are based on descriptions of sRL-automata in terms of meta-instructions.

Definition 3. *Let M be a t-sRL-automaton that is given through meta-instructions $I_1, \ldots, I_r$. Then* $\mathrm{size}_I(M) := r$ *is called the* instruction size *of M.*

The t-sRL-automata M_t and $M_t^{(n)}$ of Example 2 have instruction size 3. Obviously, each regular language L is accepted by a restarting automaton of instruction size 1 that is given through the single meta-instruction $(\mathfrak{c} \cdot L \cdot \$, \mathsf{Accept})$. It is easy to construct a sequence of languages $(L_i)_{i \geq 1}$ with growing alphabets such that any t-sRL-automaton recognizing L_i has instruction size at least i. A similar hierarchy is obtained in a simple way by the sequence of languages $LI_i := \bigcup_{j=1}^{i} \{ a^j b a^n b^{j \cdot n} \mid n \geq 0 \}$ $(i \geq 1)$. Observe that this sequence also forms an infinite hierarchy with respect to the number of delete operations per cycle.

However, we even have a sequence of 3-sRL-automata with growing instruction size and a fixed finite alphabet.

Let $\Sigma := \{a, b\}$, let $i > 1$, and let $w_j := a^j b^{i+1-j}$ $(1 \leq j \leq i)$. For each $j \in \{1, \ldots, i\}$, let E_j^i denote the language

$$E_j^i := \{w_1, \ldots, w_{j-1}, w_{j+1}, \ldots, w_i\} \subset \Sigma^{i+1},$$

and let M_i be the 3-sRL-automaton with input alphabet $\Sigma := \{a, b\}$ that is given through the following meta-instructions:

1. $(\mathfrak{c} \cdot (\sum_{j=1}^{i}(w_j \cdot a^* \cdot w_j + w_j \cdot b^+ \cdot E_j^i)) \cdot \$, \mathsf{Accept})$,
2. $(\mathfrak{c} \cdot w_j \cdot a^*, a, \{\lambda\}, b, b^* \cdot w_j \cdot \$)$, $j = 1, \ldots, i$,
3. $(\mathfrak{c} \cdot w_j \cdot a^*, a, \{\lambda\}, b, \{\lambda\}, b, b^* \cdot E_j^i \cdot \$)$, $j = 1, \ldots, i$.

Obviously, $\mathrm{size}_I(M_i) = 2i + 1$, and it is easily verified that

$$L(M_i) = \bigcup_{j=1}^{i} \{ w_j a^n b^m w_j \mid n \geq m \geq 0 \} \cup \bigcup_{\substack{j,k=1 \\ j \neq k}}^{i} \{ w_j a^n b^m w_k \mid m > 2n \geq 0 \}.$$

On the other hand, we have the following lower bound result.

Theorem 5. *If M is an sRL-automaton for the language $L(M_i)$ of the above 3-sRL-automaton M_i, then* $\mathrm{size}_I(M) \geq 2i + 1$.

Proof. Let $i > 1$ be an integer, and let M be an sRL-automaton recognizing the language $L(M) = L(M_i)$. Let $w_{k,l,\mu,\nu} := w_k a^\mu b^\nu w_l$, let p be the number of states of M, and let $n := p!$. None of the words $w_{k,k,n,n}$ $(1 \leq k \leq i)$ can be accepted by M in a tail computation, as otherwise it could be shown by using pumping techniques that M will also accept certain words which do not belong to $L(M_i)$.

Each meta-instruction which is used in an accepting computation on an input $w_{k,l,\mu,\nu} \in L(M_i)$ deletes only some of the symbols a and b in the middle. Here the fact is used that all words w_j ($1 \leq j \leq i$) have the same length, and so neither the prefix w_k nor the suffix w_l can be converted into another word w_j for any index j by applying deletions.

If there are less than i meta-instructions that are used for accepting all words of the form $w_{k,k,cn,cn}$ ($1 \leq k \leq i$, $c \geq 1$), then at least one of them applies to two different words $w_{k,k,cn,cn}$ and $w_{l,l,cn,cn}$, $l \neq k$. Hence, this instruction cannot distinguish between $w_k a^{cn} b^{cn} w_k$ and $w_l a^{cn} b^{cn} w_l$. As neither the prefixes nor the suffixes w_l and w_k are affected by this instruction, we see that this instruction also applies to the word $w_l a^{cn} b^{cn} w_k$.

Each meta-instruction which is used in an accepting computation for a word of the form word $w_l a^{cn} b^{cn} w_l$ (c a large constant) deletes at least as many symbols b as a. Now assume that, after some cycles of an accepting computation starting with the word $w_l a^{cn} b^{cn} w_l$, the number α of symbols a deleted and the number β of symbols b deleted satisfy the condition $\beta = \alpha + m$ for some integer m satisfying $m \geq n = p!$. Thus, $w_l a^{cn} b^{cn} w_l$ is reduced to a word of the form $w_l a^{cn-\alpha} b^{cn-\alpha-m} w_l$. The restarting automaton M cannot distinguish between $w_l a^{cn} b^{cn} w_l$ and $w_l a^{cn} b^{cn+n} w_l \notin L(M_i)$. However, by applying the same sequence of cycles to the latter word, M will derive the word $w_l a^{cn-\alpha} b^{cn-\alpha+n-m} w_l$, which belongs to $L(M_i)$, as $m \geq n$. This contradicts the Error Preserving Property.

Hence, for all sequences of cycles starting with a word of the form $w_l a^{cn} b^{cn} w_l$, the number α of symbols a deleted and the number β of symbols b deleted satisfy the restriction $\alpha \leq \beta < \alpha + n$. As seen above the word $w_l a^{cn} b^{cn} w_k$ can also be processed by the same sequence of cycles, and the same is true for the word $w_l a^{cn} b^{2cn} w_k \notin L(M_i)$. However, after a sufficient number of cycles $\alpha > n$ is obtained, and therewith $\beta < \alpha + n \leq 2\alpha$ holds. Hence, the resulting word is $w_l a^{cn-\alpha} b^{2cn-\beta} w_k$, which belongs to $L(M_i)$, again contradicting the Error Preserving Property.

It follows that, for each value of $j \in \{1, \ldots, i\}$, there is at least one meta-instruction with prefix and suffix w_j that is involved in the accepting computations of M for the words of the form $w_{k,k,cn,cn}$ ($1 \leq k \leq i$). Thus, there are at least i different meta-instructions of this form.

Essentially the same method also works for those meta-instructions that are used in accepting computations for words of the form $w_j a^n b^m w_k$ ($m > 2n$). At least i different meta-instructions must be used in these computations. As they differ from the meta-instructions above, and as M needs at least one accepting meta-instruction, we see that $\mathrm{size}_I(M) \geq 2i + 1$ holds.   □

4   Conclusions

Using meta-instructions for describing sRL-automata instead of describing them by elementary instructions has several advantages for the designers of sRL-automata:

1. The task of designing a particular restarting automaton can be split into several smaller tasks of designing single meta-instructions.
2. Such a design can be done incrementally. First we introduce some basic meta-instructions which do not define the whole target language, but only an important subset of it. Then we keep adding new meta-instructions to improve our approximation of the target language. In a similar way the individual rules for the analysis by reduction of Czech can be designed (see [6]).
3. If we succeed in this task, only using correctness preserving meta-instructions, then it is even possible to design the automaton for the target language in parallel, that is, two or more (correctness preserving) meta-instructions can be developed separately and finally put together to describe a single automaton. Moreover, Theorem 4 provides us with a procedure to convert a nondeterministic sRL-automaton of this form into a deterministic one. In a similar way the rule-based tagging procedure in [2] works.

The instruction size does not allow to distinguish 'complicated' regular languages from 'simple' ones. Therefore in [8] we define a finer complexity measure for sRL-automata which measures the size of a t-sRL-automaton through the size of its description in terms of meta-instructions. Actually this new measure relates the size of a meta-instruction to the length of its description in terms of regular expressions. In this way even deterministic 2-sRL-automata allow very succinct representations of (certain) regular languages, as witnessed by a non-recursive trade-off.

References

1. A. V. Aho, J. E. Hopcroft, and J. D. Ullman. A general theory of translation. *Math. Systems Theory* 3 (1969) 193-221.
2. J. Hajič, P. Krbec, K. Oliva, P. Květoň, and V. Petkevič. Serial combination of rules and statistics: A case study in Czech tagging. In: *Proceedings of the 39th Association of Computational Linguistics Conference*, Association for Computational Linguistics, Toulouse, France, 2001.
3. M. Holzer, M. Kutrib, and J. Reimann. Descriptional complexity of deterministic restarting automata. In: C. Mereghetti, B. Palano, G. Pighizzini, and D. Wotschke (eds.), *DCFS 2005, Proc.*, Università degli Studi di Milano, 2005, 158–169.
4. J. E. Hopcroft and J. D. Ullman. *Introduction to Automata Theory, Languages, and Computation*. Addison-Wesley, Reading, MA, 1979.
5. V. Kuboň and M. Plátek. A grammar based approach to a grammar checking of free word order languages. In: *COLING'94, Proc., Vol. II*, Kyoto, Japan, 1994, 906–910.
6. M. Lopatková, M. Plátek, and V. Kuboň. Modeling syntax of free word-order languages: Dependency analysis by reduction. In: V. Matoušek, P. Mautner, and T. Pavelka (eds.), *TSD 2005, Proc., LNCS 3658*, Springer, Berlin, 2005, 140–147.
7. M. Lothaire. *Combinatorics on Words*. Encyclopedia of Mathematics, Vol. 17, Addison-Wesley, Reading, 1983.
8. H. Messerschmidt, F. Mráz, F. Otto, and M. Plátek. On the descriptional complexity of simple sRL-automata. *Mathematische Schriften Kassel 4/06*, Universität Kassel, April 2006.

9. F. Mráz, F. Otto, and M. Plátek. Degrees of free word-order and restarting automata. *Grammars*, to appear.

10. F. Mráz, F. Otto, and M. Plátek. On the gap-complexity of simple RL-automata. In: O. Ibarra and Z. Dang (eds.), *DLT 2006, Proc.*, *LNCS 4036*, Springer, Berlin, 2006, 83–94.

11. M. Procházka. Concepts of syntax error recovery for monotonic reducing automata. In: D. Obdržálek and J. Štanclová (eds.), *MIS 2004, Proc.*, Matfyzpress, Praha, 2004, 94–103.

12. F. Otto. Restarting automata and their relations to the Chomsky hierarchy. In: Z. Ésik and Z. Fülöp (eds.), *DLT 2003, Proc.*, *LNCS 2710*, Springer, Berlin, 2003, 55–74.

13. G. Păun. *Marcus Contextual Grammars*, Studies in Linguistics and Philosophy, vol. 67. Kluwer, Dordrecht/Boston/London, 1997.

14. M. Plátek. Two-way restarting automata and j-monotonicity. In: L. Pacholski and P. Ružička (eds.), *SOFSEM 2001, Proc.*, *LNCS 2234*, Springer, Berlin, 2001, 316–325.

Bisimulation Minimization of Tree Automata

Parosh Aziz Abdulla[1], Lisa Kaati[1], and Johanna Högberg[2]

[1] Dept. of Information Technology, Uppsala University, Sweden
{parosh, lisa.kaati}@it.uu.se
[2] Dept. of Computing Science, Umeå University, Sweden
johanna@cs.umu.se

Abstract. We extend an algorithm by Paige and Tarjan that solves the coarsest stable refinement problem to the domain of trees. The algorithm is used to minimize non-deterministic tree automata (NTA) with respect to bisimulation. We show that our algorithm has an overall complexity of $O(\hat{r}\, m \log n)$, where $\hat{r}$ is the maximum rank of the input alphabet, m is the total size of the transition table, and n is the number of states.

1 Introduction

We present an algorithm that minimizes non-deterministic tree automata with respect to bisimulation equivalence in time $O(\hat{r}\, m \log n)$, where $\hat{r}$ is the maximum rank of the input alphabet, m is the total size of the transition table, and n is the number of states. In the construction of this algorithm, we extend the algorithm proposed in [13] to the domain of trees. Since the time complexity reduces to $O(m \log n)$ if $\hat{r}$ is constant, this retains the complexity of [13] in all cases where the maximum rank of the input alphabet is bounded. This holds in particular for monadic trees, i.e. the string case.

The minimization of finite *string* automata (FA) is a well-studied problem, where the objective is to find the unique minimal FA that recognizes the same language as a given FA. In the deterministic case, efficient algorithms are available, e.g. the algorithm proposed by Hopcroft in [9], where he uses a "process the smaller half" strategy to obtain a bound of $O(n \log n)$. However, it has been proven that minimization of non-deterministic finite automata (NFA) is PSPACE complete [10] and, what is worse, that the minimization problem for an NFA with n states cannot be efficiently approximated within the factor $O(n)$, unless P = PSPACE [8]. To avoid exponential time, the problem must either be restricted (i.e. by considering a special class of devices or requiring additional information), or no approximation guarantees can be given. Of course, this holds also for non-deterministic tree automata (NTA) because they generalize NFAs (as a string may be seen as a monadic tree). Hence, we cannot hope to find an efficient algorithm that performs well on all input NTAs.

Bisimulation minimization of tree automata is of particular interest in *tree regular model checking* (an extension of regular model checking). In this field, the verification of infinite state systems with tree-like architecture is considered, and many of the associated algorithms would benefit from an efficient method to reduce the size of non-deterministic tree automata [2,3].

O.H. Ibarra and H.-C. Yen (Eds.): CIAA 2006, LNCS 4094, pp. 173–185, 2006.

The algorithm presented in this paper takes advantage of the fact that bisimulation equivalence is computationally easier to decide than language equivalence, and that bisimulation equivalence implies language equivalence (although the converse does not hold in the general case). When minimizing an NTA, we group states that are observationally equivalent and use the blocks of the resulting partition as states in the output NTA. As mentioned above, the time complexity becomes $O(\hat{r}\, m \log n)$, as compared to $O(m \log n)$ by [13]. Thus, interestingly, the maximum rank $\hat{r}$ (which is the constant 1 in [13]) does not become an exponent. Instead, it influences the complexity rather modestly.

Related work. There does not seem to be any documented algorithm that uses bisimulation to minimize NTA, but we do know of a number of minimization algorithms that operate on various kinds of tree automata. For instance, algorithms for *guided tree automata* (GTA) are considered in [5]. A GTA is a bottom-up tree automaton equipped with separate state spaces that are assigned by a top-down automaton. According to the authors, minimization of GTA is possible in time $O(nm)$, but it is an open question whether or not tree automata can be minimized in time $O(m \log m)$. In [7], Cristau et al. claim that a deterministic bottom-up tree automaton for unranked trees can be minimized in time $O(m^2)$, using the algorithm proposed in [9]. In [6], the minimal tree automata is computed using an algorithm that construct congruences on the states of a given deterministic tree automata until a fixed point is reached. However, there are no given results regarding the complexity of the given algorithm. An alternative definition of deterministic top-down tree automata together with a minimization algorithm is given by Nivat and Podelski in [12].

Outline. Section 2 covers the preliminaries, while Section 3 generalizes a partitioning algorithm from [13] to trees. Section 4 describes the necessary calculation steps. In Section 5, the extended algorithm is applied to the minimization of NTA, and in Section 6, we show experimental results obtained from a prototype. We conclude with some directions for future work.

2   Preliminaries

Tree automata. A *ranked alphabet* is a finite set of symbols $\Sigma = \bigcup_{k \in \mathbb{N}} \Sigma_{(k)}$ which is partitioned into pairwise disjoint subsets $\Sigma_{(k)}$. The symbols in $\Sigma_{(k)}$ are said to have *rank* k. The set T_Σ of all *trees over* Σ is the smallest superset of $\Sigma_{(0)}$ that contains every $f[t_1, \ldots, t_k]$, where $f \in \Sigma_{(k)}$, $k \geq 1$, and $t_1, \ldots, t_k \in \mathrm{T}_\Sigma$. A subset of T_Σ is called a *tree language*.

A *non-deterministic tree automaton* is a quadruple $A = (Q, \Sigma, \delta, F)$ where Σ is a ranked input alphabet, Q is a finite set of *states*, δ is a finite set of *transition rules* $f(q_1, \ldots, q_n) \rightarrow q_{n+1}$ such that $f \in \Sigma_{(n)}$, and $q_1, \ldots, q_{n+1} \in Q$, for some $n \in \mathbb{N}$. Finally, $F \subseteq Q$ is a set of *accepting* states. In the obvious way, δ extends to trees, yielding a relation $\delta \colon \mathrm{T}_\Sigma \rightarrow \mathcal{P}(Q)$: For $t = f[t_1, \ldots, t_k] \in \mathrm{T}_\Sigma$,

$$\delta(t) = \{q \mid f(q_1, \ldots, q_k) \rightarrow q \in \delta \text{ and } q_i \in \delta(t_i) \text{ for all } i \in \{1, \ldots, k\}\} \ .$$

The tree language *recognized* by A is $L(A) = \{t \in T_\Sigma \mid \delta(t) \cap F \neq \emptyset\}$. Let $r = f(q_1, \ldots, q_n) \to q_{n+1}$ be a transition rule, then $|r|$ denotes its length (that is, $|r| = n + 1$), $r(i)$ denotes the state q_i, and $q \in r$ indicates that $r(i) = q$ for some $i : 1 \leq i \leq |r|$. For $B \subseteq Q$, take δ_B as the set $\{r \in \delta \mid \exists q \in B \text{ s.t. } q \in r\}$.

For technical convenience, we shall henceforth restrict ourselves to ranked alphabets containing at most one symbol of rank k for each $k \in \mathbb{N}$. We can thus leave out the input symbol when writing a transition rule, without risk of confusion. Extending the algorithm presented in Section 3 to unrestricted alphabets is straight-forward and does not effect the results in any way.

Equivalences. We consider equivalence relations on Q. Let $\simeq'$ and $\simeq$, where $\simeq' \subseteq \simeq$, be two such relations. We write $(Q/\simeq)$ to denote the set of equivalence classes (henceforth, *blocks*) of $\simeq$, and $[q]_\simeq$ to denote unique the block of $\simeq$ that contains q. For a block $B \in (Q/\simeq)$, we write $[B]_{\simeq'}$ to denote the set $\{B' \in (Q/\simeq') \mid B' \subseteq B\}$. For a block $B' \in (Q/\simeq')$, we let $[B']_\simeq$ represent the (unique) block $B \in (Q/\simeq)$ such that $B' \in [B]_{\simeq'}$.

Symbolic rules. Let $A = (Q, \Sigma, \delta, F)$ be an NTA, and $\simeq', \simeq$, where $\simeq' \subseteq \simeq$, equivalence relations on Q. To represent the set $\{([q_1]_\simeq, \ldots, [q_k]_\simeq) \to [q]_\simeq \mid (q_1, \ldots, q_k) \to q \in \delta\}$ of *symbolic rules*, we use the notation $(\delta/\simeq)$. Conversely, if $\rho = (D_1, \ldots, D_k) \to D_{k+1}$ is a symbolic rule, then the set of *instances* of ρ, denoted $[\![\rho]\!]$, is the set $\{(q_1, \ldots, q_k) \to q_{k+1} \mid q_i \in D_i, i : 1 \leq i \leq k+1\} \cap \delta$. We write $\rho(i)$ to refer to block D_i of ρ, and $B \in \rho$ to indicate that $\rho(i) = B$, for some $i \in \{1, \ldots, |\rho|\}$. The length of ρ is written $|\rho|$. For a transition rule $r \in \delta$, we use $[r]_\simeq$ to represent the unique symbolic rule $\rho \in (\delta/\simeq)$ such that $r \in [\![\rho]\!]$.

Given a rule $\rho = (D_1, \ldots, D_n) \to D_{n+1}$ in $(\delta/\simeq)$, we let $[\![\rho]\!]_{\simeq'}$ represent the set

$$\{(D'_1, \ldots, D'_n) \to D'_{n+1} \in (\delta/\simeq') \mid D'_i \in [D_i]_{\simeq'}, \text{ for all } i : 1 \leq i \leq n+1\} \ .$$

To denote the subset $\{(D'_1, \ldots, D'_n) \to D'_{n+1} \mid \exists i \in \{1, \ldots, n+1\} \text{ s.t. } D'_i = B\}$ of $[\![\rho]\!]_{\simeq'}$ we write $[\![\rho]\!]^B_{\simeq'}$. Conversely, for the symbolic rule $\rho' \in (\delta/\simeq')$, we define $[\rho']_\simeq$ to be the (unique) symbolic rule $\rho \in (\delta/\simeq)$ such that $\rho' \in [\![\rho]\!]_{\simeq'}$.

Occurrences and counts. Let $\simeq$ be an equivalence relation, and q a state, then the set of *occurrences* of q in $\simeq$, denoted $Occ(\simeq)(q)$, is the set of pairs (ρ, i) where $\rho \in (\delta/\simeq)$ and $q \in \rho(i)$ for some $i : 1 \leq i < |\rho|$. Intuitively, $Occ(\simeq)(q)$ identifies the symbolic rules in which $[q]$ occurs in the left hand side of the rule, together with the position of such an occurrence. Given a block B in $\simeq$, we define $Occ(\simeq)(B)(q)$, to be $\{(\rho, i) \mid (\rho, i) \in Occ(\simeq)(q) \text{ and } B \in \rho\}$. For a symbolic rule ρ, and a state q, we define $count(\rho)(q)$ to be the size of the set $\{r \in [\![\rho]\!] \mid \exists i \in \{1 \ldots |r|\} \text{ s.t. } r(i) = q\}$. We extend the definition to a set ϱ of symbolic rules such that $count(\varrho)(q) = \sum_{\rho \in \varrho} count(\rho)(q)$.

Stability. Let $\simeq$ and $\cong$, where $\simeq \subseteq \cong$, be equivalence relations on Q. The relation $\simeq$ is *stable* with respect to $\cong$ if whenever $q \simeq p$ then $Occ(\cong)(q) = Occ(\cong)(p)$, and *stable* if it is stable with respect to itself.

3   The Algorithm

In this section, we introduce an algorithm for solving the *coarsest stable refinement problem* for NTAs. An instance of the problem consists of an NTA A and an equivalence relation $\simeq_{init}$ on the states of A.

The equivalence relation $\simeq_{init}$ is assumed to satisfy the following conditions: (i) $\simeq_{init}$ is stable with respect to $Q \times Q$ and (ii) if $q \simeq_{init} q'$ then $q \in F$ iff $q' \in F$. The task is to find the *stable* (as defined in the previous section) refinement $\simeq$ of $\simeq_{init}$ that is *coarsest* in the sense that every other stable refinement of $\simeq_{init}$ is also a refinement of $\simeq$.

The algorithm iterates over a sequence of steps (described in detail in Section 4) generating two sequences of equivalence relations on Q, denoted by $\simeq_0, \simeq_1, \ldots, \simeq_t$ and $\cong_0, \cong_1, \ldots, \cong_t$ respectively. We define $\simeq_0$ to be $\simeq_{init}$ and $\cong_0$ to be $Q \times Q$.

In the $(i+1)$-th iteration, the equivalences $\simeq_{i+1}$ and $\cong_{i+1}$ are derived from $\simeq_i$ and $\cong_i$ as follows. Let $B_i \in (Q/\simeq_i)$ and $S_i \in (Q/\cong_i)$ be such that $B_i \subset S_i$ and $|B_i| \leq \frac{|S_i|}{2}$ (as implied by Lemma 1, $\simeq_i$ is a proper refinement of $\cong_i$ so B_i and S_i exist). We have that $q \cong_{i+1} q'$ if and only if two conditions are met. First, $q \cong_i q'$, and second, $q \in B_i$ if and only if $q' \in B_i$. Furthermore, for all $q, q' \in Q$, it holds that $q \simeq_{i+1} q'$ if and only if the following conditions are satisfied:

(1) $q \simeq_i q'$
(2) $Occ(\cong_{i+1})(B_i)(q) = Occ(\cong_{i+1})(B_i)(q')$
(3) For every $\rho \in (\delta/\cong_i)$, we have that

$$count(\rho)(q) = count\left([\![\rho]\!]^{B_i}_{\cong_{i+1}}\right)(q) \quad \text{iff} \quad count(\rho)(q') = count\left([\![\rho]\!]^{B_i}_{\cong_{i+1}}\right)(q') .$$

Intuitively, the second and third conditions refine $\simeq_i$ with respect to B_i and $S_i - B_i$ respectively. The iteration continues until we reach the termination point t, at which we have $\simeq_t = \cong_t$.

Correctness and time complexity. We now argue that the algorithm is correct and runs in time $O(\hat{r}\, m \log n)$, beginning with a simple lemma.

Lemma 1. *The relation $\simeq_i$ is a refinement of $\cong_i$, for all $i : 0 \leq i \leq t$.*

Proof. By induction on i. The base case is trivial since $\cong_0 = Q \times Q$. Suppose that $q \simeq_{i+1} q'$. By definition of $\simeq_{i+1}$ it follows that $q \simeq_i q'$. By the induction hypothesis it follows that $q \cong_i q'$. Since $q \simeq_i q$ and $B_i \in (Q/\simeq_i)$ it follows that $q \in B_i$ iff $q' \in B_i$. By definition of $\cong_{i+1}$ it follows that $q \cong_{i+1} q'$.   □

This implies that $\simeq_i$ is a *proper* refinement for all $i : 0 \leq i < t$, and that, up to the termination point, we will be able to pick $B_i \in (Q/\simeq_i)$ and $S_i \in (Q/\cong_i)$ such that $B_i \subset S_i$ and $|B_i| \leq \frac{|S_i|}{2}$. Next, we consider partial correctness of the algorithm which will follow from Lemma 2 and Lemma 5.

Lemma 2. *The relation $\simeq_i$ is stable with respect to $\cong_i$, for all $i : 1 \leq i \leq t$.*

Proof. By induction on i. The base case (when $i = 0$) follows from the definitions of $\simeq_0$ and $\cong_0$. Suppose then that $q \simeq_{i+1} q'$, and that $(\rho, j) \in Occ(\cong_{i+1})(q)$ for some $\rho \in (\delta/\cong_{i+1})$; we show that $(\rho, j) \in Occ(\cong_{i+1})(q')$. Depending on ρ, we have three cases:

First, $S_i - B_i \notin \rho$ and $B_i \notin \rho$. This means that $\rho \in (\delta/\cong_i)$, and therefore $(\rho, j) \in Occ(\cong_i)(q)$. Since $q \simeq_{i+1} q'$, we know by definition that $q \simeq_i q'$. By the induction hypothesis it follows that $\simeq_i$ is stable with respect to $\cong_i$, and hence $(\rho, j) \in Occ(\cong_i)(q')$. Since $\rho \in (\delta/\cong_{i+1})$ it follows that $(\rho, j) \in Occ(\cong_{i+1})(q')$.

Second, $S_i - B_i \in \rho$ and $B_i \notin \rho$. Let ρ be of the form $(D_1, \ldots, D_n) \to D_{n+1}$. Define $\rho^1 \in (\delta/\cong_i)$ to be the symbolic rule $(D_1^1, \ldots, D_n^1) \to D_{n+1}^1$ where, for each $k : 1 \leq k \leq n + 1$, we have that $D_k^1 = S_i$ if $D_k^1 = S_i - B_i$ and $D_k^1 = D_k$ otherwise. We observe that $\rho^1 = [\rho]_{\cong_i}$, and therefore $(\rho^1, j) \in Occ(\cong_i)(q)$. Since $q \simeq_{i+1} q'$, we know by definition that $q \simeq_i q'$. By the induction hypothesis it follows that $\simeq_i$ is stable with respect to $\cong_i$, and hence $(\rho^1, j) \in Occ(\cong_i)(q')$. From $B_i \notin \rho$ we know that $count(\rho)(q) > count\left([\rho]_{\cong_{i+1}}^{B_i}\right)(q)$. Since $q \simeq_{i+1} q'$ it follows that $count(\rho)(q') > count\left([\rho]_{\cong_{i+1}}^{B_i}\right)(q')$. Hence, $(\rho, j) \in Occ(\cong_i)(q')$.

Third, $B_i \in \rho$. This means that $(\rho, j) \in Occ(\cong_{i+1})(B_i)(q)$. Since $q \simeq_{i+1} q'$ it follows that $(\rho, j) \in Occ(\cong_{i+1})(B_i)(q')$ and hence $(\rho, j) \in Occ(\cong_{i+1})(q')$. $\square$

In the proof of Lemma 5, we use two auxiliary lemmas (Lemma 3 and Lemma 4). The proofs of these two lemmas have been omitted, but the interested reader will find these in [4].

Lemma 3. *Any stable refinement $\simeq$ of $\simeq_i$, is also a stable refinement of $\cong_{i+1}$.*

Lemma 4. *Consider equivalence relations $\simeq' \subseteq \simeq$, a symbolic rule $\rho \in (\delta/\simeq)$, a state q, and $j : 1 \leq j \leq |\rho|$. Then, we have $(\rho, j) \in Occ(\simeq)(q)$ if and only if $(\rho', j) \in Occ(\simeq')(q)$ for some $\rho' \in [\rho]_{\simeq'}$.*

Lemma 5. *If $\simeq$ is a stable refinement of $\simeq_0$, then $\simeq$ is also a refinement of $\simeq_i$, for each $i : 1 \leq i \leq t$.*

Proof. By induction on i. The base case is trivial. For the induction step, suppose that $q \simeq q'$. We show that $q \simeq_{i+1} q'$ using the three conditions in the definition of $\simeq_{i+1}$. Condition (1) is satisfied by the induction hypothesis.

For Condition (2), suppose that $(\rho, j) \in Occ(\cong_{i+1})(B_i)(q)$. Since (ρ, j) is in $Occ(\cong_{i+1})(B_i)(q)$ we know that $B_i \in \rho$ and that $(\rho, j) \in Occ(\cong_{i+1})(q)$. From the induction hypothesis we know that $\simeq \subseteq \simeq_i$, and by Lemma 3 that $\simeq \subseteq \cong_{i+1}$. By Lemma 4 there is a $\rho' \in [\rho]_\simeq$ such that $(\rho', j) \in Occ(\simeq)(q)$. Since $q \simeq q'$ and $\simeq$ is stable, we have that $(\rho', j) \in Occ(\simeq)(q')$. From $\simeq \subseteq \cong_{i+1}$ and $\rho' \in [\rho]_\simeq$, it follows by Lemma 4 that $(\rho, j) \in Occ(\cong_{i+1})(q')$. Since $B_i \in \rho$, we conclude that $(\rho, j) \in Occ(\cong_{i+1})(B_i)(q')$.

Regarding Condition (3), assume that $count(\rho)(q) \neq count([\rho]_{\cong_{i+1}}^{B_i})(q)$. We show that $count(\rho)(q') \neq count([\rho]_{\cong_{i+1}}^{B_i})(q')$. From the above assumption, we know that there are $\rho_1 \in (\rho/\cong_i)$ and j such that $B_i \notin \rho_1$ and (ρ_1, j) is an element of $Occ(\cong_{i+1})(q)$. Form the induction hypothesis we know that $\simeq \subseteq \simeq_i$, and hence by Lemma 3 it follows that $\simeq \subseteq \cong_{i+1}$. By Lemma 4 there is a $\rho_2 \in$ $[\![\rho_1]\!]_{\sim}$, such that $(\rho_2, j) \in Occ(\simeq)(q)$. Since $q \simeq q'$ and $\simeq$ is stable it follows that $(\rho_2, j) \in Occ(\simeq)(q')$. From $\simeq \subseteq \cong_{i+1}$ and $\rho_2 \in [\![\rho_1]\!]_{\sim}$, it follows by Lemma 4 that (ρ_1, j) is an element of $Occ(\cong_{i+1})(q')$, and hence the result. $\qquad \square$

Lemma 6. *There is a* $t \le n - 1$ *such that* $\simeq_t = \cong_t$.

Proof. As long as the algorithm has not terminated, we have $B_i \subset S_i$ and consequently $\cong_{i+1} \subset \cong_i$. By finiteness of Q it follows that after at most $t = |Q| - 1$ steps we reach a point where there are no $B_t \in (Q/\simeq_t)$ and $S_t \in (Q/\cong_t)$ such that $B_t \subset S_t$ and $|B_t| \le \frac{|S_t|}{2}$. This implies $\simeq_t = \cong_t$. $\qquad \square$

Now, we are ready to prove correctness. Lemma 6 guarantees that the algorithm terminates, producing $\simeq_t$. According to Lemma 2, $\simeq_t$ is stable with respect to $\cong_t$, and since $\simeq_t = \cong_t$, the equivalence $\simeq_t$ is stable. The implication of this, in combination with Lemma 5, is stated as the following theorem.

Theorem 1. *The algorithm terminates with output* $\simeq_t$, *where* $\simeq_t$ *is the coarsest stable refinement of* $\simeq_0$.

To simplify the discussion regarding time complexity, we formulate Lemma 7.

Lemma 7. *For each* $q \in Q$ *and* $i < j$ *if* $q \in B_i \cap B_j$ *then* $|B_j| \le \frac{|B_i|}{2}$.

Proof. By definition we know that B_i is a block of $\cong_{i+1}$. Since $i < j$ it follows by definition that $\cong_j$ is a refinement of $\cong_i$ and hence B_i is a union of blocks in $\cong_j$. From the fact that $q \in B_j$ we know that $q \in S_j$. Since $q \in B_i$ it follows that $S_j \subseteq B_i$. From $|B_j| \le \frac{|S_j|}{2}$, it follows that $|B_j| \le \frac{|B_i|}{2}$. $\qquad \square$

As demonstrated in Section 4, calculation steps 1 to 8 can each be performed in time $O(\sum_{r \in \delta_B} |r|)$. This is also the time required by an entire iteration. The time complexity of the algorithm can then be written as

$$\sum_{r \in \delta_{B_0}} |r| + \sum_{r \in \delta_{B_1}} |r| + \dots \sum_{r \in \delta_{B_t}} |r| \ ,$$

where B_i is the B-block chosen during the ith iteration. Now, a transition rule $r = (q_1, \dots, q_k) \to q_{k+1} \in \delta$ will only be contained in the set δ_{B_i}, $0 \le i \le t$, if state q_j is contained in B_i for some $j : 1 \le j \le k + 1$. No state occur in more than $\log n$ B-blocks (Lemma 7), and since r contains at most $|r|$ distinct states, r cannot contribute by more than $|r|^2 \log n$ to the total sum. This implies that the algorithm runs in time $O\big((\sum_{r \in \delta} |r|^2) \log n\big)$, which is bounded by $O(\hat{r}\, m \log n)$.

4   Iterations

In this section we describe the data structures used in the representation of the equivalences $\simeq_i$ and $\cong_i$ (see Section 3). Also, we use a number of auxiliary data structures which allow efficient implementation of each iteration in the algorithm. Finally, we describe how to implement each iteration.

Each state is represented by a record which we identify with the state itself. We maintain three lists of blocks:

- P corresponds to blocks in $\simeq_i$. Each block is represented by a record which we will identify with the block itself. Each block S in P contains a pointer to a doubly linked list of its elements; and each state points to the block in P containing it. Each block in P is also equipped with a natural number which indicates its size.
- X corresponds to the blocks in $\cong_i$. Each block is represented by a record which we will identify with the block itself. A block of X is *simple* if it contains a single block of P, and is *compound* otherwise. Each block in X contains a pointer to a doubly linked list of the blocks of P contained in it; and each block S in P contains a pointer to the block of X containing it.
- C is a sublist of X containing only the compound blocks in X.

The elements of the above lists are doubly linked. This allows deletion of elements in constant time. A rule r is represented by a doubly linked list of elements. The ith element of the list (corresponding to state q) is a record with:

- pointers to the next and previous elements of r (if any).
- pointers to the ith element in the previous and the next rule in $[r]_{\cong_i}$.
- a pointer to the symbolic rule $\rho = [r]_{\cong_i}$.
- pointers c, c_1, and c_2 to three counters containing natural numbers.

Intuitively, given a rule r, the pointer c points to $count(\rho)(q)$ where $\rho = [r]_{\cong_i}$. The counters c_1 and c_2 are temporary variables, used during the iterations, to point to $count(\rho')(q)$ resp. $count\left([\![\rho]\!]_{\cong_{i+1}}^B\right)(q)$, where $\rho' = [r]_{\cong_{i+1}}$. A state has a pointer to the list of rules in which it occurs. A symbolic rule ρ is represented by a record which is pointed to by all instances of ρ.

Initialization. In the initial configuration, all rules $r \in \delta$ points to (the only) symbolic rule $\rho_0 \in (\delta/\cong_0)$. Each position of r (corresponding to a state q) points to a counter $count(\rho_0)(q)$. The list X contains only one block. This block is compound and it is also the only block contained in C.

Step 1: Select compound block S. Remove a compound block S from C. Examine the first two blocks in S. Let B be the smaller one. If they are equal in size then B can be arbitrarily chosen to be anyone of them. These blocks correspond to B_i and S_i chosen during the ith iteration (Section 3). This step can be performed in constant time.

Step 2: Remove B from S. This is to maintain the invariant that $q \cong_{i+1} q'$ implies that $q \in B$ iff $q' \in B$. Remove B from S and create a new block S' in X. The block S' is simple and contains B as its only block. If S is still compound, put it back into C. Observe that the elements of X will now correspond to the blocks of $\cong_{i+1}$. This step can be performed in constant time.

Step 3: Calculate new symbolic rules. Note that each symbolic rule $\rho \in (\delta/\cong_i)$ will potentially give raise to a set of rules in $(\delta/\cong_{i+1})$, namely those in $[\![\rho]\!]^B_{\cong_{i+1}}$ and $[\![\rho]\!]^{\neg B}_{\cong_{i+1}}$, and that these rules are obtained from ρ by replacing occurrences of S in ρ either by B_i or $S - B$. The purpose of Step 3 is to derive the rules in $[\![\rho]\!]^B_{\cong_{i+1}}$, i.e., to generate those members of $(\delta/\cong_{i+1})$ in which B occurs at least once. For this purpose, we build, for each ρ with $[\![\rho]\!]^B_{\cong_{i+1}} \neq \emptyset$, a tree T_ρ which encodes the symbolic rules in $[\![\rho]\!]^B_{\cong_{i+1}}$. A list of existing trees is maintained throughout the current iteration. The rule ρ will maintain a pointer[1] to T_ρ, while each tree will maintain a pointer to the list of its leafs.

The edges of the tree are labeled with blocks in X (i.e., blocks in $\cong_{i+1}$). Each path π from the root to a leaf is of length $|\rho|$, and corresponds to one symbolic rule $\rho' = [\rho]_{\cong_{i+1}}$. More precisely, the root-to-leaf concatenation of the labels of edges along π defines the blocks which appear in ρ' from left to right. Thus, the ith edge in π is labeled by $\rho'(i)$, for $i : 1 \leq i \leq |\rho'|$. Furthermore, the leaf at the end of π points to a list $L_{\rho'}$ of rules which are instances of ρ'. The elements of different rules in $L_{\rho'}$ are also linked together: position j in each rule has a pointer to position j of the next rule in $L_{\rho'}$. This gives the list $L_{\rho'}$ a "matrix" form where the rows correspond to rules and the columns correspond to given positions in the rules. When T_ρ is completely constructed, each symbolic rule $\rho' \in [\![\rho]\!]^B_{\cong_{i+1}}$ will be represented by a path in T_ρ; and each instance of ρ' will be present in the list associated with the corresponding leaf.

To construct T_ρ, we go through the elements of B. For each element $q \in B$, we go through the list of rules r with $q \in r$. Recall that q has a pointer to this list. To prevent that a certain rule is considered twice, we mark encountered rules (and unmark them at the end of the step). For a rule r, we find the symbolic rule $\rho = [r]_{\cong_i}$. This can be done since each r has a pointer to ρ, and since the existing symbolic rules still correspond to those in $(\delta/\cong_i)$ (they have yet not been modified to reflect $\cong_{i+1}$). We also find the tree T_ρ by following pointer from each symbolic rule ρ to T_ρ. If T_ρ does not exist yet, we create it, add it to the list of currently existing trees, and add a pointer to it from ρ. Now we modify T_ρ by "adding" r to it. The addition process is carried out as follows. Let r be of the form $(q_1, \ldots, q_n) \rightarrow q_{n+1}$. We simultaneously traverse r (from left to right) and T_ρ (in a top-down manner). We start from q_1 and the root of the tree. At step j of the traversal, we consider the state q_j together with a node n_j in T_ρ. We check whether there is an edge leaving n_j which is labeled by $[q_j]_{\cong_{i+1}}$ (we can find $[q_j]_{\cong_{i+1}}$ by following the pointer to the block in P containing q_j and from there following the pointer to the corresponding block in X). If such an edge exists, we follow the edge one step down the tree to the next node n_{j+1}. We also move one step to the right in r to the state q_{j+1}. If no such an edge exists, we create a new edge n_{j+1} connected to n_j and labeled with $[q_i]_{\cong_{i+1}}$ (again moving one step to the right in r). Checking existence of the right edge takes constant time. This is due to the fact that each node may have at most two outgoing edges (in fact a node has only outgoing edge unless the edges are labeled by B

---

[1] Pointer from each symbolic rule ρ to T_ρ.

or S). Once we reach a leaf (after $|\rho|$ steps), we insert r in the list pointed to by the leaf. More precisely, we go through r from left to right. For element j in r, we remove any existing (old) links to and from elements of other lists, and add a double link to element j of the rule which was previously first in the list of rules (before the insertion of r). This is to maintain the matrix form, i.e., the invariant that corresponding elements in rules in the same list are linked. If the leaf had just been created, we add it to the list of leafs of the tree. Notice that the time complexity of the current step is $O\left(\sum_{r \in \delta_B} |r|\right)$. In fact, as we shall see all subsequent steps have the same complexity.

Step 4: Create counters. In this step, we create new counters to reflect the introduction of the new symbolic rules, and update the values of the temporary pointers c_1 and c_2 in the relevant rules . We go through the list of existing trees and through the list of leafs of each tree. For a given leaf corresponding to a symbolic rule ρ', we consider the corresponding list $L_{\rho'}$, and consider each rule r in the corresponding list. We scan the rule r, and each position (corresponding to a state q). If it is the first time we encounter q during the scanning of the current leaf, we create the counter $count(\rho')(q)$, and make both q and pointer c_1 of the current position point to it. If it is not the first time, we find $count(\rho')(q)$ by following the pointer from the current position to q, and from q to the counter. We increase its value and create a pointer to it from c_1 of the current position. We create and modify $count\left([\![\rho]\!]^B_{\cong_{i+1}}\right)(q)$ in a similar manner, with two differences, namely (i) we use c_2 instead of c_1; and (ii) we check whether it is the first time we encounter q during the scanning of the current tree (rather than the current leaf). To prevent that the same is considered twice during the scanning of r, we mark encountered states. When the scanning of r has been completed, we scan r one more time and unmark all states. When we have scanned all rules in the current leaf, we go through all rules and positions one more time and delete the pointers we have created from states q to the counters $count(\rho')(q)$ (preserving the ones from c_2). When we have scanned all leafs in the current tree, we delete the corresponding pointers to $count\left([\![\rho]\!]^B_{\cong_{i+1}}\right)(q)$.

Step 5: Refine P with respect to B. Each position $j : 1 \leq j \leq |\rho'| - 1$ may potentially give raise to a split of the blocks in P. A state q_1 which occurs in position j in the left hand side of a rule $r \in [\![\rho']\!]$ (i.e., $r(j) = q_1$ for some $j : 1 \leq j \leq |\rho'| - 1$) should not be in the same block as a state q_2 which does not occur in position j of any rule in $[\![\rho']\!]$. The reason is that this would imply $Occ(\cong_{i+1})(B)(q) \neq Occ(\cong_{i+1})(B)(q')$. To reflect this in our blocks, we go through all trees and all leafs in a tree. For a leaf corresponding to a rule ρ', we iterate over all positions $j : 1 \leq j \leq |\rho'| - 1$, and scan position j of all the rules in $L_{\rho'}$ one by one. This can be done due to the matrix form, where position j in each rule has a pointer to position j of the next rule in $L_{\rho'}$. Let q be the state in the position and rule currently under consideration. We find the block D of P containing q. We create an associated block D' if one does not already exist. We move q to D' decreasing the size of D and increasing the size of D'.

During the scanning, we construct a list which contains all blocks which have been split. After we have scanned position j of all rules in $L_{\rho'}$, we go through the new list of blocks. For each block D (and associated block D'), we remove the record for D if it has become empty (all its elements have been moved to D'); otherwise if the block of X containing D has become compound by the split, we add this block to C.

Step 6: Refine P with respect to $S - B$. For each tree T_ρ, and all of its leaves, we go through the list $L_{\rho'}$, and scan every rule r in $L_{\rho'}$. Let q be the state of r currently scanned. We determine whether the counters pointed to by c and c_1 have the same values. This corresponds to checking whether $count(\rho)(q) = count\left([\![\rho]\!]_{\cong_{i+1}}^{\neg B}\right)(q)$. If the equality holds, we find the block D of P containing q, and create an associated block D' if one does not already exist. Afterward, the new list of blocks is processed in the same way as in Step 4.

Step 7: Update the counters. This step updates the counters for every state in every rule in $[\![\rho]\!]_{\cong_{i+1}}^{\neg B}$. For each tree T_ρ in the list of trees created in Step 3, we go through all the leaves of T_ρ. For a given leaf and an associated list $L_{\rho'}$, we scan each rule r in $L_{\rho'}$ from left to right. Let q be the state that is currently scanned. We subtract the value of the counter pointed to by c_2 from that pointed to by c and put the value back in the latter. This corresponds to the assignment $count(\rho)(q) := count(\rho)(q) - count([\![\rho]\!]_{\cong_{i+1}}^{B})(q)$. To prevent that the same state is processed more than once, we mark encountered states. When the scanning of all leafs of T_ρ has been completed, we scan all leaves one more time and unmark all states. During the same scan we change the pointer c of a cell and make it point to the same counter as c_2. Now, we destroy, for each state q, the pointers c_1 and c_2 and the corresponding counters.

Step 8: Update symbolic rules. We go through each tree T_ρ. For each leaf we create a new symbolic rule ρ'. We go through the associated list of rules, and make the rules point to ρ'. After T_ρ has been processed, it is destroyed.

5   NTA Minimization with Respect to Bisimulation

We now discuss how the algorithm presented in Section 3 can be applied to the minimization of non-deterministic tree automata, with respect to bisimulation. We begin with a formal definition of bisimulation equivalence.

Let $A = (Q, \Sigma, \delta, F)$ and $A' = (Q', \Sigma, \delta', F')$ be two NTA. A relation $\simeq \subseteq Q \times Q'$ is a bisimulation relation if the following two conditions hold for all states $q \in Q$ and $q' \in Q'$ such that $q \simeq q'$. First, $q \in F$ if and only if $q' \in F'$. Second, the fact that $(q_1, \ldots, q_{i-1}, q, q_i, \ldots, q_{k-1}) \to q_k \in \delta$, where $i \leq k$, implies that there exists a rule $(q'_1, \ldots, q'_{i-1}, q', q'_i, \ldots, q'_{k-1}) \to q'_k \in \delta'$, such that $q_j \simeq q'_j$ for all $j \in \{1, \ldots, k\}$, and vice versa. States q and q' as above are said to be *bisimilar* (with respect to $\simeq$). We consider A and A' to be *bisimulation equivalent* (and write $A \sim A'$) if there is a bisimulation relation such that every state in Q is bisimilar to a state in Q', and every state in Q' to a state in Q.

Here, a brief remark is in place: When the notion of bisimulation equivalence is extended to allow alphabets containing more than one symbol of a given rank, one must require that it is the same symbol that occurs on both sides of the implication. Note also that if A and A' are bisimulation equivalent NTAs, and the relation between their states is one-to-one, then A and A' are isomorphic.

Now, to produce the unique minimal tree automaton that is bisimilar to a given tree automaton $A = (Q, \Sigma, \delta, F)$, we first apply the algorithm of Section 3 with $\simeq_0 = \simeq_{init}$ to find an equivalence relation $\simeq$ on Q, such that $Q/\simeq$ is the coarsest stable partition of Q, and then output $A_\simeq = (Q/\simeq, \Sigma, \delta/\simeq, F/\simeq)$.

In the derivation of Theorem 2, which is a non-deterministic version of a result in [6], we make use of two lemmas. To save space, the proofs have been omitted, but the interested reader will find these in [4].

Lemma 8. *Bisimulation equivalence is an equivalence relation.*

Lemma 9. *The input automaton and the output automaton returned by the minimization algorithm are bisimulation equivalent.*

Theorem 2. *Given an automaton A, the minimization algorithm returns the unique minimal bisimulation-equivalent automaton recognizing $L(A)$.*

Let $A = (Q, \Sigma, \delta, F)$ be an NTA, and $A_\simeq = (Q/\simeq, \Sigma, \delta/\simeq, F/\simeq)$ the NTA returned by the minimization algorithm. According to Theorem 1, $Q/\simeq$ is the coarsest stable refinement of $\simeq_{init}$. By Lemma 9, automata $A_\simeq$ and A are bisimulation equivalent.

Let $A' = (Q', \Sigma, \delta', F')$ be a minimal NTA bisimulation equivalent with A. Since A and A' are bisimulation equivalent, there is an equivalence relation $\simeq'$ on Q, such that $q \simeq' q'$ if q and q' are both bisimilar to the same state in Q'. The partition $Q/\simeq'$ is stable, and a refinement of $\simeq_{init}$. In combination with the assumption that A' is minimal, we have that $Q/\simeq'$ is the unique coarsest stable refinement of $\simeq_{init}$, and hence that $\simeq = \simeq'$.

Since both $A_\simeq$ and A' are bisimulation equivalent to A, they are also bisimulation equivalent to each other (Lemma 8), and since they each have $|Q/\simeq|$ states, this relation is one-to-one. Hence, $A_\simeq$ and A' are isomorphic.   □

Note that all deterministic tree automata (DTA) that recognize the same language are bisimulation equivalent to each other, because they are all bisimulation equivalent to the unique minimal DTA that recognizes this language, and bisimulation equivalence, like all equivalence relations, is transitive.

Corollary 1. *Given a DTA A, the minimization algorithm returns the unique minimal DTA recognizing $L(A)$.*

The behavior described in Corollary 1 makes it impossible to give a nontrivial approximation bound for the performance of the minimization algorithm. To see why, recall that there is a family of tree languages $\mathcal{T}$ such that if $L \in \mathcal{T}$, then the minimal DTA that recognizes L is exponentially larger than a minimal

NTA recognizing the same language. This means that given any DTA A such that $L(A) \in \mathcal{T}$, the algorithm will return a potentially smaller, but still deterministic, tree automaton, and hence misses the optimum with an exponential factor.

6   Experiments

To test our algorithm on some real life examples, we have used tree automata that arose during computations in the framework of tree regular model checking of some of the protocols described in [1]. Table 1 shows the execution time, and the size before and after running our minimization algorithm.

Tree regular model checking is the name of a family of techniques for analyzing infinite state systems in which states are represented by trees, set of states by tree automata, and transitions by tree transducers. Most tree regular model checking algorithms rely heavily on efficient methods for checking bisimulation.

Table 1. Minimization of non-deterministic tree automata

Protocol	Input		Output		Time (s)
	States	Trans.	States	Trans.	
Percolate	18	333	5	38	0.2
	21	594	5	45	1.3
Leader	25	384	9	43	0.3
	49	3081	14	167	30.6

7   Conclusion and Future Work

We have extended an algorithm by Paige and Tarjan for solving the coarsest stable partition problem to the domain of trees, and obtained a running time of $O(\hat{r}\, m \log n)$, where $\hat{r}$ is the maximum rank of the input alphabet, m is the total size of the transition table, and n is the number of states. As demonstrated, the extended algorithm can be used to minimize non-deterministic tree automata with respect to bisimulation equivalence.

One possible direction for future work is to integrate the minimization algorithm in the framework of tree regular model checking, where tree automata are encoded symbolically. Since many of the algorithms in this framework rely heavily on minimization, we believe it would improve performance if our algorithm could be integrated in this setting. We plan to implement a symbolic version of our algorithm where we consider both binary decision diagrams and SAT solvers to perform the necessary operations on the symbolic encoding.

Another possibility is to to extend the algorithm to work on hedge automata (HA). As described in [11], an XML document can be viewed as a *hedge* (a more general type of tree), and validated using a HA. We expect the size of this HA to affect the efficiency with which the validation can be performed.

References

1. P. A. Abdulla, A.Legay, J.d'Orso, and A.Rezine. Tree regular model checking: A simulation-based approach. *To appear in Jour. of Logic and Alg. Programming*, 2006.
2. P. A. Abdulla, B. Jonsson, P. Mahata, and J. d'Orso. Regular tree model checking. In *CAV*, volume 2404 of *Lecture Notes in Computer Science*, pages 555–568. Springer, 2002.
3. P. A. Abdulla, B. Jonsson, M. Nilsson, and M. Saksena. A survey of regular model checking. In *CONCUR*, volume 3170 of *Lecture Notes in Computer Science*, pages 35–48. Springer, 2004.
4. P. A. Abdulla, L. Kaati, and J. Högberg. Minimization of tree automata. UMINF 06.25, Department of Computer Science, Umeå University, 2006.
5. M. Biehl, N. Klarlund, and T. Rauhe. Algorithms for guided tree automata. In *Proceedings of the First Workshop on Implementing Automata*, volume 1260 of *Lecture Notes in Computer Science*. Springer, 1997.
6. W. S. Brainerd. The minimalization of tree automata. *Information and Computation*, 13:484–491, 1968.
7. J. Cristau, C. Löding, and W. Thomas. Deterministic automata on unranked trees. In *FCT*, volume 3623 of *Lecture Notes in Computer Science*. Springer, 2005.
8. G. Gramlich and G. Schnitger. Minimizing nfa's and regular expressions. In *STACS*, volume 3404 of *Lecture Notes in Computer Science*. Springer, 2005.
9. J. E. Hopcroft. An $n \log n$ algorithm for minimizing states in a finite automaton. In Z. Kohavi, editor, *Theory of Machines and Computations*. Academic Press, 1971.
10. A. R. Meyer and L. J. Stockmeyer. The equivalence problem for regular expressions. In *Proc. 13th Ann. IEEE Symp. on Switching and Automata Theory*, pages 125–129, 1972.
11. M. Murata. "Hedge Automata: a Formal Model for XML Schemata". Web page, 2000.
12. M. Nivat and A. Podelski. Minimal ascending and descending tree automata. *SIAM Journal on Computing*, 26:39–58, 1997.
13. R. Paige and R. Tarjan. Three partition refinement algorithms. *SIAM Journal on Computing*, 16:973–989, 1987.

Forgetting Automata and Unary Languages

Jens Glöckler

Institut für Informatik, Universität Giessen
Arndtstr. 2, D-35392 Giessen, Germany
`Jens.Gloeckler@math.uni-giessen.de`

Abstract. We consider forgetting automata, i.e., linear bounded automata which can only use the operations 'move', 'erase' (rewrite with a blank symbol) and 'delete' (remove completely). A classification of the families of languages corresponding to the possible combinations of operations has been given in [1], here we address some of the problems left open. Furthermore the unary case is being investigated.

1 Introduction

Forgetting automata were investigated by Jančar, Mráz, and Plátek in a number of papers in order to deal with linguistic models, like the *analysis by reduction* (stepwise abridgement of an input retaining the syntactical correctness). They originate from two models proposed earlier, namely *erasing automata* and *list automata*. In papers [2,3] work on erasing automata, which had been introduced in [4] as a special form of a Turing machine that is allowed to rewrite the content of an input field only a bounded number of times, was continued. Erasing automata can move bidirectionally on their input tape and rewrite the content of the tape field under the head with an auxiliary blank symbol, i.e., *erase* the field.

On the other hand, list automata that work on a doubly linked list have been investigated, e.g., in [5]. List automata operate on their input by means of the operations *move*, *write* (rewrites an input symbol), *delete* (completely deletes an input field, i.e., removes it from the doubly linked list) and *insert* (inserts a new element into the list), which interestingly enough characterizes the four levels of the Chomsky hierarchy in a uniform machine model when restricting the operations appropriately ([6]).

Forgetting automata are automata that are able to use one or more of the operations MV (move), ER (erase) and DL (delete). Associated with the possible directions left and right (indicated as a subscript) we have a total of six operations and therefore $2^6 - 1 = 63$ different automata models (see [1]) to consider.[1] Some of the corresponding language families coincide trivially, e.g.,

$$\mathscr{L}(\mathsf{MV}, \mathsf{DL}) = \mathscr{L}(\mathsf{MV}, \mathsf{DL_L}),$$

---

[1] The family of languages accepted by automata with a certain type of operations like $\mathsf{MV_R}$ and $\mathsf{DL_L}$ will be denoted by $\mathscr{L}(\mathsf{MV_R},\mathsf{DL_L})$. If both directions are allowed for one of the three operations, we will simply leave out the subscript.

O.H. Ibarra and H.-C. Yen (Eds.): CIAA 2006, LNCS 4094, pp. 186–197, 2006.

as DL_R can be simulated by consecutively performing DL_L and MV_R, while

$$\mathscr{L}(MV_R) = \mathscr{L}(DL_R) = \mathscr{L}(ER_R) = REG,$$

as only right moves are possible. Other classes coincide somewhat surprisingly with the family of context-free languages ([7]). All classes, however, are strictly included in DCSL ([8]).

In this paper we follow the aforementioned studies and concentrate on unary input. When restricting to unary input the classification of forgetting automata gets somehow more transparent. In this case, various simulations of one type of automaton by another one are possible, whereas they do not work for inputs with at least two different symbols. But also in the case of non-unary input the examination of unary strings plays in import role as forgetting automata that are able to move to the right only by erasing and deleting leave a trace of unary symbols (i.e., blank symbols) behind when moving to the right. By dealing with these strings of unary input left behind, new results can be obtained, namely the characterization of $\mathscr{L}(ER_R, DL)$ with the family of languages accepted by one-way one-counter automata and the inclusion of $\mathscr{L}(MV_L, ER, DL)$ in $\mathscr{L}(MV, ER)$, that has been left open in [1]. Instead, a direct simulation leads to the equality of $\mathscr{L}(MV_R, ER, DL_R)$ and $\mathscr{L}(MV_R, ER, DL)$ left open in [1,9].

The question whether $\mathscr{L}(MV, DL)$ is a proper subset of $\mathscr{L}(MV, ER)$, that has been put up [9] and asked again in [1,7], can at least be solved for the deterministic case, while the nondeterministic case remains open.

The remainder of this paper is organized as follows: In Section 2 some basic notations are introduced and the automata models used within the paper are defined. Section 3 deals with the non-unary case of forgetting automata but also provides some results used in Section 4, where a classification of unary forgetting automata is given.

2   Preliminaries

Let A^* denote the set of all words over the finite alphabet A. The empty word is denoted by ε. The reversal of a word w is denoted by w^R and the length of w by $|w|$. The number of occurrences of an alphabet symbol $a \in A$ in a word $w \in A^*$ is denoted by $|w|_a$. Set inclusion and strict set inclusion are denoted by $\subseteq$ and $\subset$, respectively. In figures we use arrows $\Longrightarrow$ for set inclusion and $\longrightarrow$ for strict inclusion, while dotted lines $\cdots$ mark incomparability. We use the following notations of language families: REG (regular languages), CFL (context-free languages), DCSL (deterministic context-sensitive languages), LIN (linear languages), METALIN (metalinear languages) and NL (languages accepted by a nondeterministic Turing Machine using logarithmic space). We write $\mathscr{L}(X)$ for the family of languages accepted by devices of type X and $\mathscr{L}_{det}(X)$ for the family of languages accepted by deterministic devices X. We use $\mathscr{L}^u \subseteq \mathscr{L}$ for the correspondent family of unary languages. A unary alphabet is tacitly assumed to be $\{a\}$.

2.1   Forgetting Automata

A *forgetting automaton* is a system $\mathcal{A} = \langle S, A, \triangleright, \triangleleft, \sqcup, O, \delta, s_0, F \rangle$, where S is a finite set of states, A is the input alphabet, $\triangleright, \triangleleft \notin A$ are the left and the right sentinels, $\sqcup \notin A$ is the blank symbol used for erasing, O is a set of operations (see below), $\delta : S \times (A \cup \{\triangleright, \triangleleft, \sqcup\}) \rightarrow 2^{S \times O}$ is the transition function, $s_0 \in S$ is the initial state and $F \subseteq S$ is the set of final states. O consists of one or more of the following operations:

- $\mathsf{MV_L}$, $\mathsf{MV_R}$: move head to the left and right, resp.,
- $\mathsf{DL_L}$, $\mathsf{DL_R}$: delete current field and move head to the left and right, resp.,
- $\mathsf{ER_L}$, $\mathsf{ER_R}$: erase current field with $\sqcup$ and move head to the left and right, resp.

If $\mathcal{A}$ reads $\triangleright$ (resp. $\triangleleft$), it always implies an $\mathsf{MV_R}$-operation (resp. $\mathsf{MV_L}$-operation), even if $\mathsf{MV_R}, \mathsf{MV_L} \notin O$. Generally, a forgetting automaton is nondeterministic. A forgetting automaton is deterministic if $|\delta(s, x)| \leq 1$ for all $s \in S$ and $x \in (A \cup \{\triangleright, \triangleleft, \sqcup\})$.

A configuration of a forgetting automaton $\mathcal{A}$ is a string $w_1 s w_2$, where the word $w_1 w_2 \in \triangleright(A \cup \{\sqcup\})^* \triangleleft$ is the content of the list, s is the current state and $\mathcal{A}$ reads the first symbol of w_2. By $\vdash$ we denote the relation which describes the change of configurations according to δ; $\vdash^*$ is the reflexive, transitive closure of $\vdash$. An input word is accepted by $\mathcal{A}$ if there is a computation, starting in the initial configuration $s_0 \triangleright w \triangleleft$, which reaches a configuration with an accepting state.

In case O contains both versions X_L and X_R of an operation, we write X for short. A forgetting automaton with a certain set of operations, e.g., $\mathsf{MV_R}$ and DL, is called $(\mathsf{MV_R}, \mathsf{DL})$-automaton. For the family of languages accepted by such automata we write $\mathscr{L}(\mathsf{MV_R}, \mathsf{DL})$.

2.2   Counter Automata and Register Machines

In order to be able to classify the computational capacities of forgetting automata we recall briefly some definitions of other machine models that will be dealt with:

A *one-way one-counter automaton (1CA)* is a pushdown automaton (PDA) accepting by final state, with one pushdown symbol (except for the bottom marker).

A *two-way one-counter automaton (2CA)* is a two-way finite automaton equipped with a counter (linearly bounded by the length of the input). Its input is placed between the sentinels $\triangleright$ and $\triangleleft$. The automaton can test if the counter value is zero or nonzero and can add $-1, 0$ or $+1$. The automaton accepts an input string if it halts in an accepting state.

A *two-register machine* consists of a finite control and two registers (counters) and it receives a (natural) input number in the first register (i.e., it has no input tape). It works deterministically and accepts an input by reaching an accepting state.

3   The Non-unary Case

First of all we take a closer look at the language classes between REG and CFL and compare them to the classes of linear and metalinear languages.

Theorem 3.1. $LIN \subset METALIN \subset \mathscr{L}(\mathsf{MV_R}, \mathsf{DL})$

Proof. Given a k-linear grammar, an $(\mathsf{MV_R}, \mathsf{DL})$-automaton can guess (by $\mathsf{MV_R}$-steps) the 'end points' of the k linear derivation paths and process them successively by deleting from the inside to the outside according to the given productions and moving right to the next derivation path while memorizing the (finitely many) nonterminals occurring. Furthermore the context-free language $\{w \in \{0,1\}^* \mid |w|_0 = |w|_1\} \in \mathscr{L}(\mathsf{MV_R}, \mathsf{DL})$ is not metalinear. $\square$

Lemma 3.1. *LIN and METALIN are incomparable to* $\mathscr{L}(\mathsf{ER_R}, \mathsf{DL})$.

Proof. On the one hand $\{w \in \{0,1\}^* \mid |w|_0 = |w|_1\} \in \mathscr{L}(\mathsf{ER_R}, \mathsf{DL})$ is not metalinear, on the other hand $\{wcw^R \mid w \in \{a,b\}^*\} \notin \mathscr{L}(\mathsf{ER_R}, \mathsf{DL})$ ([1]) is an (even deterministic) linear language. $\square$

Interestingly enough it was shown in [1] that $\mathscr{L}(\mathsf{MV_R}, \mathsf{ER_R}, \mathsf{DL})$ coincides with the family of context-free languages, i.e., the family of languages recognized by pushdown automata. If we leave out the $\mathsf{MV_R}$-operation, we will get another well-known family of languages:

Theorem 3.2. $\mathscr{L}(\mathsf{ER_R}, \mathsf{DL}) = \mathscr{L}(1CA)$, $\mathscr{L}_{det}(\mathsf{ER_R}, \mathsf{DL}) = \mathscr{L}_{det}(1CA)$

Proof. Nondeterministic Case: '$\subseteq$' A 1CA $\mathcal{A}$ can simulate an $(\mathsf{ER_R}, \mathsf{DL_L})$-automaton $\mathcal{B}$ ($\mathscr{L}(\mathsf{ER_R}, \mathsf{DL}) = \mathscr{L}(\mathsf{ER_R}, \mathsf{DL_L})$, see [1]) in the following way: We assume without loss of generality that $\mathcal{B}$ accepts an input by halting on $\lhd$. $\mathcal{A}$ simulates each of $\mathcal{B}$'s steps by a series of its own steps. The counter is thereby used to keep track of the number of $\sqcup$-symbols on $\mathcal{B}$'s input list while $\mathcal{A}$'s head always remains on the position of the first (unerased) input symbol. During the computation $\mathcal{B}$'s head is always positioned on one of the following list elements:

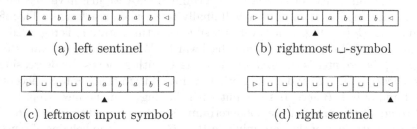

(a) left sentinel   (b) rightmost $\sqcup$-symbol

(c) leftmost input symbol   (d) right sentinel

As $\mathcal{A}$'s head is always placed on an input symbol, it needs to cope with cases (a), (b) and (d) using ε-moves. For this purpose $\mathcal{A}$ checks in every simulation step whether $\mathcal{B}$ reaches an input symbol (we call this the 'input mode') or not ('blank mode'), which can be done by looking at the operation being simulated and the counter value. Case (a) can be detected by checking the counter value for zero, case (d) needs to be handled separately (see below).

To simulate ER_R in input mode, $\mathcal{A}$ increases the counter and stays in input mode while in blank mode it simulates the state transition in an ε-move and enters the input mode. To simulate DL_L in input mode $\mathcal{A}$ also simulates the following step ($\mathcal{B}$ will be reading $\triangleright$) in advance and stays in input mode if the counter is empty; otherwise it enters the blank mode. To simulate DL_L in blank mode it decreases the counter in an ε-move and, if the counter is empty, it also simulates the next step ($\mathcal{B}$ will be reading $\triangleright$) and enters input mode again; if the counter is not empty it stays in blank mode.

In order to simulate $\mathcal{B}$'s behavior after it hits $\triangleleft$, $\mathcal{A}$ can guess the end of input after each step. $\mathcal{A}$ thereby simulates the processing of the remaining unary input $\sqcup^k$ (for some $k \in \mathbb{N}_0$) with the counter value, using only ε-moves (all transitions reading input are undefined for the states used therein). While ER_R (and the following MV_L) imply only state changes, DL_L can be simulated by decreasing the counter; the arrival at the left boundary can be detected by using the zero test. By this means $\mathcal{A}$ falls off the tape in an accepting state if and only if $\mathcal{B}$ accepts on the right sentinel (after having erased the input completely).

'$\supseteq$' An (ER_R, DL)-automaton $\mathcal{A}$ can simulate a 1CA $\mathcal{B}$ in the following way: First of all $\mathcal{B}$ can be implied to be ε-free ([10]), therefore an upper bound k of counter increase per move can be assumed. $\mathcal{A}$ needs to simulate $\mathcal{B}$'s counter including the zero test. It stores the counter value as the quotient of division by k on its list and the remainder modulo k in its states. Furthermore it keeps the information if at least one erased symbol is on the list in its states and updates it when writing or deleting erased symbols. The result of the zero test is given by this information and the remainder modulo k. By this means $\mathcal{A}$ ends up on $\triangleleft$ accepting the input if and only if $\mathcal{B}$ falls off the tape and accepts the input.

Deterministic Case: '$\subseteq$' We assume without loss of generality that a deterministic (ER_R, DL_L)-automaton always completely deletes the input before it accepts or not accepts on $\triangleleft$. As opposed to the nondeterministic case the end of input cannot be guessed, but the 'post-processing' of the remaining string $\sqcup^k$ can be performed in parallel before: As the behavior of the deterministic (ER_R, DL_L)-automaton $\mathcal{B}$ on $\sqcup^k$ can be simulated by a (unary) DFA we just have to compute the state the forgetting automaton will finally be in when reaching $\triangleleft$. Therefore a unary DFA $\mathcal{C}_i$ (see Fig. 1) for every possible (starting) state s_i is regarded and the edges are followed forwards and backwards. When going backwards from state s_{i,k_i}, the counter is checked for the value k_i with ε-moves (by decreasing k_i times, checking for zero and incrementing again). $\mathcal{A}$ then changes to an accepting state if and only if $\mathcal{B}$ accepts the input when hitting $\triangleleft$ in the next step.

'$\supseteq$' To adapt the proof of the nondeterministic case we need to make sure that within computations of the deterministic 1CA $\mathcal{B}$ only bounded chains of ε-moves can occur. In the deterministic case we cannot do without ε-moves, but we can state a linear upper bound for their usage. We therefore modify $\mathcal{B}$ to satisfy the property that after reading n input symbols the counter value is not bigger than $k \cdot n$ (for a fixed $k \in \mathbb{N}$). Whenever there occurs a series of ε-moves in $\mathcal{B}$, it can either lead into a loop or enter a state for which a state transition using an input symbol is defined again (for a DPDA only one type of transition is allowed). We

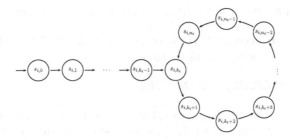

Fig. 1. DFA $\mathcal{C}_i$

obtain the desired property by removing some of the transitions as follows: In the case of a loop $s_1, s_2, \ldots, s_l, s_1$ we observe the overall change c of the counter value during one cycle. If $c < 0$ the automaton will always reach counter value zero and therefore leave the loop, if $c >= 0$ we can safely remove the transition from s_l to s_1 (counter level zero can only be reached up to the first occurrence of s_l). The language accepted by $\mathcal{B}$ remains unchanged and we can obtain k by examining the remaining state transitions.

We now know that only bounded chains of ε-moves can occur. Those can be simulated by the $(\mathsf{ER_R}, \mathsf{DL})$-automaton $\mathcal{A}$ in advance for state changes only and with DL-operations for decreasing the counter. By observing together only a number of steps such that the decrease cannot exceed k, $\mathcal{A}$ is able to perform zero check and decrease operations correctly, as it can use its modulo-k-counter and the information whether there are erased symbols on the list or not.   □

While the inclusion $\mathscr{L}(\mathsf{MV_R}, \mathsf{ER}, \mathsf{DL_R}) \subseteq \mathscr{L}(\mathsf{MV_R}, \mathsf{ER}, \mathsf{DL})$ is trivial, the question of strict inclusion or equality of the two language families was left open in [1]. We will see that the absence of the $\mathsf{DL_L}$-operation in question does not make a change in the generative power:

Theorem 3.3. $\mathscr{L}(\mathsf{MV_R}, \mathsf{ER}, \mathsf{DL_R}) = \mathscr{L}(\mathsf{MV_R}, \mathsf{ER}, \mathsf{DL})$,
$\qquad\quad \mathscr{L}_{det}(\mathsf{MV_R}, \mathsf{ER}, \mathsf{DL_R}) = \mathscr{L}_{det}(\mathsf{MV_R}, \mathsf{ER}, \mathsf{DL})$

Proof. An $(\mathsf{MV_R}, \mathsf{ER}, \mathsf{DL_R})$-automaton $\mathcal{A}$ can simulate an $(\mathsf{MV_R}, \mathsf{ER}, \mathsf{DL})$-automaton $\mathcal{B}$ in the following way: In order to deal with the $\mathsf{DL_L}$-operation unavailable to $\mathcal{A}$, it distinguishes between two different modes we call mode 1 and mode 2. In mode 1 $\mathcal{A}$ simulates the operations $\mathsf{MV_R}$, $\mathsf{ER_L}$, $\mathsf{ER_R}$ and $\mathsf{DL_R}$ directly, while it simulates $\mathsf{DL_L}$ by executing $\mathsf{ER_L}$ and entering mode 2. In mode 2 $\mathcal{A}$ simulates $\mathcal{B}$'s behavior as follows:

When $\mathcal{B}$ performs	$\mathcal{A}$	
	performs operation	enters mode
$\mathsf{MV_R}$	$\mathsf{MV_R}$, $\mathsf{DL_R}$	1
$\mathsf{ER_L}$	$\mathsf{DL_R}$, $\mathsf{ER_L}$	1
$\mathsf{ER_R}$	$\mathsf{DL_R}$, $\mathsf{MV_R}$	1
$\mathsf{DL_L}$	$\mathsf{DL_R}$, $\mathsf{ER_L}$	2
$\mathsf{DL_R}$	$\mathsf{DL_R}$, $\mathsf{DL_R}$	1

By this means $\mathcal{A}$ finally accepts the input if and only if $\mathcal{B}$ accepts.   □

Another relation left open in [1] is the one between $\mathscr{L}(\mathsf{ER}, \mathsf{DL})$ and $\mathscr{L}(\mathsf{MV}, \mathsf{ER})$, where we find the following inclusion to hold:

Theorem 3.4. $\mathscr{L}(\mathsf{ER}, \mathsf{DL}) \subseteq \mathscr{L}(\mathsf{MV}, \mathsf{ER})$

Proof. An $(\mathsf{MV}, \mathsf{ER})$-automaton $\mathcal{A}$ can simulate an $(\mathsf{ER}, \mathsf{DL_L})$-automaton $\mathcal{B}$ (note that $\mathscr{L}(\mathsf{ER}, \mathsf{DL}) = \mathscr{L}(\mathsf{ER}, \mathsf{DL_L})$ holds) as follows: essentially $\mathcal{A}$ simulates ER by MV and DL by ER, that means it does not erase the fields erased by $\mathcal{B}$ but only moves and erases fields deleted by $\mathcal{B}$ in order to treat them as deleted afterwards. The challenge is not to lose track of the 'critical' position c up to which $\mathcal{B}$ has erased the input so far in order to know if $\mathcal{B}$ reads '␣' or an input symbol throughout the simulation. The idea is to mark the symbol on position c by erasing it and to remember if currently the rightmost ␣ on the list stands for a deleted symbol or position c (note that it can always be checked whether a ␣-symbol is rightmost on the list). If $\mathcal{B}$ moves left from position c, we let $\mathcal{A}$ guess whether $\mathcal{B}$ returns with or without deleting at least one symbol in between. If we consider the partial computations performed by $\mathcal{B}$ that start in a certain state s_i on an input symbol $x \in A$ with an $\mathsf{ER_L}$-operation (resp. $\mathsf{DL_L}$-operation) and only use ER-operations (on symbols already erased), we get the behavior of a 2NFA that starts its computation on the second last (resp. last) ␣ of a unary input string $w \in \{\text{␣}\}^*$ bordered by sentinels $\triangleright$ and x. As this 2NFA can also be represented by a DFA, $\mathcal{A}$ can simulate the behavior of such an automaton $\mathcal{C}_i$ (one for each starting state s_i, see Figure 1) falling off the tape on its right sentinel x in advance and simply move right in a corresponding state. The simulation of $\mathcal{C}_i$ can be achieved by following $\mathcal{C}_i$'s edges forwards and backwards during normal movement (cf. the proof of Theorem 3.2). When going backwards from state s_{i,k_i}, $\mathcal{A}$ checks if its head is standing on position k_i (by moving k_i steps to the left, checking the presence of the boundary symbol and moving k_i steps to the right again). In this way $\mathcal{A}$ can always keep the DFA's state up to date while moving around on the tape.

If $\mathcal{A}$ instead guesses that $\mathcal{B}$ will delete some symbol before returning, we let $\mathcal{A}$ mark (i.e., erase) position c, continue simulating and halt in a non-accepting state if the guess was wrong (i.e., $\mathcal{B}$ returned without deleting in between). However, the first time $\mathcal{B}$ deletes one of the symbols left of position c, $\mathcal{A}$ simply treats the rightmost input symbol on the left of c (again, this can always be checked) as deleted. In this way the computation on the erased subword at the beginning of the list as well as its length can be simulated correctly and $\mathcal{A}$ accepts if and only if $\mathcal{B}$ does.   □

We can even add the $\mathsf{MV_L}$-operation and extend the result above:

Theorem 3.5. $\mathscr{L}(\mathsf{MV_L}, \mathsf{ER}, \mathsf{DL}) \subseteq \mathscr{L}(\mathsf{MV}, \mathsf{ER})$

Proof. Whereas $\mathsf{MV_L}$ is equivalent to $\mathsf{ER_L}$ on fields that have been erased before, it gives an $(\mathsf{MV_L}, \mathsf{ER}, \mathsf{DL_L})$-automaton the option to move left from the leftmost input symbol without erasing or deleting it. The proof of Theorem 3.4 can therefore be extended as follows: MV_L on A is simulated by MV_L (special treatment is unnecessary as position c does not change) while MV_L on '⌴' is handled like ER_L. □

The deterministic version of the preceding theorem can also be obtained:

Theorem 3.6. $\mathscr{L}_{det}(MV_L, ER, DL) \subseteq \mathscr{L}_{det}(MV, ER)$

Proof. The proof of Theorem 3.4 can be modified to suit the deterministic case as follows: If automaton $\mathcal{B}$ moves leftwards from position c, $\mathcal{A}$ does not have to guess whether $\mathcal{B}$ deletes some symbol or not. If we consider the DFA $\mathcal{C}_i$ that originates from using only ER-operations, two possibilities can emerge in the deterministic case: 1. $\mathcal{C}_i$'s state represents exactly one state of the 2DFA or 2. $\mathcal{C}_i$'s state represents the empty set of states. In the first case $\mathcal{B}$ will return to position c without deleting any symbol in between and $\mathcal{A}$ can instantly change to the corresponding state. In the second case $\mathcal{B}$ will either halt or use a DL-operation and $\mathcal{A}$ can mark position c and directly simulate $\mathcal{B}$'s steps. □

Bringing together the previous theorems with the fact from [1] that the language $\{wcw^R \mid w \in \{a, b\}^*\}$ is not contained in $\mathscr{L}(MV_L, ER, DL)$ we even have a strict inclusion:

Corollary 3.1. $\mathscr{L}(MV_L, ER, DL) \subset \mathscr{L}(MV, ER)$,
$\qquad\quad \mathscr{L}_{det}(MV_L, ER, DL) \subset \mathscr{L}_{det}(MV, ER)$

For an overview of the classification of forgetting automata see Figure 2 (the trivial classes $\mathscr{L}(MV_L), \mathscr{L}(ER_L)$ and $\mathscr{L}(MV_L, ER_L)$ below REG are omitted).

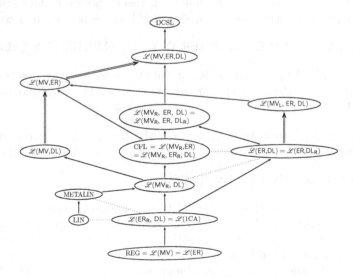

Fig. 2. The classification of (non-unary) forgetting automata

4   The Unary Case

In this chapter we examine the computational capacities of forgetting automata in the case of unary input alphabets. At the lower end of the hierarchy we can get the following immediate result: as $REG^u = CFL^u$ all language families up to CFL collapse in the unary case.

Lemma 4.1. $REG^u = \mathscr{L}^u(\mathsf{ER_R}, \mathsf{DL}) = \mathscr{L}^u(\mathsf{MV_R}, \mathsf{DL}) = \mathscr{L}^u(\mathsf{MV_R}, \mathsf{ER})$
$\qquad\qquad = \mathscr{L}^u(\mathsf{MV_R}, \mathsf{ER_R}, \mathsf{DL}) = CFL^u$

While in the general case it is still unknown if the inclusion $CFL \subseteq \mathscr{L}(\mathsf{MV}, \mathsf{DL})$ holds, in the unary case we can state:

Theorem 4.1. $REG^u = CFL^u \subset \mathscr{L}^u(\mathsf{MV}, \mathsf{DL})$

Proof. To begin with, it is clear that $REG^u \subseteq \mathscr{L}^u(\mathsf{MV}, \mathsf{DL})$ holds. Moreover the language $\{a^{2^n} \mid n \in \mathbb{N}\}$ is in $\mathscr{L}^u(\mathsf{MV}, \mathsf{DL})$, but not in REG^u. $\square$

Once more, the following relation is still unknown to hold in the non-unary case:

Theorem 4.2. $\mathscr{L}^u(\mathsf{MV_L}, \mathsf{ER}, \mathsf{DL}) \subseteq \mathscr{L}^u(\mathsf{MV_R}, \mathsf{ER}, \mathsf{DL})$,
$\qquad\qquad \mathscr{L}^u_{det}(\mathsf{MV_L}, \mathsf{ER}, \mathsf{DL}) \subseteq \mathscr{L}^u_{det}(\mathsf{MV_R}, \mathsf{ER}, \mathsf{DL})$

Proof. An $(\mathsf{MV_R}, \mathsf{ER}, \mathsf{DL})$-automaton $\mathcal{A}$ can simulate an $(\mathsf{MV_L}, \mathsf{ER}, \mathsf{DL})$-automaton $\mathcal{B}$ by first traversing the input to the right up to $\triangleleft$ and then simulating all of $\mathcal{B}$'s operations in the converse direction. $\mathcal{A}$ finally reaches an accepting state if and only if $\mathcal{B}$ does. $\square$

Note that the closure of $\mathscr{L}(\mathsf{MV_L}, \mathsf{ER}, \mathsf{DL})$ under reversal would lead to the same result for the non-unary case. The following result, however, does not hold in the non-unary case, where $\{wcw^R \mid w \in \{a, b\}^*\}$ serves as a counterexample:

Theorem 4.3. $\mathscr{L}^u(\mathsf{MV}, \mathsf{DL}) \subseteq \mathscr{L}^u(\mathsf{ER}, \mathsf{DL}),\; \mathscr{L}^u_{det}(\mathsf{MV}, \mathsf{DL}) \subseteq \mathscr{L}^u_{det}(\mathsf{ER}, \mathsf{DL})$

Proof. As an $(\mathsf{MV}, \mathsf{DL})$-automaton is not able to erase, it always reads the same symbol (apart from the sentinels) in the unary case. Therefore moving can be simulated by erasing. $\square$

In order to achieve a strict inclusion of $\mathscr{L}^u(\mathsf{MV}, \mathsf{DL})$ in $DCSL^u$ we draw a comparison between $(\mathsf{MV}, \mathsf{DL})$-automata and two-way one-counter automata:

Theorem 4.4. $\mathscr{L}^u(\mathsf{MV}, \mathsf{DL}) \subseteq \mathscr{L}^u(2CA)$

Proof. A 2CA $\mathcal{A}$ can simulate an $(\mathsf{MV}, \mathsf{DL})$-automaton $\mathcal{B}$ (processing unary input) in the following way: During the computation the counter value equals the position of $\mathcal{A}$'s head (where 1 is the position of the first input symbol) minus the number of symbols deleted by $\mathcal{B}$. In other words: the number of deleted symbols is represented by the position of $\mathcal{A}$'s head minus the counter value. This gets accomplished by simulating $\mathcal{B}$'s steps in the following manner:

$\mathcal{B}$	$\mathcal{A}$	
	head movement	counter update
MV_L	left	-1
MV_R	right	$+1$
DL_L	none	-1
DL_R	right	± 0

$\mathcal{A}$ can sense that $\mathcal{B}$ reaches the first input symbol (and therefore $\triangleright$ if MV_L or DL_L follows) if the counter value reaches zero. The right sentinel $\triangleleft$ marks the end of the input for both $\mathcal{A}$ and $\mathcal{B}$. By this means $\mathcal{A}$ accepts the input if and only if $\mathcal{B}$ accepts. $\qquad\square$

Corollary 4.1. $\mathscr{L}^u(MV, DL) \subset DCSL^u$

Proof. By Theorem 4.4 and the hierarchy for unary two-way counter automata (see [11]) we can conclude: $\mathscr{L}^u(MV, DL) \subseteq \mathscr{L}^u(2DC) \subset NL^u \subseteq DCSL^u$. $\qquad\square$

In the deterministic case we can state a stronger separation result by simulating a two-register-machine with an (MV, DL)-automaton and using a result of Ibarra and Trân:

Theorem 4.5. $\mathscr{L}^u_{det}(MV, DL) \subset \mathscr{L}^u_{det}(MV, ER)$

Proof. First of all, the inclusion $\mathscr{L}^u_{det}(MV, DL) \subseteq \mathscr{L}^u_{det}(MV, ER)$ holds, as in this case DL can be simulated by ER ([1]). In the unary case a deterministic two-register-machine $\mathcal{A}$ can simulate a deterministic (MV, DL)-automaton $\mathcal{B}$ in the following way: $\mathcal{A}$ receives the length of $\mathcal{B}$'s input string as input value in its first register. During the simulation the first register stores the number of symbols under and on the right side of $\mathcal{B}$'s head and the second register deals with the left side. MV-operations are simulated by shifting from one register to the other while DL-operations lead to a decrement of the appropriate register.

In [12] Ibarra and Trân showed that the set of numbers $L_2 = \{n^2 \mid n \geq 0\}$ (which corresponds to the language $L'_2 = \{a^{n^2} \mid n \geq 0\}$) cannot be recognized by a deterministic two-register-machine. A deterministic (MV, ER)-automaton $\mathcal{C}$ on the other hand can accept L'_2 in the following way: $\mathcal{C}$ successively marks the positions of squares, starting from 1 and 4. As the difference between two adjacent squares $(i+1)^2 - i^2$ equals $2i - 1$ it repeatedly copies a number (piece by piece) to the right and adds two. For this purpose $\mathcal{C}$ marks positions i^2 and $i^2 + 1$ with $\sqcup$-symbols and leaves them surrounded by unerased a's (i.e., on positions $i^2 - 1$ and $i^2 + 2$, see Figure 3). These subwords $a \sqcup \sqcup a$ serve as a boundary so that

Fig. 3. List contents after $\mathcal{C}$ has marked position 25

$\mathcal{C}$ can move around without losing track of its position. The copying is done by marking only every other position between two boundaries. This way the fields between the squares i^2 and $(i+1)^2$ can be used twice, first for copying $2(i-1)-1$ in it from the left (and adding two) and then for copying $2i-1$ to the right side. $\mathcal{C}$ finally accepts the input if and only if this construction finishes on a square next to the right sentinel.   □

The preceding theorem partially solves (i.e., for the deterministic case) an open problem from [1] and strengthens the claim "erasing is more powerful than deleting" (from [13]) as we have:

Corollary 4.2. $\mathscr{L}_{det}(\mathsf{MV}, \mathsf{DL}) \subset \mathscr{L}_{det}(\mathsf{MV}, \mathsf{ER})$

Moreover, in the deterministic case we can also give the following result:

Theorem 4.6. $\mathscr{L}_{det}^u(\mathsf{MV_L}, \mathsf{ER}, \mathsf{DL}) \subseteq \mathscr{L}_{det}^u(\mathsf{MV}, \mathsf{DL})$

Proof. A deterministic $(\mathsf{MV}, \mathsf{DL})$-automaton $\mathcal{A}$ is able to simulate a deterministic $(\mathsf{MV_L}, \mathsf{ER}, \mathsf{DL})$-automaton $\mathcal{B}$ as follows in the unary case: Again $\mathcal{A}$ has to keep track of the position c up to which $\mathcal{B}$ has erased the input (cf. Theorem 3.4). To simulate $\mathcal{B}$'s behavior (on sufficiently long input; input up to a certain fixed length can be handled separately) we regard loops of configurations of the following forms

$$\triangleright \sqcup^k x a^n \triangleleft \quad \vdash^* \quad \triangleright \sqcup^k x a^m \triangleleft \quad (m \leq n) \tag{1}$$

$$\triangleright \sqcup^k x a^n \triangleleft \quad \vdash^* \quad \triangleright \sqcup^l x a^m \triangleleft \quad (m < n, k < l) \tag{2}$$

where $\mathcal{A}$ will always continue with the same computation steps and loop forever (if $m = n$) or finally reach $\triangleleft$. We therefore construct $\mathcal{A}$ to simulate these loops while keeping its head on position c. In any case we first let $\mathcal{A}$ simulate the initial steps up to the loop. For form (1) we then let $\mathcal{A}$ repeat the shortening of the remaining input a^* on position c, while for form (2) we let $\mathcal{A}$ simulate the loop by moving to the right (following position c) and, if necessary, deleting the appropriate number of symbols. Moreover, in order to correctly simulate $\mathcal{B}$'s behavior when reaching $\triangleleft$, $\mathcal{A}$ needs to check the distance to the right border before simulating each cycle of the loop; as $\mathcal{B}$ can move back and forth during the loop we might not capture this only by deleting the appropriate number of symbols. $\mathcal{A}$ therefore always moves some steps (finitely many, bounded by $|S_\mathcal{B}|$) rightwards and back to see if it can calmly simulate one cycle, i.e., if $\mathcal{B}$ does not reach $\triangleleft$ in between. $\mathcal{A}$ can then directly simulate the last steps before hitting $\triangleleft$ and afterwards simulate all ER-steps by MV (as the remaining input consists only of $\sqcup$-symbols) and adopt $\mathsf{MV_L}$- and DL-steps. In that way $\mathcal{A}$ accepts if and only if $\mathcal{B}$ does.   □

Combined with Theorem 4.3 we therefore have an equality of the following language classes in the deterministic case:

Corollary 4.3. $\mathscr{L}_{det}^u(\mathsf{MV}, \mathsf{DL}) = \mathscr{L}_{det}^u(\mathsf{ER}, \mathsf{DL}) = \mathscr{L}_{det}^u(\mathsf{MV_L}, \mathsf{ER}, \mathsf{DL})$

For an overview of the classification of unary forgetting automata, in the deterministic as well as the nondeterministic case, see Figure 4.

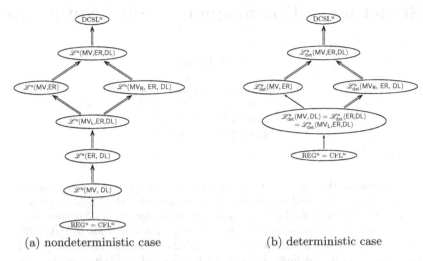

(a) nondeterministic case   (b) deterministic case

Fig. 4. The classification of unary forgetting automata

References

1. Jančar, P., Mráz, F., Plátek, M.: A taxonomy of forgetting automata. In: Proc.
   MFCS 1993. Volume 711 of LNCS. (1993) 527–536
2. Jančar, P., Mráz, F., Plátek, M.: Characterization of context-free languages by
   erasing automata. In: Proc. MFCS 1992. Volume 629 of LNCS., Springer-Verlag
   (1992) 305–314
3. Mráz, F., Plátek, M.: Erasing automata recognize more than context-free languages. Acta Mathematica et Informatica Universitatis Ostraviensis **3** (1995) 77–85
4. von Braunmühl, B., Verbeek, R.: Finite change automata. In: Proceedings of the
   Fourth GI Conference on Theoretical Computer Science. Volume 67 of LNCS.,
   Springer-Verlag (1979) 91–100
5. Plátek, M., Vogel, J.: Deterministic list automata and erasing graphs. The Prague
   bulletin of mathematical linguistics **45** (1986) 27–50
6. Chytil, M.P., Plátek, M., Vogel, J.: A note on the Chomsky hierarchy. Bulletin of
   the EATCS **27** (1985) 23–30
7. Jančar, P., Mráz, F., Plátek, M.: Forgetting automata and context-free languages.
   Acta Informatica **33** (1996) 409–420
8. Jančar, P.: Nondeterministic forgetting automata are less powerful than deterministic linear bounded automata. Acta Mathematica et Informatica Universitatis
   Ostraviensis **1** (1993) 67–74
9. Jančar, P., Mráz, F., Plátek, M.: Forgetting automata and the Chomsky hierarchy.
   In: Proc. SOFSEM 1992. (1992) 41–44
10. Greibach, S.A.: Erasable context-free languages. Information and Control **29**
    (1975) 301–326
11. Monien, B.: Two-way multihead automata over a one-letter alphabet. RAIRO –
    Theoretical Informatics and Applications **14** (1980) 67–82
12. Ibarra, O.H., Trân, N.Q.: A note on simple programs with two variables.
    Theoretical Computer Science **112** (1993) 391–397
13. Mráz, F., Plátek, M.: A remark about forgetting automata. In: Proc. SOFSEM
    1993. (1993) 63–66

Structurally Unambiguous Finite Automata*

Hing Leung

Department of Computer Science
New Mexico State University
Las Cruces, NM 88003, U.S.A.
hleung@cs.nmsu.edu

Abstract. We define a structurally unambiguous finite automaton (SUFA) to be a nondeterministic finite automaton (NFA) with one starting state q_0 such that for all input strings w and for any state q, there is at most one path from q_0 to q that consumes w. The definition of SUFA differs from the usual definition of an unambiguous finite automaton (UFA) in that the new definition is defined in terms of the transition logic of the finite automaton, and is independent of the choice of final states. We show that SUFA can be exponentially more succinct in the number of states than UFA and MDFA (deterministic finite automata with multiple initial states). Some interesting examples of SUFA are given. We argue that SUFA is a meaningful concept, and can have practical importance as it can implemented efficiently on synchronous models of parallel computation.

1 Introduction

The descriptional complexity of finite automata have been extensively studied since 1970's ([9], [11]). A recent survey on the descriptional complexity's of automata can be found in [3].

While deterministic finite automata (DFA) are more suitable for implementation, nondeterministic finite automata (NFA) can be exponentially more succinct in denoting regular languages. NFA are classified according to the amount of ambiguity used. Given an NFA M, we define the ambiguity of a string w to be the number of different accepting paths for w in M. An NFA is said to be k-ambiguous if every string in the language is accepted with at most k different accepting computations. An unambiguous NFA (UFA) is a 1-ambiguous NFA. An NFA is said to be finitely ambiguous (FNA) if the NFA is k-ambiguous for some positive integer k. There is a special class of FNA called deterministic finite automata with multiple initial states (MDFA) ([5] [4] [2] [13]) which is an NFA with deterministic transition logic. An MDFA is k-ambiguous where k is the number of starting states.

An NFA is polynomially ambiguous (PNA) if there exists a polynomial p such that every string x in the language is accepted with at most $p(|x|)$ accepting computations. Given an NFA of k states, any input string of length n can have

---

* The research is partially supported by NSF MII grant CNS-0220590.

O.H. Ibarra and H.-C. Yen (Eds.): CIAA 2006, LNCS 4094, pp. 198–207, 2006.

at most k^n different accepting computations. Thus, it follows that every NFA is exponentially ambiguous (ENA).

In Section 2, we define a variant of UFA which we call structurally unambiguous finite automata (SUFA). We present examples of interesting SUFA. We prove descriptional complexity tradeoffs results between SUFA, UFA, MDFA and reversal of MDFA. After we have established the technical results, we argue in Section 3 that the new model SUFA is a meaningful concept. It can also have practical importance as SUFA can be implemented efficiently on a synchronous model of parallel computation.

2   Structurally Unambiguous Finite Automata

A SUFA is an NFA $(Q, \Sigma, \delta, q_0, F)$, where Q is the set of states, Σ is the alphabet set, $\delta \subseteq Q \times \Sigma \times Q$, q_0 is the starting state and F is the set of final states, such that for any string $w \in \Sigma^*$ and for any $q \in Q$, there is at most one path that goes from q_0 to q for processing w.

Note that SUFA is defined by referring to the transition logic of the finite automaton, and is independent of the way the set of final states is defined. That is, SUFA is a property of the structure of the transition logic, independent from the choice of the set of final states.

If there is only one final state, that is $|F| = 1$, then a SUFA is also a UFA. However, SUFA may differ from UFA when there is more than one final state.

Similarly, we define a generalized structurally unambiguous finite automaton (GSUFA) in the same way as SUFA except that we allow more than one starting states. Specifically, a GSUFA is an NFA $(Q, \Sigma, \delta, S, F)$ such that for any $q, q' \in Q$ and for any string $w \in \Sigma^*$, there is at most one path that goes from q to q' for processing w. It is possible that in processing the same input w, two different paths beginning from different states may arrive at the same state q'.

One can see that both GSUFA and SUFA are subclasses of FNA as the amount of ambiguity of GSUFA and SUFA are bounded by n^2 and n respectively, where n is the number of states. It is interesting to compare the descriptional complexity of the new models with UFA and MDFA, which are also subclasses of FNA.

We can see that the descriptional complexity of SUFA and GSUFA in terms of the number of states are polynomially related. It is clear that a SUFA is a GSUFA. Given an n-state GSUFA $(Q, \Sigma, \delta, S, F)$ where $S = \{s_1, s_2, \ldots, s_k\} \subseteq Q$ is the set of starting states, we replicate from the GSUFA logic k disjoint copies of SUFA $M_i = (Q, \Sigma, \delta, s_i, F)$, where $1 \le i \le k$. Next, we introduce a new starting state s where $s \notin Q$ and create ϵ transitions from s to the starting state s_i of each of the k SUFA. By substituting the ϵ-moves with direct non-ϵ-moves, we obtain a $O(n^2)$-state SUFA equivalent to the given GSUFA. As a MDFA is a GSUFA, consequently neither MDFA and GSUFA can offer significant (bigger than polynomial) advantage in descriptional sizes over SUFA.

Consider an n-state NFA M with $Q = \{q_1, q_2, \ldots, q_n\}$, the alphabet set Σ and the transition function δ. Let $1 \le i, j \le n$. We define $M_{i,j} = (Q, \Sigma, \delta, q_i, q_j)$. Then M is a GSUFA iff $M_{i,j}$ is a UFA for all $i, j \in \{1, \ldots, n\}$. Stearns and

Hunt [12] showed that there is a polynomial time algorithm for checking if a given NFA is a UFA. To test if a given n-state NFA is a GSUFA, we can apply the polynomial time UFA-testing algorithm n^2 times. Similarly, we can apply the UFA-testing algorithm n times to check if a given NFA is a SUFA. Therefore, whether a NFA is a SUFA (or, GSUFA) can be determined in polynomial time.

In [12], it is shown that equivalence and containment problems for UFA can be decided in polynomially time. However, this is not the case for SUFA in general. We can show that the equivalence problem for SUFA is PSPACE-complete. In [1] (p. 266), it is known that the DFA intersection problem is PSPACE-complete. Since DFA are efficiently closed under complementation, the following *union-universe* problem [4] is also PSPACE-complete: Given a number of DFA G_1, G_2, ..., G_n over an input alphabet Σ, we ask whether the union of the languages accepted by $G_1, G_2, \ldots, G_n$ is Σ^*. One can consider the disjoint union of the n DFA as a MDFA G, which is a SUFA. We can thus reduce the union-universe problem to an instance of the SUFA equivalence problem with the instance consisting of the SUFA G and a single state DFA (which is a SUFA) accepting Σ^*. Therefore, the equivalence problem for SUFA is PSPACE-hard. As the equivalence problem for NFA is in PSPACE, we conclude that the equivalence problem for SUFA is PSPACE-complete. It is not difficult to see that the containment problem is also PSPACE-complete since the equivalence problem can be easily reduced to the containment problem, which is also PSPACE-solvable. On the other hand, if the number of final states in a SUFA is bounded by a constant k (independent of the number of states n), the equivalence and containment problems are solvable in polynomial time as Stearns and Hunt [12] had showed that the corresponding problems are polynomial time solvable for k-ambiguous finite automata.

In [8], we introduced a language of "some-register-on". Suppose there are n registers. Each register holds a value of either 0 or 1 ('off' or 'on'). Initially, register 1 is on. All other registers are off. Consider an instruction

    Copy i to j

Executing the instruction will copy the current value of register i to register j. In short, the instruction is given as $C_{i,j}$.

We define an input string to consist of a sequence of copy instructions. As copying register i to itself is a dummy instruction, we assume that $C_{i,i}$ is not allowed. As there are $n(n-1)$ possible copy instructions, the input alphabet has $O(n^2)$ letters.

An example input is $C_{1,4}C_{4,2}C_{3,1}C_{4,3}C_{1,2}$. We say that an input is in the language of some-register-on if some register is on after the sequence of copy instructions have been performed.

Consider the example input given before. Initially, register 1 is on. The first copy instruction $C_{1,4}$ will turn register 4 to on. The next instruction $C_{4,2}$ will turn on register 2. The next instruction $C_{3,1}$ sets register 1 to off as register 3 is off. Next, instruction $C_{4,3}$ turns on register 3. The last instruction $C_{1,2}$ turns register 2 to off. Thus, after all copy instructions are performed, registers 3 and 4 are on whereas registers 1 and 2 are off. Since not all registers are off, we conclude that the input belongs to the language of some-register-on.

We define an n-state SUFA for the language of some-register-on. State 1 is an initial state. The design intuition is that state i is loaded when register i is on. With respect to the input symbol $C_{i,j}$, there are transitions going from state i to state j, and transitions going from state k to state k where $k \neq j$. All states are final states. Formally, the NFA is $A = (Q, \Sigma, \delta_A, q_0, F)$ where $Q = \{1, 2, ..., n\}$, $\Sigma = \{C_{i,j} \mid 1 \leq i,j \leq n, \ i \neq j\}$, $q_0 = 1$, $F = Q$ and $\delta_A = \{(k, C_{i,j}, k) \mid 1 \leq i,j,k \leq n, \ i \neq j \neq k\} \bigcup \{(i, C_{i,j}, j) \mid 1 \leq i,j \leq n, \ i \neq j\}$. Nondeterminism occurs when the NFA is at state i given that the current input symbol is $C_{i,j}$. The NFA can remain at state i or go to state j. Other transitions are self loops.

To see that A is an SUFA, we reverse the transition directions and the roles of starting and final states from A. We denote the reversal of A as A^R. The logic after reversing the transitions is deterministic. But it differs from a DFA in that all the n states are starting states. Thus, A^R is a MDFA. Since a MDFA is a GSUFA, the reversal automaton of a MDFA is also a GSUFA. That is, A is a GSUFA with one starting state; hence, A is a SUFA.

We can show that the smallest DFA for the language of some-register-on has 2^n states. This is because all subsets of states considered by the subset construction are reachable, and any two subsets of states are distinguishable in the sense of Myhill-Nerode theorem.

In the next theorem, we show that a UFA for the language of some-register-on has at least $2^n - 1$ states.

Theorem 1. *Let $n \geq 3$. The smallest UFA for the language L of some-register-on with n registers has at least $2^n - 1$ states.*

Proof. (Sketch) The technique for proving lower bound on the size of a UFA is introduced by Schmidt [11].

For $\emptyset \neq Q' \subseteq Q = \{1, 2, \ldots, n\}$, we want to define $x_{Q'}$ such that A reaches the subset Q' of states when processing $x_{Q'}$ from the starting state 1. Let $Q' = \{q_1, q_2, \ldots, q_k\}$.

Case 1. Suppose $1 \in Q'$. Define $x_{Q'} = C_{1,q_1} C_{1,q_2} \ldots C_{1,q_k}$.

Case 2. Suppose $1 \notin Q'$. Let $q \in Q - \{1, q_1\}$. Define $x_{Q'} = C_{1,q_1} C_{q,1} C_{q_1,q_2} C_{q_1,q_3} \ldots C_{q_1,q_k}$.

Similarly, for $\emptyset \neq Q'' \subseteq Q = \{1, 2, \ldots, n\}$, we want to define $y_{Q''}$ such that A^R reaches the subset Q'' of states when processing the symbols of the string $y_{Q''}$ from right to left. Let $Q'' = \{q_1, q_2, \ldots, q_k\}$.

Case 1. Suppose $Q'' = Q$. Define $y_{Q''} = \epsilon$.

Case 2. Suppose $Q'' \neq Q$. Let $Q - Q'' = \{q_1', q_2', \ldots, q_h'\}$ where $h + k = n$. Define $y_{Q''} = C_{q_2',q_1'} C_{q_3',q_2'} \ldots C_{q_h',q_{h-1}'} C_{q_1,q_h'}$.

We can see that $x_{Q'} y_{Q''} \in L$ iff $Q' \cap Q'' \neq \emptyset$. We define a matrix M indexed by nonempty subsets of states such that entry $[Q', Q'']$ has the value 1 if $Q' \cap Q'' \neq \emptyset$, otherwise the entry has the value 0. It has been shown in [7] that M has rank $2^n - 1$. Then, by Schmidt's technique ([11] [8]), the smallest UFA equivalent to A has $2^n - 1$ states. $\square$

Theorem 1 shows that we can achieve the biggest tradeoff between SUFA and UFA. However, the language of some-register-on is over an alphabet of size

$O(n^2)$ whereas the number of states in A is only n. Using a binary encoding for the $O(n^2)$ letters, the number of states in A becomes $n + O(n^2) \cdot O(\log n^2) = O(n^2 \log n)$.

On the other hand, in [8], we have shown that there exists a family of n-state MDFA, where all states are starting states, over a binary alphabet such that the smallest UFA has $2^n - 1$ states. As explained before, a MDFA can be transformed into a $O(n^2)$-state SUFA. Therefore, we have another family of SUFA demonstrating exponential succinctness in the number of states over UFA.

As a consequence, we have

Corollary 2. *SUFA can be exponentially more succinct in the number of states than UFA.*

Not only that SUFA can be exponentially more succinct in descriptional sizes than UFA, it can also be exponentially more succinct than MDFA.

Lemma 3. *The smallest MDFA for the language L of some-register-on with n registers has at least $2^n - 2$ states.*

Proof. Suppose the contrary that there exists a k-entry MDFA with less than $2^n - 2$ states for L. The MDFA can be considered as a nondeterministic union of k DFA (named $D_1, D_2, \ldots, D_k$) each having less than $2^n - 2$ states. We consider each DFA D_i as an incompletely specified DFA such that every state in D_i are reachable from the start state and can reach some final state. Moreover, we can assume that every state in D_i is indeed an accepting state. This is because a state that can reach some final state is reached by the processing of some prefix of a string in L, where L has the property that all prefixes of strings in L are also in L.

From the subset construction of A, the state that corresponds to the subset Q is a state that once entered, the subset construction automaton will never leave the state. A string w that causes the subset construction automaton to go into this accepting "sink" state satisfies the property that $w^{-1}L = \Sigma^*$. In the following discussion, we deliberately avoid constructing strings that belong to $\{w \mid w^{-1}L = \Sigma^*\}$.

On the other hand, for all nonempty subsets of states $Q' \not\subseteq Q$, there exists a string that will cause the subset construction automaton to return to the state that corresponds to a set consisting only of the starting state 1. Thus, for any string $u \in L$ such that A reaches a nonempty subset $Q' \not\subseteq Q$ of states, there exists a string v such that $(uv)^{-1}L = L$.

Recall that the smallest DFA for L has 2^n states where one of the state is a non-accepting dead state and another state is an accepting sink state. Moreover, the rest of the $2^n - 2$ states in the DFA obtained by the subset construction are strongly connected as there is a resetting mechanism which we have discussed.

Suppose D_i arrives at state q on processing the string u from the start state. Recall that u is designed such that $u \in L - \{w \mid w^{-1}L = \Sigma^*\}$. Let v be a string such that $(uv)^{-1}L = L$. We resume the processing of D_i from state q to process v. It is possible that D_i aborts, or it may arrive at a state q'. As D_i does not have $2^n - 2$ states and the language accepted by D_i is a proper subset of

L, together with the fact that all states in D_i are accepting states, we deduce that there must exist a string $y \in L$ such that D_i aborts in processing y from state q'. We conclude that from any state q that D_i reaches on processing a string $u \in L - \{w \mid w^{-1}L = \Sigma^*\}$, there is a string z such that D_i aborts when processing z from state q, whereas $uz \in L - \{w \mid w^{-1}L = \Sigma^*\}$.

We consider DFA D_1. There exists some string $w_1 \in L - \{w \mid w^{-1}L = \Sigma^*\}$ such that D_1 aborts in processing w_1 from the starting state. On processing w_1, DFA D_2 may abort or may arrive at a state q_2. There exists w_2 such that $w_1w_2 \in L - \{w \mid w^{-1}L = \Sigma^*\}$ but D_2 aborts when processing w_2 from q_2. Similarly, on processing w_1w_2, DFA D_3 may abort or may arrive at a state q_3. There exists w_3 such that $w_1w_2w_3 \in L$ but D_3 aborts when processing w_3 from q_3. We can repeat this process to obtain a string $w = w_1w_2 \ldots w_k \in L - \{w \mid w^{-1}L = \Sigma^*\}$ such that every D_i aborts in processing w. Thus, the MDFA cannot recognize L, a contradiction to the assumption that the MDFA has less than $2^n - 2$ states. □

In fact, the above lemma can be strengthened to show that the smallest MDFA for the language of some-register-on has at least $2^n - 1$ states.

Theorem 4. *The smallest MDFA for the language L of some-register-on with n registers has at least $2^n - 1$ states.*

Proof. (Sketch) We continue with the analysis given in the previous lemma. Suppose the contrary that there is a MDFA of $2^n - 2$ states for L. Each DFA D_i (as defined in the previous proof), where $1 \leq i \leq k$, can be assumed to have at least $2^n - 2$ states. Otherwise, we can show that any DFA D_i with less than $2^n - 2$ states is not needed as we can use the same technique as in the previous proof to 'attack' D_i by a string $w \in L$ that posseses the resetting property $w^{-1}L = L$. Next, as the previous proof considers strings $w \in L - \{w \mid w^{-1}L = \Sigma^*\}$, we can argue that the $2^n - 2$ states of each D_i can be identified with the $2^n - 2$ non-sink (accepting) states of the DFA obtained by applying the subset construction to A. Moreover, all the different D_i's are functionally equivalent. Therefore, we can reduce them to only one DFA which is of $2^n - 2$ states. But this is a contradiction as we know that the smallest incompletely specified DFA for L has $2^n - 1$ states. □

As a consequence, we have

Corollary 5. *SUFA can be exponentially more succinct in the number of states than MDFA.*

Note that the SUFA A is the reversal of a MDFA. Theorem 4 also shows that the reversal of a MDFA can be exponentially more succinct than a MDFA. This should not be a surprise as the reversal of a DFA can also be exponentially more succinct than a DFA [8]. Let L^R denote the reversal of L. It is clear that L^R can be recognized by the n-state MDFA A^R. On the other hand, the statement that a MDFA requires at least $2^n - 1$ states to recognize L can be restated as L^R requires $2^n - 1$ states for the reversal of a MDFA to accept. Therefore, we have the next corollary:

Corollary 6. *The reversal of a MDFA can be exponentially more succinct than a MDFA. A MDFA can be exponentially more succinct than the reversal of a MDFA.*

In [8], it is shown that MDFA can be exponentially more succinct than UFA. On the other hand, we are going to show that UFA can also be exponentially more succinct than MDFA.

We modify the language of some-register-on. Instead of accepting a string when some register is on, we accept a string only if the register that we query at the end of the input is on. That is, the end of an input is augmented by a query instruction.

    Assert: Register i is on

An input is accepted if the register i queried is on. In short, the query instruction is denoted as Q_i. We denote the new language L_1.

We extend the previous example input by a query Q_3. The example input becomes $C_{1,4}C_{4,2}C_{3,1}C_{4,3}C_{1,2}Q_3$. Since register 3 is on after the copy instructions are performed, the input is accepted as the query is about register 3. If we query about register 1 at the end of the input as in $C_{1,4}C_{4,2}C_{3,1}C_{4,3}C_{1,2}Q_1$, then the input is not accepted since register 1 is off.

To handle the newly added query feature, we modify the SUFA for the language of some-register-on. We introduce a new state called f, which is the only final state. New transitions are added: from each state i, on processing Q_i, it will go to state f. The resulting $(n+1)$-state NFA is a UFA. We can see this as the reversal of the NFA is a DFA. In fact, it has been shown [8] that the UFA is the smallest UFA for the language.

We can argue that the smallest MDFA for L_1 has at least $2^n - 1$ states.

Corollary 7. *The smallest MDFA for L_1 has at least $2^n - 1$ states. Hence, UFA can be exponentially more succinct in the number of states than MDFA.*

Proof. Suppose the contrary that there is a MDFA A_1 for L_1 with less than $2^n - 1$ states. We can assume without loss of generality that all states in A_1 are useful in the sense that each state in A_1 can reach some final state. We can modify A_1 to give a MDFA for L. The modifications are as follows: Remove all transitions labelled with queries and define every state to be an accepting state. It is easy to see that the resulting modified automaton is a MDFA for L with less than $2^n - 1$ states. But this contradicts with the result of Theorem 4, which states that the smallest MDFA for L has at least $2^n - 1$ states.   □

In the literature, we have seen UFA designed as the reversals of DFA and FNA designed as the reversals of MDFA. Our example of SUFA, the language of some-register-on, is also the reversal of a MDFA.

As we have shown that the reversal of a MDFA is a SUFA, and a n-state MDFA can be converted to an equivalent SUFA with $O(n^2)$ states. One may wonder if SUFA is just the study of finite automata that are MDFA, or the reversals of MDFA. We answer the question by constructing a SUFA such that any equivalent MDFA, or reversal of MDFA, requires an exponential blow up in the number of states.

Recall that L denotes the language of some-register-on over the alphabet $\Sigma = \{C_{i,j} \mid 1 \leq i,j \leq n,\ i \neq j\}$. We define a language $L' = L^R \cdot b \cdot L \subseteq (\Sigma \cup \{b\})^*$, where b is a new symbol not in Σ. Note that the reversal of L' is L' itself.

An initial design of a finite automaton B for L' does not give us a SUFA. We connect A^R with a transition labelled by b, followed with A. Specifically, the copy of A^R is a MDFA with n starting states and a final state 1 (which is considered as a final state of A^R, but it is not exactly a final state of B). From the state 1 of A^R, we have a transition labelled by b that goes to the state 1 of A which is a SUFA with all n states accepting. Together, B has $2n$ states.

We replicate n copies $B_1, B_2, \ldots, B_n$ of B, each with a different starting state. That is, B_i is a SUFA with state i of A^R as the starting state. We introduce a new starting state for the nondeterministic union of $B_1, B_2, \ldots, B_n$. We call the resulting SUFA B', which has $O(n^2)$ states over the alphabet $\Sigma \cup \{b\}$ of size $O(n^2)$.

Theorem 8. *The smallest MDFA for L' has at least $2^n - 1$ states. The smallest NFA for L' that is the reversal of a MDFA has at least $2^n - 1$ states.*

Proof. Suppose there is a MDFA N for L' with less than $2^n - 1$ states. We derive from N a finite automaton for the language of some-register-on by removing all transitions that are encountered before N processes the symbol b. We define the starting states to be $\{q \mid (q', b, q)$ is a transition in $N\}$. The resulting finite automaton is a MDFA for the language of some-register-on. As N has less than $2^n - 1$ states by assumption, the resulting finite automaton is a MDFA for the language of some-register-on with less than $2^n - 1$ states, which contradicts the statement of Theorem 4.

Suppse there is a finite automaton N', which is the reversal of a MDFA, that recognizes L' with less than $2^n - 1$ states. The reversal of N' is a MDFA that recognizes the reverse of L', which is again L'. But this contradicts the previous result. □

As a consequence, we have

Corollary 9. *SUFA can be exponentially more succinct in the number of states than MDFA and the reversal of MDFA simultaneously with respect to the same language family.*

Using a binary encoding for the alphabet symbols, we obtain from B' a SUFA for L' with $O(n^3 \log n)$ states.

3   Why SUFA?

In Section 2, we have shown that SUFA can be exponentially more succinct than UFA and MDFA (also, reversals of MDFA) for denoting some family of regular languages. On the other hand, SUFA will not do worse than equivalent MDFA (or, reversals of MDFA) by more than a quadratic blow up in sizes.

From the descriptional complexity results, we see that SUFA is a stronger model than UFA and MDFA (also, reversals of MDFA). But, one may wonder whether SUFA has practical significance for the practitioners implementing finite automata for online processing of input strings.

SUFA can be implemented efficiently on a synchronous model of parallel computation. One process thread can be assigned to each state. When the state is off, the process thread is waiting to be woken up by another thread. As there is only one path arriving at a state at any moment, there will not be two messages sending to a process thread at the same time. Thus, the process thread will not require any buffer to hold the incoming messages in the synchronous computation.

NFA have been classified into UFA, FNA, PNA and ENA according to the ambiguity levels exhibited. As the amount of ambiguity is defined in terms of the number of accepting computations, the classification depends on the choice of the set of final states, which determines the language denoted.

Structural properties are obtained that offer equivalent characterizations of FNA, PNA and ENA. Suppose all states in an NFA are useful; that is, every state can reach some final state, and can be reached from some starting state. It is shown ([6] [10] [14]) that an NFA is strictly exponentially ambiguous if and only if there exists a state q and a string w such that there are more than one path from q to q processing w; an NFA is strictly polynomially ambiguous if and only if the NFA is not strictly exponentially ambiguous and there exists different states p, q and a non-empty string w such that there are paths for processing w that goes from p to itself, from q to itself and from p to q; an NFA is finitely ambiguous if and only if the NFA is not strictly polynomially ambiguous.

Observe that the structural properties are defined in terms of the transition logic of an automaton, but not on the set of final states. The characterizations for ENA, PNA and FNA show that one can replace the semantic definition of ambiguity levels exhibited by a NFA by the structural definition.

In this paper, we have shown that the structural definition of unambiguous finite automata differs from the semantic definition. That is, SUFA and UFA are not the same class. Unlike the undesirable effect that ambiguity has on the parsing of programs, ambiguity in NFA are used to reduce the descriptional size. It is therefore not necessary to demand an unambiguous finite automaton to allow only one accepting path for each string accepted. Moreover, from a practitioner's point of view, there is no drawback in adopting SUFA as the definition of unambiguous finite automata as it allows efficient synchronous parallel processing.

The classes of SUFA, FNA, PNA and ENA are forming a nice proper hierachy in that the next model in the hierachy is more general and could be exponentially more succinct than the previous model. Note that it is still a conjecture that PNA can be exponentially more succinct than FNA.

On the other hand, the models UFA, MDFA and reversal of MDFA are incomparable to each other as it has been shown that UFA can be exponentially more succinct than MDFA (Corollary 7), MDFA can be exponentially more succinct than UFA [8], MDFA can be exponentially more succinct than reversal of MDFA (Corollary 6) and reversal of MDFA can be exponentially more succinct than MDFA (Corollary 6). As the reversal of a UFA is a UFA, we can also conclude from Corollary 7 and [8] that UFA can be exponentially more succinct than reversal of MDFA, and reversal of MDFA can be exponentially more succinct than UFA.

Finally, the models UFA, MDFA and reversal of MDFA are proper subclasses of SUFA. It is shown that SUFA can be exponentially more succinct than UFA (Corollary 2), and SUFA can be exponentially more succinct than MDFA and the reversal of MDFA simultaneously (Corollary 9).

Acknowledgements

The author would like to thank Enrico Pontelli for valuable discussions.

References

1. Garey, M.R., Johnson, D.S.: Computers and intractability, W. H. Freeman and Company, San Francisco, 1970.
2. Gill, A., Kou, L.T.: Multiple-entry finite automata, J. Comput. System Sci. **9** (1974) 1–19.
3. Goldstine, J., Kappes, M., Kintala, C.M.R., Leung, H., Malcher, A., Wotschke, D.: Descriptional complexity of machines with limited resources, J. Univ. Comput. Sci. **8** (2002) 193–234.
4. Holzer, M., Salomaa, K., Yu, S.: On the state complexity of k-entry deterministic finite automata, J. Autom. Lang. Comb. **6** (2001) 453–466.
5. Kappes, M.: Descriptional complexity of deterministic finite automata with multiple initial states, J. Autom. Lang. Comb. **5** (2000) 269–278.
6. Ibarra, O., Ravikumar, B.: On sparseness, ambiguity and other decision problems for acceptors and transducers, In Proc. 3rd STACS, Orsay, France, (1986) 171–179.
7. Leung, H.: Separating exponentially ambiguous finite automata from polynomially ambiguous finite automata, SIAM J. Comput. **27** (1988) 1073–1082.
8. Leung, H.: Descriptional complexity of NFA of different ambiguity, International Journal of Foundations of Computer Science **16** (2005) 975–984.
9. Meyer, A.R., Fischer, M.: Economy of description by automata, grammars, and formal systems, IEEE Twelfth Annual Symposium on Switching and Automata Theory, (1971), 188–191.
10. Ravikumar, B., Ibarra, O.: Relating the type of ambiguity of finite automata to the succinctness of their representation, SIAM J. Comput. **18** (1989) 1263–1282.
11. Schmidt, E.M.: Succinctness of descriptions of context-free, regular and finite languages, PhD Thesis, Cornell University, Ithaca, NY (1978).
12. Stearns, R.E., Hunt, H.B.: On the equivalence and containment problems for unambiguous regular expressions, regular grammars and finite automata, SIAM J. Comput. **14** (1985) 598–611.
13. Veloso, P.A.S., Gill, A.: Some remarks on multiple-entry finite automata, J. Comput. System. Sci. **18** (1979) 304–306.
14. Weber A., Seidl, H.: On the degree of ambiguity of finite automata. Theor. Comput. Sci. **88** (1991) 325–349.

Symbolic Implementation of Alternating Automata*

R. Bloem[1], A. Cimatti[2], I. Pill[1], M. Roveri[2], and S. Semprini[2]

[1] Graz University of Technology
{rbloem, ipill}@ist.tugraz.at
[2] ITC-irst
{cimatti, roveri, semprini}@itc.it

Abstract. We show how to convert alternating Büchi automata to symbolic structures, using a variant of Miyano and Hayashi's construction. We avoid building the nondeterministic equivalent of the alternating automaton, thus save an exponential factor in space.

For one-weak automata, Miyano and Hayashi's approach produces automata that are larger than needed. We show a hybrid approach that produces a smaller nondeterministic automaton if part of the alternating automaton is one weak.

We perform a thorough experimental analysis and conclude that the symbolic approach outperforms the explicit one.

1 Introduction

In this paper we consider two closely related problems: that of model checking specifications given as alternating Büchi automata (ABWs) and that of computing language emptiness for such automata. These problems have gained importance through the advent of new temporal logics such as PSL [1] and ForSpec [2].

The standard approach for model checking and consistency checking of Linear Time Logic (LTL) properties is to convert these properties to nondeterministic Büchi word automata (NBWs). This can be done explicitly [3,4,5] or symbolically [6]. LTL properties can be seen as one-weak alternating automata, a restrictive subclass of ABWs. A one-weak alternating automaton with n states can be translated to an NBW with $n \cdot 2^n$ states [5].

Languages like PSL are not star free and are therefore translated to ABWs, not to one-weak automata [7]. For ABWs in general, conversion to an NBW is not as simple as for one-weak automata. For ABWs, we need Miyano and Hayashi's construction [8], which generates $O(3^n)$ states [9]. Thus, an efficient implementation of this construction is the key to a successful application of alternating automata and, therefore, of logics like PSL. (It should be noted that most model checkers for PSL currently accept only a subset of the language.)

This paper presents two contributions to an efficient use of Miyano and Hayashi's construction. First, through a reformulation of the construction we

---

* Supported by the European Commission under contract 507219 (PROSYD).

O.H. Ibarra and H.-C. Yen (Eds.): CIAA 2006, LNCS 4094, pp. 208–218, 2006.
© Springer-Verlag Berlin Heidelberg 2006

are able to develop a symbolic approach. Since the size of the symbolic representation is polynomial in the size of the ABW, we can avoid the $O(3^n)$ blowup associated with the conversion to an NBW[1]. The resulting symbolic representation can be used for model checking and consistency checking using either BDDs or SAT.

The second contribution is a combination of Miyano and Hayashi's construction with that of Gastin and Oddoux for one-weak automata [5]. Thus, we are able to retain full generality while increasing efficiency for automata with parts that are one-weak. Such automata occur frequently and benefit significantly from our approach.

We perform a thorough experimental evaluation of our solution using both the classic explicit approach and the symbolic one using either BDDs or SAT-based model checking.

An approach through the linear μ-calculus [10] would also be possible. However, μ-calculus formulae are expressed using parity instead of Büchi automata. This makes computing emptiness in the unbounded case (not handled in [10]) much harder.

2   Preliminaries

We denote by $\mathcal{B}(V)$ the set of Boolean formulae with variables in V. Formulae in $\mathcal{B}^+(V)$ do not use negation, formulas in $\mathcal{B}^\vee(V)$ use only disjunction. *Valuations* are denoted by subsets of V. We use $\varphi[X/Y]$ to denote that each variable in Y is replaced by the corresponding variable or expression in X. We will assume a finite set of (Boolean) atomic propositions AP. Our alphabet Σ is 2^{AP}. The i-th letter of an infinite word w on alphabet Σ, where $w \in \Sigma^\omega$, is denoted by w_i, whereby the index starts at zero. The empty word is denoted by ϵ. A Σ-labeled tree τ is a prefix-closed set $T \subseteq \mathbb{N}^*$ together with a labeling function $L : T \to \Sigma$.

Definition 1. *An* alternating generalized Büchi word automaton (AGW) *is a tuple* $A = (Q, q_0, AP, \rho, Acc)$ *where* Q *is a finite nonempty set of states,* $q_0 \in Q$ *is the initial state,* AP *is a finite set of atomic propositions,* ρ *maps every state to a disjunction of formulae* $(\varphi \wedge \psi)$ *where* $\varphi \in \mathcal{B}(AP)$, *and* $\psi \in \mathcal{B}^+(Q)$ *(the automaton is* nondeterministic *if* $\psi \in \mathcal{B}^\vee(Q)$*), and* $Acc \subseteq 2^Q$ *is the acceptance condition. (The automaton is* non-generalized *if* $|Acc| = 1$, *in which case we will take* Acc *to be a subset of* Q*.)*

We abbreviate alternating/nondeterministic generalized/non-generalized Büchi word automaton to (A/N)(G/B)W. For nondeterministic automata, we will also write $\rho : Q \times 2^{AP} \to 2^Q$, as usual.

For a given $q \in Q$, $\rho(q)$ consists of a disjunctively related set of transition formulae $\varphi \wedge \psi$, where φ defines the set of labels for which the transition is valid and ψ defines the states to which the automaton will move.

---

[1] This blowup can also be avoided by an on-the-fly approach, but that is hard to combine with symbolic model checking.

A *run* of A on an infinite word $w \in (2^{AP})^\omega$ is a (possibly infinite) Q-labeled tree τ such that the label of the root (ϵ) is q_0 and for every node t labeled q, with $|t| = i$, the conjunction of w_i and the labels of t's children models $\rho(q)$. A branch may be finite if it ends in a node t labeled q with $|t| = i$ and w_i models $\rho(q)$. A run τ on w is *accepting* if every *infinite* branch has infinitely many labels in F for all $F \in Acc$. We denote by $L(A)$ the set of words w for which A has an accepting run.

Note that in the definition of a run there is no requirement that the set of children of t be minimal. This condition can be added without changing the language. Note also that t can have an arbitrary, possibly empty set of children if $\rho(t) = \text{true}$. There is no run that contains a node labeled q if $\rho(q) = \text{false}$. A run of an NGW for word w can be viewed as sequence $r \in Q^\omega$.

A Büchi automaton induces a graph. The states of the automaton are the nodes of the graph and there is an edge from q to q' if q' occurs in $\rho(q)$. The graph is partitioned into maximal strongly connected components (SCCs), some of which may be trivial. A non-generalized alternating Büchi automaton is *weak* if each SCC contains either only accepting states or only non-accepting ones. The automaton is one weak (a.k.a. very weak or linear weak) if every SCC has size one.

Definition 2. *A* fair transition system *(FTS) [11] is a tuple* (V, A, T, Θ, F), *where V is a finite set of* state variables, *A is a finite set of* input variables, *$T \in \mathcal{B}(V \cup A \cup V')$ is the* transition relation, *$\Theta \in \mathcal{B}(V)$ specifies a single* initial *state, and $F \subseteq \mathcal{B}(V)$ specifies the* acceptance condition.

In this definition, V', the set of primed versions of variables in V, is used to denote the next state variables.

An FTS $S = (V, A, T, \Theta, \{F_1, \ldots, F_n\})$ defines an NGW N as follows: $N = (Q, I, A, \rho, Acc)$, where Q is 2^V, I is defined by Θ, $\rho(q) = \bigvee \{\varphi \wedge \psi \mid \varphi \in \mathcal{B}(A), \psi \in \mathcal{B}^+(Q) \text{ and } q \models \varphi \wedge \psi \rightarrow T\}$, and $Acc = \{Acc_1, \ldots, Acc_n\}$, where $Acc_i = \{q \mid q \models F_i\}$. Thus, we can speak of a run of an FTS and the language of an FTS as if it were an NGW.

Where convenient, we will use the obvious extension to FTSs with variables with larger finite domains.

3   Converting the Alternating Automaton

In this section, we show how to construct an NGW from an ABW. Our construction combines the full generality of Miyano and Hayashi's approach with the efficiency of Gastin and Oddoux' approach for one-weak automata where possible. Since Miyano and Hayashi's original formulation refers to individual states and can not directly be encoded symbolically, we use an alternative formulation here, more closely related to that of [12]. We also show how the same approach can be used to convert an ABW to an FTS directly, avoiding building the NGW.

3.1 From ABW to NGW

Let $A = (Q, q_0, AP, \rho, Acc)$ be an ABW. Let $Q_S \subseteq Q$ be the set of states in SCCs of size greater than one and let $Q_W = Q \setminus Q_S$ be the set of states that are SCCs of size one. We partition Q into four sets: $Q_{SN} = Q_S \setminus Acc$, $Q_{SA} = Q_S \cap Acc$, $Q_{WN} = \{q \in Q_W \setminus Acc \mid \text{SCC of } q \text{ has a self loop}\}$, and $Q_{WA} = Q_W \setminus Q_{WN}$. Assume that $k = |Q_{WN}|$ and $Q_{WN} = \{b_1, \ldots, b_k\}$.

Theorem 1. *For the ABW $A = (Q, q_0, AP, \rho, Acc)$ there exists an NGW $A' = (Q', q_0', AP, \rho', Acc')$ such that $L(A') = L(A)$. The NGW A' can be constructed as follows:*

- *Let $Q' = \mathcal{L} \times \mathcal{R} \times C$, with $\mathcal{L} = 2^Q$, $\mathcal{R} = 2^{Q_{SN}}$, and $C = \{0, \ldots, k\}$*
- *$q_0' = (\{q_0\}, \emptyset, 0)$*
- *$Acc' = \{\mathcal{L} \times \{\emptyset\} \times C, \mathcal{L} \times \mathcal{R} \times \{1\}, \ldots, \mathcal{L} \times \mathcal{R} \times \{k\}\}$*
- *The transition relation ρ' is such that $(L', R', c') \in \rho'((L, R, c), \sigma)$, where $\sigma \in 2^{AP}$ and $L = \{l_1, \ldots, l_n\}$, if $\exists L_1', \ldots, L_n'$ such that:*
  - *$\forall j : L_j' \cup \sigma \models \rho(l_j)$*
  - *$\bigcup_j L_j' = L'$*
  - *$R' \subseteq L'$*
  - *either $R = \emptyset$ and $R' = L' \cap Q_{SN}$, or $R \neq \emptyset$ and $R' \cup (L' \setminus Q_{SN}) \cup \sigma \models \bigwedge_{r \in R} \rho(r)$*
  - *for all j, either $b_c \neq l_j$ or $b_c \notin L_j'$.*

Proof. A directed acyclic graph (DAG) can be converted to a tree in the obvious way. Thus, a DAG with labels in Q can be seen as a run.

It is well known that we can convert run trees to DAGs in such a way that an accepting run yields an accepting DAG and a non-accepting run yields a non-accepting DAG. The conversion is as follows. Suppose we have a run tree τ. On every level, the DAG will have at most one node with a given label. Thus for every level and a given label, we pick one representative node in τ. Other nodes with the same label are removed, as are their subtrees. Their incoming edges are redirected to the corresponding representative nodes. In the following we will consider runs as DAGs and identify nodes for a given level by their labels.

First, we will prove that $L(A) \subseteq L(A')$. Let DAG d be an accepting run of ABW A on word w. We construct the run r of NBW A' as follows. Let $r = r_0 r_1 \ldots$ with $r_i = (L(i), R(i), c(i))$. Let $L(i) = \{q \mid q \text{ occurs at level } i \text{ of } d\}$. Assume $L(i) = \{l_1, \ldots, l_n\}$ for some n and let $L_i' = \{q \mid q \text{ is a child of } l_i\}$. Then, by the definition of a run, we have $L_i' \cup w_i \models \rho(l_i)$ and $L(i+1) = \bigcup_i L_i'$.

Let $R(0) = \emptyset$, let $R(i+1) = L(i+1) \cap Q_{SN}$ if $R(i) = \emptyset$, and let $R(i+1) = \{q \in L(i+1) \mid q \in Q_{SN}, \exists q' \in R(i) : q \text{ is a child of } q' \text{ in } d\}$ if $R(i) \neq \emptyset$.

Finally, choose $c(0) = 0$ and choose $c(i)$ such that there is no edge from $b_{c(i)}$ at level i to $b_{c(i)}$ at level $i+1$ and the level j such that $j < i$ and $c(j) = c(i)$ is minimal. (States in Q_{WN} are numbered $b_1, \ldots, b_k$.)

It should be clear that r satisfies the definition of the transition relation of A' and is therefore a run. Choose levels d_i in d such that $d_0 = 0$ and for all i, d_{i+1} is the level closest to the root such that an accepting state occurs on every path between level d_i and level d_{i+1}. Since d is an accepting run, there are infinitely many such levels, and R is empty at those levels. Furthermore, since no path gets stuck in a state b_j, for any b_j there are infinitely many levels at which the edge from b_j to b_j is not taken, and thus $c(i)$ is equal to j for infinitely many values of i. Therefore, r is accepting.

Vice-versa, we need to prove that $L(A') \subseteq L(A)$. Let $r = r_0 r_1 \dots$ be an accepting run of A' on w, with $r_i = (L(i), R(i), c(i))$. We will construct an accepting run DAG d.

By the definition of the NBW, we have

$$\forall q \in L(i) \ \exists L' \subseteq L(i+1) : Q'_L \cup w_i \models \rho(q), \text{ and} \tag{1}$$

$$\forall q \in R(i) \ R' = R(i+1) \cup (L(i+1) \setminus Q_{SN}) \Rightarrow R' \cup w_i \models \rho(q). \tag{2}$$

Let $S(i)$ denote the set of states on level i of d. We will define $S(i)$ inductively. Let $S(0) = \{q_0\}$. We define $S(i+1)$ as follows. For $q \in S(i) \setminus R(i)$, we pick as successors the states $L' \subseteq L(i+1)$ defined by 1. For $q \in S(i) \cap R(i)$ we pick as successors the states $R' \subseteq L(i+1) \cup R(i+1)$ as defined in 2. (Note that L' and R' are not uniquely defined. Any sets satisfying 1 and 2 will do.)

Note that $R(i+1) \subseteq R' \subseteq S(i+1) \subseteq L(i+1) \cup R(i+1)$. The last inclusion may be strict if $S(i) \subseteq R(i)$ and $L(i+1)$ contains redundant states in Q_{SN}.

By 1 and 2, d is a run.

Since for all i the successors of a state in $R(i)$ are all either in $R(i+1)$ or outside Q_{SN}, all paths between two levels i and j with $R(i) = R(j) = \emptyset$ must contain at least one state outside Q_{SN}.

Now, since for every j and for infinitely many i, we have $c(i) = j$, the transition from b_j to b_j is avoided infinitely often. Thus, no path in d gets stuck in any state b_j. Since every path has infinitely many states outside Q_{SN}, and does not get stuck in a state $b_j \in Q_{WN}$, it must visit an accepting state infinitely often, and the DAG is accepting. □

Intuitively, if we take $Q_{WA} \cup Q_{WN} = \emptyset$, then the construction reduces to a variant of Miyano and Hayashi's approach. A run τ of A can be mapped to a run r' of A' such that if (L, R, c) is the state of r' after i transitions, then (1) L is the set of labels of the nodes on level i of τ and (2) R consists of all labels in L that label a state v for which there is no accepting state on the path between the last level with $R = \emptyset$ and v. As Miyano and Hayashi note, a run of an ABW is accepting if and only if it has infinitely many levels such that each path between two such levels contains an accepting state. This is the case if and only if R becomes empty infinitely often.

On the other hand, if $Q_{WA} \cup Q_{WN} = Q$, then the construction reduces to that of Gastin and Oddoux. Every state in Q_{WN} has a number i, and if the self loop on state i is taken, then $c \neq i$.

Using our combined approach the state space of A' has size $|Q_{WN}| \cdot 3^{|Q \setminus (Acc \cup Q_{WN})|} \cdot 2^{|Acc \cup Q_{WN}|}$ versus $3^{|Q \setminus Acc|} \cdot 2^{|Acc|}$ using Miyano and Hayashi's approach.

Note that there is no requirement in the transition relation that the sets L' and R' be minimal. This condition can be added, but is hard to deal with in a

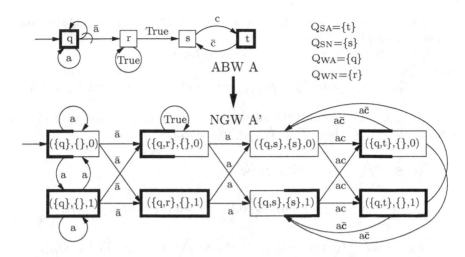

Fig. 1. ABW A and part of corresponding NGW A'

symbolic implementation. We do use the minimality condition when constructing A' explicitly.

We refer to our construction as **MHGO**, as it combines Miyano and Hayashi's with Gastin and Oddoux' construction. By setting $Q_{WN} = Q_{WA} = \emptyset$, our construction reduces to that of Miyano and Hayashi and we refer to it as **MH**.

Using this construction, accepting loops have length at least k. To remedy this drawback we introduce a simple **variant of MHGO** in which C has domain $2^{Q_{WN}}$. Intuitively a $c \in C$ contains all the states on which a self loop is not allowed, and each state in Q_{WN} should appear infinitely often. Although this expands the state space, its symbolic encoding is not larger.

The example shown in Fig. 1 illustrates the construction. (We use concatenation to denote conjunction and $\bar{a}$ (a bar) to indicate negation.) Since A' is very large, we only show a part: for most states edges labeled with $\bar{a}$ are missing. In the upper half of A' we have that $c = 0$ and in the lower one that $c = 1$. From the illustration we see that the transitions of the two halves are almost symmetric, but for the second column of states. Since r is in Q_{WN} we can take the self-loop on r only when c is 0. The NGW has two acceptance sets. One requiring infinitely many visits in states with $R = \emptyset$, the other infinitely many visits in states with $c = 1$, meaning that the self loop on r is not taken. In Fig. 1, the first acceptance set is illustrated by bold borders on the left, the second by bold borders on the right of the state.

3.2   From ABW to Fair Transition System

Let $A = (Q, q_0, AP, \rho, Acc)$ be an ABW. Let Q_{SN}, Q_{SA}, Q_{WN}, and Q_{WA} be as before. We define the symbolic fair transition system S to be (V, AP, T, Θ, F), where

- $V = Q_L \cup Q_R \cup \{c\}$ where $Q_L = \{q_L \mid q \in Q\}$, $Q_R = \{q_R \mid q \in Q_{SN}\}$, and c has domain $\{0, \ldots, k\}$,
- $T = T_I \wedge T_{LC} \wedge T_R$ (the parts are defined below),
- $\Theta = q_{0L} \wedge (c = 0)$, and
- $F = (F_0, \ldots, F_k)$, with $F_0 = \bigwedge_{q \in Q_{SN}} \neg q_R$ and $F_i = (c = i)$ for $1 \le i \le k$.

Let $[Q'_{LR}/Q]$ be the substitution that replaces $q \in Q \setminus Q_{SN}$ with q'_L and $q \in Q_{SN}$ with q'_R. We have $T_I = \bigwedge_{q \in Q_{SN}} (q'_R \to q'_L)$,

$$T_{LC} = \bigwedge_{q \in Q \setminus Q_{WN}} (q_L \to \rho(q)[Q'_L/Q]) \wedge$$

$$\bigwedge_{q = b_i \in Q_{WN}} (q_L \to \rho(q)[Q'_L/(Q \setminus \{q\}) \text{ and } (c \ne i \wedge q'_L)/\{q\}]),$$

$$T_R = (F_0 \wedge \bigwedge_{q \in Q_{SN}} (q'_L \to q'_R)) \vee (\neg F_0 \wedge \bigwedge_{q \in Q_{SN}} (q_R \to \rho(q)[Q'_{LR}/Q])).$$

The FTS is easily seen to encode the NGW A' introduced in the last section. A valuation v corresponds to a state q of the NGW: $q = (L, R, \hat{c})$, where $L = \{q \mid q_L \in v\}$, $R = \{q \mid q_R \in v\}$, and $\hat{c}$ is the valuation of variable c. Thus, by Theorem 1, we have the following theorem.

Theorem 2. $L(S) = L(A)$.

The size of the FTS depends significantly on that of ρ. In contrast to Miyano and Hayashi's approach, where T contains two copies of ρ for $Q \setminus Acc$ and one for $Q \cap Acc$, the combined approach needs only one copy for non-accepting states that are either trivial SCCs or in Q_{WN}. On the other hand, it contains additional propositions $c \ne i$ for every self-loop on a state in Q_{WN} and it has multiple fairness conditions.

Using the simple variant of MHGO in which C has domain $2^{Q_{WN}}$, it is possible to find witnesses in fewer steps than with MH, because we do not require minimality for T. For the PSL formula always$\{\{a; b\}[*n]\}$! we can find a witness in one step, whereas MH needs $2n$ steps.

4   Experimental Evaluation

We implemented the approaches on top of the NuSMV model checker [13]. We compare the **explicit** approach of building the NGW first and then converting it to an FTS against our direct **symbolic** approach of building the FTS. We use both **BDDs** and **SBMC** [14]. Finally, we compare the **MH** approach with the **variant of MHGO**. It turns out that the variant of MHGO sometimes outperforms MHGO, especially when the language of the automaton is not empty. The reason is that the latter creates accepting loops that are longer than necessary. We use the pattern $\{E, S\}_{\{MH, MHGO\}}$-$\{BDD, SBMC\}$ to denote the combinations of encodings and engines. (Where MHGO refers to the variant.) All experiments were run on a 3GHz Intel Xeon CPU with 4GB of memory, with a time out of 900s and a 1GB memory limit.

In the SAT approach we use Simple Bounded Model Checking (SBMC) since it is complete and allows for a fair comparison with BDDs, and we used MiniSAT [15] as SAT engine. The variable order chosen for the BDD experiments is such that the current and the corresponding next variables are consecutive and each q_R immediately follows the corresponding q_L. (This ordering yields good performance on average.) We first compute the set of reachable states and use it in the language emptiness algorithms to restrict the search as is common practice in model checking. Using this setting we obtained better results on average.

We experimented with two classes of ABWs: R-ABWs are random ABWs for which the number of accepting states, labels variables, transitions, and destinations of each transition are proportional to the number of states; and PSL-ABWs, which are built from typical PSL expressions used in industry [16].

The results of the experimental analysis are reported in Fig. 2: we plot the number of problems solved in a given amount of time (the samples are ordered by increasing computation time). The results show that the symbolic encoding outperforms the explicit one, and that the best approach is either S_{MH}-BDD or S_{MH}-SBMC. This is due to the construction of the explicit NBW which caused all the time-outs/memory-outs that occurred for E_{MH}-BDD on R-ABWs.

S_{MH}-SBMC outperforms S_{MH}-BDD on ABWs with $L(A) \neq \emptyset$ because of the limited number of steps needed by S_{MH}-SBMC to find a solution. (See Figs. 2(a) and 2(c).) On the other hand, BDDs perform better than SBMC on ABWs with $L(A) = \emptyset$ (Figs. 2(b) and 2(d)): SBMC needs to consider a high depth to be able to conclude that the language is empty, which results in a high consumption of resources. (Cf. [14]). Note that in these figures SBMC is either very fast or times out. A typical example of a property with an easy induction proof is $G(p \wedge X^n(\neg p \wedge X \varphi))$. A typical property for which the induction proof is hard is $G(p \wedge F(\neg p \wedge X \varphi))$. We conjecture that this is related to the fact that the encoding does not require minimality and thus the induction proof depends on φ.

Figs. 2(e) and 2(f) compare symbolic MH with MHGO on random PSL properties. No significant difference results on these formulae. In the unsatisfiable case, on average we noticed that S_{MHGO}-SBMC times out at a lower depth than S_{MH}-SBMC. The presence of multiple fairness conditions appears to blow up the SAT instance that is generated to prove that there is no witness. In the satisfiable cases S_{MHGO}-BDD performs slightly worse than S_{MH}-BDD because of the increased number of fix-points needed to perform language emptiness. On the other hand, S_{MHGO}-SBMC performs slightly better since the SAT instances are smaller and shorter witnesses are found.

Figs. 2(g) and 2(h) show the results of computing language emptiness of the combination of the Gigamax model (from the NuSMV distribution) and R-ABWs with $L(A) = \emptyset$. The language of the combination is obviously empty. The automata used in the plots of Fig. 2(g) are those for which S_{MH}-SBMC was not able to prove language emptiness. In contrast, in Fig. 2(h) we use automata for which S_{MH}-SBMC suceeded. The plots show that the BDD-based approaches

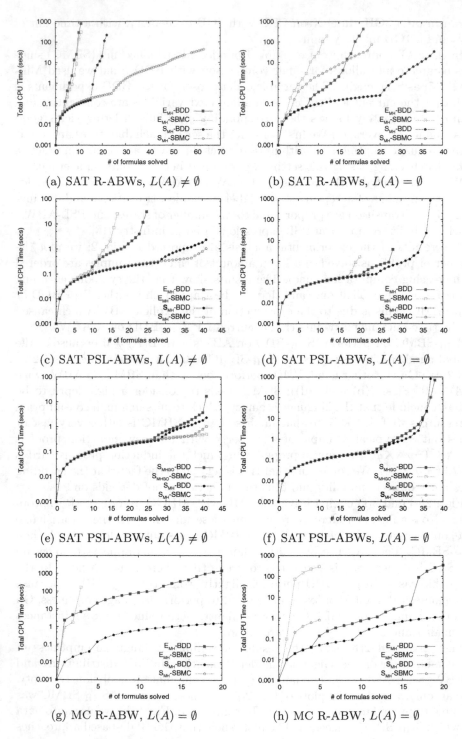

(a) SAT R-ABWs, $L(A) \neq \emptyset$

(b) SAT R-ABWs, $L(A) = \emptyset$

(c) SAT PSL-ABWs, $L(A) \neq \emptyset$

(d) SAT PSL-ABWs, $L(A) = \emptyset$

(e) SAT PSL-ABWs, $L(A) \neq \emptyset$

(f) SAT PSL-ABWs, $L(A) = \emptyset$

(g) MC R-ABW, $L(A) = \emptyset$

(h) MC R-ABW, $L(A) = \emptyset$

Fig. 2. Language emptiness and Model checking results

handle the increased complexity of the combined model well. SBMC, however shows a mixed picture. For S_{MH}-SBMC, Fig. 2(g) shows that there are three cases for which adding the Gigamax model enables language emptiness to complete. On the other hand, Fig. 2(h) shows that there are 15 examples for which S_{MH}-SBMC can not compute language emptiness on the combined model although it could do so on the automaton in separation. E_{MH}-SBMC can show language emptiness for 8 of the 20 automata used in Fig. 2(g), but only for three of the combined models. On the other hand, for the automata used in Fig. 2(h) the results for E_{MH}-SBMC are confirmed. With random models, too, BDDs are quite well behaved, but the performance of SBMC is hard to predict.

The experimental analysis clearly shows that the symbolic encoding outperforms the explicit encoding, and that on average SBMC is the most effective technique if the language is nonempty. On the other hand, BDDs are more effective than SBMC if the language is empty. Our results for SBMC confirm those of [14]: sometimes the search needs large resources to consider deep runs to prove that the property holds. (This is often the case when the language of the automaton is empty.) Finally, on the experiments considered there is no evident benefit in using the variant of MHGO over MH. We believe that a more thorough experimental analysis is needed to confirm or refute this result.

We are currently exploring the effects of optimizing both the ABW and the NBW using the techniques of [17,18]. Preliminary results are promising, but a thorough analysis must be carried out to better understand the impact of such optimizations. We are also researching ways to apply the optimizations of [17] directly to the symbolic encoding.

References

1. IEEE-Commission: IEEE standard for Property Specification Language (PSL) (2005) IEEE Std 1850-2005.
2. Armoni, R., et al.: The ForSpec temporal logic: A new temporal property-specification language. In: International Conference on Tools and Algorithms for Construction and Analysis of Systems (TACAS'02). (2002) 296–311
3. Vardi, M.Y., Wolper, P.: An automata-theoretic approach to automatic program verification. In: Proc. Logic in Computer Science. (1986) 322–331
4. Somenzi, F., Bloem, R.: Efficient Büchi automata from LTL formulae. In: Twelfth Conference on Computer Aided Verification (CAV'00). (2000) 248–263
5. Gastin, P., Oddoux, D.: Fast LTL to Büchi automata translation. In: Conference on Computer Aided Verification (CAV '01). (2001) 53–65
6. Clarke, E.M., Grumberg, O., Hamaguchi, K.: Another look at LTL model checking. Formal Methods in System Design (1) (1997) 47–71
7. Ben-David, S., Bloem, R., Fisman, D., Griesmayer, A., Pill, I., Ruah, S.: Automata construction algorithms optimized for PSL. http://www.prosyd.org (2005) Prosyd D 3.2/4.
8. Miyano, S., Hayashi, T.: Alternating finite automata on ω-words. Theoretical Computer Science **32** (1984) 321–330
9. Leucker, M.: Logics for mazurkiewicz traces. Technical Report AIB-2002-10, RWTH, Aachen, Germany (2002)

10. Jehle, M., Johannsen, J., Lange, M., Rachinsky, N.: Bounded model checking for all regular properties. In: 3rd Workshop on Bounded Model Checking (BMC'05). Volume 144.1 of Electronic Notes in Theoretical Computer Science. (2005) 3–18
11. Manna, Z., Pnueli, A.: The Temporal Logic of Reactive and Concurrent Systems, Specification. Springer Verlag, New York (1992)
12. Kupferman, O., Vardi, M.Y.: Weak alternating automata are not that weak. ACM Transactions on Computational Logic **2**(3) (2001) 408–429
13. Cimatti, A., Clarke, E., Giunchiglia, F., Roveri, M.: NuSMV: a new Symbolic Model Verifier. In: Conference on Computer-Aided Verification. (1999) 495–499
14. Heljanko, K., Junttila, T.A., Latvala, T.: Incremental and complete bounded model checking for full PLTL. In: Computer Aided Verification (CAV'05). (2005) 98–111
15. Eén, N., Sörensson, N.:   MiniSAT (2005) `http://www.cs.chalmers.se/Cs/Research/FormalMethods/MiniSat/Main.html`.
16. David, S.B., Orni, A.:   Property-by-Example guide: a handbook of PSL/Sugar examples - PROSYD deliverable d1.1/3. http://www.prosyd.org (2005)
17. Fritz, C.: Constructing Büchi automata from linear temporal logic using simulation relations for alternating Büchi automata. In: Conference on Implementation and Application of Automata. (2003) 35–48 LNCS 2759.
18. Fritz, C., Wilke, T.: Simulation relations for alternating Büchi automata. Theoretical Computer Science **338** (2005) 275–314

On-the-Fly Branching Bisimulation Minimization for Compositional Analysis

Yung-Pin Cheng, Hong-Yi Wang, and Yu-Ru Cheng

Software Engineering Lab
Department of Information and Computer Education
National Taiwan Normal University
Taipei 106, Taiwan
ypc@ice.ntnu.edu.tw

Abstract. Branching bisimulation minimization is often used to obtain a smaller but equivalent model for a complicated one. It is particularly useful in compositional analysis to replace a subsystem's behaviors with the minimal one so that the growth of states can be controlled in a hierarchical, divide-and-conquer manner. Nonetheless, branching bisimulation minimization is typically invoked after the whole state space is enumerated entirely. In practice, when the parallel composition engine drains too many memory resources during exploring reachable states, it causes operating systems to swap excessively (i.e., thrashing) due to the page replacement of virtual memory. When such a scenario occurs, the system degrades dramatically in performance and becomes unusable, albeit minimization is possible to abstract the whole state space into very small one. In this paper, we present a pragmatic approach to make branching bisimulation minimization on-the-fly. It minimizes the state space during composition and releases memory resources that are no longer used. Our approach allows larger systems to be verified by taking account of operating systems memory management.

1 Introduction

Model checking techniques [15,16,19], while dealing with large-scale concurrent software systems, typically do not scale well due to the PSPACE worst-case lower bound. Reduction methods incorporated in these tools, such as partial order or symmetry, can alleviate the state explosion problem to some extent but not in general. Approaches to increasing the size of system that can be accommodated in a single analysis step must eventually be combined with effective compositional techniques [22,7,12,6] that divide a large system into smaller subsystems, analyze each subsystem, and combine the results of these analyses to verify the full system.

The magic of compositional analysis, which allows excessive state exploration to be alleviated and controlled, relies on subsystem boundaries to prevent internal behavior (which is not concerned by outside components) from interleaving with outside behavior during parallel composition. Therefore, appropriate methods must be imposed on the subsystem state space to hide the internal behavior so that it will not participate the parallel composition in the hierarchy. These methods typically involve abstracting, reducing, or minimizing states and transitions of subsystems, while properties of interest are preserved. However, the behavior of a subsystem often comprises "pending" behavior – yet-to-synchronize behavior that appears in a subsystem's state space, but

O.H. Ibarra and H.-C. Yen (Eds.): CIAA 2006, LNCS 4094, pp. 219–229, 2006.

its reachability is uncertain in the whole state space. So, methods to hide the internal details of a subsystem must be capable of dealing with the "pending" behavior, which excludes several well-known state-space reduction or minimization methods.

Bisimulation, technologically, is very suitable for such an application. Bisimulation was first introduced by Milner [20](i.e., CCS). Milner introduced strong and weak bisimulation to relate two communicating systems. Weak bisimulation, also known as observational equivalence, is widely used in practical applications. A finer bisimulation equivalence, called branching bisimulation, was later proposed by Glabbeek[11] to improve weak bisimulation equivalence. Branching bisimulation and weak bisimulation are the same for a large class of processes. It is finer than the weak bisimulation but has some good properties, such as lower complexity and a simpler algorithm. So, in our previous work [6,5], branching bisimulation has been used as the tool to hide internal details of a subsystem. The branching bisimulation minimization (BBM) tool we use is Fc2tools from INRIA [4]. It is a solid, stable set of tools, which is well implemented. Minimizations can be invoked only after the state space is entirely explored. We call this type of minimization as *off-line*.

Although off-line BBM has been applied successfully to many tasks, we have encountered the following scenario: When the parallel composition engine consumes memory up to a certain point, the operating systems begin swapping pages between physical memory and the hard disk. This symptom is known as "thrashing." When that happens, the system's performance degrades dramatically due to the heavy disk I/Os. Beyond this point, the whole system becomes unusable, even though BBM can shrink the state-space considerably once it has the chance.

In this paper, we propose a pragmatic on-the-fly BBM approach. The minimization is incorporated with the parallel composition engine. When the shortage of memory resources is detected, branching bisimulation minimization is invoked to minimize the explored state space and then release the memories which are no longer used. Such an on-the-fly approach allows systems of larger size to be verified.

2   Related Work

Branching bisimulation equivalence was introduced by Van Glabbeek and Weijland in [11]. They argue that this equivalence relation applied on labeled transition systems (LTS) is finer than the observation equivalence of Milner[20]. Branching bisimulation is favored for the following reasons. In the view of algorithm, branching bisimulation can be decided in $O(mn)$ time complexity, where m is the number of transitions and n the number of states, and in $O(m)$ space complexity [13,4]. Nevertheless, the fastest algorithm of observation equivalence has $O(l \cdot n^{2.367})$ time complexity and $O(n+m^+)$ space complexity, where l is the number of actions and m^+ is the number of edges after taking τ^+ the transitive closure. Van Glabbeek has also shown that observation equivalence is not adequate for a modal logic with eventually operator. Therefore, if we apply the observation equivalence to minimize a process, the liveness properties will be lost. Nonetheless, branching bisimulation preserves liveness properties.

Currently, there are several branching bisimulation tools available, such as *fc2min* in [4], *ltsmin* in [8] and *bcg_min* in CADP toolset[10]. These tools perform branching bisimulation over a labeled transition system in an off-line manner. Branching bisimulation reduction based on τ-confluence can be found at [2,14,21]. τ-confluence allows to reduce on-the-fly a state space with respect to branching bisimulation but not completely.

Making reduction and minimization methods on-the-fly is a common tactic to make verification tools scale to larger systems. In [1,9], they address the application of bisimulation equivalence checking on-the-fly. In such an application, they can check the equivalence without constructing two LTSs entirely before comparisons. On-the-fly generation of minimal models for model checking can be found in [3,18]. In this application, an explicit state space is constructed from compact, implicit notations or design languages. Their objective is to obtain a reachable minimal graph on-the-fly with respect to the temporal formula.

3   Branching Bisimulation Minimization (BBM)

Formally, branching bisimulation is an equivalence relation defined as follows:

Definition 1. Let $LTS_1 = < S_1, A_1, \triangle_1, q_1 >$ and $LTS_2 = < S_2, A_2, \triangle_2, q_2 >$ be two LTS, where S_i is the set of states, A_i is the set of actions (labeled transitions), $\triangle_i$ is the transition relation, and q_i is the initial state. Let $\equiv_b$ be the branching bisimulation equivalence relation. $LTS_1 \equiv_b LTS_2$, if there exists a binary symmetric relation $\mathbf{R} \subseteq S_1 \times S_2$ such that

1. $q_1 \mathbf{R} q_2$
2. $\forall s, s' : s\mathbf{R} s', \forall a \in A \cup \{\tau\}$ if $s \xrightarrow{a} t$, then
   (a) either $a = \tau \wedge t\mathbf{R} s'$,
   (b) or $\exists t', \exists p_0, p_1, ...p_n, \exists q_0, q_1, ...q_m,$
       $s' = p_0 \xrightarrow{\tau} p_1 \cdots \xrightarrow{\tau} p_n = t_1 \xrightarrow{a} t_2 = q_0 \xrightarrow{\tau} q_1 \cdots \xrightarrow{\tau} q_m = t'$ such
       that
       $t\mathbf{R}t' \wedge s\mathbf{R}p_i \wedge t\mathbf{R}q_i, \forall i, j, 0 \le i \le n, 0 \le j \le m.$ □

The problem to obtain a minimal LTS of a given LTS is a Relational Coarsest Partition Problem (RCP for short). Kanellakis and Smolka [17] studied this problem to provide a solution on deciding equivalences over labeled transition systems. The algorithm computes equivalence classes over states of a LTS, and refines them into exclusive blocks with appropriate instability notion until all pairs of blocks are stable. Each block can be replaced by a state to form the minimal LTS.

Let S be the set of states of a LTS. Let B_i be a set of states from S, called *blocks*. The collection $\Pi = \{B_i \subseteq S \mid i \in I\}$ is a partition of S if and only if $\bigcup_{i \in I} B_i = S$ and for $j \ne i : B_i \cap B_j = \phi$. The elements in a partition are blocks. We say Π' *refines* Π if and only if $\forall B' \in \Pi', \exists B \in \Pi$ such that $B' \subseteq B$.

The basic algorithm of RCP is

```
1. Π:= Π₀
2. while (Π is not stable)
3. begin
4.     Find (B, B') unstable
5.     Π:= Refineₚ(B, B')
6. end
```

In the beginning, the algorithm initializes a partition Π to Π_0, where Π_0 is a partition with one block which contains all the states of a LTS. Then it repeats a refinement step which consists in finding an unstable pair of blocks and refining the current partition with respect to it, until a stable partition is obtained.

Definition 2. Given an action a in A of LTS, a pair of blocks (B, B') of Π is *a-unstable iff* in the setting of $(B \neq B'$ or $a \neq \tau)$ and $\phi \neq Pos_a(B, B') \neq B$, where

$$Pos_a(B, B') = \{s \in B \mid \exists s_1, s_2, ..., s_n, s' : s_0 = s,$$
$$\forall i > 0, s_i \in B \land s_{i-1} \xrightarrow{\tau} s_i, s_n \xrightarrow{a} s' \land s' \in B'\}. \qquad \square$$

The condition $(B \neq B'$ or $a \neq \tau)$ means that we cannot use τ-action to check the instability of B itself. The condition $\phi \neq Pos_a(B, B') \neq B$ means only partial states in B may reach states in B' via action a. If both conditions hold, the pair of blocks (B, B') is *a-unstable*. This instability notion is better explained in Fig. 1. In the figure, a block B is checked against a *splitter* B' with action a. The states which can use a to reach block B' is marked as grey. If the set of marked states is fewer than B, B is unstable. Therefore, B will be split into two blocks, one with the marked states and one with the unmarked states. In other words, the stability of a block is determined by its outgoing transitions to other blocks, including τ actions.

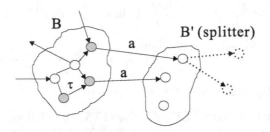

Fig. 1. The instability notion checked by a splitter block

A pair of blocks is said to be *unstable* if and only if there exists an action a for which these blocks are *a-unstable*, otherwise it is said to be *stable*. More generally, a block B of a partition Π is said to be stable *iff* for all blocks B' in Π, the pair (B, B') is stable. The partition Π is stable *iff* each of its blocks are stable.

When the BBM algorithm finds an unstable pair of blocks, it applies the refinement below in the current partition by splitting a block into two smaller blocks.

Definition 3. If a pair of blocks (B, B') of Π is *a-unstable*, then a *refinement* $Ref_\Pi^a(B, B')$ of Π is obtained by replacing B with the blocks $Pos_a(B, B')$ and $B - Pos_a(B, B')$. $\qquad \square$

For more details of the BBM algorithm, please refer to [4].

4   Making Branching Bisimulation Minimization On-the-Fly

As described in previous sections, when state exploration drains too much memory, the program begins swapping hard due to the page replacement. Therefore, minimizing a partially explored state space to save memory allows verification of larger systems. It can delay severe page replacement if the quotient of state space is indeed tractable under a computer's physical memory configuration.

According to Definition 1, the equivalence relation between two states is defined recursively. Whether two states are branching bisimulated can only be known from top to the bottom and then from bottom to the top. When a new state is newly explored, it may have more successor states to explore and these successor states determine the inequivalence. That is, we do not have backward inference of the inequivalence information to split existing blocks in an iteration for newly explored states as the applications in [3,18]. In the applications of [3,18], once a state is explored, the inequivalence can be checked immediately by its proposition formula and the splitting of blocks can be determined. So, we need to minimize a partial state space in a pragmatic way. We define the partially explored state space as a partial LTS.

Definition 4. Given an entire state space $L = < S, A, \rightarrow, q >$, $L' = < S', A', \rightarrow, q' >$ is a partial LTS with respect to L iff
$(q = q') \wedge (S' \subseteq S) \wedge (A' \subseteq A) \wedge (\rightarrow' \subseteq \rightarrow)$ such that for each state s in S' there exists a path from q' to s. $\qquad\square$

In the states of a partial LTS, we call a state which has no outgoing transitions as *terminal state*. A terminal state is either having successor states which are not yet explored or is a deadlock state. The other states in a partial LTS, which are not terminal states, are called *nonterminal states*.

The naive solution which passes a partial LTS to the BBM algorithm as an intermediate step, unfortunately, does not work. The correctness (i.e., the instability notion) is not maintained due to the unexplored states. Branching bisimulation, for example, will merge all the terminal states into one. So, we need to examine the instability notion more carefully.

Recall that in figure 1, a block B is partitioned by a splitter B' if there are specific transitions ending in the splitter. When dealing with action a, the states which can use a to reach block B' are marked. If the set of marked states is fewer than B, B is unstable. Therefore, B will be split into two blocks, one with the marked states and one with the unmarked states. In other words, the stability of a block is determined by its outgoing transitions to other blocks, including τ actions. So, whether a block should be split or not can be fully determined by its splitters. Therefore, if the states in a block B have been totally explored, the correctness of a finer instability notion is preserved. That is, once a block B is stable with respect to all its splitters, the newly explored behavior (must be from splitter blocks) will not be able to split the block anymore, though B could be merged into a bigger block in the future. Using this property, we design our pragmatic approach as follows. We first define:

Definition 5. A complete-partial LTS.
Given an entire state space $L = < S, A, \rightarrow, q >$, $L_C = < S_C, A_C, \rightarrow_C, q_c >$ is a complete-partial LTS with respect to L *iff*
L_C is a partial LTS of L and each nonterminal state in L_C has their outgoing transitions explored totally.   □

To obtain a complete-partial LTS, we need to explore the reachable states **breath-firstly**. The nature of breath-first search maintains its explored state space as a complete-partial LTS at all time. So, to cope with our approach, the parallel composition must be designed to explore states breath-firstly.

Our approach for intermediate minimization is described as follows. During state exploration, the program may pass a complete-partial LTS to the BBM module to start an intermediate minimization. In each immediate minimization, we prepare the complete-partial LTS into an initial partition which consists of a *main-block* and *splitter-blocks* (shown in figure 2). In this complete-partial LTS, the terminal states, which either have unexplored successor states or not, are made into disjoint splitter-blocks. *Splitter blocks* collects all the terminal states of a complete-partial LTS so that no outgoing transitions from main-block would end at other places.

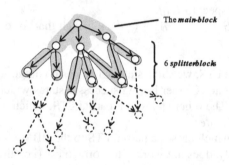

Fig. 2. The main-block and splitter blocks of a complete partial LTS

Lemma 1. Let a block B be a complete-partial LTS without terminal states. Let B be partitioned into B_i, $i \in I$ by all the actions from B that end at splitter-blocks. Then, B_i is final, i.e., it can never be split by other transitions (such as unexplored states).

Proof. By contradiction. If B_i can be split by other transitions which do not start from B and end in its splitter blocks, it would contradict the Definition 2.   □

Now, let Π_O be the partition of blocks obtained by off-line minimization. Lemma 1 shows that the instability notion holds for a complete-partial LTS, albeit B_i can be finer than that of Π_O. States in distinct block of Π_O cannot be erroneously merged by our algorithm. Some block B_i may be merged into a bigger block at a later stage, if there exist τ-actions between a main-block and the splitter-blocks.

Algorithm 1. The BFS state exploration algorithm

```
 1: list<lts> InputLtsList; /* the list of LTSs which participate
                               the parallel composition */
 2: lts complete_partial_LTS; /* a global data structure which
                                 store the complete partial LTS */
 3: void BFS_Compose() {
 4:     Let InitState be the product of initial states of LTSs in InputLtsList.
 5:     complete_partial_LTS.States.add( InitState );
 6:     complete_partial_LTS.InitStateId = InitState.Id;
 7:     Queue.addtail( InitState );
 8:     do {
 9:         CurState = Queue.delhead();
10:         for all s be successors of CurState {
11:             Let t be a transition of CurState s;
12:             complete_partial_LTS.States.add( s );
13:             complete_partial_LTS.Trans.add( t );
14:             if s is new created {
15:                 Queue.addtail( s );
16:             }
17:         }
18:         if minimization is required
19:             Minimize( Queue );
20:     } while( ! Queue.empty() );
21:     Minimize( Queue );
22: }
```

Algorithm 2. The Minimization procedure

```
 1:     Let UnstableBlockList be an empty block list;
 2:     Let complete_partial_LTS be a partially composed LTS;
 3:     void Minimization( splitterlist ) {
 4:         MergeTauCycle( complete_partial_LTS );
 5:         PrepareUnstableBlockList( splitterlist );
 6:         BranchBisim( complete_partial_LTS );
 7:     }
 8:     void PrepareUnstableBlockList( splitterlist ) {
 9:         Let MainBlock be an empty block;
10:         for all s in complete_partial_LTS.States {
11:             if s is in splitterlist {
12:                 Create an empty block b; // the splitter-block
13:                 b.BottomList.add( s );
14:                 Add all s.InTrans into b.TransitionList;
15:                 UnstableBlockList.add( b );
16:             }else {
17:                 MainBlock.BottomList.add( s );
18:                 Add all s.InTrans into MainBlock.TransitionList;
19:             }
20:         }
21:         MainBlock.resetMark();
22:         MainBlock.resetBlockPtr();
23:         MainBlock.resetBottomList();
24:         UnstableBlockList.add( MainBlock );
25:     }
```

Lemma 2. States of a complete-partial LTS which are in the same block in Π_O are eventually merged. $\square$

We explain Lemma 2 informally by introducing a *dummy* on-the-fly algorithm. This dummy algorithm always split an initial block until each state is a single block. Real minimization is actually taken place after state space is entirely explored. In this case, states in a same block of Π_O should be merged at last. This implies, a better minimization algorithm such as ours, will eventually merge the states into the same blocks in Π_O in last refinement, provided that Lemma 1 holds.

We illustrate our on-the-fly BBM algorithm in Algorithm 1 and Algorithm 2.

5   Experiments

In this section, we discuss how the memory resources are saved in our approach. In principle, the parallel composition engine can output the explored states directly to files, if no minimization method or analysis algorithm is invoked. The required memory storage is the hash table which keeps the information of explored states so that when a new reachable state is generated, it can be checked if it is already explored before.

In a straightforward implementation of explicit state enumeration, a state and a transition require the least memory structure as follows:

```
struct state_type {
    BITSTATE state_no ; // the bit representation
    struct edge_type * transitions ;
};
struct edge_type {
    struct state_type *to ; // the destination state
    struct edge_type * next ; // the pointer to link the transitions
};
```

Let the length of BITSTATE be S bits. A pointer in most platforms occupies 4 bytes. So, a state with 3 outgoing transitions can occupy $(\lceil \frac{S}{8} \rceil + 4) + 3 * 8$ bytes. In the hash table, a state needs to store $\lceil \frac{S}{8} \rceil + 4$ bytes, where 4 bytes are the pointer to the state. When a state is merged, the memory resources of its state and transitions can be freed and re-allocated but it still needs to keep a copy of BITSTATE ($\lceil \frac{S}{8} \rceil + 4$ bytes) in the hash table and its pointer in the hash table is redirected to the representative state of all the merged ones.

By the analysis above, let the number of states being merged be n. Assume each state has 3 transitions. The total memory occupied (including hash table) by these states are $n * ((\lceil \frac{S}{8} \rceil + 4) + 24 + (\lceil \frac{S}{8} \rceil + 4))$ bytes. After these states are merged, there are $n * (\lceil \frac{S}{8} \rceil + 4)$ bytes need to be kept in the hash table. Take $S = 32$ for example. 4/5 of the memory is returned for reallocation. So, using our strategy, it could approximately have a factor 5 gain.

An essential question unanswered in the previous section is the timing for triggering minimization. If there is plenty of memory, it is unnecessary to invoke an intermediate minimization. So, our tool allows two kinds of threshold to be specified - *number of new states* (NNS) and *memory size of states and transitions* (MSST). In the case of NNS, a counter is increased for each newly enumerated state. When the counter exceeds the given NNS, minimization is invoked and the counter is reset. In the case of MSST, users can manually specify the upper bound of the size of new states and transitions in bytes. When that limit is reached, minimization is invoked. Compared to NNS, MSST is more accurate. It can be used to count how much memory has been used by the newly explored states and transitions in the unit of pages.

Table 1. The results of of applying different NNS thresholds

Two-elevator system		
state space without minimization	3600 states	7951 transitions
state space with minimization	53 states	199 transitions
upper bound (states)	Max. State Num.	Time Spent (sec.)
10,000	3600	2.693
1,000	1464	4.567
500	963	5.978
100	601	16.422
50	573	29.331
10	534	125.96

In table 1, we show a two-elevator system minimized on-the-fly with different NNS values and the time spent. The middle column is the maximum number of states that ever generated in each experiment. Undoubtedly, on-the-fly BBM will produce longer elapse time. However, in the case of verification application, the primary concern is to lower memory usage and prevent the program from thrashing. Additional computation time is often acceptable, as long as it is not an increase in hours or days. In the extreme case of NNS = 10, the maximum number of states ever generated is not close to minimal 53 states. So, there is a root cost for the intermediate minimization in this example.

In figure 3(b), we show the distribution of the maximum number generated for a larger example – three-elevator system. During the on-the-fly minimization, with NNS = 5000, the maximum number of states generated has never exceed 7803. In figure 3(a), we show the subtasks performed in an intermediate minimization cycle.

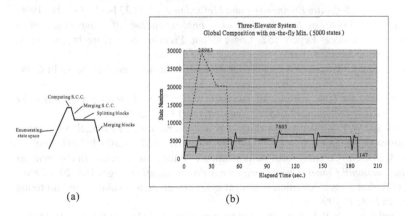

(a)   (b)

Fig. 3. A comparison of analyses with/without on-the-fly BBM by the maximum number of states ever generated

6   Conclusions

In this paper, we propose a pragmatic approach to achieve on-the-fly BBM which allows larger systems to be verified. In our approach, BBM algorithm needs not be modified. We have shown that a partially explored LTS can be minimized by the BBM algorithm if its state exploration is enumerated breath-firstly and an initial partition is prepared in a specific way. In our future research, we will seek approaches to determine the thresholds of triggering intermediate minimization automatically so that BBM is only triggered at the precise timing. The thresholds apparently may vary from a system to a system.

References

1. D. Bergamini, N. Descoubes, C. Joubert, and R. Mateescu. Bisimulator: A modular tool for on-the-fly equivalence checking. In *TACAS*, pages 613–618, 2005.
2. S. Blom and J. van de Pol. State space reduction by proving confluence. In *Proc. of 14th Int. Conf. on Computer Aided Verification, LNCS 2404*, pages 596–609, 2002.
3. A. Bouajjani, J.-C. Fernandez, and N. Halbwachs. Minimal model generation. In *Proceedings of International Conference on Computer-Aided Verification(CAV), Volume 531 of Lecture Notes in Computer Science*, pages 197–203, 1990.
4. A. Bouali. Weak and branching bisimulation in fctool. Technical Report Technical Report 1575, INRIA, Sophia Antipolis, Valbonne Cedex, France, 1992.
5. Y. Cheng. Refactoring design models for inductive verification. In *Proceedings of International Symposium on Software Testing and Analysis (ISSTA2002)*, pages 164–168, Rome, Italy, July 2002.
6. Y.-P. Cheng, M. Young, C.-L. Huang, and C.-Y. Pan. Towards scalable compositional analysis by refactoring design models. In *Proceedings of the ACM SIGSOFT 2003 Symposium on the Foundations of Software Engineering*, pages 247–256, 2003.
7. S. C. Cheung and J. Kramer. Context constraints for compositional reachability analysis. *ACM Transactions on Software Engineering and Methodology*, 5(4):334–377, October 1996.
8. D. Dams and J. Groote. *Specification and implementation of components of a £gCRL toolbox*. Technical Report 152, Logic Group Preprint, SeriesUtrecht University, http://homepages.cwi.nl/ mcrl, 1995.
9. J.-C. Fernandez and L. Mounier. A tool set for deciding behavioral equivalences. In *CONCUR*, 1991.
10. H. Garavel, F. Lang, and R. Mateescu. An overview of cadp 2001. *European Association for Software Science and Technology (EASST) Newsletter*, 4:13–24, 2002.
11. R. V. Glabbeek and W. P. Weijland. Branching time and abstraction in bisimulation semantics (extended abstract). In *Information Processing 89*, pages 613–618, North-Holland, 1989.
12. S. Graf and B. Steffen. Compositional minimization of finite state systems. In *Proceedings of the 2nd International Conference of Computer-Aided Verification*, pages 186–204, 1990.
13. J. Groote and F. Vaandrager. An efficient algorithm for branching bisimulation and stuttering equivalence. In *ICALP*, 1990.
14. J. F. Groote and J. van de Pol. State space reduction using partial τ-confluence. In *MFCS, LNCS 1893*, pages 383–393, 2000.
15. G. J. Holzmann. *Design and Validation of Computer Protocols*. Prentice-Hall, Englewood Cliffs, NJ 07632, 1991.
16. G. J. Holzmann. The model checker SPIN. *Software Engineering*, 23(5):279–295, 1997.

17. P. C. Kanellakis and S. A. Smolka. CCS expressions, finite state processes, and three problems of equivalence. *Information and Computation*, 86:43–68, 1990.
18. D. Lee and M. Yannakakis. Online minimization of transition systems. In *Proceedings of 24th ACM Symposium on Theory of Computing*, pages 264–274, Victoria, May 1992.
19. K. L. McMillan. *Symbolic model checking*. Kluwer Academic Publishers, Massachusetts, 1993.
20. R. Milner. *A Calculus of Communicating Systems*, volume 92 of *Lecture Notes in Computer Science*. Springer-Verlag, New York, 1980.
21. G. Pace, F. Lang, and R. Mateescu. Calculating tau-confluence compositionally. In *Proceedings of the 15th Computer-Aided Verification conference CAV'2003*, pages 446–459, 2003.
22. W. J. Yeh and M. Young. Compositional reachability analysis using process algebra. In *Proceedings of the Symposium on Software Testing, Analysis, and Verification (TAV4)*, pages 49–59, Victoria, British Columbia, October 1991. ACM SIGSOFT, ACM Press.

Finite-State Temporal Projection

Tim Fernando

Computer Science, Trinity College, Dublin 2, Ireland

Abstract. Finite-state methods are applied to determine the conse-
quences of events, represented as strings of sets of fluents. Developed
to flesh out events used in natural language semantics, the approach
supports reasoning about action in AI, including the frame problem and
inertia. Representational and inferential aspects of the approach are explored, centering on conciseness of language, context update and constraint application with bias.

1 Introduction

What follows, given that certain events happen? This question is addressed below
through finite-state methods. Automata and their runs are basic to temporal
logic (e.g. Eme92). In Linear Temporal Logic (LTL), for instance, an infinite
string $x_1 x_2 \cdots$ of sets x_i of atomic propositions specifying *all* atomic propositions
true at time i extends uniquely to an infinite string $\hat{x}_1 \hat{x}_2 \cdots$ of sets $\hat{x}_i$ of formulae
true at i. To capture events that make up the string $x_1 x_2 \cdots$, it is convenient to
consider fragments $a_n a_{n+1} \cdots a_{n+m}$ of $\hat{x}_1 \hat{x}_2 \cdots$, where $a_k \subseteq \hat{x}_k$ for $n \leq k \leq n+m$.
These fragments cover only finite stretches of $\hat{x}_1 \hat{x}_2 \cdots$ and may include only some
formulae true over those stretches.

In general, let Φ be a set of formulae called *fluents*. A fluent may or may not
be atomic, and may or may not belong to LTL. We identify an event with a
string $a_1 a_2 \cdots a_n$ over the alphabet 2^{Φ} of sets of fluents, drawing boxes, instead
of curly braces, to enclose a set of fluents when it is intended as a symbol of
the alphabet. This notation reinforces the intuition that an event is a film strip
assembled from partial snapshots $\in 2^{\Phi}$, and helps, for instance, distinguish the
string $\square$ (that we conflate with the language $\{\square\}$) from the empty language $\emptyset$
(containing no strings). As an event, the string $\boxed{\varphi}\,\square$ is as much a part of $\boxed{\varphi}\,\boxed{\varphi}$
as it is of $\boxed{\varphi}\,\boxed{\overline{\varphi}}$, where $\overline{\varphi}$ is the negation of φ. Henceforth, we assume negation
$\overline{}$ is a map on fluents such that $\overline{\overline{\varphi}} = \varphi \neq \overline{\varphi}$ for every fluent φ.

We shall see shortly that identifying an event (instance) with a string has
certain defects. We will finesse the problem by focusing less on the conception
of an event-as-string and more on that of an event-type-as-language. Much of
what follows concerns operations and relations on languages over the alphabet
2^{Φ} that build up and relate event-types in useful ways.

1.1 Superposition and the Allen Interval Relations

A natural conjunction of languages L, L' over 2^{Φ} is the *superposition of L and
L'* (Fer04) obtained from the componentwise union of strings in L and L' of the
same length

O.H. Ibarra and H.-C. Yen (Eds.): CIAA 2006, LNCS 4094, pp. 230–241, 2006.

$$L\&L' \stackrel{\text{def}}{=} \bigcup_{n\geq 0}\{(a_1 \cup b_1)\cdots(a_n \cup b_n) \mid a_1\cdots a_n \in L \text{ and } b_1\cdots b_n \in L'\} .$$

For instance, we can compose a language for *rain from dawn to dusk* as

$$\boxed{\text{rain}}^{+} \ \& \ \boxed{\text{dawn}}\,\square^{+} \ \& \ \square^{+}\boxed{\text{dusk}} \ = \ \boxed{\text{rain, dawn}}\boxed{\text{rain}}^{*}\boxed{\text{rain, dusk}}$$

(suppressing parentheses, as $\&$ is associative) consisting for $n \geq 0$ of strings $\boxed{\text{rain, dawn}}\boxed{\text{rain}}^{n}\boxed{\text{rain, dusk}}$ with $(n+2)$ snapshots, all of rain, the first at dawn, and the last at dusk. The different values of n support models at different levels of temporal granularity (the larger the n, the finer the grain). It is not obvious, however, that we should think of each of these infinitely many strings as distinct events. And surely we can reduce the infinite language to some finite core that captures its essence: three snapshots, $\boxed{\text{rain, dawn}}$, $\boxed{\text{rain}}$ and $\boxed{\text{rain, dusk}}$, arranged in a particular order.

Indeed, it is tempting to reduce every string $\boxed{\text{rain, dawn}}\boxed{\text{rain}}^{n}\boxed{\text{rain, dusk}}$ with $n \geq 1$ to the string $\boxed{\text{rain, dawn}}\boxed{\text{rain}}\boxed{\text{rain, dusk}}$ of length 3. More generally, we define the *interval reduction* $\text{ir}(s)$ of a string $s \in (2^{\Phi})^{*}$ inductively

$$\text{ir}(s) \stackrel{\text{def}}{=} \begin{cases} s & \text{if length}(s) \leq 1 \\ \text{ir}(as') & \text{if } s = aas' \\ a\,\text{ir}(a's') & \text{if } s = aa's' \text{ where } a \neq a' \end{cases}$$

(for all $a, a' \subseteq \Phi$), reducing a block aa of two a's to one, in line with the dictum "no time without change" (KR93, page 674). What does the modification "interval" in ir have to do with Allen's 13 interval relations, tabulated below?

p before q	$\boxed{p}\ \square\ \boxed{q}$		p after q	$\boxed{q}\ \square\ \boxed{p}$
p meets q	$\boxed{p}\boxed{q}$		p met-by q	$\boxed{q}\boxed{p}$
p overlaps q	$\boxed{p}\boxed{p,q}\boxed{q}$		p overlapped-by q	$\boxed{q}\boxed{p,q}\boxed{p}$
p starts q	$\boxed{p,q}\boxed{q}$		p started-by q	$\boxed{p,q}\boxed{p}$
p during q	$\boxed{q}\boxed{p,q}\boxed{q}$		p contains q	$\boxed{p}\boxed{p,q}\boxed{p}$
p finishes q	$\boxed{q}\boxed{p,q}$		p finish-by q	$\boxed{p}\boxed{p,q}$
p equals q	$\boxed{p,q}$			

It turns out we can extract each of the 13 strings in the language

$$\text{Allen}(p,q) \stackrel{\text{def}}{=} \boxed{p}(\epsilon + \square)\boxed{q} + \boxed{q}(\epsilon + \square)\boxed{p} +$$
$$(\boxed{p} + \boxed{q} + \epsilon)\boxed{p,q}(\boxed{p} + \boxed{q} + \epsilon)$$

(where ϵ is the null string) from the superposition

$$\square^{+}\boxed{p}^{+}\square^{+} \ \& \ \square^{+}\boxed{q}^{+}\square^{+} \ = \ \text{ir}^{-1}(\square\boxed{p}\square) \ \& \ \text{ir}^{-1}(\square\boxed{q}\square))$$

by applying ir

$$\mathrm{ir}(\mathrm{ir}^{-1}(\square\boxed{p}\square) \ \& \ \mathrm{ir}^{-1}(\square\boxed{q}\square)) \ = \ \square\mathrm{Allen}(p,q)\square$$

where $\mathrm{ir}(L) \overset{\mathrm{def}}{=} \{\mathrm{ir}(s) \mid s \in L\}$. Without the intervention of ir^{-1},

$$\mathrm{ir}(\square\boxed{p}\square \ \& \ \square\boxed{q}\square) \ = \ \mathrm{ir}(\square\boxed{p,q}\square) \ = \ \square\boxed{p,q}\square$$

and a lot of structure gets lost.[1] Going back to $\boxed{\text{rain, dawn}}\,\boxed{\text{rain}}^{*}\,\boxed{\text{rain, dusk}}$, we may, anticipating further superpositions, wish to live with its infinitely many strings, whether or not they correspond to distinct events.

1.2   Subsumption and Constraints

If we &-superpose $\boxed{\text{rain, dawn}}\,\boxed{\text{rain}}^{*}\,\boxed{\text{rain, dusk}}$ with $\square^{+}\boxed{\text{noon}}\square^{+}$, we get

$$\boxed{\text{rain, dawn}}\,\boxed{\text{rain}}^{*}\,\boxed{\text{rain,noon}}\,\boxed{\text{rain}}^{*}\,\boxed{\text{rain, dusk}}$$

which filters out the string $\boxed{\text{rain, dawn}}\,\boxed{\text{rain, dusk}}$ of length 2, and fleshes out the remaining strings in $\boxed{\text{rain, dawn}}\,\boxed{\text{rain}}^{+}\,\boxed{\text{rain, dusk}}$ by including noon in the middle. To capture the growth of information here, let us say that L *subsumes* L' and write $L \trianglerighteq L'$ if the superposition of L and L' includes L

$$L \trianglerighteq L' \overset{\mathrm{def}}{\Longleftrightarrow} L \subseteq L\&L'$$

(roughly: L is at least as informative as L'). Conflating a string s with the singleton language $\{s\}$, it follows that L subsumes L' exactly if each string in L subsumes some string in L'

$$L \trianglerighteq L' \quad \text{iff} \quad (\forall s \in L)(\exists s' \in L') \ s \trianglerighteq s'$$

where $\trianglerighteq$ holds between strings of the same length related componentwise by inclusion

$$a_1 a_2 \cdots a_n \trianglerighteq b_1 b_2 \cdots b_m \quad \text{iff} \quad n = m \text{ and } a_i \supseteq b_i \text{ for } 1 \le i \le n \,.$$

For example, $\boxed{p,q} \trianglerighteq \boxed{p} \trianglerighteq \boxed{p}+\boxed{q}$. As a type with instances $s \in L$, a language L is essentially a disjunction $\bigvee_{s \in L} s$ of conjunctions s (as is clear from the model-theoretic interpretations spelled out in Fer04).

---

[1] Another way of making sense of Allen's relations in the present set-up is to replace intervals i and j by languages L and L' (respectively), and then turn $before(i,j)$ to $L\square^{+}L'$, $meets(i,j)$ to LL', $equals(i,j)$ to $L\&L'$, $finishes(i,j)$ to $\square^{+}L \ \&L'$, etc. These constructions are all finite-state.

Pausing to consider the finite-state character of the preceding notions, note that for finite Φ and $L \subseteq (2^\Phi)^*$, we can construct a finite-state transducer for the relation

$$\&_L \stackrel{\text{def}}{=} \{(s_1, s_2) \mid s_2 \in s_1 \& L\}$$

provided L is regular. (Given a finite automaton for L, form a transducer with the labeled state transitions

$$q \stackrel{a:b}{\to} q' \stackrel{\text{def}}{\iff} (\exists c)\ q \stackrel{c}{\to} q' \text{ and } a \cup c = b$$

with initial and final states unchanged.) Hence, if L and L' are regular, then so is

$$L\&L' = \{s_2 \mid (\exists s_1 \in L')\ (s_1, s_2) \in \&_L\}\ .$$

The relation

$$\{(s, s') \mid s' \trianglerighteq s\} = \&_{(2^\Phi)^*}$$

is also regular. Moreover, if L is regular, so is the *subsumption closure* $L^{\trianglerighteq}$ of L

$$L^{\trianglerighteq} \stackrel{\text{def}}{=} \{s \mid s \trianglerighteq L\} = L \ \& \ (2^\Phi)^*$$

consisting of strings that subsume some string in L.

In addition to the unary operation mapping a language L to $L^{\trianglerighteq}$, subsumption $\trianglerighteq$ induces a binary operation $\Rightarrow$ on languages. Given L and L', let the *constraint* $L \Rightarrow L'$ be the set of strings s such that whenever $s \trianglerighteq \Box^n L \Box^m$, $s \trianglerighteq \Box^n L' \Box^m$

$$L \Rightarrow L' \stackrel{\text{def}}{=} \{s \in (2^\Phi)^* \mid (\forall n, m \geq 0)\ s \trianglerighteq \Box^n L \Box^m \text{ implies } s \trianglerighteq \Box^n L' \Box^m\}\ .$$

As explained in FN05, $\Rightarrow$ is adapted from a similar construct called *restriction* in BK03, with

$$L \Rightarrow L' = \overline{(2^\Phi)^* \ (L^{\trianglerighteq} \cap \overline{L'^{\trianglerighteq}}) \ (2^\Phi)^*}$$

where $\overline{L}$ is the set-theoretic complement $(2^\Phi)^* - L$. (To make sense of the expression to the right, recall the Boolean equivalence between $A \supset B$ and $\neg(A \wedge \neg B)$; the counterexamples in $L \Rightarrow L'$ corresponding to $A \wedge \neg B$ are strings with substrings that subsume L but not L' — that is, substrings from $L^{\trianglerighteq} \cap \overline{L'^{\trianglerighteq}}$.) We can use $\Rightarrow$ to define the φ-*bivalent* language

(φ-biv) $\qquad\qquad\qquad\qquad \Box \ \Rightarrow \ \boxed{\varphi} + \boxed{\overline{\varphi}}$

consisting of strings $a_1 a_2 \cdots a_n \in (2^\Phi)^*$ such that for each i from 1 to n (inclusive), $\varphi \in a_i$ or $\overline{\varphi} \in a_i$. While we may want to work with strings that do not belong to this language (allowing a string to be silent on φ), it makes sense to restrict our events to strings in the φ-*consistent* language

$(\varphi\text{-con})$ $\qquad\qquad\qquad$ $\boxed{\varphi, \overline{\varphi}} \Rightarrow \emptyset$

requiring that no symbol in a string contain both φ and its negation $\overline{\varphi}$. Similarly, to pick out a unique position in a string by a fluent r (e.g. r = speech time "now" or some other reference point), the constraint

$$\boxed{r}\,\square^*\,\boxed{r} \Rightarrow \emptyset$$

precludes the occurrence of r in two different positions in a string. Again, observe that in general $L \Rightarrow L'$ is regular if L and L' are (and Φ is finite).

1.3   Inertia, Force and STRIPS Actions

Next, given a fluent φ, we introduce a fluent $f\varphi$ to mark the application of a force to make φ true (at the next step). Hence, the fluent $f\overline{\varphi}$ says a force is applied to make φ false. Accordingly, the constraint

$$\boxed{\varphi}\,\square \Rightarrow \square\,\boxed{\varphi} + \boxed{f\overline{\varphi}}\,\square \qquad\qquad (1)$$

states that φ persists (forwards) unless some force is applied against it, while

$$\square\,\boxed{\varphi} \Rightarrow \boxed{\varphi}\,\square + \boxed{f\varphi}\,\square \qquad\qquad (2)$$

states that φ persists backward unless it was previously forced. (1) and (2) are similar to inertial constraints formulated in FN05 except that we distinguish $f\varphi$ from $f\overline{\varphi}$ here (the previous fluents $F\varphi$ amounting essentially to $f\varphi \vee f\overline{\varphi}$) in order to formulate the constraint

$$\boxed{f\varphi}\,\square \Rightarrow \square\,\boxed{\varphi} + \boxed{f\overline{\varphi}}\,\square \qquad\qquad (3)$$

saying an unopposed force on φ brings φ about at the next moment. We could derive (1) from (3) and the constraint

$$\boxed{\varphi} \Rightarrow \boxed{f\varphi} \qquad\qquad (4)$$

but (4) would, under ($f\varphi$-con), rule out snapshots $\boxed{\varphi, \overline{f\varphi}, f\overline{\varphi}}$ that make $\overline{\varphi}$ true at the next step, assuming (3) for $\overline{\varphi}$. Instead of (4), we use $f\varphi$ to encode the representation of an action A in STRIPS (FN71) by the constraints

$$\boxed{\text{try(A)}} \Rightarrow \boxed{f\varphi_1, \ldots f\varphi_n} \text{ where Add-List(A)} = [\varphi_1, \ldots, \varphi_n]$$

$$\boxed{\text{try(A)}} \Rightarrow \boxed{f\overline{\psi_1}, \ldots, f\overline{\psi_m}} \text{ where Delete-List(A)} = [\psi_1, \ldots, \psi_m]$$

alongside

$$\boxed{\text{try(A)}} \Rightarrow \boxed{\chi_1, \ldots, \chi_k} \text{ where Precondition-List(A)} = [\chi_1, \ldots, \chi_k]$$

(borrowing the notation try(A) from AF94, with the temporal parameter implicit). In STRIPS, only one action is performed at a time, with deterministic post-conditions provided by constraints of the form (3) asserting that an unopposed force succeeds. The constraints above go beyond STRIPS in allowing multiple actions to execute simultaneously, and the effects of an action to be non-deterministic.

1.4 The Remainder of This Paper

Building on §§1.1 and 1.2 above (which draw on Fer04 and FN05, in pursuit of a line of research derived from Ste00), we consider the conciseness of representation in §2, the contribution context as a language makes to entailments in §3, and the application of constraints for inference rules in §4.

2 Concise Representations and Minimal Strings

In this section, we examine the conciseness of our string/language representations, starting with an observation worked out in Kar05 that we can unpack the symbols in our alphabet 2^Φ as strings. In a string $a_1 \cdots a_n \in (2^\Phi)^*$, each addition a_{i+1} to $a_1 \cdots a_i$ is understood as describing a succeeding moment of time. But, of course, the sequential structure in a string need not mark the passage of time. Instead, assuming Φ is finite, as henceforth we do, we can define a surjective function $\pi : \Phi^* \to 2^\Phi$ by

$$\pi(\epsilon) \stackrel{\text{def}}{=} \Box$$
$$\pi(\varphi s) \stackrel{\text{def}}{=} \boxed{\varphi} \cup \pi(s)$$

so for example $\boxed{\varphi, \psi} = \pi(\varphi\psi) = \pi(\varphi\psi\varphi)$. We then introduce a new symbol "tick" $\wr \notin \Phi^+$ to advance the clock so that we can encode, for instance, $\boxed{\psi, \psi \mid \varphi}$ as the string $\psi\psi \wr \varphi$, or as $\psi\varphi\psi \wr \varphi\varphi$.

2.1 Snapshots-as-Symbols Versus Snapshots-as-Strings

Given an ordering of the fluents, we can pick out for each $a \in 2^\Phi$ a canonical representative $\hat\pi(a) \in \Phi^*$ such that $\pi(\hat\pi(a)) = a$. Extending $\hat\pi$ to strings over 2^Φ, we can define $\hat\pi : (2^\Phi)^* \to (\Phi \cup \{\wr\})^*$ by

$$\hat\pi(\epsilon) \stackrel{\text{def}}{=} \epsilon$$
$$\hat\pi(as) \stackrel{\text{def}}{=} \hat\pi(a) \wr \hat\pi(s)$$

so for example $\hat\pi(a_1 a_2 a_3) = \hat\pi(a_1) \wr \hat\pi(a_2) \wr \hat\pi(a_3) \wr$. It is easy to build a finite-state transducer for $\{(s, \hat\pi(s)) \mid s \in (2^\Phi)^*\}$.

Proposition 1. If $L \subseteq (2^\Phi)^*$ is regular then so is

$$L_{\hat\pi} \stackrel{\text{def}}{=} \{\hat\pi(s) \mid s \in L\} .$$

Indeed, if $R \subseteq (2^\Phi)^* \times (2^\Phi)^*$ is regular, so is

$$R_{\hat\pi} \stackrel{\text{def}}{=} \{(\hat\pi(s), \hat\pi(s')) \mid sRs'\} .$$

Proof. $R_{\hat\pi} = \hat\pi^{-1}; R; \hat\pi$ where ; is sequential composition. ⊣

By Proposition 1, we can work with the alphabet 2^{Φ} without worrying if regularity is preserved when switching over to the alphabet $\Phi \cup \{\wr\}$. Equally, a regular relation R over the alphabet $\Phi \cup \{\wr\}$ remains regular when translated to $\hat{\pi}; R; \hat{\pi}^{-1} \subseteq (2^{\Phi})^* \times (2^{\Phi})^*$. The choice between snapshots-as-symbols and snapshots-as-strings is a matter of taste, as far as regularity is concerned. From a processing perspective, it is noteworthy that working with $\Phi \cup \{\wr\}$ makes greater use of the finite-state machinery. But for that very reason, the theory is arguably simpler to describe in terms of 2^{Φ} (with the unwinding of a snapshot to a string over $\Phi \cup \{\wr\}$ kept in the background).

2.2   Minimal Strings and Weak Subsumption

Given a language L and string s over 2^{Φ}, let us call s $\trianglerighteq$-*minimal in* L if $s \in L$ and for all $s' \in L - \{s\}$, not $s \trianglerighteq s'$. Let $L_{\trianglerighteq}$ be the set of strings $\trianglerighteq$-minimal in L

$$L_{\trianglerighteq} \stackrel{\text{def}}{=} \{s \in L \mid (\forall s' \in L - \{s\}) \text{ not } s \trianglerighteq s'\} \ .$$

For example, $(2^{\Phi})_{\trianglerighteq} = \square$, and recalling the constraint (φ-biv) of φ-bivalence

$$(\square \Rightarrow \boxed{\varphi} + \boxed{\overline{\varphi}})_{\trianglerighteq} \ = \ (\boxed{\varphi} + \boxed{\overline{\varphi}})^*$$

or in words: $(\boxed{\varphi} + \boxed{\overline{\varphi}})^*$ is the set of $\trianglerighteq$-minimal φ-bivalent strings.

Proposition 2. *Let L be a language over the alphabet 2^{Φ}.*

(a) $L_{\trianglerighteq}$ *is the $\subseteq$-least language $\trianglerighteq$-equivalent[2] to L, while $L^{\trianglerighteq}$ is the $\subseteq$-greatest.*
(b) *If L is regular, then so are $L_{\trianglerighteq}$ and $L^{\trianglerighteq}$.*

Proof. Straightforward, where a finite automaton for L can be turned into one for $\{s \mid (\exists s' \in L) \ s \trianglerighteq s' \text{ and } s \neq s'\}$, making

$$L_{\trianglerighteq} \ = \ L - \{s \mid (\exists s' \in L) \ s \trianglerighteq s' \text{ and } s \neq s'\}$$

regular (by the closure properties of regular languages). $\dashv$

We can minimize L further by "unpadding" $L_{\trianglerighteq}$. More precisely, for every string $s \in (2^{\Phi})^*$, let $\mathsf{unpad}(s)$ be s with all initial and final $\square$'s stripped off

$$\mathsf{unpad}(s) \stackrel{\text{def}}{=} \begin{cases} s & \text{if } s \text{ neither begins nor ends with } \square \\ \mathsf{unpad}(s') & \text{if } s = \square s' \text{ or else if } s = s'\square \ . \end{cases}$$

For example, $\mathsf{unpad}(\square\square\boxed{\varphi}\square\boxed{\psi}\square) = \boxed{\varphi}\square\boxed{\psi}$. Next, for every language L over 2^{Φ}, let $\mathsf{unpad}(L) \stackrel{\text{def}}{=} \{\mathsf{unpad}(s) \mid s \in L\}$ and call L *unpadded* if $\mathsf{unpad}(L) = L$. Let $L^{\square}$ consist of all strings in L with any number of leading and trailing $\square$'s deleted or added

$$L^{\square} \stackrel{\text{def}}{=} \square^* \mathsf{unpad}(L)\square^* \ = \ \{s \mid \mathsf{unpad}(s) \in \mathsf{unpad}(L)\} \ .$$

---

[2] Given a relation $\mathcal{R}$ (such as $\trianglerighteq$) between languages, we say L is $\mathcal{R}$-*equivalent* to L' if $L\mathcal{R}L'$ and $L'\mathcal{R}L$.

Incorporating unpadding into subsumption $\trianglerighteq$, let *weak subsumption* $\blacktriangleright$ be $\trianglerighteq$ with the second argument L' weakened to $L'^{\square}$

$$L\blacktriangleright L' \overset{\text{def}}{\iff} L \trianglerighteq L'^{\square} .$$

Weak subsumption $\blacktriangleright$ compares information content in the same way as $\trianglerighteq$

$$L\blacktriangleright L' \quad \text{iff} \quad (\forall s \in L)(\exists s' \in L') \; s\blacktriangleright s' .$$

but without insisting that strings have the same length

$$s\blacktriangleright s' \quad \text{iff} \quad (\exists s'') \; \mathsf{unpad}(s'') = \mathsf{unpad}(s') \text{ and } s \trianglerighteq s'' .$$

Insofar as $L\blacktriangleright L'$ says every instance of L contains some instance of L', it is natural to say L' *happens in* L when $L\blacktriangleright L'$. For the record, we have

Proposition 3. *Let $L \subseteq (2^{\Phi})^*$.*

(a) $\mathsf{unpad}(L_{\trianglerighteq})$ *is the $\subseteq$-least unpadded language $\blacktriangleright$-equivalent to L.*

(b) *The relations $\{(s, \mathsf{unpad}(s)) \mid s \in (2^{\Phi})^*\}$ and $\{(s, s') \mid s'\blacktriangleright s\}$ are regular. Hence, $\mathsf{unpad}(L)$ and $L^{\square}$ are regular if L is.*

3   Context as Language

It is a truism that information should be understood relative to context. But what does this mean for information and context represented as languages over the alphabet 2^{Φ}? If we regard strings over 2^{Φ} as epistemic possibilities much like possible worlds except that strings are finite and their snapshots non-exhaustive, then we can turn weak subsumption $\blacktriangleright$ into an inference relation $\vdash^C$ factoring in background information encoded by a context $C \subseteq (2^{\Phi})^*$. Let

$$L \vdash^C L' \overset{\text{def}}{\iff} C[L]\blacktriangleright L'$$

for some notion $C[L] \subseteq (2^{\Phi})^*$ of C *updated by* L. Precisely what $C[L]$ might be depends on what we assume about C and L. In this section, we will assume C describes the "big picture" with *global* constraints such as $\boxed{\varphi, \overline{\varphi}} \Rightarrow \emptyset$ providing the background for the more *local* events (with bounded temporal extents) described by L. For example, we might expect an event $L = \boxed{\text{rain,now}}$ of *raining now* to update a background

$$C \;=\; (\square + \boxed{\text{rain}} + \boxed{\overline{\text{rain}}})^{+} \; \& \; (\square^{+}\boxed{\text{now}}\square^{+})$$

to give

$$C[L] \;=\; (\square + \boxed{\text{rain}} + \boxed{\overline{\text{rain}}})^{*}\boxed{\text{rain,now}}(\square + \boxed{\text{rain}} + \boxed{\overline{\text{rain}}})^{*} .$$

The asymmetry assumed above between C and L means that neither the intersection $C \cap L$ nor the superposition $C\&L$ will do for $C[L]$.

3.1   Context Updated by L

Keeping the previous example in mind, let us define

$$C[L] \stackrel{\text{def}}{=} \{s \in C \mid s \blacktriangleright L\}$$

thereby ensuring that the update $C[L]$ preserves C and L. We write $s \in C$ for "s complies with the global constraint C," and $s \blacktriangleright L$ for "s complies with the local conditions L" (admittedly, a rather long-winded way of saying L happens in s).

Proposition 4. Let $C, L \subseteq (2^{\Phi})^*$.

(a) $C[L] \blacktriangleright L$ and $C[L] = (C[L])[L]$ and $C[C] = C$.
(b) $C[L] = \bigcup_{s \in L} C[s]$ and the relations

$$\{(s, s') \mid s' \blacktriangleright s \text{ and } s' \in C\} = \{(s, s') \mid s' \blacktriangleright s\} \; ; \; \{(s', s') \mid s' \in C\}$$
$$\{(s, s') \in L \times C \mid s' \blacktriangleright s\} = \{(s, s) \mid s \in L\} \; ; \; \{(s, s') \mid s' \blacktriangleright s \text{ and } s' \in C\}$$

and language $C[L]$ are regular if C and L are.
(c) $(C[L])[L'] = (C[L'])[L]$ for any $L' \subseteq (2^{\Phi})^*$.
(d) $C[L] = C[L']$ for every language L' $\blacktriangleright$-equivalent to L. In particular, $C[L] = C[L_{\triangleright}]$.
(e) $C[L] = (L^{\square} \& C) \cap C$. Hence, if $C = C^{\triangleright}$, then $C[L] = L^{\square} \& C$.

Proof. All parts are routine, with the regularity in part (b) a corollary of Proposition 3(b), part (d) following from the biconditional

$$s \blacktriangleright L \quad \text{iff} \quad s \blacktriangleright L'$$

for every L' $\blacktriangleright$-equivalent to L, and part (e) from

$$C \blacktriangleright L \quad \text{iff} \quad C \subseteq L^{\square} \& C .$$

$\dashv$

3.2   The C-Negation of L

What part of a context C would be *unable* to support an update by L? Calling that part $\text{neg}_C L$, we require that $(\text{neg}_C L)[L] = \emptyset$. An obvious candidate for $\text{neg}_C L$ is $C - C[L]$. The problem is that for say, $C = (\square + \boxed{p} + \boxed{\overline{p}})^+$,

$$C[\boxed{p}] = (\square + \boxed{p} + \boxed{\overline{p}})^* \boxed{p}(\square + \boxed{p} + \boxed{\overline{p}})^*$$
$$C - C[\boxed{p}] = (\square + \boxed{\overline{p}})^+$$
$$(C - C[\boxed{p}])[\boxed{p}] = (\square + \boxed{\overline{p}})^* \boxed{p}(\square + \boxed{\overline{p}})^* \neq \emptyset .$$

So instead, let us define $\text{neg}_C L$ to be the $\subseteq$-largest sublanguage L' of C such that $L' \& L^{\square}$ is disjoint from C

$$\text{neg}_C L \stackrel{\text{def}}{=} \{s \in C \mid (s \& L^{\square}) \cap C = \emptyset\} .$$

Proposition 5. Let $C, L \subseteq (2^{\Phi})^*$.

(a) For any $L' \subseteq (2^{\Phi})^*$, the following are equivalent.
   (i) $C[L'] \subseteq neg_C L$
   (ii) $(C[L'])[L] = \emptyset$
   (iii) $(C[L])[L'] = \emptyset$
   (iv) $C[L] \subseteq neg_C L'$
(b) $neg_C L$ is regular if C and L are.

Proof. For part (a), the equivalence of (ii) and (iii) follows from the commutativity expressed in Proposition 4(c). Note that (i) fails iff for some $s \in C[L']$, there is an $s' \in (s \& L^{\square}) \cap C$. Such a pair s, s' is what is precisely needed for (ii) to fail, by Proposition 4(b,e).

For part (b), the trick, as with $L_{\triangleright}$, is to use the closure of regular languages under complementation

$$neg_C L = C - \{ s \in C \mid (\exists s' \in L^{\square})(\exists s'' \in C) \, s \& s' \simeq s'' \}$$

where $s_1 \& s_2 \simeq s_3$ abbreviates $\{s_1\} \& \{s_2\} = \{s_3\}$. ⊣

Armed with the definition of $neg_C(L)$ above, we can for many languages L associate a complement $\neg L$ such that for contexts C meeting minimal conditions, $C[\neg L] = neg_C L$. More in §4.3 below.

4   Constraints as Inference Rules

If the previous section is about changes to context when a language is asserted or denied, this (final) section is about changes to a language L when constraints C from context are applied to L. We start by injecting L into C

$$inject(L, C) \stackrel{\text{def}}{=} \{ s \in C \mid s \trianglerighteq L \} = L^{\trianglerighteq} \cap C$$

(so $C[L] = inject(L^{\square}, C)$) before taking the strings $\trianglerighteq$-minimal in that set for the result of applying C to L

$$apply(C, L) \stackrel{\text{def}}{=} (inject(L, C))_{\trianglerighteq} .$$

Recall from §3.1 that L is presumed to be local, and from Proposition 4(d) that we can reduce L to $L_{\triangleright}$. If C has the form $L \Rightarrow L'$, then $apply(L \Rightarrow L', L)$ looks very much like the rule of inference *modus ponens* and indeed we will see that $apply(L \Rightarrow L', L) \trianglerighteq L'$. We will proceed more generally, allowing the lefthand side of C to differ (or not differ) from L, and paying special attention to the case where the righthand side of C has the form $B_1 + B_2$.

4.1   Minimal Changes

For a constraint C of the form $A \Rightarrow B$, let us define a relation $\langle\!\langle A, B \rangle\!\rangle$ between strings where fragments in A are superposed with strings in B

$$s \langle\!\langle A, B \rangle\!\rangle s' \stackrel{\text{def}}{\iff} (\exists x \in A, y \in B, n, m \geq 0) \, s \trianglerighteq \square^n x \square^m, \, s \& \square^n y \square^m \simeq s'.$$

Let $\langle\!\langle A, B \rangle\!\rangle^*$ be the reflexive transitive closure of $\langle\!\langle A, B \rangle\!\rangle$.

Proposition 6. For $A, B, L \subseteq (2^{\Phi})^*$, apply$(A \Rightarrow B, L)$ is the set of strings $\trianglerighteq$-minimal in

$$\{s' \in A \Rightarrow B \mid (\exists s \in L)\ s\ \langle\!\langle A, B \rangle\!\rangle^*\ s'\}\ .$$

It is regular if A, B and L are.

4.2 Biased Changes

Suppose further that the constraint C has the form $A \Rightarrow (B_1 + B_2)$, such as the constraints (φ-biv) and (1)-(3) from §1.3. We can arrange a language L to satisfy C by adding, as stated in Proposition 6, fragments of B_1 or of B_2. Introducing a bias for B_1, let us restrict $\langle\!\langle A, B_1 + B_2 \rangle\!\rangle$ to a variant $\langle\!\langle A, B_1, B_2 \rangle\!\rangle$ that can be read: "if A then add B_1 unless B_2"

$$s\ \langle\!\langle A, B_1, B_2 \rangle\!\rangle\ s' \overset{\text{def}}{\iff} (\exists x \in A, y \in B_1, n, m \geq 0)\ s \trianglerighteq \square^n x \square^m,$$
$$s \ntrianglerighteq \square^n B_2 \square^m \text{ and } s \& \square^n y \square^m \simeq s'\ .$$

To implement this restriction, we must constrain the step to $L^{\trianglerighteq}$ in apply(C, L) to satisfy C, introducing a new parameter L' to define

$$\text{app}(C, L, L') \overset{\text{def}}{=} ((L \& L') \cap C)_{\trianglerighteq}$$
$$\text{ap}(A, B_1, B_2, L) \overset{\text{def}}{=} \text{app}(A \Rightarrow (B_1 + B_2), L, (2^{\Phi(B_1)})^*)$$

where $\Phi(B_1)$ is the set $\{\varphi \in \Phi \mid (\exists s \in B_1)\ s \trianglerighteq \square^* \boxed{\varphi} \square^*\}$ of fluents occurring in B_1. Notice that for the constraints (φ-biv) and (1)-(3), $\Phi(B_1)$ adds nothing to B_2 inasmuch as B_2 is disjoint from $\overline{B_2}$ & $(2^{\Phi(B_1)})^*$.

Proposition 7. For $A, B_1, B_2, L \subseteq (2^{\Phi})^*$, ap$(A, B_1, B_2, L)$ is the set of strings $\trianglerighteq$-minimal in

$$\{s' \in A \Rightarrow (B_1 + B_2) \mid (\exists s \in L)\ s\ \langle\!\langle A, B_1, B_2 \rangle\!\rangle^*\ s'\}$$

assuming B_2 is disjoint from $\overline{B_2} \& (2^{\Phi(B_1)})^*$. The language ap$(A, B_1, B_2, L)$ is regular if A, B_1, B_2 and L are.

4.3 Refinements Based on Consistency

Bias applied blindly can lead to trouble, as illustrated by the case of (1)

$$\boxed{\varphi} \square \Rightarrow \square \boxed{\varphi} + \boxed{f\overline{\varphi}} \square$$

in the presence of the consistency constraint

$$\Phi\text{-con} \overset{\text{def}}{=} \bigcap_{\psi \in \Phi} (\boxed{\psi, \overline{\psi}} \Rightarrow \emptyset) = \{a \subseteq \Phi \mid (\forall \psi \in a)\ \overline{\psi} \notin a\}^*\ .$$

When imposing (1) on $\boxed{\varphi \mid \overline{\varphi}}$, we must take the second disjunct $\boxed{\mathsf{f}\overline{\varphi} \mid \square}$ on the righthand side of (1). But on $\boxed{\varphi, \overline{\mathsf{f}\overline{\varphi}} \mid \square}$, we must opt for the first disjunct $\boxed{\square \mid \varphi}$.

To cover such contingencies, let us refine our transformation $\mathrm{ap}(A, B_1, B_2, L)$ of L, rewriting $A \Rightarrow (B_1 + B_2)$ as two constraints,

$$(A \& \neg B_1) \Rightarrow B_2 \quad \text{and} \quad (A \& \neg B_2) \Rightarrow B_1$$

where $\neg B_1$ and $\neg B_2$ are defined from Φ-con and A as follows. Let $A\text{-con} \overset{\text{def}}{=} A^{\trianglerighteq} \cap \Phi\text{-con}$ and

$$\neg B_i \overset{\text{def}}{=} \{s \in A\text{-con} \mid (s \& B_i) \cap A\text{-con} = \emptyset\}_{\trianglerighteq}$$

for $i \in \{1, 2\}$. (So for (1), $\neg B_1 = \boxed{\varphi \mid \overline{\varphi}}$ and $\neg B_2 = \boxed{\varphi, \overline{\mathsf{f}\overline{\varphi}} \mid \square}$.) Continuing to keep the notation simple, we form in sequence the languages

$$L_1 \overset{\text{def}}{=} \mathrm{apply}((A \& \neg B_1) \Rightarrow B_2, L)$$

$$L_2 \overset{\text{def}}{=} \mathrm{ap}(A, \neg B_2, B_2, L_1)$$

$$L_3 \overset{\text{def}}{=} \mathrm{apply}((A \& \neg B_2) \Rightarrow B_1, L_2)$$

which are regular if A, B_1, B_2 and L are. The idea is to settle the question of B_2 versus $\neg B_2$ given A, minimizing B_2 in L_2 before reducing $A \Rightarrow (B_1 + B_2)$ to $(A \& \neg B_2) \Rightarrow B_1$ in L_3. The bias favoring B_1 in $A \Rightarrow (B_1 + B_2)$ is derived from a bias favoring $\neg B_2$ in $A \Rightarrow (\neg B_2 + B_2)$ after giving B_2 its due in L_1. The general point is to subject the non-determinism in constraints $A \Rightarrow (B + B')$ to some default preference between B and $\neg B$.

References

Allen, J.F., Ferguson, G.: Actions and events in interval temporal logic. *Journal of Logic and Computation*, 4(5):531–579, 1994.

Beesley, K.R., Karttunen, L.: *Finite State Morphology*. CSLI, Stanford, 2003.

Emerson, E.A.: Temporal and modal logic. In J. van Leeuwen, editor, *Handbook of Theoretical Computer Science*, volume B: Formal Methods and Semantics, pages 995–1072. MIT Press, 1992.

Fernando, T.: A finite-state approach to events in natural language semantics. *Journal of Logic and Computation*, 14(1):79–92, 2004.

Fernando, T., Nairn, R.: Entailments in finite-state temporality. In *Proc. 6th International Workshop on Computational Semantics*, pages 128–138. Tilburg University, 2005.

Fikes, R.E., Nilsson, N.J.: STRIPS: a new approach to the application of theorem proving to problem solving. *Artificial Intelligence*, 2:189–208, 1971.

Kamp, H., Reyle, U.: *From Discourse to Logic*. Kluwer, Dordrecht, 1993.

Karttunen, L.: `www.stanford.edu/~laurik/fsmbook/examples/YaleShooting.html`, 2005.

Steedman, M.: *The Productions of Time*. Draft, `ftp://ftp.cogsci.ed.ac.uk/pub/steedman/temporality/temporality.ps.gz`, July 2000. Subsumes 'Temporality,' in J. van Benthem and A. ter Meulen, editors, *Handbook of Logic and Language*, pages 895–935, Elsevier North Holland, 1997.

Compiling Linguistic Constraints into Finite State Automata

Matthieu Constant[1] and Denis Maurel[2]

[1] Université de Marne-la-Vallée, Institut Gaspard Monge, France
[2] Université François-Rabelais de Tours, Laboratoire d'Informatique, France

Abstract. This paper deals with linguistic constraints encoded in the form of (binary) tables, generally called lexicon-grammar tables. We describe a unified method to compile sets of tables of linguistic constraints into Finite State Automata. This method has been practically implemented in the linguistic platform Unitex.

1 Motivation

Finite State Models have been intensively used in Natural Language Processing [13]. Nevertheless, because of the complexity of languages, it is often more convenient for linguists to describe linguistic constraints with simpler and more ergonomic representations. For instance, simple regular expressions are sometimes used to express morphological rules [6], inflected forms of dictionaries are preferred to be written in a textual form [3] and syntactic constraints depending on lexicon are represented in the form of binary matrices [4]. Finite State linguistic phenomena are sometimes described with more powerful and more compact formalisms such as (weighted) context-free grammars [10] and recursive transition networks[5]. These representations are then compiled into Finite State Automata or Transducers in order to optimize processing.

This paper deals with linguistic constraints encoded in the form of (binary) tables made of rows and columns, generally called lexicon-grammar tables. A row of such table corresponds to the formal description of the lexical and syntactic properties accepted by a lexical item. Each column corresponds to a property. At the intersection of a row and a column, the encoded value indicates whether or not a lexical entry (row) accepts a property (column)[1]. In this paper, we will describe a unified method to compile sets of tables of linguistic constraints into Finite State Automata. We will also show how it has been practically implemented in the linguistic platform Unitex [11].

2 State-of-the-Art

The first idea of combining binary matrices and automata was pointed out in [7], but the first compilation method has been found in [12] and has been implemented in the linguistic platforms INTEX [14] and Unitex [11]. It was limited

---

[1] Usually, symbol + stands for `True` and symbol - stands for `False`.

O.H. Ibarra and H.-C. Yen (Eds.): CIAA 2006, LNCS 4094, pp. 242–252, 2006.

to systems of constraints encoded in one table such as the ones in [4]. It used hand-built parameterized reference automata, representing the sets of the possible syntactic constructions where can enter a fictive lexical entry accepting all properties of the table. Each path is parameterized by one or several parameters that refer to properties that correspond to syntactic constructions (e.g. `Prep Det Noun`[2]) or lexical information (e.g. if the constituent `Prep` accepts the lexical value *in*). The compilation process consists, for each lexical entry (or raw), in resolving the parameters according to the encoding in the tables. For instance, a false value at a given column indicates that the transitions labeled with the parameter associated with the column, must be removed. A true value indicates that these transitions must be made epsilon-transitions. Then, a specific automaton is constructed for each lexical entry. The automaton representing all described phenomena is simply the union of all constructed automata. It is then optimized by a deterministic minimization operation for text processing efficiency.

Several linguistic studies have shown that it is sometimes more convenient to encode constraints of a same linguistic phenomena into systems of multiple tables because some properties can be factorized in different tables to avoid encoding duplication [7,1]. In this case, Roche's compilation does not work because it does not handle multiple tables. [8] implemented an algorithm compiling systems of multiple tables of specific constraints. These constraints were limited to very local constraints. Tables described the restrictions on the combinations of pairs of lexical elements in sequences where both elements occur consecutively (or sometimes with a grammatical word in between). For instance, for French time expressions, sequence *milieu de matin* (middle of morning) is forbidden while sequence *milieu d'après-midi* (middle of afternoon) is accepted. A schemata automaton is used to represent all possible patterns for a type of expressions. This automaton also recognizes bad sequences because it does not take lexical restrictions into account. All forbidden sequences encoded in the tables are put in an automaton that is then applied using the failure algorithm [9] that cuts all forbidden paths in the schemata automaton. [2] proposed an algorithm with no restrictions on the constraints; constraints were represented in relational systems of tables. The algorithm consisted in directly constructing the automaton that recognizes accepted sequences, by using a parameterized reference automaton with parameters resembling Roche's ones. Nevertheless, the complexity of the construction of the parameterized automaton could grow very fast with the number of tables. For instance, it is not well adapted to Maurel's time expressions.

In this paper, we present a unified algorithm for compiling systems of tables of constraints with no restrictions on the type of constraints.

3   Set of Constraints and Parameterized Automaton

This section focuses on the general description of inputs of our algorithm, that are a set of linguistic constraints and a parameterized schemata. They are respectively described in section 3.1 and in section 3.2.

---

[2] `Prep Det Noun` stands the construction `preposition determiner noun`

3.1   Sets of Linguistic Constraints

A syntactic construction is a sequence of syntactic symbols (and sometimes of lexical symbols): for instance, the syntactic construction N0 V N1 is composed of a noun phrase (N0) followed by a verb (V) and then another noun phrase (N1). Each syntactic symbol have a set of possible lexical realizations, e.g. V could be eat or walk. Though, syntactic constructions have lexical restrictions; their acceptability can depend on the lexical realizations of a syntactic element. For example, the transitive verb eat can enter the constructions N0 V N1, while the intransitive verb walk cannot[3]:

> John is eating an apple.
> *John is walking an apple.

Such constraint is called a one-dimensional constraint because it depends on only one element (the verb).

There can also exist lexical restrictions on the combination of two syntactic elements in the context of a construction. For instance, in the construction N0 V N1 Prep N2[4], there exist lexical constraints on the pair (V,Prep): pairs (receive,from) and (give,to) are acceptable, while (receive,to) and (give,from) are forbidden as it is shown in the sentences below.

> John received a present (*to+from) Mary.
> John gave a present (to+*from) Mary.

Such constraint is called a two-dimensional constraint because it depends on the combination of two elements (the pair verb-preposition).

Practically, a given constraint is not only limited to a single construction, but also a set of equivalent constructions. For instance, the constraint on the pair (V,Prep) in the example above is available as well for the equivalent interrogative construction :

> Who received a present (*to+from) Mary ?

Moreover, linguistic constraints can also restrict the combination of more syntactic elements cooccurring in a same construction. Theoretically, such constraints can be decomposed into elementary constraints that are one-dimensional and two-dimensional ones, all related with logical AND operators. For example, the acceptability of frozen constructions of the form N0 be Prep N Prep1 N1, can depend on the lexical combination of Prep, N and Prep1 such as in:

> The text is (in+*on) contradiction (with+*to) the law.

Verifying if this constraint is valid is equivalent to checking if elements in and contradiction can cooccur in this context and if contradiction and with

---

[3] In linguistic examples, the symbol * is the forbidden symbol and symbol + is the disjonction symbol.
[4] N0, N1 and N2 are noun phrases, V is a verb and Prep a preposition.

cooccur. Thus, in the next sections, we will consider that there exist only one-dimensional and two-dimensional constraints. One-dimensional ones are encoded in the form of binary vectors, each element corresponding to a lexical value; two-dimensional lexical constraints are encoded in the form of binary matrices, encoding the restrictions on the combination of pairs of lexical values.

Examples of such representations are given in figure 1. The binary representations describe lexical constraints on geographical names. Such names can enter two constructions `Detc Npr Nc` (labeled NN) and `Detc Nc of Npr` (labeled NPN), where `Detc` is a definite determiner (e.g. `the`), `Npr` is a proper name such as `Adriatic`, `Marmara`, `Paris`... and `Nc` is a location noun classifier like `city`, `sea`... Figure 1(a) presents two-dimensional constraints between lexical realizations of `Nc` and `Npr` (`sea` and `Adriatic`); figure 1(b) and figure 1(c) present one-dimensional constraints depending on `Npr`, indicating whether or not it can enter constructions NPN (`city of Paris`) or NN (`Adriatic sea`).

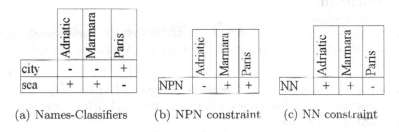

(a) Names-Classifiers   (b) NPN constraint   (c) NN constraint

Fig. 1. One- and two-dimensional constraints

3.2 Parameterized Schemata Automaton

A parameterized schemata automaton is a hand-built acyclic automaton that explicitly represents all possible syntactic realizations that the studied linguistic phenomenon can have. It is used as a basis to build an automaton representing all accepted constructions of this phenomenon, taking encoded lexical restrictions into account. Each path represents a possible construction. Labels of this automaton are either lexical or syntactic elements, or parameters. Syntactic elements that may cause lexical constraints in the construction are marked as parameters. They are called syntactic parameters. Such parameters are denoted with the name of the syntactic element preceded by symbol @: for instance, @X is the parameter associated with the syntactic symbol X. Sets of constructions (i.e. sets of paths) can also be parameterized because their acceptability may depend on the lexical realizations of some syntactic "parameterized" elements. We call them construction parameters. They are denoted with the label assigned to the set of constructions, preceded and followed by symbol @: for example, @P@ is the parameter associated with the constructions labeled P. An example of such automaton is given in figure 2: it consists of the parameterized schemata automaton used for geographical names. @Nc@ and @Npr@ are syntactic parameters; @NN@ and @NPN@ are construction parameters.

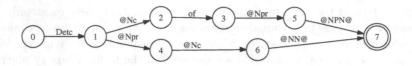

Fig. 2. A parameterized schemata automaton

A pair of parameters defines a set of lexical constraints. A pair composed of a syntactic parameter @X and a construction parameter @P@ defines all 1-dimensional lexical constraints depending on the syntactic element X in the context of the constructions parameterized with P[5]. A pair composed of two syntactic parameters (@X and @Y) defines all 2-dimensional lexical constraints for combining the syntactic elements X and Y in the studied linguistic phenomenon[6].

4   Algorithm

Our algorithm for compiling a set of constraints into a finite state automaton (A^+) is based on the use of a parameterized schemata automaton (Ap). It consists of 3 steps:

1. building the automaton of all possible sequences (A) from Ap;
2. constructing the forbidden sequence automaton A^-, from Ap and the sets of different constraints;
3. constructing automaton A^+ defined by $L(A^+) = L(A) - L(A^-)$, where $L(A)$ stands for the language recognized by automaton A.

One can wonder why the desired automaton A^+ is not directly constructed from Ap. It is simply due to the fact that adding a new path requires checking all constraints it undergoes. In case of complex systems like the one proposed by [8] for date adverbials, the cost would be very important. At worse, the construction process would have exponential complexity. The idea to build first the automaton of forbidden constructions is because a path is invalid if it undergoes only one forbidden constraint. Its construction is then linear with the number of constraints[7]. The construction of the automaton of accepted sequences is simply implemented using an intersection-type algorithm.

4.1   Construction of the Automata of All Possible Constructions

Automaton A (step 1) is built by replacing the syntactic parameters of Ap by their actual associated symbols (standing for word classes), and replacing construction parameters by ϵ symbol. The automaton produced for geographical

---

[5] Path 5-7 comes from Fig. 1 (b) and path 6-7 comes from Fig. 1 (c).

[6] Paths 1-2-3-5 and 1-4-6 come from Fig. 1 (a).

[7] One should remark that the determinization operation computed after the automata construction is theoretically exponential in complexity. Nevertheless, it has been observed that, practically, it is very often not the case for natural language automata.

names is given in figure 3. Symbol <E> stands for ε symbol. Note that syntactic symbols are references to classes of words; they are also represented with automata. These automata are automatically built from the set of lexical realizations used in the set of constraints. Automaton A is obtained by replacing all syntactic symbols by their actual word class and then computing some optimization operations as it is shown in figure 4.

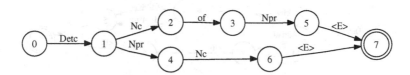

Fig. 3. A schemata automaton

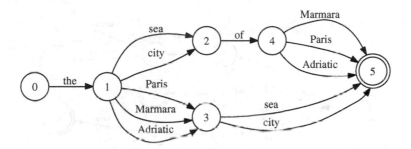

Fig. 4. A lexicalized schemata automaton

4.2 Construction of the Automaton of Forbidden Syntactic Forms

The construction of A^- consists in building, automatically from Ap, a parameterized automaton for each pair of parameters (X,Y) that undergoes lexical restrictions; and then in lexicalizing this automaton according to the restrictions encoded in the corresponding vectors or tables.

The construction of the pair-specific parameterized schemata automaton, called $Ap(X, Y)$, consists in keeping only paths of Ap where X and Y cooccur. Marking such paths is based on an automaton transversal-type algorithm: for each parameter of the pair, we mark the states and transitions of Ap, which can be reached from transitions labeled by the parameter, or from which such a transition can be reached. Then, $Ap(X, Y)$ is obtained by keeping states and transitions of Ap marked for both parameters. Finally, other parameters are either replaced by an ε (<E>) if they are construction parameters, or replaced by their associated syntactic symbol (refering to a word class) if they are syntactic parameters. An example of such automaton for the pair (Nc,Npr) is given in figure 5.

The construction of the automaton of forbidden syntactic forms is then based on the lexicalization of such pair-specific parameterized schemata automata. Such an automaton is associated with a binary vector or a binary table. In case

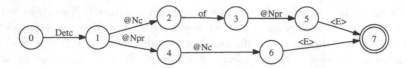

Fig. 5. the (Nc,Npr) parameterized schemata automaton

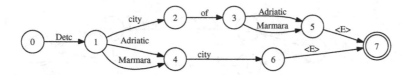

Fig. 6. the (Nc,Npr) lexicalized schemata automaton for entry `city`

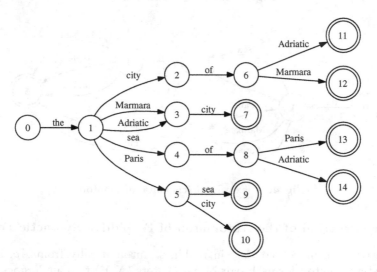

Fig. 7. Automaton of forbidden constructions for geographic names

of a binary vector associated with a parameter pair (`@X,@Y@`), for each lexical entry x that are lexical realization of X, a new automaton is created from $Ap(X, Y)$. Parameters $@X$ are replaced by x. If the constructions labeled Y are not accepted, parameters $@Y@$ are replaced by ϵ (`<E>`). If they are, transitions labeled by $@Y@$ are removed. In case of a binary table associated with a parameter pair (`@X,@Y`), for each lexical realization x of X, a new automaton is created from $Ap(X, Y)$. Transitions $(q, @Y, p)$, where p and q are states of the new automaton, are removed. For each lexical realization y of Y, if the combination between x and y is forbidden, a new transition (q, y, p) is added. Figure 6 shows an example of a lexicalized automaton specific to the pair (`Nc,Npr`) for the lexical entry `city` in the case of geographic names.

All obtained lexicalized automata are then unioned; all syntactic symbols are replaced by their actual automata; and finally, an optimization operation is computed (useless state removal and determinization). The global lexicalized automaton of forbidden constructions for geographic names is given in figure 7.

4.3   Construction of the Automaton of Possible Syntactic Forms

Given deterministic automata A and A^-, it is then possible to compute automaton A^+ representing all possible constructions, taking all lexical restrictions into account. The process consists in computing the automaton that recognizes the language $L(A^+)$ defined such that $L(A^+) = L(A) - L(A^-)$. It implements a variant of the standard algorithm for computing the intersection between two automata. The automaton obtained for geographical names is given in figure 8.

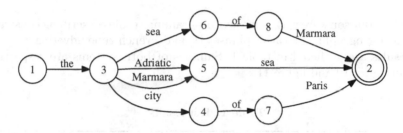

Fig. 8. Automaton of accepted constructions for geographic names

5   Implementation

Our algorithm has been implemented in C in Unitex, a GPL linguistic platform [11]. The implementation was eased by the use of some modules, data structures on finite state automata and common operations on them, already implemented in Unitex. Parameterized schemata automata can be drawn with a graph editor included in the platform. Unitex automata are recursive automata (automata that can call other automata) that are equivalent to Recursive Transition Networks (RTN) [15]. Therefore, syntactic symbols are simply calls to automata that represents their associated word classes. Automata can be unioned by simply creating an automaton that concurrently call all of them. There also exists a "Flatten" operation that computes the equivalent finite-state automaton of a given RTN (when recognizing a regular language).

Besides, it is often more convenient for linguists to have different parameter-pair constraints encoded in a same table in order to have a better view of the studied linguistic phenomenon[8]. Moreover, tables are not always binary: they can contain lexical values. For example, the example table and vectors (figure 1) are practically gathered in one table as in figure 9. We therefore implemented a module that transforms real tables into several binary vectors or tables.

---

[8] As it has been shown in [2], elementary constraints can be also gathered in several real tables.

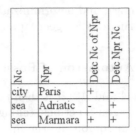

Fig. 9. A real table of linguistic constraints

6   Evaluation and Discussion

We tested[9] our software with some lexicon-grammar tables describing constraints on French geographical locative phrases [1] and French time adverbials [8]. The test results are gathered in table 1. Samples of both systems are respectively given in figure 10 and figure 11.

Table 1. Test results

type	# of lexical constraints	# of parameter pairs	# of A^- states	# of A^- transitions	# of A^+ states	# of A^+ transitions	Compiling time
Loc	1,420	15	47,822	81,760	253	782	29 s
Time	818	5	2,868	27,280	100	694	2 s

Our unified algorithm has the advantage of working for all different types of systems of lexicon-grammar tables. Although compiling times are reasonable (cf. table 1), our algorithm is not always the most efficient one. For instance, the conversion of simple systems of relational tables like geographical phrases ones is faster using a process based on Roche's algorithm preceded by a merge operation on the related tables: 4s instead of 29s for our converter. Comparison is not feasible for time adverbials because Roche's algorithm and its extensions do not work in that case.

Constructing automaton A^- is the main factor for slowing down the process because A^- tends to be much bigger than the final A^+ (cf. table 1). Roche's algorithm and its extension (to systems with multiple tables) directly deal with A^+. Maurel's algorithm simply constructs the automaton recognizing forbidden subsequences, which is clearly a smaller automaton than A^- (542 states and 4191 transitions for 50 tables or parameter pairs [8]). The determinization of these automata makes the difference clearer because of the exponential complexity of this operation. Nevertheless, we consider that this relative lack of efficiency is not really important because compiling can be done once for all before applying

---

[9] Pentium III, 1.6 GHz, 512 Mb RAM.

Detc pluriel	Nc	Prep	Det	Npr	LE Nc de Npr	LE Nc Npr	dans Det Npr	à Det Npr
+	île	-	-	Aléoutiennes	-	+	+	+
-	île	de	la	Ascension	-	-	-	-
+	île	-	-	Bahamas	-	+	+	+
+	île	de	les	Baléares	-	+	+	+
-	île	de	la	Barbade	-	-	-	+
-	île	de	-	Beauté	+	-	-	-
+	île	-	-	Bermudes	-	+	+	+

(a) Islands

Nc	Prep	Det	Npr	LE Nc de Npr	en Npr	dans Det Npr
département	de	l'	Ain	-	-	+
département	de	l'	Aisne	-	-	+
département	de	l'	Allier	-	-	+
département	de	les	Alpes-de-Haute-Provence	-	+	+
département	de	les	Hautes-Alpes	-	-	+
département	de	les	Alpes-Maritimes	-	-	+
département	de	l'	Ardèche	+	+	+

(b) French Departments

Loc = :à	Loc =: dans	Loc =:sur	Loc =: en	Loc =:E	Nc
-	+	+	-	-	département
+	+	+	-	-	île

(c) Prepositional distribution

Fig. 10. Locative geographical phrases

	matin (morning)	midi (12 a.m.)	soir (evening)
aujourd'hui (today)	-	+	-
hier (yesterday)	+	+	+
demain (tomorrow)	+	+	+

	aujourd'hui (today)	hier (yesterday)	demain (tomorrow)
à	-	-	-
après	+	+	-
d'ici	+	-	+

Fig. 11. Time adverbials

the compiled automata on different texts. We are more interested in the fact that the algorithm works for all types of systems.

7   Conclusion

In this paper, we have shown that linguistic constraints encoded in the form of (binary) tables can be compiled into finite state automata. We have describe a unified method, implemented in the linguistic platform Unitex, in three steps: building the automaton of all possible sequences, the forbidden sequence automaton and the resulting automaton.

References

1. Constant, Matthieu. 2002. On the Analysis of Locative Phrases with Graphs and Lexicon-Grammar: the Classifier/Proper Noun Pairing. In Advances in Natural Language Processing, Proceedings of PorTAL, Lecture Notes in Artificial Intelligence (LNAI) 2389, Berlin: Springer, 33-42.
2. Constant, Matthieu. 2003. Converting Linguistic Systems of Relational Matrices into Finite-State Transducers. Proceedings of the EACL Workshop on Finite-State Methods in Natural Language Processing, Budapest, 75-82
3. Courtois, Blandine. 1990. Un système de dictionnaires électroniques pour les mots simples du français. Langue Française 87, Paris: Larousse
4. Gross, Maurice. 1984. Lexicon-Grammar and the Syntactic Analysis of French. In Proceedings of the 10 th International Conference on Computational Linguistics (COLING'84), Stanford, California.
5. Gross, Maurice. 1997. The Construction of Local Grammars. In Finite-State Language Processing, E. Roche & Y. Schabès (eds.), Language, Speech, and Communication, Cambridge, Mass.: MIT Press, 329-354.
6. Karttunen, Lauri, Jean-Pierre Chanod, Gregory Grefenstette and Anne Schiller. 1996. Regular Expressions for Language Engineering. CUP Journals: Natural Language Engineering 2 (4), Cambridge University Press, 305-328.
7. Maurel, Denis. 1989. Reconnaissance de séquences de mots par automates, Adverbes de dates du français. PhD. thesis, Paris: Université Paris 7.
8. Maurel, Denis 1996. Building automaton on Schemata and Acceptability Tables. First Workshop on Implementing automata (WIA'96), London, Ontario, 29-31 août, in LNCS 1260, 72-86.
9. Mohri, Mehryar. 1994. Syntactic Analysis by Local Grammars Automata: an Efficient Algorithm. In Proceedings of COMPLEX 94, Budapest, Hungary.
10. Mohri, Mehryar and Fernando C. N. Pereira. 1998. Dynamic compilation of weighted context-free grammars. 36th Annual Meeting of the ACL and 17th International Conference on Computational Linguistics, Vol. 2, 891-897.
11. Paumier, Sébastien. 2003. De la reconnaissance de formes linguistiques à l'analyse syntaxique. PhD. thesis, Université de Marne-la-Vallée.
12. Roche, Emmanuel. 1993. Une représentation par automate fini des textes et des propriétés transformationnelles des verbes. Lingvisticae Investigationes XVII:1Amsterdam/Philadelphia, John Benjamins, 189-222.
13. Roche, Emmanuel and Yves Schabes. 1997. Finite-State Language Processing, Cambridge, Mass./London, The MIT Press, 241-281.
14. Silberztein, Max D. . 1999. INTEX: a Finite State Transducer Toolbox". Theorical computer science. Vol. 231:1, 33-46.
15. Woods, William A.. 1970. Transition Network Grammars for Natural Language Analysis, Communications of the ACM, 13:10

Shift-Resolve Parsing: Simple, Unbounded Lookahead, Linear Time

José Fortes Gálvez[1], Sylvain Schmitz[2], and Jacques Farré[2]

[1] Universidad de Las Palmas de Gran Canaria, Spain
jfortes@dis.ulpgc.es
[2] Laboratoire I3S, Université de Nice - Sophia Antipolis, France
schmitz@i3s.unice.fr, Jacques.Farre@unice.fr

Abstract. This paper introduces a mechanism for combining unbounded lookahead exploration with linear time complexity in a deterministic parser. The idea is to use a *resolve* parsing action in place of the classical reduce. The construction of shift-resolve parsers is presented as a two-step algorithm, from the grammar to a finite nondeterministic automaton, and from this automaton to the deterministic parser. Grammar classes comparisons are provided.

1 Introduction

Common deterministic parser generators [1] provide a parser developer with two interesting static guarantees: that the input grammar is unambiguous, and that the resulting parser will process its input string in linear time. There is however a major issue with these parser generation algorithms: they cannot provide a deterministic parser for an arbitrary context-free grammar, resulting in the infamous *conflicts* between possible parsing actions. Their inability to deal with parsing decisions that need more than the pre-established k lookahead terminal symbols is to blame for a large part of it.

Two different parsing techniques allow to circumvent this limitation to bounded lookaheads in bottom-up parsers, but to keep the unambiguity guarantee. The first, called regular lookahead parsing, uses a finite state automaton to explore an unbounded right context [2,3,4]. The linear time guarantee is however lost. The second, called noncanonical parsing, explores the right context using the parser itself. The latter can thus perform some reductions in this right context, return to the conflict point, and use a bounded number of the newly reduced symbols to yield a deterministic decision [5,6,7]. However, the preset bound on the reduced lookahead length—in practice the bound is $k = 1$—hampers the power of the noncanonical methods.

We want to have our cake and eat it too: we want linear time parsing, ambiguity detection, and no user defined bound on the lookahead length. Shift-resolve parsing is a new combination of the regular and noncanonical strategies that achieves all these properties. To this end, we make the following contributions.

- We propose a new parsing action, *resolve* (Section 2.1), which combines the classical reduction with a pushback, *i.e.* it rewinds the stack down to the

O.H. Ibarra and H.-C. Yen (Eds.): CIAA 2006, LNCS 4094, pp. 253–264, 2006.
© Springer-Verlag Berlin Heidelberg 2006

point where the reduction should take place. The exact amount of pushback is not fixed, but computed for each reduction as a minimal necessary length.

- By promoting the resolve action as a replacement for the reduce action, our parsers properly integrate noncanonical resolutions in the right context exploration (Section 2.2). One could fear that a quadratic time complexity would stem from this combination. We avoid it by ensuring that the pushback lengths remain bounded.
- We present the construction of shift-resolve parsers as the determinization of a phrase recognizer (Section 4). The algorithm generalizes similar constructions for LR parsers. The choice of the approximations used in order to have a finite recognizer is left open, and we use a lattice of possible approximations (Section 3.2). Hence, our method is highly generic and allows for tradeoffs between descriptional complexity and classes of accepted grammars.

2   Shift-Resolve Parsing

A bottom-up parser operates by reverting the derivations that led from the axiom of the grammar to the input string. Each of these reversions is the *reduction* of a *phrase* α to a nonterminal A, where $A{\rightarrow}\alpha$ is a rule of P. A canonical parser always reduces the leftmost phrase in a given sentential form, called the *handle* of the sentential form, but a noncanonical parser partially ignores this ordering. It is able to reduce a phrase further right from a handle, and to use the additional information provided by the newly reduced nonterminals to infer its parsing decisions. Indeed, a single nonterminal symbol describes a complete context-free language, and, using only a few nonterminals as lookahead, a noncanonical parser has an impressive amount of right context information at its disposal.

2.1   The Approach

We make here the simplifying choice of always using completely reduced lookahead symbols: symbols as they appear in the grammar rule we are exploring, and cannot be reduced without reducing the entire rule.

As usual in noncanonical parsing [8], a deterministic two-stack model is used to hold the current sentential form. The parsing (or left) stack corresponds to the traditional LR stack, while the input (or right) stack initially contains the input string. Two operations allow to move symbols from the top of one stack to the top of the other: a *shift* of a symbol from the input stack to the parsing stack, and a *pushback* of a bounded number of symbols the other way around. A *reduction* using rule $A{\rightarrow}\alpha$ removes the topmost $|\alpha|$ symbols from the parsing stack and pushes A on top of the input stack.

We compute, for each reduction, the minimal bounded reduced lookahead length needed to discriminate it from other parsing actions. This lookahead exploration is properly integrated in the parser. Once the parser succeeds in telling which action should have been done, we either keep parsing if it was a shift, or need to reduce at an earlier point. The pushback brings the parser back at this point; we call the combination of a pushback and a reduction a *resolution*.

Table 1. Shift-resolve parsing table for $\mathcal{G}_1$

	$	a	b	c	S	A	B	C	D
q_0		s_4	s_5		s_1	s_2	s_3		
q_1	$r_1'0$								
q_2				s_8				s_6	s_7
q_3				s_8				s_9	s_{10}
q_4				s_8				$r_5'0$	$r_5'0$
q_5				s_8				$r_7'0$	$r_7'0$
q_6		s_{11}		s_8					
q_7				s_8				$r_4'0$	$r_4'0$
q_8		$r_8'0$	$r_9'0$	s_8				s_{12}	s_{13}
q_9				s_8				$r_6'0$	$r_6'0$
q_{10}			s_{14}	s_8					
q_{11}	$r_2'0$								
q_{12}		$r_9'1$		s_8				$r_8'1$	$r_8'1$
q_{13}			$r_8'1$	s_8				$r_9'1$	$r_9'1$
q_{14}	$r_3'0$								

No cost is paid in terms of computational complexity, since shift-resolve parsers are linear in the length of the input text. A simple proof is that the only re-explored symbols are those pushed back. Since pushback lengths are bounded, and since each reduction gives place to a single pushback, the time linearity is clear if the number of reductions is linear with the input length. This last point stems from the fact that our method detects and rejects cyclic grammars.

2.2 Parsing Example

Let us consider the extended grammar with rules

$$S' \xrightarrow{1} S, \ S \xrightarrow{2} ACa, \ S \xrightarrow{3} BDb, \ A \xrightarrow{4} AD,$$
$$A \xrightarrow{5} a, \ B \xrightarrow{6} BC, \ B \xrightarrow{7} b, \ C \xrightarrow{8} c, \ D \xrightarrow{9} c. \tag{$\mathcal{G}_1$}$$

Grammar $\mathcal{G}_1$ can require an unbounded lookahead if we consider approximated parsing methods, like for instance a LR(0) approximation, which provides the basis for most practical parsing methods. A single *inadequate* state with items $C \rightarrow c\bullet$ and $D \rightarrow c\bullet$ can be reached after reading both prefixes Ac and Bc. After reading Ac, the lookahead for the reduction to C is a, while the one for the reduction to D is c^+a. After reading Bc, the lookaheads are c^+b and b respectively. Thus, if we use a LR(0) approximation, we need an unbounded terminal lookahead length in order to choose between the reduction to C or D, when seeing the last input symbol a or b after a sequence c^+.

Grammar $\mathcal{G}_1$ is not LALR(1). If we try to use more advanced parsers, $\mathcal{G}_1$ is not NSLR(1) [6]—it is NSLR(2)—, and the time complexity of XLR(∞) parsing [2] —LR-Regular using a LR(0) approximation—according to $\mathcal{G}_1$ is quadratic.

Table 1 contains the parse table for shift-resolve parsing according to $\mathcal{G}_1$. The table is quite similar to a LR(1) table, with the additional pushback length information, but describes a parser with much more lookahead information. States are denoted by q_i; shift entries are denoted as s_i where i is the new state of the parser; resolve entries are denoted as $r_i'j$ where i is the number of the rule for the

Table 2. The parse of the string *acca* by the shift-resolve parser for $\mathcal{G}_1$

parsing stack	input stack	actions
q_0	$acca\$$	s_4
$q_0 a q_4$	$cca\$$	s_8
$q_0 a q_4 c q_8$	$ca\$$	s_8
$q_0 a q_4 c q_8 c q_8$	$a\$$	$r_8'0$

We have reached the first phrase in *acca*$ that we can resolve with a completely reduced lookahead. This lookahead is *a*, and indeed it cannot be reduced any further in the rule $S \rightarrow ACa$. The lookahead allows the decision of resolving $C \rightarrow c$. The newly reduced nonterminal is pushed on the input stack, as usual in noncanonical parsing.

$q_0 a q_4 c q_8$	$Ca\$$	s_{12}
$q_0 a q_4 c q_8 C q_{12}$	$a\$$	$r_9'1$

We have here a non-null pushback: the resolve action $r_9'1$, which would have needed an unbounded terminal lookahead, is solved using the stacked C and the lookahead *a*. The pushback of length 1 emulates a reduced lookahead inspection of length 2.

$q_0 a q_4$	$DCa\$$	$r_5'0$
q_0	$ADCa\$$	s_2
$q_0 A q_2$	$DCa\$$	s_7
$q_0 A q_2 D q_7$	$Ca\$$	$r_4'0$
q_0	$AC\$$	s_2
$q_0 A q_2$	$Ca\$$	s_6
$q_0 A q_2 C q_6$	$a\$$	s_{11}
$q_0 A q_2 C q_6 a q_{11}$	$\$$	$r_2'0$
q_0	$S\$$	s_1
$q_0 S q_1$	$\$$	$r_1'0$, accept

reduction and j the pushback length. The reduction according to rule $S' \overset{1}{\longrightarrow} S$ indicates that the input is successfully parsed. Table 2 details the parsing steps on the valid input *acca*. Symbols are interleaved with states in the parsing stack in order to ease the reading, and are not actually used.

The originality of shift-resolve parsing resides in that Table 1 is not the result of a very precise computation; in fact, we used the worst approximation we tolerate. Still, the parsing time is linear and no preset lookahead length was necessary.

3   Grammatical Representation

The shift-resolve parsing table presented in Table 1 is the result of a two-steps process: the first step builds a finite nondeterministic automaton from the grammar, and the second generates the deterministic shift-resolve parser from it.

3.1   Position Graph

We consider here a graph representation of a context-free grammar. This graph can be seen as the set of all left to right walks in all possible derivation trees

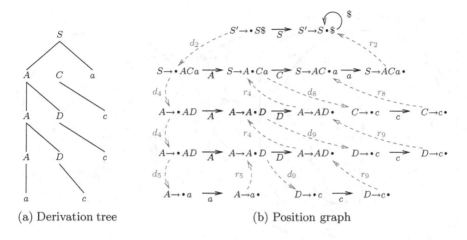

(a) Derivation tree   (b) Position graph

Fig. 1. Representing the derivation of string $accca$ in $\mathcal{G}_1$

for the grammar. The nodes of this graph are *positions* to the immediate left or immediate right of a derivation tree node. The vertices tell which other positions are reachable. We label each position with a dotted rule giving its local context.

For instance, with $\mathcal{G}_1$, any tree node ν_A with symbol A can nondeterministically derive a node ν_a with symbol a from $A{\to}a$, or two nodes ν'_A and ν_D with symbols A and D from $A{\to}AD$. Following this idea, we find that the local context of ν'_A provides us with more information than the mere symbol A: the symbol A in question is in front of a dot in the position $A{\to}{\bullet}AD$.

If we make this local context explicit in the labels of the positions, then the relations between these positions become visible. These transitions are of three types: symbol transitions $\overset{X}{\longleftarrow}{\to}$, and a two kinds of ε-transitions: derivation transitions $\overset{d_i}{\longleftarrow}{\to}$ and reduction transitions $\overset{r_i}{\longleftarrow}{\to}$ where i is a rule number. Figure 1 presents the portion deriving $accca$ of the position graph for $\mathcal{G}_1$, along with the traditional derivation tree representation. We emulate an infinite number of end of file markers with a looping transition $\overset{\$}{\longleftarrow}{\to}$.

We introduce the *parenthesis grammar* $p(\mathcal{G})$ of a context-free grammar $\mathcal{G}$ as the grammar with rules $A\overset{i}{\longrightarrow}d_i\alpha r_i$ whenever $A\overset{i}{\longrightarrow}\alpha$ is a rule of $\mathcal{G}$. We also define a homomorphism h that removes all the d_i and r_i symbols from a string. An immediate consequence is that $\mathcal{L}(\mathcal{G}) = h(\mathcal{L}(p(\mathcal{G})))$.

In order to uniquely identify a single position in the position graph, we define *valid positions* for a grammar $\mathcal{G}$ as triples $\delta d_i[A\overset{i}{\longrightarrow}\alpha{\bullet}\alpha']r_iy$ such that

$$S\underset{\mathrm{rm}}{\overset{*}{\Rightarrow}}\delta Ay\underset{\mathrm{rm}}{\Rightarrow}\delta d_i\alpha\alpha'r_iy \text{ in } p(\mathcal{G}). \tag{1}$$

For instance, the position labeled by $C{\to}{\bullet}c$ in Figure 1b is identified by the expression $d_2Ad_8[C\overset{8}{\longrightarrow}{\bullet}c]r_8ar_2$.

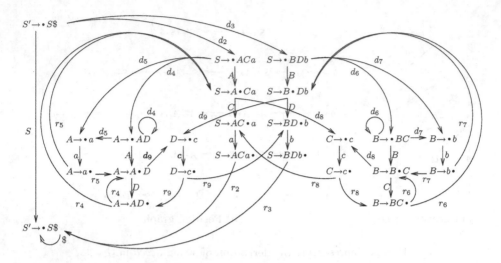

Fig. 2. Nondeterministic automaton for Grammar $\mathcal{G}_1$ using κ_0

Definition 1. *The* position graph $\mathcal{I} = \langle \mathcal{N}, \longmapsto \rangle$ *of grammar* $\mathcal{G}$ *associates the (potentially infinite) set* $\mathcal{N}$ *of valid positions for* $\mathcal{G}$ *with the labeled relation* $\longmapsto$ *defined by*

$$\delta[A \xrightarrow{i} \alpha \cdot X\alpha']y \xrightarrow{X} \delta[A \xrightarrow{i} \alpha X \cdot \alpha']y, \tag{2}$$

$$\delta[A \xrightarrow{i} \alpha \cdot B\alpha']y \xrightarrow{d_j} \delta\alpha d_j[B \xrightarrow{j} \cdot \beta]r_j uy \quad \text{if } \alpha' \Rightarrow^* u \text{ in } p(\mathcal{G}), \text{ and} \tag{3}$$

$$\delta\alpha d_j[B \xrightarrow{j} \beta \cdot]r_j uy \xrightarrow{r_j} \delta[A \xrightarrow{i} \alpha B \cdot \alpha']y \quad \text{if } \alpha' \Rightarrow^* u \text{ in } p(\mathcal{G}). \tag{4}$$

3.2 Position Equivalences

We are eager to put explicit labels on our positions because we intend to collapse the position graph into a finite graph. The equivalence relations defined to this end will preserve the local context, and thus use the position labels.

Definition 2. *The* collapsed position graph $\Gamma_\kappa = \langle [\mathcal{N}]_\kappa, \longmapsto_\kappa \rangle$ *of a position graph* $\mathcal{I} = \langle \mathcal{N}, \longmapsto \rangle$ *associates* $[\mathcal{N}]_\kappa$ *the finite set of equivalence classes* $[p]_\kappa$ *over* $\mathcal{N}$ *modulo* κ *with the labeled relation* $\longmapsto_\kappa$ *defined by*

$$[p]_\kappa \xrightarrow{X}_\kappa [q]_\kappa \quad \text{iff} \quad \exists p' \in [p]_\kappa, q' \in [q]_\kappa, p' \xrightarrow{X} q'. \tag{5}$$

Simple Equivalence Relation. Figure 2 is not a Rorschach test but the collapsed position graph Γ_{κ_0} for $\mathcal{G}_1$ using a simple equivalence relation κ_0 between positions.

Definition 3. *Two positions are* simply equivalent *if and only if they have the same dotted rule as label, i.e.*

$$\delta[A \rightarrow \alpha \cdot \alpha']y \ \kappa_0 \ \gamma[B \rightarrow \beta \cdot \beta']z \quad \text{iff} \quad A \rightarrow \alpha \cdot \alpha' = B \rightarrow \beta \cdot \beta'. \tag{6}$$

While very basic, this equivalence relation is fine enough to yield a working shift-resolve parser for $\mathcal{G}_1$. It is the simplest equivalence relation we will use for shift-resolve parsing.

Lattice of Equivalence Relations. The usual partial order on $\mathrm{Eq}(\mathcal{N})$—the complete lattice of all equivalence relations on $\mathcal{N}$—is the inclusion relation $\subseteq$. For any two elements κ_a and κ_b of $\mathrm{Eq}(\mathcal{N})$, $\kappa_a \wedge \kappa_b$ is the greatest lower bound or *meet*, defined as

$$\kappa_a \wedge \kappa_b = \kappa_a \cap \kappa_b. \tag{7}$$

Finer equivalence relations are obtained when using the meet of two equivalence relations; they result in larger collapsed position graphs.

Let $\mathcal{K}$ be the set of all equivalence relations that are included in κ_0; $\mathcal{K}$ is an obvious interval sublattice of $\mathrm{Eq}(\mathcal{N})$, ordered by the inclusion relation. We will only make use of equivalence relations in $\mathcal{K}$: if κ is in $\mathcal{K}$, then $\kappa = \kappa_0 \wedge \kappa'$ for some κ' in $\mathrm{Eq}(\mathcal{N})$. Equivalence relations in $\mathcal{K}$ abound: for instance, a relation κ_k with $\mathrm{LR}(k)$ precision could be written as $\kappa_0 \wedge l_k$ with

$$\delta[A{\rightarrow}\alpha\bullet\alpha']y \; l_k \; \gamma[B{\rightarrow}\beta\bullet\beta']z \text{ iff } k : h(y) = k : h(z); \tag{8}$$

the set of equivalence classes using l_k is $[\mathcal{N}]_{l_k} = T'^k$—the set of different sequences of k terminals. An experimental parser generator with a much finer equivalence relation is currently available from the Internet at the following address: `http://serdis.dis.ulpgc.es/~ii-pl/ftp/dr`.

3.3   Nondeterministic Automaton

We call a collapsed position graph Γ_κ using an equivalence relation κ in $\mathcal{K}$ a *nondeterministic automaton.*

Preserving Grammar Derivations. Let us denote by $\nu_0 = [\varepsilon[S'{\rightarrow}\bullet S\$]\varepsilon]_\kappa$ the equivalence class on $\mathcal{N}$ using κ containing $\varepsilon[S'{\rightarrow}\bullet S\$]\varepsilon$, and by $\nu_1 = [\varepsilon[S'{\rightarrow}S\bullet\$]\varepsilon]_\kappa$ the one containing $\varepsilon[S'{\rightarrow}S\bullet\$]\varepsilon$. We also denote by $\xmapsto{\chi}{}^*_\kappa$ the transitive reflexive closure of $\longmapsto_\kappa$, labeled with χ the sequence of labels on the individual relations. We show here a simple result: paths in a nondeterministic automaton correspond to derivations in the parenthesis grammar.

Theorem 1. *If* $S{\Rightarrow}^*\delta A\rho{\Rightarrow}\delta r_i\alpha\alpha'd_i\rho = \gamma\alpha'd_i\rho = \gamma\sigma$ *holds in* $p(\mathcal{G})$, *then* $\nu_0\xmapsto{\gamma}{}^*_\kappa[\delta r_i[A\xrightarrow{i}\alpha\bullet\alpha']d_ix]_\kappa\xmapsto{\sigma}{}^*_\kappa\nu_1$ *with* $\rho{\Rightarrow}^*x$ *holds in* Γ_κ.

Proof. A straightforward induction on the length of γ.

Size of the Nondeterministic Automaton. The index of κ_0 is $|\mathcal{G}|$, thus, the size of $\Gamma_{\kappa_0 \wedge \kappa'}$ is in the worst case $O(|[\mathcal{N}]_{\kappa'}|.|\mathcal{G}|)$ where $|[\mathcal{N}]_{\kappa'}|$ is the index of κ'.

4   Shift-Resolve Parsers

4.1   Shift-Resolve Parser Construction

We now describe how to extract a deterministic shift-resolve parser from a nondeterministic automaton Γ_κ. The algorithm is based on a subset construction.

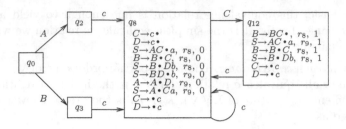

Fig. 3. Item sets of some states of the shift-resolve parser for Grammar $\mathcal{G}_1$

States of the Shift-Resolve Parser. The states of the shift-resolve parser are sets of *items* $[\nu, sr, d]$, where ν is an equivalence class on $\mathcal{N}$ using κ—i.e. a state in Γ_κ—, sr a parsing action—either a production number or 0 to code a shift—, and d is a nonnegative integer to code the distance to the resolution point. By convention, we assume that d is null whenever sr denotes a shift.

Initial state's item set is computed as $I_{q_0} = \mathcal{C}(\{[\nu_0, 0, 0]\})$, where the closure $\mathcal{C}$ of an item set I is the minimal set such that

$$\mathcal{C}(I) = I \,\cup$$
$$\{[\nu', 0, 0] \mid [\nu, sr, d] \in \mathcal{C}(I), \nu \xmapsto{d_i}_\kappa \nu'\} \,\cup$$
$$\{\iota \mid [\nu, sr, d] \in \mathcal{C}(I), \nu \xmapsto{r_i}_\kappa \nu', \neg(null(i) \text{ and } null(I)),$$
$$((sr = 0 \text{ and } \iota = [\nu', i, 0]) \text{ or } (sr \neq 0 \text{ and } \iota = [\nu', sr, d]))\},$$

where, by noting $\mathcal{L}$ the terminal language produced by a sequence of symbols, we discard superfluous ε-reductions with the help of the conditions

$$null(i) \text{ iff } A \xrightarrow{i} \alpha, \ \mathcal{L}(\alpha) = \{\varepsilon\}$$
$$null(I) \text{ iff } [[\delta[A \rightarrow \alpha X \bullet \beta]y]_\kappa, sr, d] \in I, \ \mathcal{L}(X) = \{\varepsilon\}.$$

Transition from state item set I with symbol X is defined as follows.

$$\Delta(I, X) = \mathcal{C}(\{[\nu', sr, d'] \mid [\nu, sr, d] \in I, \nu \xmapsto{X}_\kappa \nu',$$
$$((sr = 0 \text{ and } d' = 0) \text{ or } (sr \neq 0 \text{ and } d' = d + 1))\})$$

Figure 3 presents the details of the item sets computations for states q_8 and q_{12} of the shift-resolve parser presented in Table 1.

Parser Table. Parser table entries, *i.e.*, shifts and resolves, are computed from the item set I_q of each state q as follows.

$$T(q, X) =$$
$$\text{if } \forall \iota = [[\delta[A \rightarrow \alpha \bullet X \beta]x]_\kappa, sr, d] \in I_q,$$
$$sr = r: \textbf{resolve } r \textbf{ with pushback } d \text{ (if } r = 1 \text{ and } d = 0, \textbf{accept})$$
$$\text{otherwise: } \textbf{shift} \text{ to } q' \text{ such that } I_{q'} = \Delta(I_q, X)$$

4.2 Shift-Resolve Grammars

Rejection Condition. A grammar is *inadequate* if and only if two different state item sets are built with identical item sets except for some pushback length(s); otherwise, we write it is a ShRe(κ) grammar.

It follows that the worst-case space complexity of the shift-reduce parser for $\mathcal{G}$ is $O(2^{|\Gamma_\kappa||P|})$. More powerful shift-resolve parsers can be obtained at the price of descriptional complexity if we add to the condition that one such state should be Δ-reachable from the other.

Theorem 2. *If $\mathcal{G}$ is ambiguous, then it is not ShRe(κ) for any κ in $\mathcal{K}$.*

Proof. We merely outline the proof.

Since $\mathcal{G}$ is an ambiguous context-free grammar, we can find two leftmost derivations $S \underset{\mathrm{lm}}{\Rightarrow}^* xA\rho \underset{\mathrm{lm}}{\Rightarrow} x\alpha\alpha'\rho = x\alpha\sigma$ and $S \underset{\mathrm{lm}}{\Rightarrow}^* yB\sigma \underset{\mathrm{lm}}{\Rightarrow} y\beta\sigma$ in $\mathcal{G}$, with $A\alpha\alpha' \neq B\beta$, and such that there is a z in T^* with $x\alpha \Rightarrow^* z$ and $y\beta \Rightarrow^* z$.

Such derivations are mirrored in the nondeterministic automaton Γ_κ by two positions $\nu = [\delta[A \rightarrow \alpha \bullet \alpha']s]_\kappa$ and $\nu' = [\gamma[B \rightarrow \beta \bullet]t]_\kappa$ such that $\nu_0 \overset{u}{\longmapsto}{}^*_\kappa \nu \overset{\chi}{\longmapsto}{}^*_\kappa \nu_1$ and $\nu_0 \overset{u'}{\longmapsto}{}^*_\kappa \nu' \overset{\chi'}{\longmapsto}{}^*_\kappa \nu_1$, with

$$h(u) = h(u') = z \tag{9}$$
$$h(\chi) = h(\chi') = \sigma. \tag{10}$$

In such a situation, there is a prefix φ in V^* such that some items $[\nu, sr, d]$ and $[\nu', sr', d']$ are included in the item set of $\Delta(I_{q_0}, \varphi)$. The right context of this shift-resolve parser state is $\sigma\$^*$, an infinite regular language. Since $\nu \neq \nu'$ ($A\alpha\alpha' \neq B\beta$ and $\kappa = \kappa_0 \wedge \kappa'$), we are bound to find two item sets only differing on the pushback lengths, and therefore $\mathcal{G}$ is found inadequate.

Grammar Classes. The problem of deciding whether there exists an equivalence relation κ in $\mathcal{K}$ such that a given context-free grammar is ShRe(κ) is obviously not decidable, otherwise we could answer to the ambiguity problem in context-free grammars using Theorem 2.

The classes of ShRe(κ_k)—κ_k is defined as the meet of k_0 and l_k from Equation (8)—grammars are not comparable with the classes of LR(k) grammars. For instance, we can produce a shift-resolve parser for the grammar with rules

$$S \rightarrow AC \mid BCb, \quad A \rightarrow d, \quad B \rightarrow d, \quad C \rightarrow aCb \mid c \tag{$\mathcal{G}_2$}$$

using κ_0, but $\mathcal{G}_2$ is not LR(k) for any value of k—as a matter of fact, it is not LR-Regular either.

Conversely, for $k > 0$, we can put an unbounded number of null nonterminals between a conflict and its resolution. For instance, the grammar with rules

$$S \rightarrow Aa \mid Bb, \quad A \rightarrow cAE \mid c, \quad B \rightarrow cBE \mid c, \quad E \rightarrow \varepsilon \tag{$\mathcal{G}_3$}$$

is LR(1) but not ShRe(κ) for any κ: once we reach the a or b symbol allowing to resolve, we would need to pushback an unbounded number of E symbols in order to have the c we intend to reduce on top of the parsing stack.

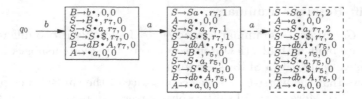

Fig. 4. Item sets exhibiting the inadequacy of Grammar $\mathcal{G}_4$ using κ_0

A simplification we made in the shift-resolve construction makes it possible for a LR(0) to be inadequate using κ_k. This is the case for the grammar with rules

$$S\rightarrow Sa\,|\,B,\ A\rightarrow a,\ B\rightarrow dBA\,|\,b. \tag{$\mathcal{G}_4$}$$

Figure 4 shows how the resolution in a shift-resolve state with a single possible reduction (here $B\rightarrow b$) can be tricked into an useless exploration of the right context caused by the κ_k approximations. The issue can be tackled on the nondeterministic automaton level by choosing a finer equivalence relation, for instance $\kappa = \kappa_0 \wedge c_1$ where

$$\delta[A\rightarrow\alpha\bullet\alpha']y\ c_1\ \gamma[B\rightarrow\beta\bullet\beta']z \text{ iff } h(\delta):1 = h(\gamma):1. \tag{11}$$

The issue can also be tackled on the subset construction level if we test whether following r_i transitions in the nondeterministic automaton is necessary for a resolution, and if not, fill the entire parser table line with this resolution.

5   Related Work

Shift-resolve parsing is related to two areas: parsing techniques and nondeterministic grammatical representations.

Parsing Techniques. The presence of conflicts in deterministic parsers is a widely acknowledged issue. Transforming an input grammar until no more conflicts can be found is a tedious task, can obfuscate the grammar, and may result in convoluted semantic actions. It is therefore tempting for a parser developer to trade the two static guarantees—unambiguity and linear time recognition—for his confidence in his own skill in the handling of ambiguities and a reasonable chance of having a linear time parser [9]. Another line of research is to see how far one can go without sacrificing the static guarantees.

This line has given birth to the LR-Regular [10] and noncanonical [5] parser families. To the best of our knowledge, the only other combination of the two families [11] is an extension to DR(k) parsing [12]. It suffers from a worst-case quadratic parsing time complexity inherent to DR(k) parsing with non LR(k) grammars.

Using only completely reduced symbols in noncanonical parsing was already investigated with the Leftmost SLR(1) parsers [6], and discarded as less powerful than Noncanonical SLR(1) parsing. We improve on LSLR(1) parsers by allowing a non-predefined lookahead length and more powerful approximations in our grammatical representations.

Finally, to the extent of our knowledge, Grammar $\mathcal{G}_1$ is the first published instance of a quadratic parsing time complexity with a regular lookahead parser.

Nondeterministic Grammatical Representations. Before becoming a classical presentation [13] and a classical implementation [1] for LR(k) parser constructions, nondeterministic grammatical representations were used for efficient LR(k) testing [14]. Item grammars are a very similar representation [15]. They have also been used as a unifying framework for parsing methods [16]. Our idea of using the lattice of equivalence relations for the various possible approximations seems to be new, though there are many similarities with the theory of abstract interpretation [17].

6   Conclusion

Shift-resolve parsing is a novel parsing method with an attractive combination of properties: the produced parsers are deterministic, they can use an unbounded lookahead, and they run in linear time. Their generation is the result of a highly generic algorithm working on a nondeterministic automaton. It is easy to design new approximations for the automaton in order to improve the grammatical coverage.

The next logical step is the investigation of which conditions would yield shift-resolve parsers that keep running in linear time even if we allow unbounded pushback lengths.

References

1. Donnely, C., Stallman, R.: Bison, The YACC-compatible Parser Generator. The Free Software Foundation (2002)
2. Baker, T.P.: Extending lookahead for LR parsers. Journal of Computer and System Sciences **22**(2) (1981) 243–259
3. Bermudez, M.E., Schimpf, K.M.: Practical arbitrary lookahead LR parsing. Journal of Computer and System Sciences **41**(2) (1990) 230–250
4. Farré, J., Fortes Gálvez, J.:   A bounded-connect construction for LR-regular parsers. In Wilhelm, R., ed.: CC'01. Volume 2027 of Lecture Notes in Computer Science., Springer (2001) 244–258
5. Szymanski, T.G., Williams, J.H.: Noncanonical extensions of bottom-up parsing techniques. SIAM Journal on Computing **5**(2) (1976) 231–250
6. Tai, K.C.: Noncanonical SLR(1) grammars. ACM Transactions on Programming Languages and Systems **1**(2) (1979) 295–320
7. Schmitz, S.:   Noncanonical LALR(1) parsing.   In Dang, Z., Ibarra, O.H., eds.: DLT'06. Volume 4036 of Lecture Notes in Computer Science., Springer (2006) 95–107
8. Aho, A.V., Ullman, J.D.: The Theory of Parsing, Translation, and Compiling. Volume I: Parsing of Series in Automatic Computation. Prentice Hall, Englewood Cliffs, New Jersey (1972)

9. Tomita, M.: Efficient Parsing for Natural Language. Kluwer Academic Publishers (1986)

10. Čulik, K., Cohen, R.: LR-Regular grammars—an extension of LR(k) grammars. Journal of Computer and System Sciences **7** (1973) 66–96

11. Farré, J., Fortes Gálvez, J.: Bounded-connect noncanonical discriminating-reverse parsers. Theoretical Computer Science **313**(1) (2004) 73–91

12. Fortes Gálvez, J.: A Discriminating Reverse Approach to LR(k) Parsing. PhD thesis, Universidad de Las Palmas de Gran Canaria and Université de Nice-Sophia Antipolis (1998)

13. Grune, D., Jacobs, C.J.H.: Parsing Techniques: A Practical Guide. Ellis Horwood Limited (1990)

14. Hunt, III, H.B., Szymanski, T.G., Ullman, J.D.: On the complexity of LR(k) testing. Communications of the ACM **18**(12) (1975) 707–716

15. Heilbrunner, S.: A parsing automata approach to LR theory. Theoretical Computer Science **15**(2) (1981) 117–157

16. Schöbel-Theuer, T.: Towards a unifying theory of context-free parsing. In Pighizzini, G., San Pietro, P., eds.: Proceedings ASMICS Workshop on Parsing Theory. Technical Report 126-1994, Università di Milano (1994) 89–100

17. Cousot, P., Cousot, R.: Abstract interpretation: a unified lattice model for static analysis of programs by construction or approximation of fixpoints. In: POPL '77, ACM Press (1977) 238–252

A Family of Algorithms for Non Deterministic Regular Languages Inference*

Manuel Vázquez de Parga, Pedro García, and José Ruiz

Universidad Politécnica de Valencia
Departamento de Sistemas informáticos y Computación, Camino de Vera s/n
46022 Valencia, Spain
{mvazquez, pgarcia, jruiz}@dsic.upv.es
http://www.dsic.upv.es/users/tlcc/tlcc.html

Abstract. We present in this paper a new family of algorithms for regular languages inference from complete presentation.

Every algorithm of this family, on input of the sets of words (D_+, D_-), obtains for every x in D_+ at least a non deterministic finite automaton (*NFA*) which accepts x and is consistent with D_-. This automaton is, besides, irreducible in the sense that any further merging of states accepts words of D_-. The output of the algorithm is a *NFA* which consists of the collection of *NFAs* associated to each word of D_+. Every algorithm of the family converges to a automaton for the target language.

We also present the experiments done to compare one of the algorithms of the family with two other well known algorithms for the same task. The results obtained by our algorithm are better, both in error rate as in the size of the output.

1 Introduction

The classical algorithms for regular languages identification typically output a deterministic finite automaton (*DFA*). One of the best known algorithms of this kind is the *RPNI* (Regular Positive and Negative Inference) algorithm [8], which converges to the minimal *DFA* of the target language. Its method is to merge the states in the prefix tree Moore machine of the sample in lexicographical order and to propagate the merges to keep the automaton deterministic, under the condition of not merging states that represent positive samples with those which represent negative ones.

Starting up from the idea that a non deterministic automaton (*NFA*) is generally a smaller description for a regular language than its equivalent *DFAs*, it has recently been proposed an algorithm called *DeLeTe2* [3] whose output is a special type of *NFA* called *RFSA* (Residual Finite State Automata) characterized by the fact that its states are residuals of the language it recognizes.

The authors of *DeLeTe2* show that when the target automaton is a randomly generated *DFA*, this algorithm behaves worse than *RPNI*, but the opposite way

---

* Work partially supported by Spanish CICYT under TIC2003-09319-C03-02.

O.H. Ibarra and H.-C. Yen (Eds.): CIAA 2006, LNCS 4094, pp. 265–274, 2006.

happens if the target automaton is generated using random regular expressions or *NFAs*.

We propose in this work a family of algorithms such that each of them, on input of a sample, outputs a non deterministic automaton. They all infer the class of regular languages in the limit. The method is to obtain, for each word of the positive sample, at least an irreducible consistent automaton (the merging of any two states in it, makes the resulting automaton to accept negative words). The way to do it is merging states in the automaton that just recognizes the word. The method is flexible as things like the number of subautomata inferred for each word or the order of state merging can be changed without affecting to the convergence of the process. The experiments done clearly show that this method obtains better results than both the classical *RPNI* and *DeLeTe2* algorithms.

The article is structured as follows: After this introduction, section 2 contains some preliminary definitions and notation, section 3 contains the theoretical basis of the method while section 4 contains the method itself and section 5 contains two examples for better understanding of the method. Finally, the experiments done (section 6) and the conclusions (section 7) end the job.

2   Preliminary Definitions and Notation

2.1   Finite Automata

An *alphabet* is any non empty finite set of symbols. A word over an alphabet Σ is any finite sequence of symbols in Σ, the *empty word* is denoted as λ, Σ^* is the set of all the words over Σ, which is a *free monoid* under the concatenation of words. Given a word $x = uv$, with $u, v \in \Sigma^*$, u is called prefix of x. The set of the prefixes of x is called $Pr(x)$.

A *language* over Σ is any subset of Σ^*. The *concatenation* of two languages L_1 and L_2 will be denoted as $L_1 L_2$. The residual language of L associated to x is $x^{-1}L = \{y \in \Sigma^* | xy \in L\}$.

A *non deterministic finite automaton* (NFA) is a 5-tuple $\mathcal{A} = (Q, \Sigma, \delta, I, F)$, where Q is a finite set of states, Σ is an alphabet, $I, F \subseteq Q$ are respectively the set of initial and final states and $\delta : Q \times \Sigma \to 2^Q$ is the transition function, which will also be denoted as $\delta \subseteq Q \times \Sigma \times Q$.

Given $P \subseteq Q$ and $a \in \Sigma$, $\delta(P, a) = \bigcup_{q \in P} \delta(q, a)$. The function δ is extended to words writing $\delta(P, \lambda) = P$ and $\delta(P, xa) = \delta(\delta(P, x), a)$, for every $a \in \Sigma$, $x \in \Sigma^*$. The language accepted by $\mathcal{A}$ will be denoted as $L(\mathcal{A})$, that is, $L(\mathcal{A}) = \{x \in \Sigma^* : \delta(I, x) \cap F \neq \emptyset\}$. The *left language* of a state q with respect to $\mathcal{A}$ is $L_q = \{x \in \Sigma^* : q \in \delta(I, x)\}$. Two automata are equivalent if they accept the same language.

A finite automaton $\mathcal{A}$ is *deterministic* if $Card(I) = 1$ and for every state q and every symbol a, $Card(\delta(q, a)) \leq 1$.

A *subautomaton* of a non deterministic finite automaton $\mathcal{A} = (Q, \Sigma, \delta, I, F)$ is any finite automaton $\mathcal{A}' = (Q', \Sigma, \delta', I', F')$ where $Q' \subseteq Q$, $I' \subseteq I \cap Q'$, $F' \subseteq F \cap Q'$ and $\delta' \subseteq \delta \cap Q' \times \Sigma \times Q'$.

It is easily seen that if $\mathcal{A}'$ is a subautomaton of $\mathcal{A}$ then $L(\mathcal{A}') \subseteq L(\mathcal{A})$.

Given $\mathcal{A} = (Q, \Sigma, \delta, I, F)$ and $\mathcal{B} = (Q', \Sigma, \delta', I', F')$ the function $\varphi : Q \rightarrow Q'$ is a *homomorphism* from $\mathcal{A}$ to $\mathcal{B}$ if $\varphi(I) \subseteq I'$, $\varphi(F) \subseteq F'$ and $\varphi(\delta(q, a)) \subseteq \delta'(\varphi(q), a)$ for any q in Q and a in Σ.

The subautomaton of $\mathcal{B}$ induced by $\varphi(Q)$ is denoted as $\varphi(\mathcal{A})$. It follows that $L(\mathcal{A}) \subseteq L(\varphi(\mathcal{A})) \subseteq L(\mathcal{B})$.

The *merge* of states p and q in a finite automaton $\mathcal{A} = (Q, \Sigma, \delta, I, F)$ is defined as follows: $merge(\mathcal{A}, p, q) = (\varphi(Q), \Sigma, \delta', I', F')$ where $\varphi(q) = p$ and $\forall r \neq q, \varphi(r) = r$, also $I' = \varphi(I)$, $F' = \varphi(F)$ and $(r, a, s) \in \delta$ if and only if $(\varphi(r), a, \varphi(s)) \in \delta'$.

It follows that $L(\mathcal{A}) \subseteq L(merge(\mathcal{A}, p, q))$.

Given a language L, let $\mathsf{U} = \{u_1^{-1}L \cap \ldots \cap u_k^{-1}L : k \geq 0, u_1, \ldots, u_k \in \Sigma^*\}$. The *universal automaton* [1,2,7,9] for L is defined as $\mathcal{U} = (\mathsf{U}, \Sigma, \delta, I, F)$ with:

- $I = \{q \in \mathsf{U} : q \subseteq L\}$.
- $F = \{q \in \mathsf{U} : \lambda \in q\}$.
- The transition function is such that $q \in \delta(p, a)$ iff $q \subseteq a^{-1}p$.

Related to the universal automaton we have the following:

Theorem 1. *[2] Let $\mathcal{U} = (U, \Sigma, \delta, I, F)$ the universal automaton for $L \subseteq \Sigma^*$. Then:*

1. $L(\mathcal{U}) = L$.
2. *For any automaton $\mathcal{A} = (Q, \Sigma, \delta_{\mathcal{A}}, I_{\mathcal{A}}, F_{\mathcal{A}})$ such that $L(\mathcal{A}) \subseteq L$, the function $\varphi : Q \rightarrow U$ defined as $\varphi(q) = \bigcap_{u \in L_q} u^{-1}L$ is an automata homomorphism.*

2.2 Grammatical Inference

Grammatical inference is the discipline that deals with learning formal languages from either a positive or a complete sample.

A positive (resp. negative) sample of L is any finite set $D_+ \subseteq L$ (resp. $D_- \subseteq \overline{L}$). In the case it contains positive and negative words it will be denoted as (D_+, D_-).

An *inference algorithm* is an algorithm that on input of any sample outputs a representation of a language. The algorithm is *consistent* if the output contains D_+ and is disjoint with D_-.

The type of convergence that we will use in our algorithms was defined by Gold [5,6] and is called *identification in the limit*.

An algorithm A identifies a class of languages $\mathcal{L}$ by means of hypothesis in $\mathcal{H}$ *in the limit* if and only if for any $L \in \mathcal{L}$, and any presentation of L, the infinite sequence of hypothesis output by A converges to h such that $L(h) = L$, that is, there exists t_0 such that $(t \geq t_0 \Rightarrow h_t = h_{t_0} \wedge L(h_{t_0}) = L)$, where h_t denotes the hypothesis output by A after processing t examples.

One of the best known algorithms that identifies $\mathcal{L}_3$ (the family of regular languages) using deterministic finite automata is the *RPNI* (Regular positive and negative inference) [8]. Given a sample, the algorithm builds the prefix tree Moore machine, whose states are the prefixes of the sample and whose transitions are of the form $\delta(x, a) = xa$. An output 1, 0 or ? is assigned to every state depending whether it is associated to a positive sample, to a negative one or to a prefix of a word of the sample which is not itself a word of it. The algorithm merges every state with the previous ones in lexicographical order and propagates the merges to keep the determinism under the condition that no state with output 0 can be merged with a state with output 1. The merging of a state with output s with a state with output ? gives out a state with output s.

Among the recently proposed algorithms that output non deterministic finite automata is the algorithm *DeLeTe2* [3]. It outputs a special type of automata called *RFSA* (Residual finite state automaton). A finite automaton $\mathcal{A} = (Q, \Sigma, \delta, I, F)$ is a *RFSA* if for every $q \in Q$ the language $\{x | \delta(q, x) \cap F \neq \emptyset\}$ is a residual language of $L(A)$.

3   Subautomata Associated to a Word in a Language

Definition 1. *An automaton $\mathcal{A} = (Q, \Sigma, \delta, I, F)$ is irreducible in a regular language L if and only if $L(\mathcal{A}) \subseteq L$ and for any pair of states p and q in Q we have that $L(merge(\mathcal{A}, p, q)) - L \neq \emptyset$.*

Proposition 1. *Let $\mathcal{A} = (Q, \Sigma, \delta, I, F)$ irreducible in a regular language L. Then $\mathcal{A}$ is isomorphic to a subautomaton of $\mathcal{U}$, the universal automaton for L.*

Proof. Let $\varphi : Q \to \mathsf{U}$ the homomorphism of Theorem 1. As $\mathcal{A}$ is irreducible in L so is irreducible in $L(\mathcal{A})$. As $\mathcal{A}$ does not have mergible states φ is injective [4], then given states p and q in Q with $p \neq q$ it holds that $\varphi(p) \neq \varphi(q)$. The automaton $\varphi(\mathcal{A})$ induced in $\mathcal{U}$ by $\varphi(Q)$ is a subautomaton of $\mathcal{U}$. Let δ' the transition function of $\varphi(\mathcal{A})$ and let δ'' be the restriction of δ' such that for every q in Q and a in Σ, $\delta''(\varphi(q), a) = \varphi(\delta(q, a))$. The automaton $\mathcal{B} = (\varphi(Q), \Sigma, \delta'', \varphi(I), \varphi(F))$ is isomorphic to $\mathcal{A}$ and is a subautomaton of $\mathcal{U}$.

Definition 2. *A decomposition of a finite automaton $\mathcal{A}$ is any collection $(\mathcal{A}_i)_{i \in I}$ of subautomata of $\mathcal{A}$ such that $L(\mathcal{A}) = \bigcup_{i \in I} L(\mathcal{A}_i)$.*

Definition 3. *Given a word x, we will denote $\mathcal{A}_x$ the minimal deterministic finite automaton without useless states for the language $\{x\}$, that is, $\mathcal{A}_x = (Q, \Sigma, \delta, I, F)$ where $Q = Pr(x)$, $I = \{\lambda\}$, $F = \{x\}$ and for any u, ua in $Pr(x)$ $\delta(u, a) = ua$.*

Definition 4. *Let L be a language over the alphabet Σ and let $x \in L$. A subautomaton associated to x in L is any finite automaton $\mathcal{A}$ obtained by means of any sequence of state merging in $\mathcal{A}_x$ and such that $\mathcal{A}$ is irreducible in L.*

It is clear that for every automaton $\mathcal{A}$ associated to x in L, $x \in L(\mathcal{A})$.

Proposition 2. *Let L be a regular language and $x \in L$. A subautomaton associated to x in L can be obtained knowing a finite number of words in $\Sigma^* - L$.*

Proof. Let x be a word in L and let u, v, z be a factorization of x, that is, $x = uvz$. If the states related to u and to uv can not be merged, any word in $uv^*z - L$ will prevent to do so. If n is the number of states of $\mathcal{A}_x$, the number of words enough to guarantee that a subautomaton associated to x in L is obtained is bounded above by n^2.

Proposition 3. *Let L be a regular language. There exists a finite set M of words in L such that L is accepted by the NFA defined by the collection of subautomata associated to the words in M.*

Proof. As any subautomaton associated to any word in M is a subautomaton of $\mathcal{U}$, the collection of all the subautomata associated to the different words of L recognizes L. The finiteness is deduced from the fact that if $\mathcal{A}$ is the subautomaton of $\mathcal{U}$ associated to x in L and $y \in L - L(\mathcal{A})$, the subautomaton $\mathcal{A}'$ associated to y is different from $\mathcal{A}$. Then, as the number of subautomata of $\mathcal{U}$ is finite, M is finite.

4 A Family of Algorithms for Inference of $\mathcal{L}_3$ Using Non Deterministic Finite Automata

4.1 The Family WASRI

Based on the concepts that have been previously exposed, we describe now a family of algorithms that will be called *WASRI* (word associated subautomata regular inference). Every member of this family infers the class of regular languages in the limit and is described in Algorithm 1.

Algorithm 1. WASRI Scheme

Input: (D_+, D_-).
Output: *NFA* consistent with (D_+, D_-).
Method:
$\mathcal{A} = (Q, \Sigma, \delta, I, F)$ with $Q = \delta = I = F = \emptyset$
For every $x \in D_+$
    If $x \notin L(\mathcal{A})$
        Obtain at least a finite automaton irreducible for x in $\Sigma^* - D_-$.
        For every $\mathcal{A}' = (Q', \Sigma, \delta', I', F')$ so obtained, where $Q \cap Q' = \emptyset$
            $\mathcal{A} = (Q \cup Q', \Sigma, \delta \cup \delta', I \cup I', F \cup F')$
        End For
End For
Returns $(\mathcal{A})$
End

Theorem 2. *Any algorithm of the WASRI family infers the class of regular languages in the limit.*

Proof. Let $L \subseteq \Sigma^*$ and suppose we have a complete presentation of L. From Proposition 3, there exists a finite set of words in L that give a collection of subautomata that recognizes L, and for every word, the number of words in $\overline{L}$ needed to obtain those subautomata is also finite (Proposition 2), these two facts assure the convergence of the process, as after a finite amount of time those words will appear and L will be identified.

As it can be deduced from the above scheme, what will make the algorithms in *WASRI* differ from each other will be facts like:

- The number of subautomata which are inferred for each word.
- The order in the process of merging states in the way to obtain each subautomata.

Although it has been omitted in the above scheme an algorithm of the family may introduce a subsequent selection in the collection of automata obtained so far. For example, if we have obtained several automata for each word (using different merging order criteria), it is possible to select one or some of them (for example the smallest in size). Some of the automata in the output collection may also be eliminated, when the resulting automaton doing so still accepts D_+.

Let us see next the description of one of the most basic members of the family:

4.2 WASRI1

Let $D = (D_+, D_-)$ be a complete sample of the language, with $D_+ = \{x_1, ..., x_n\}$. The Algorithm 2 describes one of the elements of the family, that will be called *WASRI1*.

WASRI1 obtains a finite automaton $\mathcal{A}$ compatible with (D_+, D_-) in the following way: For every word $x \in D_+$ which is not recognized by the current automaton, it starts building $\mathcal{A}_x$ and obtains a subautomaton associated to x merging states in $\mathcal{A}_x$ following the lexicographical order, under the condition that the state merging does not make the resulting automaton to accept any of the negative samples. The subautomaton for that word is added to the current one.

Finally, it checks if the automaton resulting from the deletion of the subautomata obtained for any of the words of D_+ still recognizes D_+. If that is the case the subautomaton is effectively deleted.

The complexity of the algorithm *WASRI1* is $kn^2|D_-|$, where k is an integer, n is the length of the longest word of D_+ and $|D_-|$ is the sum of the lengths of the negative words of the sample. It is worth to mention that the temporal complexity depends on the length of every word and not on the sum of the lengths of the input (i. e. the size of the prefix tree acceptor of the sample). This fact makes *WASRI1* to run much faster, under the same conditions, than the rest of the algorithms that will be compared to it in this work.

If $\mathcal{A} = (Q, \Sigma, \delta, I, F)$ and $\mathcal{A}_i = (Q_i, \Sigma, \delta_i, I_i, F_i)$ by $\mathcal{A} = \mathcal{A} \cup \mathcal{A}_i$ we mean that the automaton $\mathcal{A}$ becomes $(Q \cup Q_i, \Sigma, \delta \cup \delta_i, I \cup I_i, F \cup F_i)$. Under the same conditions as before, by $\mathcal{A} = Delete(\mathcal{A}, \mathcal{A}_i)$, we mean that the automaton $\mathcal{A}$ becomes $(Q - Q_i, \Sigma, \delta - \delta_i, I - I_i, F - F_i)$.

Algorithm 2

WASRI1(D_+, D_-)
$\mathcal{A} = (Q, \Sigma, \delta, I, F)$ with $Q = \delta = I = F = \emptyset$
$list = \emptyset$
For $i = 1$ **to** $i = n$
If $x_i \notin L(\mathcal{A})$
    $\mathcal{A}_i = \mathcal{A}_{x_i}$ with $Q_i = \{q_{i_0}, ..., q_{i_m}\} = Pr(x_i)$
    For $j = 1$ **to** $j = m$
        For $k = 0$ **to** $k = j - 1$
            If $q_{i_k} \in Q_i$
                If $L(merge(\mathcal{A}_i, q_{i_k}, q_{i_j})) \cap D_- = \emptyset$
                Then $\mathcal{A}_i = merge(\mathcal{A}_i, q_{ik}, q_{ij})$
                End If
            End If
        End For
    End For
$\mathcal{A} = \mathcal{A} \cup \mathcal{A}_i$
$list = Add(list, \mathcal{A}_i)$
End For
For $i = 1$ **to** Length$(list)$
    If $D_+ \subseteq L(Delete(\mathcal{A}, \mathcal{A}_i))$ **Then** $\mathcal{A} = Delete(\mathcal{A}, \mathcal{A}_i)$
End For
Return$(\mathcal{A})$
End

---

5   Two Examples

We present in this section two examples of run for better understanding of *WASRI1*, the first one describes most of the situations that may appear in it, that is, besides the merging of states it reflects the fact that some of the input words may be recognized by the previous automaton and also the fact that some of the subautomata may be deleted and the automaton still recognizes D_+. The second is an example to show that this algorithm may treat some situations in a much more efficient way than the rest of algorithms that have been compared with it.

5.1   Example of Run

Let us suppose that the input to *WASRI1* is $D_+ = \{0, 000011, 001, 0101010\}$ and $D_- = \{01000010\}$.

We will describe the process of the word 0101010 as if this word were the first input to *WASRI1*. The automaton A_x for $x = 0101010$ is depicted in Fig. 1 (A). States 2,3 and 4 can be merged with state 1 as the resulting automaton does not accept the negative sample. The output to these first merges is in Fig. 1 (B). The next states that can be merged in lexicographical order are states 6 and 7, as the previous possible merges would give an automaton that accepts the

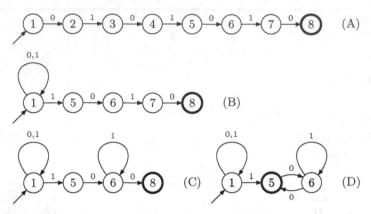

Fig. 1. Successive merges done by algorithm WASRI1 while processing the word 0101010 on input $D_+ = \{0101010, 0, 001, 000011\}$ and $D_- = \{01000010\}$

negative sample. The resulting automaton is Fig. 1 (C). Finally, merging states 5 and 8 gives automaton in Fig. 1 (D), which is minimal for this word.

Considering the complete input $D_+ = \{0, 000011, 001, 0101010\}$, the automaton for the first word 0 is in Fig. 2 (A), while Fig. 2 (B) and (C) are respectively the outputs for the words 000011 and 0101010. You should observe at this point that the word 001 produces no output as it is recognized by the current automaton so far (Fig. 2 (A) and (B)).

Finally, as the deletion of the automaton corresponding to the word 000011 still recognizes D_+, *WASRI1* algorithm outputs automata (A) and (C) in Fig.2.

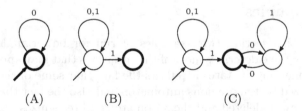

Fig. 2. Non deterministic automata on input $D_+ = \{0, 000011, 001, 0101010\}$ and $D_- = \{01000010\}$ before deleting superfluous automata.

5.2   A Nice Example

Let us suppose that the target language is $L = \{x \in 0^* : |x| \text{ is a multiple of } 2, 3 \text{ or } 5\}$. The minimal *DFA* for L has the same number of states than its canonical *RFSA* (30 states). If the input for *WASRI1* algorithm is $D_+ = \{0^2, 0^3, 0^5\}$ and $D_- = \{0, 0^{11}\}$, it outputs the automaton depicted in Fig. 3 which recognizes L, while algorithms like *RPNI* or *DeLeTe2* are far away from convergence with this input.

Fig. 3. Output automata given by WASRI on input $D_+ = \{0^2, 0^3, 0^5\}, D_- = \{0, 0^{11}\}$

6   Experiments

The aim of the experiments is to analyze the behavior of one of the implementations of the algorithm *WASRI* and to compare it with the *DeLeTe2* algorithm, which has been reported as to have a better behavior than the classical inference algorithms if the target automata are randomly generated as NFAs. We also include the recognition rates obtained by *RPNI* algorithm using the same set of experiments. Both the training/test samples and the *DeLeTe2* program used in these experiments are provided by their authors and are available at Aurélien Lemay's web page http://www.grappa.univlille3.fr/~lemay/.

Two kinds of experiments are reported in Table 1, depending on the source of the training and test samples: er_* if they come from regular expressions and nfa_* from NFAs. The number in the identifier of the experiment represents the number of training samples. Each experiment consists of 30 different languages to be learned and has 1000 test samples. Table 1 reports the recognition rate and the average size of the inferred hypothesis. These results are calculated as follows: each test sample is presented to the inference program, the program tags the sample as belonging to the target language or not, if this classification agrees with the real sample tag, the sample is considered correct and increases a counter; at the end, the number of correct samples is divided by 1000 (the total of test samples) and this value is reported as recognition rate. The average size is computed adding up the number of states of the 30 hypothesis generated in each experiment and dividing by 30.

The algorithm implemented for experiments obtains, for every word in D_+, two automata: The first one is obtained applying *WASRI1* (the order is lexicographical and every state tries to get merged with the previous ones). The

Table 1. Inference results with *RPNI*, *DeLeTe2* and *Wasri* algorithms

Iden.	RPNI		DeLeTe2		WASRI	
	Recogn. rate	Avg. size	Recogn. rate	Avg. size	Recogn. rate	Avg. size
er_50	76.36%	9.63	81.3%	32.43	89.15%	15,93
er_100	80.61%	14.16	91.4%	30.73	93.0%	25,36
er_150	84.46%	15.43	92.0%	60.96	95.88%	25,73
er_200	91.06%	13.3	95.7%	47.73	95.79%	35,5
nfa_50	64.8%	14.3	69.3%	71.26	74,76%	39,3
nfa_100	68.25%	21.83	74.4%	149.13	76.46%	79,83
nfa_150	71.21%	28.13	76.7%	218.26	77.27%	121,1
nfa_200	71.74%	33.43	78.9%	271.3	81.16%	148,13

second uses the same algorithm with an inverse order (the word x_i corresponds to state q_{i_0} and λ to state q_{i_m}). Once the whole set D_+ has been processed, the algorithm outputs the automata with less number of states.

Table 1 resumes the recognition rates and the average size of the automata obtained by the three algorithms to be compared, that is, *RPNI*, *DeLeTe2* and *WASRI*. As it can be seen, the recognition rates obtained by *WASRI* are higher than those obtained by the other algorithms. It can also be seen that the number of states of the automata obtained by *WASRI* is smaller than those obtained by *DeLeTe2*.

7   Conclusions

We describe in this paper a family of algorithms that, each one of them, infers the class of regular languages in the limit. We have made the same experiments as in [3] to compare the error rate and the size of the output automata of one of the algorithms of the family, the *WASRI1*, with the results obtained by the algorithm *DeLeTe2*. The results obtained by *WASRI1* are better both in error rate as in smaller size of the output.

Some work needs to be done to complete the comparisons. It has been reported in [3] that *RPNI* behaves better than *DeLeTe2* when the source of the target language is generated in a deterministic way. The comparisons between *RPNI* and *WASRI1* remain to be done with this type of source. Also, some effort to characterize the type of the output produced by our algorithm would probably lead us to determine some languages for which its performance might not be so good.

References

1. Arnold, A. Dicky, A. Nivat, M. *A note about minimal non-deterministic automata.* Bull. EATCS 47, pp 166-169, 1970.
2. Carrez, C. *On the minimalization of non-deterministic automata.* Laboratoire de Calcul de la Faculté des Sciences de L'Université de Lille, 1970.
3. Denis, F. Lemay, A. and Terlutte, A. *Learning regular languages using RFSAs.* Theoretical Computer Science 313(2), pp 267-294 (2004).
4. García, P. and Vazquez de Parga, M. *A Note about mergible states in large NFA.* Bull. of the EATCS 87 pp. 181-184 (2005).
5. Gold, E.M. *Language identification in the limit.* Information and Control 10, pp 447-474 (1967).
6. Gold, E.M. *Complexity of Automaton Identification from Given Data.* Information and Control 37, pp 302-320 (1978).
7. Lombardy, S. *Approche structurelle de quelques problémes de la théorie des automates.* Ph.D. Thesis, Ecole N.S. des Télécomunications. (2001).
8. Oncina, J. and García, P. *Inferring Regular Languages in Polynomial Updated Time.* In Pattern Recognition and Image Analysis. Pérez de la Blanca, Sanfeliú and Vidal (Eds.) World Scientific (1992).
9. Polák, L. *Minimalizations of NFA using the universal automaton.* LNCS 3317 pp 325-326 (2005).

XSLT Version 2.0 Is Turing-Complete: A Purely Transformation Based Proof

Ruhsan Onder and Zeki Bayram

Department of Computer Engineering and Internet Technologies Research Center
Eastern Mediterranean University
Famagusta, Cyprus
{ruhsan.onder, zeki.bayram}@emu.edu.tr
http://cmpe.emu.edu.tr/ruhsan/
http://cmpe.emu.edu.tr/bayram/

Abstract. XSLT version 2.0 has the full power of a Turing machine, i.e. it is "Turing-complete." We show this is so by implementing a universal Turing machine emulator stylesheet in XSLT. We use only the constructs available in the official XSLT version 2.0 recommendation of the World Wide Web Consortium. Furthermore, we do not resort to string functions (which are also available in XSLT) but rather rely on the innate transformational capabilities of XSLT.

1 Introduction

Recently, we showed that XSLT can be used as an interpreter for a simple imperative language [1]. Here, we show that XSLT can be used to implement the functionality of a universal Turing machine.

Formally, a Turing machine (TM) is denoted M=$(Q, \Sigma, \Gamma, \delta, q_0, B, F)$ where Q is a finite set of states, Σ is the set of *input symbols*, Γ is the set of tape symbols, δ is a mapping from QxΓ to QxΓx$\{L, R\}$, $q_0 \in Q$ is the *start state*, B is the *blank symbol* and $F \subseteq Q$ is the set of final states [2]. A *universal Turing machine* accepts the language {<M,w> | M is an encoding of a TM, w is an encoding of the input to M, and M accepts w}. A programming language or any other logical system is called *Turing-complete* if it has a computational power equivalent to a universal Turing machine. In other words, the system and the universal Turing machine can emulate each other [3].

2 The "Universal Turing Machine Emulator Stylesheet" UTMES

UTMES is an XSLT version 2.0 [4] stylesheet. It takes as input an XML encoded definition of a TM that accepts by final state, as well as the input for the TM, and "runs" the TM on the provided input, making use of the temporary tree construct of XSLT version 2.0. This proves the Turing-completeness of XSLT version 2.0.

The specification of a TM is structured under a <TM> root which has <Spec> and <input> elements. The <Spec> element has the state set, input symbols, tape symbols, start state, blank symbol, final states and transition function specifications as sub-elements. The transition rules in the <TransitionFunction> element are enclosed

O.H. Ibarra and H.-C. Yen (Eds.): CIAA 2006, LNCS 4094, pp. 275–276, 2006.

in `<Delta>` elements, having `@CurrentState`, `@read`, `@NextState`, `@write` and `@direction` attributes, which indicate the current state, symbol read from tape, next state, the symbol to overwrite the symbol read and the direction that the tape head will move (left or right), respectively.

UTMES transforms the TM specification, together with its initial input, into an internal format, which represents the instantaneous description (ID) [2] of the TM in its initial configuration. Execution then proceeds by successively generating a new ID, using the current ID and the transition function of the TM. The full code of our implementation, documentation, as well as sample Turing machines can be found at [5].

In related work, there have been several approaches to proving Turing-completeness of XSLT version 1.0. Kepser [6] coded *mu-recursive* functions in XSLT, which are themselves Turing-complete. Lyons [7] implemented a universal TM which takes the initial tape as an input *string* parameter from the command line at execution time. Korlyukov [8] used the transformation oriented approach with recursive templates like we did, but made use of non-standard features of the XML processor *XT* developed by Clark [9].

3   Conclusion

We showed the Turing-completeness of XSLT version 2.0, by developing an XSLT stylesheet, called UTMES, that emulates a universal Turing machine using only native XSL transformations (as opposed to non-standard features or string manipulation functions). XSLT version 2.0 is backwards compatible with version 1.0, and previous completeness results for XSLT 1.0 generally apply to version 2.0. However, our work seems to be the only one so far that shows the Turing-completeness of the *official* XSLT version 2.0 recommendation of the W3C using a *purely transformation based approach*.

References

1. Onder, R., Bayram, Z.: Interpreting imperative programming languages in XSLT. In: Proceedings of the Ninth IASTED International conference on Internet and Multimedia Systems and Applications (EuroIMSA2005), IASTED (2005) 131–136
2. Hopcroft, J., Motwani, R., Ullman, J.: Introduction to Automata Theory, Languages, and Computation. Addison-Wesley (2001)
3. Brainerd, W., Landweber, L.: Theory of Computation. Wiley (1974)
4. Michael Kay (Editor): XSL transformations (XSLT) version 2.0 of W3C working draft. Available at http://www.w3.org/TR/xslt20 (2005)
5. Onder, R., Bayram, Z.: Universal Turing Machine Emulator Stylesheet UTMES. Available at http://itrc.emu.edu.tr (2006)
6. Kepser, S.: A simple proof for the Turing-completeness of XSLT and XQuery. In: Proceedings of the Extreme Markup Languages, Montreal, Quebec. (2004)
7. Lyons, B.: Universal Turing machine in XSLT. Available at http://www.unidex.com/turing/utm.htm (2001)
8. Korlyukov, A.: Turing machine. Available at http://www.refal.net/~korlukov/tm/ (2001)
9. Clark, J.: XT: an XSLT processor in Java. Available at http://www.blnz.com/xt/index.html (2002)

A Finite Union of DFAs in Symbolic Model Checking of Infinite Systems

(Extended Abstract)

Suman Roy[1] and Bhaskar Chakraborty[2],[*]

[1] Honeywell Technology Solutions Lab. (HTSL),
151/1, Doraisanipalya, Bannerghatta Road, Bangalore 560 076, India
suman.roy@honeywell.com
[2] Indian Statistical Institute
203 Barrackpore Trunk Road, Kolkata 700108, India
2bhaskar@gmail.com

We address the model-checking problem of *viz. communicating finite-state machines* (in short, CFSMs) [1,2,6], an infinite system which are modelled as a collection of finite state automata communicating messages through FIFO queues. Several verification methods have been developed for CFSMs. Since all interesting verification problems are undecidable [4], there is in general no completely automatic verification procedure for this class of systems.

Generally state-space exploration techniques are used for verifying properties of CFSMs; they spread the reachability information along the transitions of the system to be analyzed. The exploration process starts with the initial global state of the system, and tries at every step to enlarge its current set of reachable states by propagating these states through transitions. The search terminates when a stable set is reached, *i.e.*, for every control state, the new queue contents are included in the current ones associated with that control state. In order to use this state-space exploration paradigm for verifying properties of systems with infinite state spaces, one needs a finite representation for an infinite sets of states, as well as a search technique that can explore an infinite number of states in a finite amount of time. A solution to the first problem is to use global state by representing the control part *explicitly* and the queue contents *symbolically*. To solve the second problem, techniques such as, *meta-transitions* [2] or *accelerations* [6] have been used.

We use a Finite Union of Deterministic Finite Automata (FUDFA) to represent (possibly infinite) set of queue contents as introduced in [8]. Quite a few operations needed to symbolically analyze such systems can be implemented on the union of DFAs in polynomial time. The advantage gained by this approach is that the inclusion between finite unions DFAs can be checked efficiently. In [9], it was showed that FUDFAs can be used for the forward and backward reachability analysis of the systems. It also lifts this approach for the case of a CFSM with n queues. Using this fact a generic algorithm for reachability analysis

---

[*] The author did this work when he was a summer intern at HTSL, Bangalore during May-July'05.

O.H. Ibarra and H.-C. Yen (Eds.): CIAA 2006, LNCS 4094, pp. 277–278, 2006.
© Springer-Verlag Berlin Heidelberg 2006

parameterized by a set of cycles Θ was defined. Finally we implement a state space search algorithm using FUDFAs as the representation of queue contents for a version of Alternating Bit Protocol. For this we developed our own library in C for symbolic manipulation of DFAs.

We also formulate a partial decision procedure based on this reachability analysis for model checking LTL-formulas. We know that the LTL model-checking problem is undecidable for CFSMs [1]. We adapt a partial decision procedure from [3]. We build a Büchi automaton $\mathcal{B}_{\neg\Pi}$ for the negation (complement) of the LTL formula Π. We compute the product of the protocol P (which is modelled by a CFSM) and $\mathcal{B}_{\neg\Pi}$. The result is a protocol enhanced by a set of accepting states. We call such a machine *Büchi automaton with queues*. The property Π is satisfied by every run of P if and only if the set of accepting runs of $\mathcal{B}_{P,\neg\Pi}$ is empty. An accepting run of $\mathcal{B}_{P,\neg\Pi}$ is a run containing an infinite number of occurrences of some accepting control state c, the queue contents at each visit to c being allowed to vary. Since it is impossible to check all the runs of $\mathcal{B}_{P,\neg\Pi}$, our procedure will search for only runs containing an infinite number of occurrences of c produced by the infinite execution of a sequence of transitions forming a cycle from c to c. We use a testing procedure for checking the unboundedness of queue contents following a a result by Jérone. In [7] Jéron has developed a semi-decision procedure to check whether some sequences can be infinitely repeated for transition systems representing CFSMs. This reduces the model checking problem to calculating few derivative operations [5] for regular languages.

References

1. Abdulla, P., A., Jonsson, B.: Undecidable Verification Problems for Programs with Unreliable Channels. In: Proc. ICALP-94, **vol. 820**, LNCS, Springer-Verlag, (1994) 316-327.
2. Boigelot, B., Godefroid, P.: Symbolic Verification of Communication Protocols with Infinite State Spaces using QDDs. In: Proc. 8th Conferences on Computer Aided Verification. LNCS Springer-Verlag. vol. **1102** (1996) 1–12.
3. Boigelot, B., Godefroid, P., Willems, P., Wolper, P.: The power of QDDS. In: Proc. 4th Intl.Symp. of Static Analysis, Paris, vol. **1302**, LNCS, (1997) 172-186.
4. Brand, D., Zafiropulo, P.: On Communicating Finite-state Machines. Journal of the ACM. **2(5)** (1983) 323–342.
5. Brzozowski, J. A.: Derivatives of Regular Expressions. Journal of the ACM. **11(4)** (1964) 481–494.
6. Finkel, A., Purushothaman Iyer, S., Sutre, G.: Well-Abstracted Transition Systems: Application to FIFO Automata. In: Proc. 11th Int. Conf.on Concurrency Theory (CONCOUR 2000), USA, LNCS Springer vol. **1877** (2000). Also, Information and Computation **181(1)** (2003) 1–31.
7. Jéron, T.: Testing for unboundedness of FIFO Channels. Theoretical Computer Science, **113**, (1993) 93-117.
8. Roy, S.: A Symbolic Representation of Unbounded Queue Contents by a Finite Union of DFAs. In: International Workshop AVIS (ETAPS), Warsaw, (2003).
9. Roy, S.: Symbolic Verification of Infinite Systems using a Finite Union of DFAs. In: 2nd IEEE International Conference on Software Engineering and Formal Methods (SEFM), Beijing, September (2004).

Universality of Hybrid Quantum Gates and Synthesis Without Ancilla Qudits

Guowu Yang[1,2], Fei Xie[1], Xiaoyu Song[3], and Marek Perkowski[3]

[1] Dept. of Computer Science, Portland State University, Portland, OR 97207, USA
[2] School of Computer Science and Engineering, University of Electronic Science and Technology of China, Chengdu, Sichuan 610054, China
[3] Dept. of ECE, Portland State University, Portland, OR 97207, USA

Abstract. This paper investigates the synthesis of quantum networks built to realize hybrid switching circuits in the absence of ancilla qudits. We prove that all mixed qudit, binary/ternary, circuits can be constructed by hybrid Not and Multiple-Controlled-Not gates without any ancilla qudits.

1 Introduction

Quantum computation quantum information theory have become one of most interesting and productive fields [1]. Computer and communication systems using quantum effects have remarkable efficient properties [1,2,3]. Recently, Hybrid quantum computing is studied [4]. Multiple-qudit gates, such as Not, Swap, and hybrid Toffoli gates are studied in [2,3,4,5]. But the universality of these gates and synthesis arbitary hybrid circuits by these gates without ancilla qudits are not studied.

In this paper, we constructively prove that hybrid Not and Multiple-Controlled-Not gates are universal to realize all hybrid reversible circuits. Based on this proof process, a construction based synthesis algorithm for any hybrid reversible circuits is proposed in our technique report [6].

2 Universality of Hybrid Reversible Gates

This section begins by presenting some basic definitions of hybrid reversible switching gates and we prove that hybrid Not gate and Multiple-Controlled-Not gate are universal for realization of arbitrary hybrid reversible circuits without using ancilla qudits.

Definition 1 (Hybrid reversible function). *Let $B = \{0, 1\}$, $T = \{0, 1, 2\}$. A hybrid logic function f with n input variables, $A_1, \ldots, A_n$, and n output variables, $P_1, \ldots, P_n$, is denoted by $f : T^{n_1} \times B^{n_2} \to T^{n_1} \times B^{n_2}$, where $n = n_1 + n_2, n_1 \geq 1, n_2 \geq 1$, A_i and P_i are ternary variables when $1 \leq i \leq n_1$, A_i and P_i are binary variables when $n_1 + 1 \leq i \leq n_1 + n_2$. There are $2^{n_1} \times 3^{n_2}$ different n-dimension hybrid assignments for the input vectors. A hybrid logic*

O.H. Ibarra and H.-C. Yen (Eds.): CIAA 2006, LNCS 4094, pp. 279–280, 2006.
© Springer-Verlag Berlin Heidelberg 2006

function f is reversible if it is a one-to-one and onto function (bijection), called $((n_1, 3), (n_2, 2))$ hybrid reversible circuit. A hybrid reversible logic circuit is also called a hybrid reversible gate when it is used to synthesize other hybrid reversible circuits. There are a total of $(3^{n_1} \times 2^{n_2})!$ different n-qudit hybrid reversible functions.

Definition 2 (Hybrid Not gate). *A hybrid Not gate N_j is defined as: $P_j = A_j \oplus_3 1$, where $\oplus_3$ denotes addition modulo 3, if $1 \leq j \leq n_1$; $P_j = A_j \oplus_2 1$ if $n_1 + 1 \leq j \leq n_1 + n_2$; $P_i = A_i$, if $i \neq j$.*

Definition 3 ('$(n-1)$'-Controlled-Not hybrid gate). *A '$(n-1)$'-Controlled-Not hybrid gate C_j, briefly called '$(n-1)$'-CNot gate, is defined as :*

If $m \neq j$, then $P_m = C_j(A_m) = A_m$. If $m = j$, and if $A_1 = \ldots = A_{n_1} = 2$, and $A_{n_1+1} = \ldots = A_{n_1+n_2} = 1$, then $P_j = C_j(A_j) = A_j \oplus_3 1$ if $1 \leq j \leq n_1$, or $P_j = C_j(A_j) = A_j \oplus_2 1$ if $n_1 + 1 \leq j \leq n_1 + n_2$; else, $P_j = A_j$.

Theorem 1. *All n-bit ($n \geq 2$) hybrid reversible functions can be realized by using Not and '$(n - 1)$'-CNot gates without ancilla qudits. And the number of ternary '$(n - 1)$'-CNot gates is no more than $14n_1 \times 3^{n_1} \times 2^{n_2}$, the number of binary '$(n - 1)$'-CNOT gates is no more than $2n_2 \times 3^{n_1} \times 2^{n_2}$, the number of ternary Not gates is no more than $6n \times n_1 \times 3^{n_1} \times 2^{n_2}$, and the number of binary Not gates is no more than $4n \times n_2 \times 3^{n_1} \times 2^{n_2}$.*

Theorem 2. *The computational complexity of our synthesis algorithm is no higher than $n(2n + 1)3^{n_1} \times 2^{n_2}$.*

Remark 1. The computational complexity of breadth-first search based synthesis algorithm is greater than $(3^{n_1} \times 2^{n_2})!$, because in the worst case, it at least needs to compute all $(3^{n_1} \times 2^{n_2})!$ reversible circuits. In fact, it also has to do a lot of comparisons of equality to determine whether the calculated circuit is the given circuit or not. Therefore, the computational complexity of our construction based synthesis algorithm is exponentially lower than any breadth-first search based synthesis algorithm.

References

1. M. Nielsen and I. Chuang, *Quantum Computation and Quantum Information*, Cambridge Univ. Press (2000).
2. H. B. Pasquinucci and A. Peres, *Quantum Cryptography with 3-state Systems*, Phys. Rev. Lett. 85 (2000) 3313.
3. S. S. Bullock, D. P. O'Leary and G. K. Brennen, *Asymptotically Optimal Quantum Circuits for d-level Systems*, Physical Review Letters, volume 94, 230502 (2005).
4. J. Daboul, X. Wang and B. C Sanders, *Quantum gates on hybrid qudits*, Journal of Physics A: Mathematical and General, 36 (2003), 2525-2536.
5. G. Yang, X. Song, M. A. Perkowski, and J. Wu, *Realizing Ternary Quantum Switching Networks without Ancilla Bits*, Journal of Physics A: Mathematical and General, 38(2005) 9689-9697.
6. G. Yang, F. Xie, X. Song, and M. A. Perkowski, *Universality of Hybrid Quantum Gates and Synthesis without Ancilla Qudits*, Technique report. http://www.cecs.pdx.edu/guowu/.

Reachability Analysis of Procedural Programs with Affine Integer Arithmetic*

Michael Luttenberger

Institute for Formal Methods in Computer Science, University of Stuttgart
luttenml@informatik.uni-stuttgart.de

Abstract. We present a tool for reachability analysis of procedural programs whose statements consist of affine equations and inequations. We use finite automata for representing the possibly infinite sets of stack configurations and memory valuations.

Let $\wp$ be any procedural program with the following restrictions: (1) variables take only integer ($\mathbb{Z}$) values, (2) every right-hand side of an assignment is an affine equation over $\mathbb{Z}$, (3) every condition of an if-statement or a while-loop is a boolean combination of affine inequations over $\mathbb{Z}$. A *configuration* of $\wp$ consists of a string of labels $l_0 l_1 \ldots l_n$ and a sequence of memory valuations $\sigma_0 \sigma_1 \ldots \sigma_n$ where l_0 is the label of the statement to be executed next, l_1 to l_n are labels marking re-entry points, σ_0 describes the values of the variables in scope at l_0 before the execution of l_0, and σ_1 to σ_n describe the memory contents saved on the stack. Given a set of configurations $\mathcal{C}_0$, we are interested in calculating all reachable successors (post*($\mathcal{C}_0$)) or predecessors (pre*($\mathcal{C}_0$)). As it is in general undecidable, whether a given configuration is reachable from $\mathcal{C}_0$, we only give an algorithm which calculates in each step a subset of reachable states but may not terminate. We use the framework of *weighted pushdown systems* introduced in [1] for representing $\wp$, allowing us to apply the algorithms mentioned there.

Definition 1. *A* pushdown system (PDS) *is a tuple* (Q, Γ, Δ) *where* Q *and* Γ *are finite sets and* Δ *is a relation between* $Q \times \Gamma$ *and* $Q \times \bigcup_{k \leq 0} \Gamma^k$. *The elements of* Δ *are called* rules. *A* weighted PDS (wPDS) (Q, Γ, Δ, w) *is a PDS* (Q, Γ, Δ) *extended with a function* $w : \Delta \to \mathcal{S}$ *which assigns to each rule of* Δ *a weight in the set* $\mathcal{S}$.

For translating $\wp$ into a wPDS $\mathcal{P}$, let $\mathcal{V}$ be the set of variables used in $\wp$. We introduce additional variable identifiers $\mathcal{V}' := \{x' \mid x \in \mathcal{V}\}$, $\mathcal{V}_s := \{x_s \mid x \in \mathcal{V}\}$, $\mathcal{V}'_s := \{x'_s \mid x \in \mathcal{V}\}$. $x \in \mathcal{V}$ is used for representing the value of the variable x before a given statement is executed, x' for its value after execution. Similarly, we use x_s and x'_s for the values of x saved in the top-most activation record (σ_1). Assume that a procedure call (1) proc(x); (1') ... in $\wp$ where l, l' are unique labels. Further assume, that x and y are the local variables in scope at l. Let the first statement of the procedure proc(z) be labeled by l_p, and let l_{wb} be an unused label up to now. We then represent this procedure call by two

---

* Partially funded by the DFG project Algorithms for Software Model Checking.

rules $r_{\text{call}} = (q, l, q, l_p l_{\text{wb}})$ and $r_{\text{wb}} = (q, l_{\text{wb}}, q, l')$. We assign r_{call} the relation $w(r_{\text{call}}) = \{(x, y, z', y'_s) \mid z' = x \wedge y'_s = y\}$, and set $w(r_{\text{wb}})$ to $\{(z, y_s, x', y') \mid x' = z \wedge y' = y_s\}$. We only include those variables in the relation $w(l)$ which are read or written by l. $\mathcal{S}$ therefore becomes the set of relations over the variables $\mathcal{V} \cup \mathcal{V}' \cup \mathcal{V}_s \cup \mathcal{V}'_s$ definable by Presburger formulae.

We instantiate the algorithms of [1] in order to calculate $\text{post}^*(\mathcal{C}_0)$, resp. $\text{pre}^*(\mathcal{C}_0)$. For this, we need an operation which, given two statements represented by the rules r_1, r_2, calculates the weight representing their serial execution. In our case, this becomes the concatenation of relations where we have to take into account that the relations only describe the changes of variables accessed by the represented statement. In the case of post^*, we additionally need an unary operator for restricting the values on which a procedure call is evaluated (cf. [2]). We finally require that $\mathcal{C}_0$ can be represented as a $\mathcal{P}$-automaton:

Definition 2. *Let $\mathcal{P} = (Q, \Gamma, \Delta, w)$ be a wPDS. $\mathcal{A} = (Z, \Gamma, \delta, Q, F, g)$ is a (weighted) $\mathcal{P}$-automaton where Z is the set of states, a finite superset of Q, $F \subseteq Z$ is the set of final states, Q is the set of initial states, $\delta \subseteq Z \times \Gamma \times Z$ is the transition relation, and $g : \delta \to \mathcal{S}$ assigns each transition a weight in $\mathcal{S}$. $z' \notin Q$ hast to hold for $(z, a, z') \in \delta$. $\mathcal{C}(\mathcal{A})$ denotes the set of configurations represented by $\mathcal{A}$.*

With this at hand, we get the following result for post^*, and similarly for pre^*:

Theorem 1. *Given a wPDS $\mathcal{P}$ and a $\mathcal{P}$-automaton $\mathcal{A}$ representing the set $\mathcal{C}_0$ of initial configurations, the algorithms of [1] calculate a sequence $(\mathcal{A}_i)_{i \in \mathbb{N}}$ of $\mathcal{P}$-automata with either $\mathcal{C}(\mathcal{A}_i) \subsetneq \mathcal{C}(\mathcal{A}_{i+1}) \subseteq \text{post}^*(\mathcal{C}_0)$ or $\mathcal{C}(\mathcal{A}_i) = \mathcal{C}(\mathcal{A}_{i+1}) = \text{post}^*(\mathcal{C}_0)$. In the latter case the algorithm terminates.*

We use *number decision diagrams (NDD)*, a subclass of finite automata (cf. [3]) for compactly representing the elements of $\mathcal{S}$. We have implemented our own NDD-library, as we needed to support the operations described above. Special care was taken for an efficient implementation of these operations, especially in the case of concatenation (cf. [2]). Further, we adapted the technique of path compression used for BDDs, which allows us to dispense with states of a NDD that do not carry any information (in the sense that they have exactly one successor). We have implemented these algorithms in a tool. As a case study we computed the complete input-output relation of a faulty quicksort-implementation allowing us to locate the error ([2]).

References

1. Reps, T., Schwoon, S., Jha, S.: Weighted pushdown systems and their application to interprocedural dataflow analysis. In: Proceedings of SAS '03. (2003)
2. Luttenberger, M.: Reachability analysis of procedural programs with affine integer arithmetic. Technical report, Universität Stuttgart (2006) http://www.fmi.uni-stuttgart.de/szs/tools/bnddwpds/.
3. Wolper, P., Boigelot, B.: On the construction of automata from linear arithmetic constraints. In: Proceedings of TACAS '00. (2000)

Lexical Disambiguation with Polarities and Automata

Guillaume Bonfante, Joseph Le Roux, and Guy Perrier

Universités de Nancy

Abstract. We propose a method for lexical disambiguation based on polarities for Interaction Grammars (IGs), well suited for coordination.

1 Introduction

We deal with lexical disambiguation using lexicalized IGs[2]. An IG is defined by a lexicon which associates to every word a set of lexical items specifying its grammatical behaviors. The number of lexical selections for a sentence is the product of the number of lexical entries for each word.

Lexical items are polarized. They may be seen as bags of polarized features and this simplification, as an abstraction. In the abstract grammar, parsing amounts to counting polarities and we use it to filter the initial grammar because of a homomorphism, presented in [1], from the initial to the abstract grammar: every parse in the former is transposed in a parse in the latter.

2 Interaction Grammars

IGs are based on *underspecification*, expressed by using *tree descriptions* rather than trees, and *polarities*. Polarized features decorating nodes express valences: positive (resp. negative) features represent available (resp. expected) resources. Syntactic composition consists of superposing tree descriptions while respecting polarities: a negative feature must encounter a dual positive feature to be neutralized. A feature is a triple (f, p, v) such that f is a feature name taken from $\mathcal{F}$, v is a finite disjunction $(v_1 | \ldots | v_n)$ of atoms and p is a polarity from $\{\rightarrow, \leftarrow, =\}$.

3 Polarity Automata

We first need a function p_D that count polarities in a description for particular f and v. We assign $+1$ to $\rightarrow$, -1 to $\leftarrow$ and 0 to $=$ or if a the value is not present in a description. Feature values being disjunctions, this function returns the set of all possible countings. It can be shown that it is a $\mathbb{Z}$ interval.

Let $w_1 \ldots w_n$ be a sentence to parse with an IG G given by its lexicon Lex_G. For each word w_i we know $Lex_G(w_i) = \{D_{i,1} \ldots D_{i,k_i}\}$. A *lexical selection* is a sequence $S = D_{1,s_1} \ldots D_{n,s_n}$, where $D_{i,s_i} \in Lex_G(w_i)$. We extend function p to selections as the sum of p_D for all D in S.

Here is the a *global neutrality criterion* (GNC) verified by valid selections: if a selection S is valid, for every f and v then $0 \in p_S(f, v)$.

O.H. Ibarra and H.-C. Yen (Eds.): CIAA 2006, LNCS 4094, pp. 283–284, 2006.

Polarity Automata. For any $f \in \mathcal{F}$ and value v, the automaton $A(f, v)$ is defined as follows. States are pairs (i, p), where i represents the position between w_i and w_{i+1} and p is an interval of $\mathbb{Z}$ which represents the counting of polarities. Transitions have the form $(i, p) \xrightarrow{D_{i+1, s_k}} (i + 1, q)$, where q is a $\mathbb{Z}$ interval of the sums of any element of p added to any element of $p_{D_{i+1, s_k}}(f, v)$. The initial state is $(0, \{0\})$ and accepting states are (n, p) such that $0 \in p$.

A lexical selection accepted by $A(f, v)$ verifies GNC. Hence, the intersection of polarity automata contains the good solutions. Furthermore, a (bad) lexical selection not contained in all initial automata will disappear from the intersection. Actually, this process pursues the filtering.

Selection of Feature Values. If a value does not appear with an active ($\rightarrow$ or $\leftarrow$) polarity in any description, the automaton will not filter. So, the first optimization is to consider only values with active polarity within some descriptions.

Then, the size of the automaton depends on the choice of the value. If $v \subseteq v'$ the automaton for v will be larger than the one for v'. So we order feature values.

Let us pay attention to maximal values for that order. If $v \cap v' \neq \emptyset$ then $A(f, v \cup v')$ may be smaller than $A(f, v)$ and $A(f, v')$. As a conclusion, we add any value $v1 \cup v2$ such that $v_1 \cap v_2 \neq \emptyset$ until we reach a fix point.

Refinement. Coordination shows so much ambiguity that GNC is not sufficient but we can take advantage of the syntactic modelisation. Two conjoinable segments must be on the left and on the right of a coordination and have the same active polarities. We can show that if D_i is associated with a coordination for two segments between position h and j then we have the following invariants: $\sum_{n=1}^{i} p_{D_n}(f, v) = \sum_{n=1}^{h-1} p_{D_n}(f, v)$ and $\sum_{n=1}^{j} p_{D_n}(f, v) = \sum_{n=1}^{i-1} p_{D_n}(f, v)$.

Our invariants can be applied on states. For every transition t labelled with a coordination from (i, p) to $(i + 1, q)$ in $A(f, v)$ we check that: (1) there exists (h, q) in the path from the initial state to (i, p) and (2) there exists (k, p) in the path from $(i+1, q)$ to a final state. If these states cannot be found, the transition t should be removed.

4   Conclusion

We presented a symbolic method for lexical selection. We used IGs but this method can be extended to other formalisms, see [1]. We also go beyond a simple counting of polarities by incorporating syntactical information for coordination.

References

1. G. Bonfante, B. Guillaume, and G. Perrier. Polarization and abstraction of grammatical formalisms as methods for lexical disambiguation. In *20th Conference on Computational Linguistics, CoLing'2004, Genève, Switzerland*, pages 303–309, 2004.
2. G. Perrier. La sémantique dans les grammaires d'interaction. *Traitement Automatique des Langues*, 45(3):123–144, 2004.

Parsing Computer Languages with an Automaton Compiled from a Single Regular Expression

Adrian D. Thurston

Software Technology Laboratory, Queen's University, Kingston, Canada
thurston@cs.queensu.ca

When a programmer is faced with the task of producing a parser for a context-free language there are many tools to choose from. We find that programmers avoid such tools when making parsers for simpler, domain-specific computer languages, such as file formats, communication protocols and end-user inputs. Since these languages often meet the criteria for regular languages, the extra run-time effort required for supporting the recursive nature of context-free languages is wasted.

Existing parsing tools based on regular expressions such as Lex, TLex, Re2C, Sed, Awk and Perl focus on building parsers by combining small regular expressions using some form of program logic. For example, Lex defines a token sequence model. None of these tools support the construction of an entire parser using a single regular expression. Doing so has a number of advantages. From the regular expression we gain a clear and concise statement of the solution. From the state machine we obtain a very fast and robust executable that lends itself to many kinds of analysis and visualization. In this work we present the machine construction and action execution model of Ragel, which allows the embedding of user code into regular expressions to support the single-expression model.

The Ragel language provides the regular expression operators *union, concatenation, kleene star, difference* and *intersection* for constructing parsers. The full set of operators is given in the manual, available from Ragel's homepage.

User actions can be embedded into regular expressions in arbitrary places using action embedding operators. The *entering transition* operator > isolates the start state, then embeds an action into all transitions leaving it. The *finishing transition* operator @ embeds an action into all transitions going into a final state. The *all transition* operator $ embeds an action into every transition. The *pending out transition* operator % enqueues an embedding for the yet-unmade leaving transitions. It allows the user to specify an action to be taken upon the termination of a sequence, prior to the definition of the termination characters.

When a parser is built by combining expressions with embedded actions, transitions which need to execute a number of actions on one input character are often synthesized. To yield an action ordering that is intuitive and predictable for the user, we recursively traverse the parse tree of regular expressions and assign timestamps to action embeddings. When the traversal visits a parse tree node it assigns timestamps to all *entering* action embeddings, recurses on the

O.H. Ibarra and H.-C. Yen (Eds.): CIAA 2006, LNCS 4094, pp. 285–286, 2006.
© Springer-Verlag Berlin Heidelberg 2006

children, then assigns timestamps to the remaining embedding types in the order in which they appear.

During the composition of a parser, the programmer must be careful to ensure that only the intended sub-components of the parser are active at any given time. Otherwise, there is a danger that actions which are irrelevant to the current section of the parser will be executed. In the context of embedded actions, unintended nondeterminism causes spurious action execution.

In most situations, regular expression operators are adequate for segmenting the components of a parser, but they sometimes lead to complicated and verbose parser specifications. In one case, there is no regex-based means of controlling nondeterminism; when we attempt to use the standard kleene star operator to parse a token stream we create an ambiguity between extending a token and wrapping around the machine to begin a new token.

A priority mechanism was devised and built into the determinization process, specifically for the purpose of allowing the user to control nondeterminism. Priorities are integer values embedded into transitions. When the determinization process is combining transitions that have different priorities, the transition with the higher priority is preserved and the transition with the lower priority is dropped. To avoid unintended side-effects, priorities were made into named entities; only priority embeddings with the same name are allowed to interact.

Using priority embeddings for controlling nondeterminism can be tedious and confusing for the programmer. Fortunately, the use of priorities has been necessary only in a small number of scenarios. This allows us to encapsulate the priority functionality into a set of operators and hide priority embeddings from the user.

The *left-guarded concatenation* operator, given by the <: compound symbol, places a higher priority on all transitions of the first machine. This is useful if one must forcibly separate two lists that contain common elements. The *entry-guarded concatenation* operator, given by :>, terminates the first machine when the second machine begins. The *finish-guarded concatenation* operator, given by :>>, terminates the first machine when the second machine moves into a final state. The *longest-match kleene star* operator, given by **, first embeds a high priority into all transitions and a low priority into pending out transitions. When it makes the epsilon transitions from the final states into the start state, they will be given a lower priority than the existing transitions.

```
header_list := ( lower+ ':' ' '* <: (
    ( lower ( lower | digit )* ) >mark %id |
    [ \t]+ >mark %ws |
    '\n\t' @cont )** '\n' )*;
```

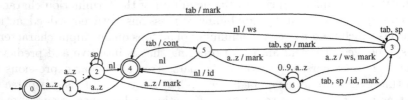

Tighter Packed Bit-Parallel NFA for Approximate String Matching

Heikki Hyyrö

Department of Computer Sciences, University of Tampere, Finland
heikki.hyyro@cs.uta.fi

Given a length-m pattern P and an error threshold k, the bit-parallel NFA of Baeza-Yates and Navarro uses $(m - k)(k + 2)$ bits of space. In this paper we decrease this to $(m - k)(k + 1)$ by modifying the NFA simulation algorithm. As a side-effect, also the original NFA simulation is slightly improved.

For a string A, let A_i denote the ith character, and $A_{i..j}$ denote the substring whose endpoints are A_i and A_j (for $i \leq j$). We consider the task of approximate matching where we wish to find from a text T all locations j where $ed_L(P, T_{j-h..j}) \leq k$ for some $h \geq 0$. Here k is an error threshold and $ed_L(A, B)$ denotes Levenshtein edit distance between strings A and B.

The Bit-Parallel by Diagonals (BPD) algorithm of Baeza-Yates and Navarro [1] is the fastest verification capable approximate string matching algorithm for a wide range of moderate values of m and k [2]. BPD encodes the type of NFA shown in Fig. 1 into a length-$(k+2)(m-k)$ bit-vector $D = 0\ D_1\ 0\ D_2\ 0...0\ D_{m-k}$. Each D_i is a sequence of $k + 1$ bits that describes the status of the $k + 1$ states $i + d$ on rows $d = 0...k$. BPD also preprocesses vectors M_λ that describe matching transitions for character λ (see [1]). The core of BPD is an efficient algorithm for updating the automaton status bit-vector D at text character T_j. See Fig. 2 (*Left*). Here '&', '|', and '^' denote bitwise "and", "or", and "xor", respectively, and '$<<$' and '$>>$' denote shifting the bit-vector left and right. Superscript denotes repetition in bit-vectors (e.g. $1^2(01)^2 = 110101$). The segments D_i in D are separated by a 0 bit to avoid overflow in the arithmetic addition of the update algorithm. The following Lemmata enable removing the separator bits.

Lemma 1. *The operation $(((x + (0^{k+1}1)^{m-k}) \wedge x) >> 1)$ in algorithm BPD is equivalent to $(((x + (0^{k+1}1)^{m-k}) \wedge x)\ \&\ x)$.*

Lemma 2. *If operation $(((x + (0^{k+1}1)^{m-k}) \wedge x) >> 1)$ is replaced by $(((x + (0^{k+1}1)^{m-k}) \wedge x)\ \&\ x)$ in BPD, the separator bits do not need explicit resetting.*

Lemma 3. *Let y be an arbitrary bit-sequence of length q, and set $z = y\ \&\ 01^{q-1}$. Then $u = ((y + 1) \wedge y)\ \&\ y)$ is equal to $v = ((z + 1) \wedge z)\ \&\ y)$.*

The modification of Lemma 1 does not alter the number of operations in BPD. Lemma 2 enables removing the operation that resets the separator bits (last line in Fig. 2 (*Left*)). Lemma 3 gives a modification that makes the separator bits obsolete: The algorithm remains correct if we perform the arithmetic addition on a version of D where the $(k + 1)$th bit in each D_i is set to 0 (avoiding overflow).

O.H. Ibarra and H.-C. Yen (Eds.): CIAA 2006, LNCS 4094, pp. 287–289, 2006.
© Springer-Verlag Berlin Heidelberg 2006

We can now form the complete update algorithm for D of form $D_1 D_2...D_{m-k}$. It is shown in Fig. 2 (*Right*). Now M_λ must be built without the separator bits. We implemented both BPD variants in C and performed tests on a 32-bit SUN Sparc Ultra 2 with 128 MB RAM and GCC 4.0.2 compiler (using '-O3' switch). Fig. 3 shows the results. The methods used horizontal partitioning (see [1]) when the NFA required more than one computer word. Our BPD used separator bits (removing 2nd last line in our code) if it did not increase the number of words.

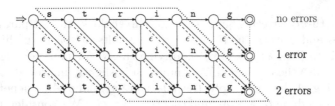

Fig. 1. NFA for approximate string matching with $P = $ "string" and $k = 2$

$$x \leftarrow (D >> (k+2)) \mid M_{T_j}$$
$$D' \leftarrow ((D << 1) \mid (0^{k+1}1)^{m-k})$$
$$\& ((D << (k+3)) \mid (0^{k+1}1)^{m-k-1}01^{k+1})$$
$$\& (((x + (0^{k+1}1)^{m-k}) \wedge x) >> 1)$$
$$\& (0 \ 1^{k+1})^{m-k}$$

$$x \leftarrow (D >> (k+1)) \mid M_{T_j}$$
$$D' \leftarrow ((D << 1) \mid (0^k1)^{m-k})$$
$$\& ((D << (k+2)) \mid (0^k1)^{m-k-1}1^{k+1})$$
$$z \leftarrow x \ \& \ (0 \ 1^k)^{m-k}$$
$$D' \leftarrow D' \ \& \ (((z + (0^k1)^{m-k}) \wedge z) \ \& \ x$$

Fig. 2. Algorithms for updating D. (*Left*) Original BPD. (*Right*) Our tight BPD.

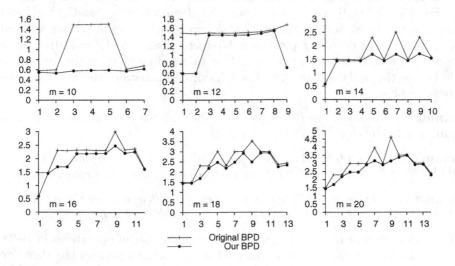

Fig. 3. Average time in seconds for approximate search in 8 MB English text

References

1. Baeza-Yates, R., and Navarro, G. Faster Approximate String Matching. *Algorithmica*, 23:127–158, 1999.
2. Navarro, G., and Raffinot, M. *Flexible Pattern Matching in Strings – Practical on-line search algorithms for texts and biological sequences.* Cambridge University Press, Cambridge, UK, 2002.

References

Author Index

Lecture Notes in Computer Science

For information about Vols. 1–4007

please contact your bookseller or Springer